Diverse Development Paths and Structural Transformation in the Escape from Poverty

This volume analyses the experiences of developing countries in Asia, Latin America, and Sub-Saharan Africa, and examines how they might catch up.

Based on growth performance across the developing world over the last five decades, it offers a thorough account of the possibilities to engage in such processes in an increasingly globalized world. Together, the chapters highlight the diversity and variation of development pathways and provide valuable lessons and implications for how to approach this difficult question. The book shows the importance of acknowledging that the process of development is dynamic and that the possibilities for catch up are situation dependent. At the same time it makes clear that without structural change, and in particular agricultural transformation, sustained catch up is unlikely to happen.

The volume demonstrates how analysis of current growth processes in developing countries can be enriched by paying closer attention to the multi-faceted nature of both economic backwardness and successful pathways to escape it.

Martin Andersson, Associate Professor, Department of Economic History, Lund University.

Tobias Axelsson, Senior Lecturer, Department of Economic History, Lund University.

T0323321

Diverse Development Paths and Structural Transformation in the Escape from Poverty

Edited by
Martin Andersson and Tobias Axelsson

OXFORD
UNIVERSITY PRESS

OXFORD
UNIVERSITY PRESS

Great Clarendon Street, Oxford, OX2 6DP,
United Kingdom

Oxford University Press is a department of the University of Oxford.
It furthers the University's objective of excellence in research, scholarship,
and education by publishing worldwide. Oxford is a registered trade mark of
Oxford University Press in the UK and in certain other countries

© the various contributors 2016

The moral rights of the authors have been asserted

First published 2016
First published in paperback 2017

Published in the United States of America by Oxford University Press
198 Madison Avenue, New York, NY 10016, United States of America

British Library Cataloguing in Publication Data
Data available

Library of Congress Cataloging in Publication Data
Data available

ISBN 978–0–19–873740–7 (Hbk.)
ISBN 978–0–19–880370–6 (Pbk.)

Preface and Acknowledgements

We had two objectives when we started to sketch the outline of this volume. First, to gather world-leading scholars with interests in long-term economic dynamics in the borderland between Economic History and Development Economics to reflect upon the development gap in the world economy and the prospects for less advantaged economies to move ahead. We asked the contributors to discuss approaches to and patterns of economic development of today in a longer-term perspective. What are the lessons learned, to be discovered, or perhaps, rediscovered? We proposed to the authors to freely revisit analytical concepts such as advantages and disadvantages of backwardness, acts of substitution, the role of initial conditions, social capabilities etc. in process-oriented perspectives in the tradition of Gerschenkron, Hirschman, Abramovitz, to name a few. We thought, and still think, that this fills a significant gap in the current development discussion.

A second objective was to honour Professor Christer Gunnarsson who has devoted his academic career, in both teaching and research, to discussing these very issues. We are both, as former students and current colleagues, indebted to his urging and effort to focus on social change, to be relevant to current affairs, to let the research questions guide the choice of methods and always to keep a sound scepticism towards the fads in the field. With Christer being a big fan of the Gerschenkronian approach—at least until asked to contribute with a chapter using such a perspective to this volume—we thought a fitting dedication would be to ask scholars with similar inclinations to delve into the very questions he himself has grappled with. It is our hope that this book will inspire thinking about experiences of and possibilities for catching up in the developing world, in a cohesive way and without being in thrall to pre-set universal models.

To complete a project like this is impossible without the devotion of the contributors. Our deepest thanks go to all of you for all the work you have put into this volume.[1] We also thank our colleagues in the 'development group' at

[1] In January 2016, as this book went through its final stages, Lennart Schön sadly passed away. With his structural-analytical approach he made a profound intellectual impression in Lund and beyond. With humble sharpness and depth he was a source of inspiration to many of us.

the department of Economic History, Lund University, for stimulating and constructive discussions. Special thanks go to Montserrat López Jerez. Cristián Arturo Ducoing Ruiz deserves a special mention.

At Oxford University Press, we would like to thank Adam Swallow, who right from the start believed in our proposal, and Aimee Wright, for their guidance and assistance. Without financial support we could not have carried out this project. We would like to thank The Swedish Research Council, The Crafoord Foundation, Rektor Nils Stjernquists forskningsfond, and Per Westlings Minnesfond.

Martin is grateful to Teresia Rindefjäll and Tobias to Sarah Hill. Thank you for always being there for us, providing encouragement, invaluable comments, and suggestions along the way.

Martin and Tobias
Lund 28 January 2016

Table of Contents

List of Figures

List of Tables

Notes on Contributors

Lee Alston is the Ostrom Chair, professor of economics and law, and director of the Ostrom Workshop at Indiana University. He is a Research Associate at the NBER. Alston is past president of the International Society for the New Institutional Economics, and president of the Economic History Association. He is the author of eight books and more than 70 scholarly articles. His research interests include: the roles of institutions, beliefs, and contracts in shaping economic and political outcomes in the United States and Latin America. Issues examined include the role of the US South in shaping the welfare system in the 1960s; titles and land conflict in the Amazon; and the governance and use of natural resources, historically and today. Alston has held faculty positions at Williams College, the University of Illinois, and the University of Colorado and visiting positions at the University of Washington, UC-Davis, Australian National University, University of Paris-Sorbonne, Stockholm School of Economics, and Princeton University.

Martin Andersson researches and publishes on the reasons behind the success and failure of development from a variety of geographical contexts. He has published on East Asia, Southeast Asia, Latin America, Africa, and Sweden. His research interests include agricultural development and the relation between economic growth, poverty reduction, and distribution of income in the developing world. He has been the editor of one book on the lessons from the economic transformation in Pacific Asia and written two others. He has worked as a consultant for the World Bank and African Center for Economic Transformation and has been a Marie Curie post-doc at EUI in Florence and a visiting scholar at UC Berkeley and University of Queensland and is currently Associate Professor in Economic History at Lund University.

Gareth Austin specializes in African and comparative economic history. His publications include *Labour, Land and Capital in Ghana: From Slavery to Free Labour in Asante, 1807–1956* (2005) and *Labour-Intensive Industrialization in Global History* (edited with K. Sugihara, 2013). After teaching at a *harambee* school in Kenya, he did his BA at Cambridge and PhD at Birmingham. His past employers include the University of Ghana and the London School of Economics. He taught at the Graduate Institute of International and Development Studies, Geneva. In 2016 he became a professor of economic history in the history faculty at Cambridge.

Tobias Axelsson is senior lecturer at the Department of economic history, Lund University. He has his BA in Indonesian studies also from Lund University. He researches and publishes on agricultural transformation processes and the colonial origins of inequality. He has been a guest researcher at ISEAS in Singapore and a guest research fellow at the International Institute for Asian Studies, Leiden. Axelsson is a cofounder of the Bachelor programme in development studies at Lund University.

Luis Bértola is a PhD in Economic History (University of Gothenburg), Professor at Universidad de la República, Uruguay, where he teaches on the Master and Doctoral Programme in Economic History. His research is mainly focussed on comparative long-run development in Latin America, with special interest in structural change, income distribution, and institutions. He has taught postgraduate courses in several universities and been advisor for several international organizations such as ECLAC, ILO, IADB.

OUP has published his *The Economic Development of Latin America since Independence*, written together with José Antonio Ocampo.

Anne Booth was Professor of Economics (with reference to Asia) in the School of Oriental and African Studies, University of London between 1991 and 2013. She is now a Professor Emerita at the University of London. She grew up in New Zealand and holds degrees from Victoria University of Wellington and the Australian National University in Canberra. Between 1976 and 1991, she held research and teaching positions in Singapore and Australia.

She has published extensively on the modern economic history of Southeast Asia, and has also published a comparative study of the economic legacy of colonialism in East and Southeast Asia. A book on the economic development of Indonesia will be published by Cambridge University Press next year.

She has recently been awarded a Lee Kong Chian NUS-Stanford Distinguished Fellowship on Contemporary Southeast Asia, and will spend several months in 2015/16 at Stanford University and at the National University of Singapore.

Christer Gunnarsson, PhD, Chair of Economic History, and Professor of International Economics with a focus on Asia, at Lund School of Economics and Management, Lund University. His research is focussed on the economic history of developing regions, including the impact of colonialism on institutions and long-run economic growth. Gunnarsson has led research and done his own extensive research on industrialization in East and Southeast Asia. His publications include Tillväxt, Stagnation, Kaos (*Growth, Stagnation, Chaos,* with Mauricio Rojas and Martin Andersson), *Capacity Building, Institutional Crisis and the Issue of Recurrent Cost, and Development and Structural Change in Asia-Pacific* (with Martin Andersson). Gunnarsson has done extensive consultancy work for development agencies such as the World Bank, the Swedish International Development Cooperation Agency, and for the Ministry of Foreign Affairs.

Justin Yifu Lin is professor and honorary dean, National School of Development at Peking University. He was the Senior Vice President and Chief Economist of the World Bank, 2008–2012. Before this, Mr. Lin served for fifteen years as Founding Director of the China Centre for Economic Research at Peking University. He is the author of twenty-three books including *Against the Consensus: Reflections on the Great Recession; The Quest for Prosperity: How Developing Economies Can Take Off; Demystifying the Chinese Economy*; and *New Structural Economics: A Framework for Rethinking Development and Policy*. He is a Corresponding Fellow of the British Academy and a Fellow of the Academy of Sciences for the Developing World.

Bernardo Mueller has been a lecturer at the University of Brasília since 1995. He received his undergraduate degree in economics at the University of Brasília in 1987, his Masters at the University of Illinois at Champaign-Urbana in 1993 and his PhD at the University of Illinois at Champaign Urbana in 1994. From 2015 to 2016 he is a visiting scholar at the Ostrom Workshop at Indiana University. He has been an associate editor at *Environment and Development Economics* and at the *Journal of Economic Behavior and Organization*. His areas of interest are Political Economy, Economic Development, Institutional Analysis, and Complex Adaptive Systems. Major publications include political economy of land reform in Brazil, political institutions in Brazil, Executive-Legislative relations, political economy of regulation. A book on the development of Brazil will be published in 2016.

Yusi Ouyang joined the University of Tulsa as an assistant professor of economics after receiving her PhD in Applied Economics from Cornell University in 2013. She has researched minority welfare in China during her doctoral study and published in *World Development*. She remains interested in the welfare of the disadvantaged groups in China and the Chinese economy in general, but has also extended her research into the study of economic development in sub-Saharan Africa. Before earning her PhD, Yusi received a Master's degree in economics and management science and a Master's degree in British Studies from Humboldt University in Berlin.

Lennart Schön was professor at the Department of Economic History, Lund University, between 1992 and 2016. His research focussed on long term economic growth and the role of structural and technological change, long cycles and crisis in a Swedish, European, and international context over the last two centuries. He also constructed detailed Historical National Accounts back to the sixteenth century and was a member of the international Advisory Board of the Maddison Project. Schön has also been trustee and president of the European Historical Economics Society.

Erik Thorbecke is the H.E. Babcock Professor of Economics and Food Economics Emeritus and former Director of the Program on Comparative Economic Development at Cornell University. He is presently a Graduate School Professor. His past positions include chairman of the Department of Economics at Cornell, a professorship at Iowa State University, and associate assistant administrator for program policy at the Agency for International Development. He has made contributions in the areas of economic and agricultural development, the measurement and analysis of poverty and malnutrition, the Social Accounting Matrix and general equilibrium modeling, and international economic policy.

The Foster-Greer-Thorbecke poverty measure (Econometrica, 1984) has been adopted as the standard poverty measure by the World Bank and practically all UN agencies and is used almost universally by researchers doing empirical work on poverty. In recent years he has co-directed a large scale research project on 'The Impact of Globalization on the World's Poor' under the auspices of the United Nations University's World Institute for Development Economics Research; continued his research on multidimensional poverty; and undertaken research on inclusive growth in Africa and Asia.

He is the author or co-author of more than twenty five books and over one hundred and fifty articles.

C. Peter Timmer is an authority on agricultural development, food security, and the world rice economy who has published scores of papers and books on these topics. He has served as a professor at Stanford, Cornell, three faculties at Harvard, and the University of California, San Diego, where he was also the dean of the Graduate School of International Relations and Pacific Studies. Timmer is now the Cabot Professor of Development Studies, emeritus, at Harvard University.

A core advisor on the World Bank's World Development Report 2008: *Agriculture for Development*, Timmer is a non-resident fellow at the Center for Global Development.

Timmer's research and advisory work focuses on three main themes: lessons from the historical experience of structural transformation in Europe and Asia for the role of agriculture in currently developing countries; the impact of modern food supply chains on smallholder farmers and poor consumers; and approaches to stabilizing rice prices in Asia with minimum spillover to the world market and to producers and consumers in Africa and Latin America.

Part 1
Structural Transformation and Catching up

1

Diversity of Development Paths and Structural Transformation in Historical Perspective—an Introduction

Martin Andersson and Tobias Axelsson

1.1 Development Thinking and Catching up Experiences

What poor countries should do to escape relative economic backwardness and catch up with the rich is unquestionably subject to one of the most intense and long-standing debates in the social sciences. Since the birth of Development Economics after World War II it has forwarded a wealth of contesting ideas and solutions. Developing countries both in the past and today are often told that certain necessary prerequisites need to be in place and that without, for instance, initial entrepreneurial skills, good governance structures and tropical disease control they will not be able to make it. If we are to look back at the history of development policies, the ever-increasing list of alleged necessary prerequisites is intimidating and not seldom reflecting the whim of the time. Support for mono-causal and universal recipes for success are derived from fundamental theoretical assumptions of the importance of free and open markets or, alternatively, an asserted necessity to delink from them. Others are empirical generalizations of one or a few successful cases, found in the history literature, ranging from emphasizing good institutions (typically well-defined individual property rights), supreme cultural attributes (for instance Protestant ethics) or favourable geography (for example possession of coal).

The discussion about prospects for economic development among low-income countries is further complicated by the fact that the study of development has both positive and normative ambitions difficult or even impossible to separate from each other. The positive objective to explain the process of economic development, the principal task of the economic historian, is made more relevant if it conforms with the second objective, a primary concern of the development economist, to propose to the policy maker an agenda for change. Unfortunately the desire to find the silver bullet to kill the beast of economic backwardness is sometimes too strong, which to a certain extent explains why universal templates and mono-causal narratives characterize the development discussion. However, this aspiration tends to violate the dynamic and complex nature of social change and sometimes obscures the possibilities to see the variety of the mechanisms at play (Hirschman 1958; Gerschenkron 1962 and 1968; Adelman and Morris 1997; Pritchett 1997; Kenny and Williams 2001).

The objective of this volume is to elaborate on the recognition that the development process is not uniform over time and space while highlighting that sustained catching up is dependent to a large degree on the extent to which structural changes are activated. Two of the currently most influential approaches in the discussion of how and why development fails or succeeds tend to neglect either the diverse nature of development or the importance of structural transformation. On the one hand, the highly influential writings of Acemoglu et al. (2001; 2002; 2012) stressing the persistence of fundamental institutions for long-term development possibilities, have put focus on the origins of growth to explain why some countries have succeeded while most have not. Although this has stimulated the rise of a large body of literature in Economic History on historical determinants of growth, the basic causality given by the model's appreciation of the role of fundamental institutions in history has not given due attention to the variation and diversity found in development experiences. This is a procrustean approach that has led to what Austin (2008) calls a *compression of history*. On the other hand, in Development Economics, development dynamics are to an increasing extent derived from Randomized Controlled Trials (RCT) that have been geared towards the question of 'what works' without necessarily having to use a priori theoretical propositions or possibly intangible historical lessons (Banerjee and Duflo 2011). It is an attempt, in many ways commendable, to find hard evidence of measures and policies to be implemented to attack the development problem at hand. Although the RCT-method has been questioned on the account that it is unable to produce knowledge with greater accuracy than traditional estimation techniques (see Deaton 2009), another major concern is that by focussing on the impacts of rather well-specified policies, it does not inform us about structural changes or the more fundamental sources of development. As Ravallion (2012) has complained, the method of RCT does not allow the bigger questions to be addressed and therefore the method runs the risk of deciding the question rather than the other way around. In neither of the two approaches are empirical patterns of historical processes an important part of the analysis of how opportunities for catching up might evolve.

4

The use of core concepts also varies in the broad literature on economic development. In order to discuss, assess and ultimately explain the diverse processes of economic development and to approach an understanding of how relatively backward economies might catch up, there needs to be a general agreement of concepts. Economic development should therefore be regarded as the long-term process of sustained and widely shared increase in income per capita in which substantial parts of the economy and society undergo marked and rapid structural and institutional changes, even in periods of strong population growth. Catching up is the process whereby which a less economically developed country approaches the level of general standards of living and efficiency in the productive structure and organization of the more economically developed ones. For historical appreciations of economic development, however, the measure available is sometimes only average income per capita, then constituting a proxy. It is within these conceptual frames the following discussion is situated.

Since the dawn of the first industrial revolution tendencies of falling behind have clearly been stronger than processes of catching up indicated by a widening of the income gap between poor and rich countries, for a long time dividing the world between the West and the Rest. If we rely on the classic estimates by Angus Maddison (2003), the GDP per capita in Africa in the early nineteenth century was about one third of the level in Western Europe and less than one tenth by the turn of the millennium. At the same time, even if the distance between the top and the bottom nations in the global income hierarchy has increased, the divergence is not clear-cut. While some countries relatively well-to-do at the beginning of the twentieth century, such as Argentina, Chile, and Uruguay in the Southern Cone of Latin America, fell behind during the course of the century, other initially poorer countries have been taking steps up the income ladder, strongly suggesting that the development process is neither linear nor pre-determined. The average GDP per capita in Africa and Asia was almost on a par at the beginning of the twentieth century but by the end of the century countries in East and Southeast Asia were already advancing and had escaped the league of poor nations, while growth in South Asia and Latin America was stagnant and had collapsed in most parts of sub-Saharan Africa. A description of the developing world as being characterized by *growth* (East Asia), *stagnation* (Latin America) and *chaos* (Africa) seemed highly relevant at the end of the twentieth century (Gunnarsson et al. 2008; see also Nayyar 2013). Although most developing countries have failed to achieve sustained economic growth over the past half century and that many have encountered recurrent and long-lasting crises, the global income distribution as regards differences of average national per capita income between countries has changed dramatically, especially since the mid 1980s. Some developing nations, most notably the four East Asian 'tigers' South Korea, Singapore, Taiwan and Hong Kong, have already developed and become high-income countries, while others are moving either out of the ranks of the poorest low-income countries into middle-income status or are on the verge of graduating from middle-income to high-income status (for instance Malaysia, Chile). A new global middle class is now made up of people residing outside the industrialized North.

Hence, during the first decade of the new millennium we have seen increased growth in the global South that makes it relevant to ask whether we are in the midst of a game-changer. The recent growth experience of a substantial number of emerging economies in the developing world appears to defy commonly held views of, and explanations for, the state of play in the global economy. The world can no longer be seen as divided between the West and the Rest and the Rest is not to the same extent marked by stagnation and chaos. More than a billion people have escaped extreme poverty in the last quarter of a century and income growth has on average been fast in low and middle-income countries while slowing down across many high-income countries. Therefore, considering the last couple of decades in a historical perspective the growth across the developing world is clearly impressive and we find many examples of low-income countries growing faster than the world average. The reasons behind the growth performance across the developing world over the last decades might be many; for example, the increasing role of China as a locomotive of growth and the related increase in the flow of investments and trade within the South, which has taken advantage of better international prices and increased demand for commodities. Also signs of improved governance and management of macro-economic fundamentals are recognized as important factors. One question is of course whether these conditions are sufficient prerequisites for developing countries to speed up structural change and continue to move ahead. As potential signs of catching up are emerging, the challenge for research is to measure and assess to what extent, and where, catching up might be sustained. Although growth is recurrent in the developing world, it should be remembered that the sustainability of the growth process remains uncertain and that the process of growth might not translate into economic development as defined above. The 'bottom billion' of people living under a dollar a day still remains but is now to be found in countries where the average income has increased quite dramatically, suggesting that growth is not always inclusive. After half a century of attempted development models and occasional growth spurts, it is only in countries in East Asia where improvement of development indicators been sustained over at least twenty-five years. In any case, gloomy predictions about the future of the poorest countries of the world have given way to more optimistic scenarios. Now the poorest countries are no longer seen as doomed to eternal poverty. Some even argue that by 2035, there will be almost no poor countries left in the world (Gates and Gates 2014). This could quite possibly be too rosy a prediction, but it does none the less emphasize the need to reorient our thinking towards finding new ways to approach and assess different trajectories from a longer time perspective with regard to the capability for sustained catch-up.

One of the key themes of this volume is that this capability is closely connected to the extent to which growth is accompanied with structural changes in the relative weight and productivity of the sectors of the economy and possibilities to be gainfully employed in higher productivity activities. Due regard should then be paid to the particular initial conditions, for instance in terms of balance of factor endowments and distribution of assets and opportunities, that exist in individual countries at the beginning of such transformation affecting the direction of the development pathway. Over the last half century, however, the most influential development paradigms have been promoting universal templates.

1.2 One-eyed Paradigms of Catching up

In many ways, almost the entire body of the development literature, particularly in the writings of the immediate post-World War II, is directly related to the question of how economically backward countries might catch up. One of the most influential paradigms, connected to the thinking of Raul Prebisch and Hans Singer, making its mark for a broad cross-section of the developing world, in particular in Latin America but also in Africa and Asia, is the structuralist perspective. It suggested that long-term deteriorating terms of trade for primary goods production, in large part caused by specialization in lower value-added goods subject to destabilizing price volatilities, was causing the technological gap between rich and poor to grow. It argued for the necessity for economically backward and primary export-dependent countries to speed up the process of industrialization by nurturing and diversifying domestic industry towards capital goods and consumer durables. The consequent policy prescription for catch-up, captured by the import-substitution industrialization (ISI), was built on state-induced nurturing of infant industries, by imposing import tariffs and quotas, as well as multiple exchange rates and other protective measures. Even if the strategy was relatively successful in generating both growth of production and industrial employment, by the 1980s the process could be characterized as 'growth without development' and as such it turned out to be a model of temporary rather than sustained catch-up in most parts of the developing world. In Latin America deficits caused by weak development of competitive industries ultimately led to inflationary pressure and popular unrest. The lack of autonomous state capacity and inclusive democratic procedures and traditions was surely important for this strategy to turn economically inefficient and politically repressive. Both as a mode of explanation and as a development strategy, the ISI-model can be characterized as a universal prescription, as indeed can the radical neo-liberal strategy emphasizing openness, privatization and deregulation that followed. Both failed to take into account differences in initial conditions and were unable to address some of the structural heterogeneities that constituted part of the reason why Latin America had fallen behind in the first place. For instance, inter-sectoral duality between agriculture and industry and substantial inequality of personal income and wealth limited the development of domestic market dynamics and internationally competitive industries.

The literature on *ex-post* successful catching up of the developing countries has naturally been confined to lessons from development experiences in Asia. It may well be argued that the transformation of East and Southeast Asia has forced some previously influential hypotheses of development and underdevelopment to step back. Explanations that stressed cultural traits specific to East Asia as particularly harmful for economic progress (for instance Fairbank 1982), only to be forwarded later as explanations to account for the contrary (for instance Fei 1986), has in all likelihood lost analytical credibility. Similarly, the dependency paradigm (Frank 1969; Amin 1990), which predicted a practical impossibility for poor countries to develop unless they delinked from the global market forces, became perhaps even more damaged when it became apparent that countries in East Asia both grew at an unprecedented rate and were closely connected to the market demand of the Western world. Instead, assessments of the Asian miracle have created a tug of war between market friendly and state interventionist standpoints. Interpretations of the 'miracle' have formed a battlefield between two conventional schools of thought; between advocates of openness and free market in line with the so-called Washington Consensus on the one hand and believers in the necessity and advantage of government intervention on the other.

To explain the rise of East Asia, reference was routinely made to factors such as openness to the global economy, macroeconomic stability, high saving and investment rates and reliance on market allocation (World Bank 1983; Growth Commission 2008). The standard policy recommendations for technological catch-up consisted of dismantling quantitative restrictions on imports, the reduction of import tariffs and their dispersion, making the currency convertible to current account transactions, elimination of bureaucratic red tape and the establishment of the rule of law. Basically, recipes for success were commonly oriented towards 'getting prices right'. At the same time, the East Asian miracle story also complies well with the statist standpoint nicely captured by the title of Robert Wade's study on Taiwan 'Governing the Market' (1990; see also Amsden 1989, and Chang 2002). In a similar vein, Rodrik (1994) has suggested that an investment boom of the 1960s is the core explanation behind the East Asian miracle. This was launched by a successful co-ordination of investment decisions by the state and facilitated through a combination of a well-educated population and relative equality of income. Although initially met with strong resistance, this perspective has become integrated with neo-classical economics and no longer constitutes a red rag to a bull even among the major development organizations such as the World Bank. As such, the task for policy makers is 'getting interventions right'.

Without doubt, in reference to East Asia, both interpretations still carry substantial weight and might even be possible to combine and synthesize further, but since both explanations have their focus on policy instruments the driving forces are referred to in terms of leadership and governance; i.e. agency. As such they are less concerned with inner dynamics or more deeply rooted causes of growth stemming from initial conditions and structural changes (Andersson and Gunnarsson 2003). Consequently, the returns from attempts to forge workable and transferable development policies from the success stories of East Asia seem to have been surprisingly low. Therefore, understanding and exploring a possible replication of the strategies, policies and mechanisms that have allowed East Asian economies to catch up with the most advanced economies still remains a major challenge for research and policy. The question of which lessons one may draw from historical cases or how much a latecomer is able to imitate forerunners is subject to constant discussion also beyond stressing policy instruments. A perspective that accommodates both the diverse dynamics given by historical and structural conditions as well as an analysis of what policy choices with a coherent logic that might promote change under certain circumstances could be a potentially rewarding research agenda. Although the tide of the times seems to be running in the other direction, as suggested by the predominance of approaches stressing institutional persistence or randomized controlled trials, the seeds of such an agenda are firmly rooted in other strands of the literature on catching up.

1.3 The Case for Structural Transformation and Diversity in the Development Process

An early hypothesis of catching up, coined by Akamatsu as the theory of the 'flying geese' (Akamatsu 1962), argues from the viewpoint of more secular and structural conditions that backward economies under certain conditions may have particular advantages to progress. In this theory—restricted to intra-Asian catch-up—spillovers and the division of labour predict the sequential development pattern of emulation of many Asian countries following, and catching up with, the 'lead goose', Japan. Non-market, or non-economic, institutions were part of the dynamics, since massive application of techno-logical innovations requires a learning process for making efficient use of available technology. This, in turn, required the formation of strong financial, educational and legal systems. It was suggested that following the footsteps of such sequencing is a step-by-step recipe for growth.

In the catching-up literature there are also approaches challenging the idea that outright imitation à la 'flying geese' is possible by arguing that the nature of catching-up processes to a large extent depend on contextual conditions and that the lessons from success-cases should not be seen as standard recipes to be imitated for best result. Rather the general mechanisms and processes of change might be better understood if sufficient attention is given to differ-ences in endowments and other initial conditions. When Abramovitz (1986) revisited the question of the potential advantage of backwardness—the so-called convergence thesis, suggesting that the growth rates of productivity tend to be inversely related to the initial levels of productivity—he suggested that making full use of technological advances made elsewhere is determined by the 'social capability' of the developing country (see also Ohkawa and Rosovsky 1973). He proposed that 'social capability is what separates less developed countries from advanced countries today and which, in the past, separated the late-comers among the countries that are now industrialized from the early entrants into what Kuznets called "modern economic growth". The upshot is that a country's potential for growth is strong not when it is backward in all respects but rather when it is technologically backward but socially advanced.' (Abramovitz 1990:3). This concept, vague as it is, might include the components of educational levels, the quality of institutions, state capacity and social unity.

For Abramovitz, the less social capability a developing country was endowed with, the more inhibited was the potential to catch up. In the language of Alexander Gerschenkron, one could argue that it corresponds with the *degree of backwardness*. But in Gerschenkron's approach the focus is not on what the successful and less developed countries had in common respectively, but rather to understand the options available to overcome backwardness. Par-ticularly in the field of Economic History, Gerschenkron became highly influ-ential for the study of European patterns of industrialization and his work came to inspire entire research agendas (see for instance Sylla and Toniolo 1991). Gerschenkron sketched an analytical framework influenced by patterns of industrialization in Europe that allows for a deeper study of the structural changes in both the production process and institutional arrangements. In addition, it highlights the increased market exchange and sectoral shifts in relative shares of employment and value that takes place when higher value added activities gain ground through the adoption of new technology and a general rise of skills. Most importantly it directs attention to the variety of mechanism and processes at work on the road towards modern economic growth. The strong point is that the prerequisites of the first movers cannot be replicated but rather substituted. Thus Germany and France managed to create a great spurt and break with the old order but we cannot assume that this was done by following an English blueprint. The Gerschenkronian approach is still largely unexplored since its original scope is restricted to economies that have been successful or at least have made real efforts for full-scale industrialization, as was the case in parts of Eastern Europe. It has rarely been used for discussing what backward economies of today should do to break away from this state of affairs. Neither is the perspective explicit about one of the major concerns of today, inclusive growth. To the extent the Gerschenkron approach has been applied in the analysis of industrialization outside Europe it has served as an argument for the *necessity* of state intervention for late-comers, supported by the post-World War II East Asian development experience. This is, however, a selective reading of Gerschenkron, whose major claim was that missing prerequisites can be substituted for, of which the state taking the lead was but one possibility. Rather, the act of substitution corresponded to the specific degree of backwardness that the economy represented. This *situational relativism*, as Adelman and Morris (1997) labelled it, represents the notion that development is better perceived as non-linear and that different development mechanisms apply depending on circumstance, situation and degree of development. While the end objective is similar, the road to it is determined by country specific circumstances and preconditions stemming from the backwardness itself. This view is also present in the works of Hirschman (for instance 1958; 1981) who forcefully argued that growth is typically unbalanced and that sequences of development need not follow a pre-determined path but could be inverted depending on what linkages are activated in the process itself.

The writings in this tradition attempt to draw general implications from the variety of individual country experiences but while the number of ways to accomplish the great spurt towards modern economic growth are several, the list is not endless. The development path is not totally unique to each case and we have learnt from Kuznets (as well as Syrquin/Chenery, Timmer, and others) that structural change is a common characteristic of the development process. To make up for missing markets, deficient institutions or lack of agricultural surplus production the need for certain mechanisms to be activated becomes stronger, such as the role of financial institutions, foreign capital, or the state. The challenge is then how to analytically approach diversity in a systematic fashion and how to relevantly relate current developments to historical experiences even when external conditions, for instance possibilities to interact with the global economy, have changed. One of the most important and inspiring insights of this intellectual tradition, in the absence of manuals for change that can easily be converted into policy advice, might be the reminder that the development process is both dynamic and multifaceted and therefore not easily moulded into fixed models. At the same time a careful analysis of initial conditions has implications with regard to how we systematically think about possibilities for economic development. It is within this spirit that leading scholars in the fields of global and developing country economic dynamics in this book reflect upon past experiences and prospects for the future for the developing world. It attempts to complement our understanding of the development process and possibly provide a bridge between the two disciplines of Economic History and Development Economics that very much share the subject matter—to understand the reason behind why some countries are poor and others not—but have become methodologically separated.

1.4 The Content

The compilation of chapters is intended to stimulate the discussion on a big question on global development and what is in it for the developing world. Although standard economic theory postulates late-comer advantages due to the possibilities of emulating well-tried technologies and know-how, as well as comparative cost advantages, the potential advantage of backwardness has in reality shown to be conditional on various factors. We also need to look into greater detail why countries with the potential advantages of backwardness more often than not fall short of expectations. The chapters are divided under the two broad themes of this volume. In part one, three chapters are devoted to the continuing importance of the role of structural transformation. Part two consists of six chapters which, both individually and combined, show the diverse nature of both successful and less successful pathways of development.

The new global economic dynamics of recent decades make some of the authors pose the question whether there is an advantage of being late or if it is a gradually increasing disadvantage. It is argued by Lennart Schön that countries endowed with a skilled work force and relatively flexible institutions are more prone to structural change and therefore are more likely to reap the benefits of interacting with the global markets. According to a comparison of structural change made possible by using different benchmark years for purchasing power parity (PPP), the small, open, and relatively rich economies tend to take better advantage of changing relative prices on the world markets. However, most developing countries are not knowledge-intensive and by definition not rich, implying that narrowing of inter-sectoral productivity gaps, that is, to increase the average productivity of the lagging sectors is crucial for catch-up. If the large Indian and Chinese economies structurally upgrade and deepen their domestic markets, new opportunities might arise for the developing countries taking advantage of increasing purchasing power in India and China, a point also stressed by Justin Lin. While it is too early to say if low-income countries will be able to exploit these potential possibilities, a related question is whether and to what extent structural changes have been made over the last decades in terms of production structure and organization. As Lin argues, all low-income countries are in possession of latent latecomer advantage to be used if they succeed in making a correct self-identification of their own relative structural strengths and let the image of inspiration be a case with which the developing country in question shares similar development features. It allows for a closer scrutiny and greater understanding of why some Asian countries have not only been living up to expectations but also exceeded them.

One fundamental dimension of the structural aspect of the catching up process often overlooked is the role played by agriculture for conditioning not only the possibilities but also the speed and scope of the process. As Peter Timmer argues, with personal recollections from his days as a student of Gerschenkron, one of the neglected areas in the understanding of the development process, both in the catching up literature and among policy makers, is to acknowledge the central role of agricultural development. Not only is agricultural productivity growth important for improving the livelihood of rural populations but perhaps even more for providing linkages to other activities and in that sense easing the need for large scale substitutive efforts that may backfire. For Timmer, taking more careful note of historical experiences of agricultural transformation would provide policymakers with stronger evidence of how the development process might be encouraged than ever the results from randomized controlled trials could.

In part two Christer Gunnarsson provides an interpretation of how East Asian cases broke the traditional developing country pattern and achieved modern economic growth at a rapid pace. These economies utilized the advantage of 'being late' by adopting modern technology occasionally with the help of forceful substitution but also, as emphasized by Gunnarsson, with less substitutive forms. It can be argued that this not only set the East Asian experience apart from that of its European predecessors, but also that pathways differed within East Asia. To lay out the complexities of this dynamic story, Gunnarsson proposes that insights given by a retake on the Gerschenkronian perspective, stressing agricultural backwardness, provide different implications for our understanding of the development process than either the old state vs. market interpretations or the more Asian-style explanations. Similarly, as Anne Booth suggests, even within Asia it may be argued that although China and the Southeast Asian countries are rapidly catching up, the prerequisites are fundamentally different. With the Abramovitz argument of how economic growth and social capability are mutually intertwined, she finds that the most advanced ASEAN economies fifty years ago remain ahead also today and that very little intra-regional catch-up has taken place. Despite periods of rapid growth in some countries, for instance Thailand, this process has not automatically converted into capabilities in a virtuous fashion envisaged by the Abramovitz hypothesis. The variety of pathways, and sudden reversals of such paths in the region is quite notable, partly for reasons going back to pre-colonial conditions but also in the way individual countries designed their development strategies along the way.

As is well recognized, East and Southeast Asia over the last fifty years stand in sharp contrast to the development of Latin America. Luis Bértola takes a bird's eye perspective on long-term trends to assess whether the relatively progressive advances made over the last couple of decades might constitute a continent-wide shift in terms of structural change. Admittedly, he finds some signs of systematic change in terms of economic and political inclusiveness but is hesitant to subscribe to the view that fundamental changes have been made. Latin America seems to still be unable to pilot its own development pathway and reduce its propensity for volatility imposed by a high concentration on a limited number of export goods. This implies that the window of opportunity given by the commodity boom of the recent decades might not have been converted into sufficient changes in either the policy environment or the production structure. Somewhat at odds with this view, Lee Alston and Bernardo Mueller attempt to explain the underlying reasons for why Brazil has become a 'global agricultural powerhouse'. They argue that after a new belief system based on 'fiscally sound social inclusion' was credibly established in Brazil in the late 1990s, it released agricultural entrepreneurial spirit hitherto subdued. With the help of fitness landscapes, they stress that institutional change brought about by the abandonment of previous mismatched belief systems was the result of self-reflection. These economically more efficient institutions follow from a change in belief system that is better aligned with the reality of what this system promises. Alston and Mueller find support and reason in the Gerschenkron/Hirschman-inspired approach of contextualizing the development process to local circumstances rather than imitating a prescript.

Gareth Austin picks up on the argument of Gerschenkron that advances made in economies elsewhere alter the state of play for other late-comers. By focusing on sub-Saharan Africa, he argues that backwardness for a long time and for many reasons has been a great disadvantage, with colonial legacy and undesirable factor endowments strongly delaying structural change and economic progress. But population expansion and rising skill levels are now perhaps shifting opportunities in Africa's favour. To seize such opportunities and overcome other remaining hindrances, at least now acts of substitution are potentially possible compared to previously when the windows were perhaps more or less shut. For this to happen, for improving both human and environmental conditions, governments need to be more active in the developmental rather than patrimonial sense in help guiding the way for the demographic dividend to be absorbed in productive employment, not least in the manufacturing sector. Erik Thorbecke and Yusi Ouyang more explicitly make an attempt to approach the latest trends of sub-Saharan development and finds that typical vicious circle dynamics and poverty traps that plagued African growth for decades have been reduced. A combination of an improved policy environment and better terms of trade have increased investments, not least in the agricultural sector, resulting in more inclusive growth. These are signs of the ability to capitalize on globalization. For the trends to be sustained, structural change, in particular in the form of increased manufacturing, continues to be highly important.

References

Abramovitz, M., 1986. 'Catching up, forging ahead and falling behind.' *Journal of Economic History* vol. 46 number 2: 385–406.

Abramovitz, M., 1990. 'The Catch-up Factor in Postwar Economic Growth: Presidential Address to the Western Economic Association, June 21, 1989'. *Economic Inquiry* vol. 28 number 1: 1–18.

Acemoglu, D., S. Johnson, and J.A. Robinson, 2001. 'The Colonial Origins of Comparative Development: an Empirical Investigation'. *American Economic Review* vol. 91 number 5: 1369–401.

Acemoglu, D., S. Johnson, and J.A. Robinson, 2002. 'Reversal of fortune: geography and institutions in the making of the modern world income distribution'. *Quarterly Journal of Economics* vol. 117 number 4: 1231–79.

Acemoglu, D. and J.A. Robinson, 2012. *Why Nations Fail: The Origins of Power, Prosperity, and Poverty*, New York: Crown.

Adelman, I. and C.T. Morris, 1997. 'Editorial: Development History and its Implications for Development Theory'. *World Development*, vol. 25 number 6: 831–84.

Akamatsu, K., 1962. 'Historical pattern of economic growth in developing countries'. *The Developing Economies* vol. 1: 3–25.

Amin, S., 1990. *Delinking:Towards a Polycentric World*, London: Zed Books Ltd.

Amsden, A., 1989. *Asia's Next Giant: South Korea and Late Industrialization*, New York: Oxford University Press.

Andersson, M. and C. Gunnarsson, 2003. *Development and Structural Change in Asia-Pacific: Globalising Miracles or End of a Model?* London: Routledge.

Austin, G., 2008. 'The "Reversal of Fortune" Thesis and the Compression of History: Perspectives from African and Comparative Economic History'. *Journal of International Development* vol. 20 number 8: 996–1027.

Banerjee, A.V. and E. Duflo, 2011. *Poor Economics—A Radical Rethinking of the Way to Fight Global Poverty*, New York: Public Affairs.

Chang, H-J., 2002. *Kicking Away the Ladder: Development Strategy in Historical Perspective*, London: Anthem Press.

Deaton, A.S., 2009. 'Instruments of Development: Randomization in the Tropics, and the Search for the Elusive Keys to Economic Development'. NBER WP 14690.

Fairbank, J.K., 1982. *Chinabound: A Fifty-year Memoir,* New York: Harper and Row.

Fei, J.C.H., 1986. 'Economic Development and Traditional Chinese Cultural Values'. *Journal of Chinese Studies*, vol. 3 number 1: 109–30.

Frank, A.G., 1969. *Capitalism and Underdevelopment in Latin America: Historical Studies of Chile and Brazil*, New York: Monthly Review Press.

Gates, B. and M. Gates, 2014. 'Three Myths That Block Progress for the Poor'. 2014 Gates Annual Letter.

Gerschenkron, A., 1962. *Economic Backwardness in Historical Perspective: A Book of Essays*, Cambridge MA.: Harvard University Press.

Gerschenkron, A., 1968. *Continuity in History and Other Essays*, Cambridge MA.: Harvard University Press.

Growth Commission 2008. *The Growth Report: Strategies for Sustained Growth and Inclusive Development*, Washington DC: World Bank.

Gunnarsson, C., M. Rojas, and M. Andersson, 2008. *Tillväxt, Stagnation, Kaos—En Institutionell Studie av Underutvecklingens Orsaker och Utvecklingens Möjligheter* (3rd edition), Stockholm: SNS.

Hirschman, A.O., 1958. *The Strategy of Economic Development*, New Haven: Yale University Press.

Hirschman, A.O., 1981. 'A Generalized Linkage Approach to Development, with Special Reference to Staples', in (Hirschman) *Essays in Trespassing: Economics to Politics and Beyond*, New York: Cambridge University Press.

Kenny, C. and D. Williams, 2001. 'What Do We Know About Economic Growth? Or, Why Don't We Know Very Much?' *World Development,* vol. 29 number 1: 1–22.

Maddison, A., 2003. *The World Economy: Historical Statistics*. OECD: Development Centre Studies, France: OECD Publications.

Nayyar, D., 2013. *Catch up: Developing Countries in the World Economy*, Oxford: Oxford University Press.

Ohkawa, K. and H. Rosovsky, 1973. *Japanese Economic Growth: Trend Acceleration in the Twentieth Century*, Stanford: Stanford University Press.

Pritchett, L., 1997. 'Divergence, big time'. *Journal of Economic Perspectives* vol. 11 number 3: 3–17.

Ravallion, M., 2012. 'Fighting Poverty one Experiment at a Time: A Review of Abhijit Banerjee and Esther Duflo's, Poor Economics: A Radical Rethinking of the Way to Fight Global Poverty'. *Journal of Economic Literature* vol. 50 number 1: 103–14.

Rodrik, D., 1994. 'Getting Interventions Right: How South Korea and Taiwan Grew Rich'. NBER WP: 4964.

Sylla, R. and G. Toniolo (eds.), 1991. *Patterns of European Industrialization: The Nineteenth Century*, London: Routledge.

Wade, R., 1990. *Governing the Market: Economic Theory and the Role of Government in East Asian Industrialization*, Princeton: Princeton University Press.

World Bank, 1983. *World Development Report*, Washington D.C: World Bank.

2

Structural Change and Catching up—the Relative Small Country Advantage

Lennart Schön

2.1 Introduction

This chapter raises one overarching question: How has economic development since 1990—with globalization and the ICT revolution—affected possibilities to catch-up or to forge ahead in different corners of the world?

Since the early 1990s, global development has turned to new directions in a quite dramatic way. The two accelerating megatrends, globalization and ICT revolution, have been strongly interconnected and have shaped both recent events and future perspectives on economic growth. In this chapter, the aspects of catching up and forging ahead will be discussed from a viewpoint that is not very common among economists today but can be found and explored among the traditional work tools of economic historians, namely measures of structural change and adjustments of economic growth rates based upon different price bases. In the present case, it is the comparative GDP levels from the Purchasing Power Parity (PPP) constructions in 1990 and 2005—reported for a great number of countries—that will be analyzed. The analysis changes some perspectives on recent development and provides a positive role to small, open, and relatively rich countries.

In the first section, continental and major regional growth rates of the period 1990–2013 will be presented in a long term perspective, from the postwar decades onwards. The presentation follows well-known trends from the commonly used growth rates, based upon one fixed PPP base for all countries. The next section presents the principles of using two PPP-benchmarks in order to adjust growth rates and to evaluate direction of structural change. The theoretical inspirations for this methodology are also presented. The third section reports the adjustment effects. The concern is particularly whether the effect of PPP adjustments on the growth rates of a country, a region, or a continent is positive or negative. In the following section, the structural backgrounds to these effects are analyzed, using an econometrical exercise. In the last section, implications for catching up and forging ahead processes are discussed. Furthermore, some comparisons are made between the situations following the Great Recession around 2010 and the Great Depression in the early 1930s, in both cases underlining a possible positive role for small open economies.

2.2 Global Development Since 1990 in a Long Term Perspective—a Dramatic Chapter

The postwar decades of the 1950s and 1960s represented a golden age of economic growth globally and particularly in Europe and Asia. Europe, both east and west, converged with the world-leading USA. In Asia, convergence was driven by the phenomenal growth rates of Japan and the initial catch-up processes of South Korea and Taiwan. The following two decades were however plagued by crises and unstable growth worldwide. As shown in Table 2.1, rising energy prices during the 1970s and debt crises in the early 1980s combined with new directions in economic growth and incipient radical technological change around microelectronics slowed down growth everywhere. In particular, peripheral low-income countries in Eastern Europe, Africa and Latin America ran into political instability and economic stagnation.

From the 1990s, as shown in Table 2.2, economic growth picked up again globally and in almost every region. The ICT revolution passed into a more mature phase with the supply of standardized PC and mobile phone equipment at dramatically falling prices. Above all, a new infrastructure arose around Internet and the World Wide Web. Technological diffusion increased rapidly. At the same time, globalization took a giant leap forward with the opening of formidable regions such as China, India, and the former socialist Eastern Europe. Political and technological change complemented each other to radically lower transaction costs. In fact, the global economy went through, what has been named, a 'Great Doubling' (Freeman, R. 2005) within only a couple of years in terms of potentially available labour at lower wages.

2.2.1 The American 1990s

The two decades from the breakthrough of the new globalization around 1990 up to the Great Recession around 2010 were however very different in character and growth pattern, as can also be seen in Table 2.2. In the 1990s, growth rates picked up almost everywhere but stood particularly strong in rich regions

Table 2.1 Annual growth rates per capita in major global regions 1950/54–2009/13. Five-year averages over periods of two decades.

	Western Europe	North America	Australia New Zealand	Eastern Europe	Latin America	Asia	Africa	World
1950/54–1970/74	3.8	2.3	2.5	3.8	2.6	3.7	1.8	2.8
1970/74–1990/94	1.9	1.9	1.5	0.5	1.0	3.0	0.1	1.5
1990/94–2009/13	1.3	1.5	2.1	1.9	1.7	4.4	2.0	2.4

Note: Computation from regional total population and total production, aggregated from GDP in 1990 US$ (converted at Geary Khamis PPPs).
Western Europe: Austria, Belgium, Cyprus, Denmark, Finland, France, Germany (East Germany linked pre-1990), Greece, Iceland, Ireland, Italy, Luxemburg, Malta, Netherlands, Norway, Portugal, Spain, Sweden, Switzerland, Turkey, United Kingdom.
North America: Canada, USA.
Eastern Europe: 1950–1990: Albania, Bulgaria, Czechoslovakia, Hungary, Poland, Romania, USSR, Yugoslavia; 1990–2013: Albania, Armenia, Azerbaijan, Belarus, Bosnia-Herzegovina, Bulgaria, Croatia, Czech Republic, Estonia, Georgia, Hungary, Kazakhstan, Kyrgyz Republic, Latvia, Lithuania, Macedonia, Moldova, Poland, Romania, Russian Federation, Serbia & Montenegro, Slovak Republic, Slovenia, Tajikistan, Turkmenistan, Ukraine, Uzbekistan.
Asia: Bahrain, Bangladesh, Cambodia, China, Hong Kong, India, Indonesia, Iran, Iraq, Israel, Japan, Jordan, Kuwait, Malaysia, Omar, Pakistan, Philippines, Qatar, Saudi Arabia, Singapore, South Korea, Sri Lanka, Syria, Taiwan, Thailand, Vietnam, United Arab Emirates, Yemen.
Latin America: Argentina, Barbados, Bolivia, Brazil, Chile, Colombia, Costa Rica, Dominican Republic, Ecuador, Guatemala, Jamaica, Mexico, Peru, St Lucia, Trinidad Tobago, Uruguay, Venezuela.
Africa: Algeria, Angola, Burkina Faso, Cameroon, Cote d'Ivoire, DR Congo, Egypt, Ethiopia, Ghana, Kenya, Madagascar, Malawi, Mali, Morocco, Mozambique, Niger, Nigeria, Senegal, South Africa, Sudan, Tanzania, Tunisia, Uganda, Zambia, Zimbabwe.
Source: The Conference Board January 2014, *Total Economy Database Output, Labour and Labour Productivity, country details, 1950–2013*.

Table 2.2 Annual growth rates per capita in major global regions 1991/95–2009/13. Five-year averages over periods of one decade.

	Western Europe	North America	Australia New Zealand	Eastern Europe	Latin America	Asia	Africa	World
1990/94–2000/04	1.9	2.3	2.5	−1.1	1.1	3.4	1.3	2.0
2000/04–2009/13	0.7	0.8	1.7	5.2	2.4	5.6	2.8	3.0

Note: Computation from regional total population and total production, aggregated from GDP in 2013 US$ (converted to 2013 price level with updated 2005 EKS PPPs).
Regional division as in table 2.1.
Source: See table 2.1.

such as North America, Western Europe and Australia. Only Asia could compete thanks to the incipient catch-up in China and India. Overall, however, poor peripheries lagged behind the rich leaders in a global divergence.

The new position of the USA was most noticed (e.g. Rhode/Toniolo 2006). For about forty years since 1950, Western Europe and Japan had converged with the USA. During the 1990s, the situation was seen to change into a new divergence when the US economy advanced ahead of Europe and Japan. This was ascribed mostly to the effects of the ICT revolution and to the greater flexibility of the American economy to meet new demands in work organizations and to supply more human capital into innovation processes (Crafts 2006). Optimism increased in the American society and in its economic policy. It is also a distinctive pattern that English-speaking countries advanced during the early breakthrough of Internet in the 1990s—this goes not only for USA but also for UK, Ireland and Australia as well as for countries proficient in English such as Scandinavia and India. But overall, Europe and Japan were said to suffer from sclerosis. Within the European Union, new political agendas were formulated to enable a return to the catch-up process.

2.2.2 The Chinese 2000s

The following decade, after the turn of the millennium, was very different. The 2000s saw the profound effects of globalization, technological diffusion and increased competition. Economic giants with increased efficiency and lower wages, such as China, took the lead with all non-Western regions advancing on a broad front. In Western Europe and North America, growth rates fell dramatically. Rates fell as well in Australia and New Zealand. Thus, economic growth faltered in rich economies—particularly so in Western Europe. At the other end of the scale, economic growth accelerated strongly in all peripheral regions, most notably in China. Economic growth shifted from the centre to the periphery of the global economy. All economies were hit by the financial crisis in 2008, followed by the Great Recession, but USA and parts of EU were hit the hardest. Peripheral economies bounced back more directly, although dropping some percentages in annual growth rates.

As a summary of the two decades from 1990 to 2010, two giant economies put their imprints on global development—USA in the 1990s and China in the 2000s.

2.3 Purchasing Power Parity and the Index Problem

The general picture may seem clear with the shift of economic growth from USA and Europe to Asia and to the periphery in general, with Europe as the prime laggard. This is, however, the picture one receives from traditional accounts of economic growth rates internationally. These are based on domestically calculated GDP series at fixed prices in each country which for international comparative purposes are adjusted to the same level of purchasing power per unit of value added at one PPP benchmark.

2.3.1 The Index Problem

This procedure provides a major problem for the evaluation of economic growth over time. For economic growth rates to be fully comparable, you have to assume that either structures or prices in the different economies move in the same directions. If there are changes in the economies or in the market, different yardsticks (price bases) will give different results.

This problem is relevant in the present context, since two sets of international market prices have been provided by two different PPP benchmarks, in 1990 and 2005. These have been applied to the national GDP series for a large number of countries in two sets of series, aligned to the same purchasing power in international dollars, either at 1990 or at 2005. The annual growth rate of each country is identical between the two series but their levels in relation to each other shift between the two series. Thus, different PPP benchmarks give different relationship between countries despite the use of the same national series at fixed prices.

This result is a version of the old Index Number Problem, stating that calculations in constant prices from different price bases (or with different deflators) will result in different growth rates as long as there are changes of production structures or of relative prices in the economy. To statisticians and many economists, this is a nuisance in the search for a 'true' or at least a 'best' measure of economic growth. Efforts have been made by economists and economic historians to reconcile benchmark estimates with time series growth (see discussion in Johnson et al. 2009). To the famous economic historian Alexander Gerschenkron, however, the index number problem instead provided an important method to pinpoint structural changes in industrializing economies (Gerschenkron 1962). The present investigation follows this method.

2.3.2 Lessons from Gerschenkron and Dahmén

In Gerschenkron's analysis, the basic assumption was that industrialization concurred with technological changes in crucial branches that supplied increasing volumes of goods at lower prices. Central suppliers of inputs 'downstream' such as iron and steel works were of particular importance to nineteenth century industrialization. Innovations in this sector led to changes in the price and quantity structure, lowering prices and increasing volumes in the innovating sector. Such changes would result in higher growth rates if the price structure before the spurt was used in a constant price estimate instead of prices from after the spurt. Gerschenkron used the index number problem as a method to identify crucial moments of industrial spurts. The idea corresponds to the concept of market widening of innovating branches, launched by the Swedish economic historian/economist Erik Dahmén (1950, 1988). The market widening led in turn to increasing demand for complementary goods and services at rising relative prices as long as these were supplied less elastically. The reaction in complementary industries represented Dahmén's concept of market suction or demand pull within a development block around the innovation.

In a one-country framework, the Gerschenkronian structural change indicates a favourable industrial development of increased supply at lower prices of strategic goods.[1] In a multi-country analysis, including foreign trade, the analysis is more complex. A country may as well be favoured by the positive demand effect from other countries for complementary goods and services or from rising income generally.

In the construction of GDP series at national levels, the index number problem is usually reduced, although not eliminated, through the use of annual links of two-year averaged national prices (Fischer Index). This procedure is not available at the international level to accommodate growth rates between PPP benchmarks. In the Conference Board database, used in the present investigation, the growth rates of each country are not affected, when shifting between series based on 1990 and 2005 PPP benchmarks. The benchmark price structure affects, however, the purchasing power provided from a certain volume. With shift of PPP benchmark, the purchasing power levels are shifted and the shift factor differs considerably between countries. This means that the same volume growth rate may result in a different growth rate of purchasing power and consequently have different income effects. Thus, if nationally constructed GDP growth rates at constant prices are adjusted for the relative shift in purchasing power, we reach two objects in the analysis. We acquire firstly better measures of the income effect of volume growth and, secondly, Gerschenkronian or Dahmenian viewpoints on structural changes.

Analyses from these angles of the period from the early 1990s to the early 2010s may also give perspectives on conditions for catching up or forging ahead in the decades to come—perspectives we will return to.

2.4 The Measurement Principles

A simple aggregation of all national GDP series into two Gross World Production series, based on PPPs from 1990 and 2005 respectively, gives a first indication of the Index Number problem. Even if the two series develop quite similarly, their relationship is not fully stable but changes over time. The series with PPP base 1990 shows a somewhat higher growth rate over the period 1990/94–2009/13 than the series based on PPP 2005[2]—the two growth

---

[1] These may also be part of substitutions possibilities in a catch-up process where crucial, even fundamental, preconditions for industrialization are missing.

[2] Since business cycles are not simultaneous over the global economy, five-year averages are used at benchmarks to even out these differences in calculation of annual growth rates. Furthermore,

rates for world production per capita are on average 2.4 per cent and 2.1 per cent respectively. This is the traditional Gerschenkronian effect of aggregation indicating that goods and services with a falling relative price had an increasing volume over the period, i.e. the weight (relative price) of the advancing section of production was higher at the beginning than at the end of the period. Thus, advancing industries had a greater weight in the production index with prices at the beginning than at the end. This is an anticipated effect from rapid technological change, globalization and accelerated economic growth in emerging economies with a lower price level. As can be seen from Figure 2.1, the effect was rather weak during the 1990s but increased in strength after the turn of the millennium and became particularly strong at the onset of the Great Recession.

The comparison between the two series on Gross World Production also gives a measure of global inflation over the period, on average a rise of 50 per cent or slightly below 3 per cent annually, which corresponds to the shift factor between the 1990 and the 2005 series. In short, within the framework of generally rising prices, goods and services with relatively falling prices

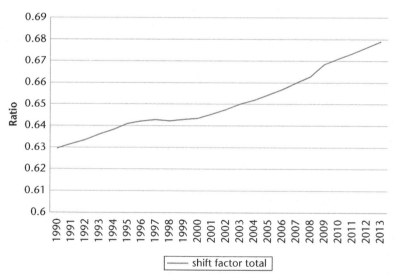

Figure 2.1 Ratio between World Gross Production 1990–2013 aggregated in PPP 1990 to aggregated in updated PPP 2005.

Source: Conference Board January 2014.

the 2005 PPP has been updated annually by The Conference Board. Differences between the updates are rather slight. In the present investigation, the update of 2011 is used, being the middle year of the last five-year period. In the text, however, it is referred to as 2005 PPP which is the basic construction.

increased their share and, thus, lowered the inflation pressure globally, particularly after the turn of the millennium.

2.4.1 Shift Factors Differ between Countries

These effects differ considerably though, between the countries. As long as constant prices with a fixed deflation procedure are applied in the calculation of GDP at a national level, global price changes will not interfere in the calculation of national growth rates. The growth rates of each country are unaffected, regardless whether we use the 1990 or 2005 PPP benchmark. Relative price shifts will, however, affect the purchasing power generated from a certain volume growth, due to changes in the world price structure, and thus affect the position of a country between two PPP benchmarks. The levels of the two curves are shifted and the shift factor differs considerably between countries. In Figure 2.2, these two effects are demonstrated with the

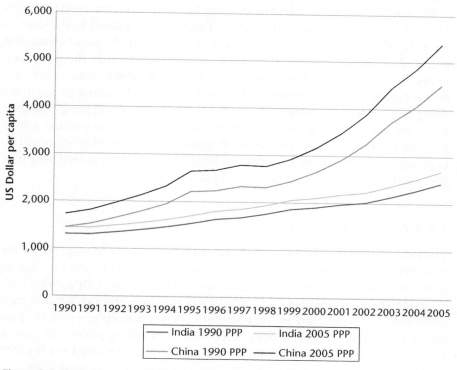

Figure 2.2 GDP per capita 1990–2005 in China and India—levels of 1990 PPP (lower curves) and 2005 PPP (upper curves). US Dollar per capita. Log scale. Ratio between World Gross Production 1990–2013 aggregated in PPP 1990 to aggregated in updated PPP 2005.

Source: Conference Board January 2014.

two PPP series for China and India respectively. In both cases the two lines follow each other perfectly, so the annual growth rates are unchanged using 1990s or 2005s PPPs. The shift factor differs remarkably however between China and India. The shift is greater between the two Chinese than between the two Indian series. From this follows that national GDP growth rates at constant prices ought to be adjusted for the shift in purchasing power between benchmarks to get a better measure of the income effect at world prices of the volume growth. When the shifts are determined in a great number of countries, roads are opened for analyses of what factors lay behind the differences in shift.

2.4.2 Analytical Aspects

Difference in shift is the primary object of the present analysis. By analyzing how each country behaved in the shift from 1990 PPP to 2005 PPP, one gets a measure of what purchasing power has been generated by GDP growth.

The starting point is to calculate the shift factor between the 1990 and 2005 PPP series for each country. The national shift is then related to the shift in total global supply, i.e. in aggregated world production. As noted above, the global shift factor indicates the global inflation rate, while the difference between the global and the country shift factor indicates whether a country on average has supplied goods and services at relatively falling or relatively rising prices. Thus, the relationship between the national and the global shift factor shows whether a country has increased its global purchasing power more or less than indicated by the GDP growth rate alone. This result will be expressed in a PPP adjusted growth rate which is the country growth rate plus the country shift factor minus the world shift factor.[3]

2.4.3 Causes Behind Shifts

The next question is obvious: what causes the shift factor to vary? There are basically three circumstances that may make the growth of the purchasing power of a country at the international level differ from its GDP growth rate.

Firstly, there are changes in relative prices on the world market that may affect national purchasing power differently, depending upon a nation's production structure. A specialization on products at falling prices will have a negative effect upon the shift factor and thus a negative effect on the PPP

---

[3] An alternative procedure is to recalculate the 1990 GDP for every country in 2005 price level but with 1990 PPP share of global production according to this formula: ((Country share of world production 1990 in 1990 PPP) x (world production 1990 in 2005 PPP)) and then calculate the difference in growth rates between series with the adjusted and non-adjusted base year of 1990.

adjusted growth rate—and vice versa of course if the nation is specialized in production segments of rising prices. An even more dynamic cause to the variation in the shift factor may be a structural change within the national economy between the two benchmarks. The country may move its specialization in the direction of sectors of either rising or falling prices. The dynamic interaction between production volumes and prices is similar to what were described above as Gerschenkronian or Dahmenian effects. A country may be active in a supply push or react to a demand pull and these two shifts may interact through the world market.

Secondly, there is an effect from estimating volumes of non-traded (domestic) sectors at world prices. In many developing countries, such goods or services are supplied at lower prices domestically than at the estimated world price level. In those cases, a PPP measurement enhances the traditional sector and thus the size of the economy, but if the traditional sector grows at a slower rate than the modern sector, a PPP adjustment will reduce overall growth rates, i.e. the shift effect will be negative. Once again, the effect may be the opposite if a slow growing sector is relatively highly valued domestically. In that case, a PPP measurement reduces the weight of the slowing growing sector and raises the adjusted growth rates. This might be the case with e.g., the public sector in some developed countries.

The different effects of measuring non-traded sectors at an estimated purchasing power parity level is clear from a comparison between GDP measured at PPP and at exchange value of the currency. In Western Europe, North America, Australia, New Zealand and Japan the relationship is close to one which means that modernized countries have a largely integrated price structure. In low-income or emerging economies, such as in South and East Asia, the situation is different. Except for Japan, all economies have considerably higher GDP at PPP than at exchange value levels. In Singapore, South Korea and Taiwan the ratio is in the interval of 1.5–2 while in the rest of this large region the ratio is in the interval of 2.5–3.5.

This means for instance that the size of Chinese total GDP in PPP terms is at about the same level as world-leading USA or as the whole of Western Europe. In exchange value, however, the Chinese GDP is no more than roughly a third of the US economy and about the same as the French and German economies together. These examples underline that national prices and national weights in GDP calculations may differ substantially from the weighting procedure in the PPP estimates, particularly concerning non-traded sectors in countries with great differences in price levels and growth rates between modern and traditional sectors.

A third, and unavoidable, factor is measurement errors. One can assume that these are more prevalent in poor countries at an early stage of modernization than in the developed world, which is highly integrated in the global economy. One can also assume that measurement practices were less system-atized in 1990 than in 2005. It is, though, beyond the scope of this investiga-tion to go into these details. Another method will be applied instead, namely to check the consistency between the shift factor and the structure of the economies in a number of cross-section regressions, including a total of 120 countries. The explanatory factors include income level and population size (in combination these also function as indirect measure of openness), the share of the agricultural sector in total employment and the structure of exports (share of fuels, low-tech manufactured goods and services respect-ively) as an indication of specialization in relation to the world market. If shift factors are significantly related to the explanatory variables and with expected signs, the relevance of the data is strengthened.

2.5 Adjustments of GDP Growth Rates to PPP Benchmarks

The result of the adjustment procedure is clear-cut (see Table 2.3). The com-paratively rich world had an overwhelmingly positive PPP adjustment effect, while low-income and middle-income countries overall had a negative effect. The positive impact includes all of the Western European countries (excluding Turkey) and almost all Central-Eastern European countries (excluding the new

Table 2.3 Annual growth rates in GDP per capita in major regions 1990/94–2009/13. Traditional growth rates and PPP-adjusted growth rates—adjusted from PPP 1990 to PPP 2005 (updated to 2011).

Region	Growth rates 1990/ 94–2009/13 with one benchmark (2005)	Effects of PPP adjustment to two benchmarks (1990 and 2005)	Growth rates adjusted to benchmarks 1990 and 2005
Western Europe	1.4	+0.9	2.3
Central-Eastern Europe	3.2	+1.9	5.1
Russia	1.8	+1.5	3.3
USA	1.5	+0.1	1.6
Middle East	2.4	+1.9	4.3
Asia, South & East	4.2	−0.7	3.5
Row above, excl. of Japan	5.7	−1.8	3.9
Latin America	1.7	−0.2	1.5
Africa	1.9	−0.9	1.0

Notes: On computation of adjustment effects, see text.
Western Europe: See table 2.1.
Central-Eastern Europe: Albania, Bosnia-Herzegovina, Bulgaria, Croatia, Czech Republic, Hungary, Macedonia, Poland, Romania, Serbia & Montenegro, Slovak Republic, Slovenia.
Middle East: Bahrain, Iran, Iraq, Israel, Jordan, Kuwait, Omar, Qatar, Saudi Arabia, Syria, United Arab Emirates, Yemen.
Asia, South and East: Bangladesh, Cambodia, China, Hong Kong, India, Indonesia, Japan, Malaysia, Pakistan, Philip-pines, Singapore, South Korea, Sri Lanka, Taiwan, Thailand, Vietnam.
Latin America and Africa: See table 2.1.
Source: See table 2.1.

republics in former USSR), North America and Oceania (Australia and New Zealand). It also includes the oil states in the Middle East. In all these countries, purchasing power grew ahead of the GDP volume growth.

Very significant is the positive PPP adjustment effect in the former socialist republics in Central and Eastern Europe. Countries such as Poland, Czech Republic, Slovakia, Slovenia, Hungary and Croatia all expanded strongly after the political revolution in the early 1990s. With the PPP adjustment effect, the region became a hothouse of income growth even at a global level.

A strong positive effect also goes for Russia, aided by mineral resources such as oil and gas, clearly similar to the positive effects in the Middle East oil states. In the rest of the former USSR, almost all states (12 out of 14) had a negative effect which was very different from the outcome in the former independent socialist states in Central-Eastern Europe.

On a global scale, the negative effect is particularly noteworthy in the fast-growing emerging economies in Eastern and Southern Asia, including China and India. The overall negative effect is much accentuated when the rich economy of Japan is excluded from the region's aggregated GDP. Actually, in this part of the world there were only three economies that had a positive impact from the PPP adjustment. Together with Japan, it was Singapore and Taiwan. All others were negatively affected. Most severely negative among large economies were Indonesia and India.

In Latin America, the only large economy with a positive effect was Mexico—also some small tourism orientated islands in the Caribbean were on the positive side. As a generalization, economies close to USA had a more positive outcome. The whole of South America, on the other hand, was on the negative side. The situation in Africa was similar. Of the 25 African nations in this investigation, only 5 were on the positive side—these were the relatively rich Algeria and South Africa, the oil or mineral rich Angola and Zambia and the fast growing Cameroon.

Thus, in the southern hemisphere only a few countries had a positive impact from the PPP adjustment while the outcome in the northern hemisphere was more mixed with strong positive zones.

2.5.1 *Europe Comes out Stronger*

A major result of the PPP adjustment process is the strengthened position of Europe relative to both USA and to the emerging economies of Asia. The positive effect in Western Europe is particularly noteworthy. All Western European countries (excluding Turkey) have a positive PPP effect and in all cases the effect is stronger than in the USA. The result is important in a longer perspective on relations between these continents. From 1950 to about 1990, Europe had been converging with the USA but from the 1990s US growth was said to have accelerated in a new process of divergence to Europe. As mentioned above, this was referred to as an effect of the ICT-revolution and the differing abilities in Europe and USA to adapt organizations to the new technology. The PPP adjustment effect points, however, in another direction. It reverses commonly received views on European and American economic growth of the past decades into continued convergence.

The PPP adjustment also puts new light on the convergence process between Western Europe, on one hand, and Southern and Eastern Asia excluding Japan, on the other hand. If the traditionally measured growth rates over the last two decades (1.4 and 5.7) were to continue, it would take about 40 years for Southern and Eastern Asia as a whole to catch up with Western Europe in terms of GDP per capita. If, however, growth in income were to follow the respective PPP adjusted growth rates (2.3 and 3.9), it would take more than a hundred years. The very large region would still be in convergence but at a considerably slower rate. The effect is also drastic, if not as strong, in the comparison between Western Europe and China. With the traditional growth rates (1.4 and 8.3), it would take China only about 20 years to reach Western European per capita levels. With the PPP adjusted growth rate levels (2.3 and 6.6) the time period of full catch-up would be about 40 years. It is still a very rapid catch-up but the difference between the two projections is significant.

Above all, the present investigation of the PPP adjustment effects points to the importance of analyzing factors behind the different results and their role for development beyond 2010 in terms of structural change and further catch-up or forge-ahead processes.

2.6 Explanatory Factors to PPP Adjustment Effects

The PPP adjustment factor of 120 countries is the dependent variable in an econometric exercise with two main objectives. The first objective is, of course, to analyze what factors made adjustment to PPP positions in 1990 and 2005 drive growth rates upwards or downwards. Secondly, the aim is to check whether regressions give reasonable and significant results that should strengthen trust in the data source. Two models were set up in order to meet these aims.

One model basically aims at exploring the importance of openness of an economy to the adjustment factor. The model combines the income level per capita of each country at the beginning of the period (i.e. GDP in 1990 PPP per inhabitant) with its size in terms of population or total GDP. The start year was chosen since income level should be seen as a precondition for and not as an effect of adjustment. The idea behind the model is that small economies are assumed to be more open to foreign trade than large ones and that rich economies should have more intensive trade than poor ones. In what direction these factors work on PPP adjustment over the last two decades is an open question. Small and open economies ought to be more sensitive to world market trends than large ones with huge domestic markets, but it is not a priori clear whether the small ones should be more effective or more vulnerable in relation to those trends. One could expect, however, that small and rich (open) economies have been relatively successful in adapting their structure to the world market.

The second model aims at analyzing the importance of the economic structure of each country in two ways. One is the share of agriculture in GDP. The idea is that the size of agriculture indicates the role of the traditional sector in the economy with an assumed negative relation to the PPP adjustment. The other way is the structure of foreign trade. The trade structure is measured by three variables: fuel as a proportion of total exports, low-skilled and labour-intensive products as a proportion of total manufactured exports, service exports as a proportion of GDP. There are reasons for formulating these export ratios in different ways. If all were formulated as proportions of exports, one would receive a strongly correlated triangle for each country. If all were formulated as proportions of GDP there would be a downward bias on the size of exports in rich countries. Instead, the fuel variable expresses an export specialization, the manufacturing variable a specialization within the manufacturing industry while the service variable combines the role of services both in exports and in the economy at large.

2.6.1 Small, Rich, Open and Ahead

The results of the econometric investigations are quite reassuring. The model on income and size gives high statistical determination of the adjustments effects and strong significance for the two variables—both of them in the expected direction. Thus, income is positively and size negatively, related to the PPP adjustments. Rich and small (open) economies have had a purchasing power that grew at a higher rate than their volume growth rates indicated. The income variable is particularly strong both in statistical significance and in impact on adjustments.

The model works even better when Latin America, Africa and the former USSR republics are excluded. Thus, in the OECD countries, the Middle East and the emerging South and East Asian parts of the world, the positive effects of being small and rich are even stronger—despite the reduction of the sample to the half. The adjusted R-square rises from about 0.42 to 0.52 with the reduction and it is particularly the size-factor that strengthens both in terms of impact and significance. One conclusion is that the interaction between openness and PPP-adjustment has been strong and predominantly positive in the part of the world that is most actively engaged in trade and industrialization.

When running the regression restricted to the rest of the world, the results are different. Statistically the model works less efficiently and the effect of country size is turned around. Large economies tend to have a somewhat more positive adjustment effect, although in an environment of mostly negative effects. Although the positive size coefficient has low significance, the result may point for small economies in the poorer part of the world at weaker positions at the market and weaker institutions to drive a catch-up process. This seems to be the case e.g., in most of the small republics that sprang from the former USSR. The weaker econometric results in statistical terms may also indicate less robust or lower quality in PPP estimates for these countries, especially for the 1990 benchmark.

2.6.2 Specialization Patterns Support PPP Analysis

The agricultural variable gives the expected negative relation to the PPP adjustment effect. As noted above, large agricultural sectors go together with large traditional or non-traded sectors and the greater weights in the PPP estimates to slow-growing traditional sectors have negative effects on the adjusted growth rates.

The foreign trade structure model also points in expected directions, having in mind the development of relative prices on the world market over the decades since 1990. Fuel, as part of exports has had a very significant positive effect on purchasing power in relation to volume growth. The impact of standardized manufactured goods as part of total manufactured exports is negative, while services exports as share of GDP have a positive impact. The outcome is about the same in the full global sample and the restricted sample with adjusted R-squared coefficients of 0.28 and 0.30 respectively. Thus, the structural model indicates that changes in relative prices have affected all economies in a similar fashion.

Fuel is a rather specific resource—either a nation has it or not and it may be central to catching up strategies—but its effect on the purchasing power of different countries over the last decades of rising relative fuel prices has to be taken into account. Development during 2014 shows, however, that oil is an economically unstable asset. Low-skilled or labour-intensive manufactured goods and services in exports are variables of another character. They indicate more of interaction between the internal development in terms of labour supply, industrial policy and institutions, on one hand, and the global market development, on the other.

To conclude, relatively large economies at a low or medium income level have supplied the world market with standardized goods—and also standardized services as in the case of India—at falling relative prices over the last two decades. Small and rich economies, on the other hand, have supplied more complex manufactured goods and services at relatively rising prices. These different structures go a long way to explain the overall pattern in PPP adjustment effects since 1990.

2.7 On the Role of Structural Change for Catching up or Forging Ahead

The investigation of the adjustment effects to purchasing power parity benchmarks has underlined the importance of a number of factors—both through the geographical distribution of positive and negative effects and through their relation to explanatory factors, formulated in models and estimated in cross-country regressions. Two main results are salient.

2.7.1 *The Increasing Need for Structural Change*

One overall reflection is the role of structures in an era when the weight of creative and knowledge-intensive work has increased in relation to standardized or mundane work. This is indicated by changes in relative prices and their impact upon the distribution of adjustment effects that is in accordance with country specialization and structure of foreign trade. This fairly positive outcome for rich countries might be seen as a paradoxical effect of the Great Doubling of the world market labour force—a doubling that was feared by some American economists a few years ago. The outcome, however, is a logical effect as long as developed countries are open for structural change.

The structural change to more knowledge-intensive, creative work puts a number of requirements on nations. While the economy becomes more globalized overall, particularly in standardized work, creative work producing more complex or customized products and services becomes more localized and dependent upon direct human contacts between many contributors. Thus, having well-functioning regions with intensive interaction becomes a necessity that raises new demands on institutions and policy in terms of infrastructure, culture and diversity; i.e. social capabilities or the fundamental determinants of growth become increasingly important (Abramovitz 1986, 1989; Maddison 1988) Deficiencies in these respects limit the efficiency of any catch-up oriented development policy.

Thus, the outcome of the investigation underlines the need for a great number of countries with catching-up ambitions to perform structural changes in direction of more qualified work. Otherwise, further volume growth in exports on mundane or standardized products will increase the price pressure in this area and undermine their income. All catching-up countries meet this challenge but it falls particularly heavily on economic giants such as China and India.

2.7.2 The Chinese and Indian Cases

Even if the PPP adjustment effects reduced growth rates in China, these are still very high and the adjustment effects fairly limited (minus 1.7 per cent annually). But the limited adjustment effect on growth and the still very high effect of going from GDP in exchange value to PPP estimate puts the finger on another Chinese problem for catching up over the next decades—the great regional and social imbalances produced by economic growth so far. Economic growth has been extremely high in Eastern China with enormous investments in export production and material infrastructure with increasing costs and with incipient structural change towards more qualified work. The social infrastructure, however, has deteriorated in the shift from the old to the new regime. In particular, Central and Western China has fallen behind. New five-year plans taken by the Chinese leadership in the beginning of the 2010s sought to ameliorate this situation by reducing inequality both regionally and socially. Diverting income flows from one region and from one interest group to another is, however, a politically risky undertaking that may increase instability in the enormous country for a couple of years—a major adversity for the political leadership. The immediate reaction to the Great Recession rather led to further support for the traditional growth mechanisms in the eastern regions—exports and investments—to keep up economic growth and employment. A rebalancing of the Chinese economy would, however, have a great impact upon the global—and surrounding Asian economy, by increasing Chinese demand and reducing its export surplus. It would above all provide impetus to further catch-up in Asia.

The Indian case has similarities with the Chinese but is in many ways different. As in China, political reforms led to acceleration in economic growth from the 1980s and 1990s but at a lower level and, in particular, India did not see such a huge increase in growth rates during the 2000s as China did. Indian growth has followed a more stable curve with less political injections although India has a history of ambitious state planning as well. One great difference, however, that comes out of the present investigation is the considerably more negative adjustment effect for India (minus 2.3 per cent annually) that reduces Indian economic growth from a high to medium position globally. This indicates that the traditional sector is even greater in India with less influence from modernization than in China—maybe the

Green Revolution has been too limited regionally and maybe its momentum has petered out on the Indian countryside—and that the much appraised, even feared, modernization of the ICT service sector around e.g., Bangalore and New Delhi, has not reached out very far regionally and has had one mainstay in standardized, large-scale undertakings. Further catch-up growth raises a number of challenges in India as well as in China.

2.7.3 *Small and Rich Leading in Both Asia and Europe*

The second main result of the investigation is the greater ability in small and comparatively rich countries to keep up with new market possibilities and perform structural changes. The greater dependence upon the global market in open economies might be one reason for this capacity that may be imbued in attitudes and institutions. Both market mechanisms in effective interplay with institutions may lead the way. That seems to be the case both in Asia and in Europe. As mentioned, only a few countries were on the positive side in Asia in terms of PPP adjustment effects but the positive list is clearly headed by Singapore—a small and rich country that early on went through a politically-led and market-attached catch-up process, based on structural change directed to more qualified work. The process seems to have continued over the last two decades with an adjusted annual per capita growth rate of about 5 per cent, not far below the Chinese rate. Singapore may very well continue as a node in Asian catch-up together with countries such as South Korea and Taiwan, especially if China reduces its export pressure over the region.

Europe gives a very articulate result in the investigation. All Western countries have a positive adjustment effect and it is particularly strong in small countries such as Luxemburg, Norway, Cyprus, Malta, Iceland, and Switzerland. These are countries with a high service orientation (finance and tourism) and in the Norwegian case also orientation to fuel. They contribute to the global pattern of small, open and service orientated economies as leading in structural adjustment. To the overall Western European result it is also important that comparatively large economies such as Germany, Austria, Spain, and Greece show considerable positive effects of the PPP adjustment. Table 2.4 distinguishes three different zones in Western Europe in terms of economic growth—all show similar adjustment effects on average (plus 0.8–0.9 per cent annually) but have different growth rates and characteristics. Northwestern Europe has been clearly leading in terms of economic growth since the 1990s with the British Isles, the Netherlands and the Nordic countries favoured by early adaptation to ICT and globalization. The Continental countries are lagging, partly due to slow growth in Germany in the 1990s after unification and sluggish growth in France. Even further

Table 2.4 Annual growth rates in GDP per capita in major European regions 1990/ 94–2009/13. Traditional growth rates and PPP-adjusted growth rates—adjusted from PPP 1990 to PPP 2005 (updated to 2011).

Region	Traditional growth rate	PPP adjusted rate
Northwestern Europe	1.9	2.7
Continental Europe	1.2	2.1
Southern Europe	0.9	1.7
All Western Europe	1.4	2.3

Notes: Northwestern Europe: Denmark, Finland, Iceland, Ireland, Netherlands, Norway, Sweden, United Kingdom. Continental Europe: Austria, Belgium, France, Germany, Luxemburg, Switzerland.
Southern Europe: Cyprus, Greece, Italy, Malta, Portugal, Spain.
See further notes to table 2.3.
Sources: See table 2.1.

behind is Southern Europe, very much as an effect of the Euro crisis, but there are great differences within the zone between Portugal and Italy, on one hand, and Spain and Greece, on the other.

2.7.4 Factors Behind European Divergence

Some investigations provide deeper insights into national and regional characteristics behind this pattern. These insights indicate important factors for catch-up or forging ahead processes. During the first decade of the 2000s, ICT diffusion and contribution to economic growth was the highest in the Nordic countries (Sweden on par with the USA) and in Northwestern Europe generally, while it was lagging specifically in Southern Europe. (Oulton 2012) Furthermore, a sociological investigation of working organization within EU15 from two criteria—complexity of learning processes and discretion for the employees—showed a similar spatial distribution (Lorenz/Valeyre 2006). Complexities in learning processes and discretion for individuals or groups of employees were characteristic features of the more horizontally organized work processes in Northern Europe with much communication both internally and externally. This opened up for the provision of complex services, combining many competencies, and for easier adoption of ICT in organizations. Further to the west, hierarchies became more prevalent and in Southern Europe even fordist mass production together with pure handicraft was still pervasive. Therefore, Southern Europe was more at the mercy of the new price competition in standardized goods from both East Asia and Eastern Europe; in a European perspective, the more affluent northern part forged ahead in recent decades, which in its turn creates new catch-up possibilities within Europe, once Southern Europe more thoroughly adapts to new conditions. That may be the case when the present drawn out Euro crisis is overcome.

The next question on Southern Europe and the Euro crisis presents itself almost automatically. Why have Spain and Greece, two of the most afflicted economies, both high traditional growth rates up to the crisis and high positive adjustment effects? Both traits may be connected to the crisis. The modernization of the economies with heavy investments in infrastructure and residential constructions incurred increasing debts at a vulnerable moment when the global economy contracted while Spanish and Greek competitive power was still too low on standardized markets. The positive adjustment effect may also partly be linked to the possibility that relatively slow-growing private and public services were highly-priced domestically in Southern compared to Northern Europe which gives a positive effect on the PPP adjustment. At the same time, a highly priced service sector may contribute to the financial pressure on public finances.

The opening of markets and modernizing of industries in Central-Eastern Europe was an integral part of the structural change since 1990. Investments from German companies especially, propelled capital exports and high savings ratios in Germany, while competitive power in manufacturing increased rapidly in the liberalized states—their growth rate in exports of manufactured products was on the same level as in Chinese manufactured exports over the period. Proximity to Western Europe and not too distant experiences of market institutions were probably important for these countries, in contrast to the new republics in former USSR.

The extremely fuel-based economies in the Middle East were partly modernized, in e.g. finances and tourism, but the high adjusted growth rates can so far hardly be seen as a basis for catch-up processes on a broader scale. Modernization and unequal wealth has rather brought conflicts high up on the agenda in the region.

2.8 The 2010s and the 1930s—a Long Historical Perspective

The concluding discussion puts the present Great Recession in a longer time perspective, as a structural crisis that will make up a turning point in global development—partly as a reaction to the profound changes in the global economy over the last decades but also as a crisis in a quite regular sequence of structural crises in modern economic history. The discussion also puts up a Scandinavian mirror that emphasizes historically the role of small open economies in crises of corresponding character that may be relevant for the present crisis and for the question: can small countries catch-up?

2.8.1 *Long Cyclical Similarities between the 1930s and the 2010s*

The long term perspective on the crisis is based on a comparison between the crises of the 1930s and 2010s from a structural and a long cyclical rather than a financial or business cycle point of view. The focus is especially on political and institutional challenges, on Scandinavian responses in the 1930s and their relevance for small countries today.

A basic similarity between the two crises is their critical role of finding roads for social and economic adaptation to radical technological and organizational change at a global level, after two epochs of industrial revolutions—the so called second and third industrial revolutions that took off about 40 years earlier, at the beginning of the 1890s and the 1970s.

The breaking points between industrial revolutions and their adaptive crises 1890s–1930s–1970s–2010s indicate a periodicity of a long-cyclical character that has been quite pronounced in the Swedish economy and studied in more detail (Schön 1991, 1998, 2000, 2012). This pattern differs from most periodization of long cycles or long waves that have been proposed in the international literature from Kondratieff onwards (See e.g. Kondratieff 1926, van Duijn 1983, Freeman and Louca 2001). Differences go back to different traditions in economic and historical analysis. While the international literature is dominated by technological perspectives (such as the advent of new techno-economic regimes, the appearance of radical innovations or General Purpose Technologies (Bresnahan & Trajtenberg 1995)), the Swedish pattern is based on an analysis of the behaviour of the economy and society in response to technological change, much in the traditions of Erik Dahmén and Alexander Gerschenkron. This has been possible thanks to a rich annual database back to the early nineteenth century, indicating breaks in behaviour with new growth patterns following upon global crises since the Barings crises of the early 1890s. The analysis goes even further back with another breaking point in the 1850s—following upon the 1848 financial and social crisis mainly in Europe. Development from the 1850s was characterized by infrastructural and institutional adaptations to the new possibilities that sprang from the first industrial revolution, following the same logic as from the 1930s and 2010s.

2.8.2 *Relevance of a Swedish Pattern*

A full sequence appears from Swedish data of three industrial revolutions (or radical innovations with the early breakthrough of new General Purpose Technologies), followed after some 40 years of another period characterized by a broader social and political change. The prolonged crisis after the Great Recession fits very well into this rhythm.

At this point it is certainly appropriate to ask what relevance a Swedish pattern should have for the much wider global economy. One can argue from different positions. A first argument holds that the Swedish breaking points are clearly related to well-known wider crises at the international or global level, even with documented effects on structural and institutional change. Secondly, even if Sweden is a small economy, it is very dependent upon the international/global economy as an open economy with a large export sector. Furthermore, ever since the nineteenth century Swedish exports have been highly related to demand from investments abroad, thus a dependence upon the most volatile and structurally sensitive sector of foreign markets. One can argue that the Swedish economy has acted as a thermometer of broader structural change in the international economy in conjunction with the major crises that deserve to be denominated as structural crises.

Financial factors were certainly important as an initiator of most of these crises (the 1970s being an exception) but the longevity of the crises were occasioned by their structural basis, i.e. of the need to develop new forces of economic growth and to meet new demands on political/institutional change. While periods of industrial revolutions have a strong bent for establishing radically new growth forces, the following periods (from the 1850s, 1930s and 2010s) are characterized by a more political agenda.

In the 1930s, Scandinavian countries were important in formulating a political response to the radical changes that had occurred in previous decades—in the first instance it was rather a response to the crisis itself but it contained the seeds to a broader adaptation in small and open economies to global economic and social change, that were to develop into the Swedish or the Scandinavian model of policy and institutions. Despite their modest size, Scandinavian countries were important in developing a social-liberal alternative in the fierce ideological struggles that characterized the interwar period. What factors contributed to this role of the Scandinavian countries from the 1930s?

Firstly, being small and open they had to follow trends in the international market, providing major impetus to structural changes that were in line with technological opportunities and market demand (the two primary factors in Erik Dahmén's central concept 'development blocks' in his analysis of Sweden's economy in the interwar period). The strength of the development blocks was dependent upon a number of complementary factors, including entrepreneurs, financial institutions and politicians. Secondly, the Scandinavian countries had comparatively strong and stable political institutions, important not only for the advancement of development blocks with heavy infrastructural components (such as roads, electrification, residential constructions) but also for developing a social security system to complement the openness of the small economy. Thus, Scandinavia had a structure highly appropriate for meeting the challenges of social adaptation to prior radical change, the main component of the structural crisis of the 1930s. Thirdly, Scandinavia was part of a relatively strong region of the world economy. Northwestern Europe comprised leading countries such as UK, Germany and the Netherlands. Despite substantial differences between these countries in the 1930s, they all acted as stimuli for innovations as well as demand for Scandinavian exports.

2.8.3 Are Experiences of the 1930s Still Relevant?

The last question comes naturally. Are the 1930s experiences still relevant for the road out of the Great Recession and for accomplishing the social adaptations to the Third Industrial Revolution with intensified globalization and ICT revolution? Following the main lines in earlier adaptations, a new complementarity is needed between institutions, infrastructures and innovative growth trajectories that stimulate economic growth and increase participation and equality broadly in economic and social development.

Some of the factors for earlier successful adaptation are certainly present also today—such as being small and open and highly dependent on the global economy—as prerequisites for flexible structural change. The world is, however, different from the 1970s. The traditional Scandinavian model had one of its bases in the equalizing force of capital intensive fordist technologies but that model is no longer efficient in highly developed or postindustrial societies.

The model may, however, still be relevant for catching-up economies. The drive for equalization of productivity also increased the pressure for structural change which is still important as the PPP analysis indicated. Increased globalization and technological change, however, create also new preconditions. The world economy is much more open in the 2010s than in the 1930s. Growth in the global economy may act as a locomotive for catching-up economies, particularly if giants like China or India upgrade their structures with increased domestic demand and less output pressure on markets for standardized goods and services. That could stimulate industrial development and service exchange in catch up processes in Asia and even more so in Africa, if a number of countries can upgrade their economies from natural resource based growth to modern industrialization. However, there is another but. Technological change may take a new jump from the 2010s into the robotization of standardized work that threatens to hit specialized low-wage countries the hardest and to increase the demand for programming, product development, logistics, and other complementary competencies to robotization, which developed countries may provide more efficiently, leading rather to reindustrialization in the centre (Brynjolfsson/McAfee 2014).

Structural change with a shift over the last decades towards knowledge-intensive activities and demand for labour with more human capital has, furthermore, contributed to an increasingly uneven income distribution in rich countries that puts up a primary challenge for social policy and infrastructural development over the next decades. This is an enigma also in catch-up processes. Fundamentals in terms of social capabilities become increasingly important up the ladder in that process, while capital intensive substitution policies may come to reside in the backwaters of economic growth.

The present Great Recession presents this enigma in different proportions at different stages of the ladder between catching up and forging ahead. Whether political institutions in small and open economies are ready to play the role of avant-garde in providing directions for the future, as in the 1930s, is still an open question.

References

Abramowitz, M., 1986. 'Catching Up, Forging Ahead, and Falling Behind'. *Journal of Economic History* vol. 46:385–406.

Abramovitz, M., 1989. *Thinking about growth and other essays on economic growth and welfare.* Cambridge: Cambridge University Press.

Bresnahan, T. F. and M. Trajtenberg, 1995. 'General purpose technologies: engines of growth?' *Journal of Econometrics* vol. 65 number 1:83–108.

Brynjolfsson, E. and A. McAfee, 2014. *The Second Machine Age. Work, Progress and Prosperity in a Time of Brilliant Technologies*, New York and London 2014: W.W. Norton & Company.

Crafts, N., 2006. 'The world economy in the 1990s: a long-run perspective'. In *The Global Economy in the 1990s. A long-run perspective*, edited by Rhode, P. W. and G. Toniolo, Cambridge: Cambridge University Press, 21–42.

Dahmén, E., 1950. *Svensk industriell företagarverksamhet. Kausalanalys av den industriella utvecklingen 1919–1939. Part I–II.* Stockholm: IUI.

Dahmén, E., 1988. 'Development blocks in industrial economics'. *Scandinavian Economic History Review*, 36, 3–14.

Freeman, R., 2005. 'What Really Ails Europe (and America): The Doubling of the Global Workforce.' *The Globalist*, June 3, 2005. <http://www.theglobalist.com/StoryId.aspx?StoryId=4542>.

Freeman, C. and F. Louca, 2001. *As Time Goes By: From the Industrial Revolution to the Information Revolution*, Oxford: Oxford University Press.

Gerschenkron, A., 1962. *Some Aspects of Industrialization in Bulgaria, 1878–1939*, in *Economic Backwardness in Historical Perspective*, Cambridge, Ma: Harvard University Press.

Johnson, S., W. Larson, C. Papageorgiou, and A. Subramanian, 2009. *Is newer better? Penn World Table revisions and their impact on growth estimates*, NBER Working Paper 15455, October 2009.

Kondratieff, N. D., 1926. 'Die lange wellen der konjunktur'. *Archiv für Sozialwissenschaft und Sozialpolitik*, Band 56:3: 573–609.

Lorenz, E. and A. Valeyre, 2006. 'Organizational forms and innovative performance: a comparison of the EU-15'. In: *How Europe's economies learn. Coordinating competing models*, edited by Lorenz, E. and B.Å. Lundvall, New York: Oxford University Press.

Maddison, A., 1988. 'Ultimate and proximate growth causality: A critique of Mancur Olson on the rise and decline of nations.' *Scandinavian Economic History Review* Vol. 36 number 2.

Oulton, N., 2012. 'Long term implications of the ICT revolution: Applying the lessons of growth theory and growth accounting.' *Economic Modelling* vol. 29, 2012:1722–36.

Rhode, P. W. and G. Toniolo, 2006. *The Global Economy in the 1990s. A long-run perspective*, Cambridge: Cambridge University Press.

Schön, L., 1991. 'Development blocks and transformation pressure in a macro-economic perspective—a model of long-term cyclical change.' *Skandinaviska Enskilda Banken Quarterly Review* Number 3–4:67–76.

Schön, L., 1998. 'Industrial crises in a model of long cycles: Sweden in an international perspective.' In *Economic crises and restructuring in history*, edited by Myllyntaus, T., Stuttgart: Scripta Mercaturae Verlag.

Schön, L., 2000. 'Electricity, technological change and productivity in Swedish industry, 1890–1990.' *European Review of Economic History* vol. 4 number 2:175–94.

Schön, L. 2012. *An Economic History of Modern Sweden*, London: Routledge.

The Conference Board, 2014 (January). *Total Economy Database Output, Labor and Labor Productivity, country details, 1950–2013*. Retrieved in March 2014, <https://www.conference-board.org/retrievefile.cfm>.

van Duijn, J., 1983. *The Long Wave in Economic Life*, London: George Allen & Unwin.

3

The Latecomer Advantages and Disadvantages

A New Structural Economics Perspective

Justin Yifu Lin

3.1 Introduction

Before the industrial revolution in the eighteenth century the world was quite stagnant and flat in terms of the speed of growth and difference in per capita income across countries. Most countries lived on their agriculture and were poor. According to Maddison's estimates it took about 1400 years to double per capita income in Western Europe before the eighteenth century and the per capita GDP of the Netherlands, the richest and most prominent trading power at the beginning of the eighteenth century, was 2130 international dollars, about five times the average of 421 international dollars in Africa (Maddison 2010).[1] The industrial revolution, referred to as the only event in human history by the historian Clark (2007), started in the UK in the mid-eighteenth century, marking a dramatic turning point in the economic progress of the world's nations. Rapid technological innovation after the arrival of the first industrial revolution created new tools with higher productivity and new industries with higher values that made it possible not only to break the Malthusian trap but also a dramatic increase in per capita income (Kuznets 1966). During the nineteenth century, a number of the pioneers of the industrial revolution in Western Europe and North America leapt ahead of the rest of the world. By 1851 the UK had overtaken the Netherlands to become the

---

[1] Unless indicated otherwise, all estimates of GDP and per capita GDP, cited in this paper, are taken from Maddison (2010) and measured in 1990 Geary-Khamis PPP adjusted dollars.

richest country in the world and at the beginning of the twentieth century, its per capita GDP had reached 4492 dollars, just over eight times that of China, the poorest country in the world at that time in Maddison's table of historical statistics of the world economy.

It is the dream of every backward country to become an advanced industrialized country. Gerschenkron's seminal studies of the industrialization in continental Europe and Russia found that the latecomer countries have the advantage of backwardness in industrialization because a backward country can borrow from a large store of technological innovations from the advanced countries and can adopt the latest technology without facing the resistance put up by users of old technologies (Gerschenkron 1962).[2]

Gerschenkron also summarizes his findings in six propositions for countries starting industrialization with different degrees of backwardness (Gerschenkron 1962, pp. 353–4):

1. The more backward a country's economy was initially, the more likely was its industrialization to start discontinuously as a sudden great spurt proceeding at a relatively high rate of growth of manufacturing output.

2. The more backward a country's economy, the more pronounced was the stress placed on bigness of both plant and enterprise in its industrialization.

3. The more backward a country's economy, the greater was the stress placed upon producers' goods as against consumers' goods.

4. The more backward a country's economy, the heavier was the pressure upon the levels of consumption of the population.

5. The more backward a country's economy, the greater was the part played by special institutional factors designed to increase supply of capital to the nascent industries and, in addition, to provide them with less decentralized and better informed entrepreneurial guidance; the more backward the country, the more pronounced was the coerciveness and comprehensiveness of those factors.

6. The more backward a country, the less likely was its agriculture to play any active role by offering to the growing industries the advantages of an expanding industrial market based in turn on the rising productivity of agricultural labour.

From the point of view of the advantages of backwardness, the government of a backward country can adopt various institutional arrangements to mobilize

[2] Gershenkron's first article, 'Economic Backwardness in Historical Perspective', was published in 1952. A collection of fourteen related essays, together with an introduction, a postscript and three appendixes, was published in 1962 with the same title of the first article 'Economic Backwardness in Historical Perspective'.

capital with which to develop advanced industries and make the country grow faster than the high-income countries. The country will achieve convergence by tapping into that potential. Indeed, there was a small group of countries achieving 'catch-up' in the colonial offshoots of Central and Western European countries in the late nineteenth century and, again, in East Asia in the post World War II period. For most backward countries, though, the twentieth century was instead an unfortunate period of continued and accelerated divergence in income level and living standards between them and the advanced countries. Instead of the advantage of backwardness, there seems to be in reality a disadvantage of backwardness in catch-up.

This historical record challenges economists to rethink the issue of industrialization and convergence. This chapter is organized as follows: The next section (3.2) provides a history of twentieth century divergence. This is followed in Section 3.3 by a critique of two previous waves of development thinking, structuralism and neoliberalism, examining how they have failed to guide developing countries to catch up with the developed countries. Section 3.4 introduces the new structural economics as an alternative to previous thinking. Section 3.5 discusses how governments apply new structural economics to realize the advantage of backwardness. Section 3.6 concludes with a few remarks.

3.2 The Challenge of Economic Development: Historical Antecedents and Twentieth Century Divergence

Before the industrial revolution, there was little growth in the world economy and the income gap between countries was extremely small.[3] In 1820, the between-country income differences represented less than fifteen per cent of income inequality across people in the world (whereas the between-country share rose to well over half of global inequality by 1950),[4] and per capita GDP of the richest country was not quite four times higher than that of the poorest (Maddison 2010). The industrial revolution led to the Great Divergence: world growth was driven by a few Western industrialized countries before and after World War II, with the exception that in the post-war period Japan joined the group of advanced industrialized nations.

---

[3] This section draws on Lin and Rosenblatt (2012).

[4] See Bourguignon and Morrisson (2002) for a calculation of global inequality since the start of the industrial revolution and a decomposition between within country and between country inequality. The figures referred to here are from Theil Index and Mean Logarithmic Difference measures. The between country share is larger for the 'standard deviation of logarithm' method; however, the same trend is followed: a lower share of between-country differences that then grows dramatically in the twentieth century. See Table 2 of Bourguignon and Morrisson for more details.

Before the industrial revolution, the global economic landscape was dramatically different. Economies were largely based on agriculture and scientific progress was largely divorced from technological innovation in production (Lin 1995). Growth was driven mainly by population expansion and frequently threated by the Malthusian trap (Kuznets 1966).

All of this changed with the industrial revolution. Scientific progress began to be applied to the means of production as machines were developed that both increased productivity in firms, but also dramatically reduced transportation costs. This created the possibility for the countries that developed those technologies, or that adapted the technologies first, to grow much faster than the less technologically advanced ones.

In the case of Britain, the Industrial Revolution generally refers to the period 'that witnessed the application of mechanically powered machinery in the textile industries, the introduction of James Watt's steam engine, and the "triumph" of the factory system of production' (Cameron, 1997, page 166). It was the outcome of the idea born during the Middle Ages and developed thereafter that science should be applied to industry and the practical affairs of humankind. As Azariadis and Stachurski (2005) point out, 'While the scientific achievements of the ancient Mediterranean civilizations and China were remarkable, in general there was little attempt to apply science to the economic problems of the peasants. Scientists and practical people had only limited interaction.' Lin (1995) argues that the key factor was the transition from innovation based on the experiences of artisan/farmers in the pre-industrial revolution period to innovation based on controlled experiments guided by science after the industrial revolution. Societal incentives embedded in the civil service examination in pre-modern China did not encourage the human capital accumulation needed for the new system of innovation, inhibiting the industrial revolution from originating in China.

The result of this process was that (at least before the year 2000) the global economy was dominated by the few industrialized economies that existed in the world, and most of these few economies had become industrialized either as leaders or earlier followers of the nineteenth century industrial revolution.[5] Historical data (Figure 3.1) dramatically reveal the divergent pattern of growth across country groupings. In the late nineteenth century, the western European countries and their colonial 'offshoots' began to experience a historic take-off in incomes per capita, as did Japan in the middle of the twentieth century. The world economy was driven by several large Western European countries (Germany, France, Italy, the United Kingdom) and Anglophone

[5] There is a tectonic shift in the pattern of global growth after 2000. China and other emerging market economies become the main growth drivers in the world (Lin and Rosenblatt 2012).

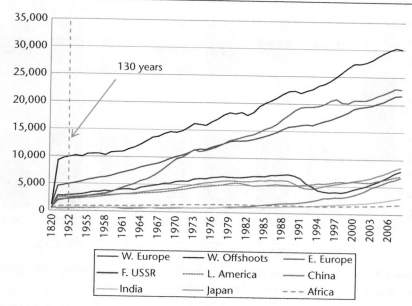

Figure 3.1 Development since the Industrial Revolution.
Source: Maddison (2010) database.

'offshoots' (Australia, New Zealand, the United States, and Canada), plus Japan. Many other countries, including the former Soviet Union, were able to rise to middle-income status and experience levels of average economic welfare that far surpassed earlier centuries; however, these standards of living still lagged badly behind the leading countries.

In theory, based on Gershenkron's advantage of backwardness hypothesis, one would expect, and certainly hope, that the poorer countries in the world can catch up with the richer ones. But in reality, there seems to be a *disadvantage* of backwardness. Few countries have experienced 'convergence' on a sustained basis. A famous paper that discusses the performance during the twentieth century is entitled 'Divergence, Big Time' (Pritchett 1997).

One approach to measuring relative progress is to look at per capita GDP relative to the United States, which has been the exemplar of all advanced industrialized countries after World War II. Figure 3.2 shows that the shares of countries in each ratio range has been fairly stable, with some growth in the share of countries in the upper Middle Income Country (MIC) range (say, roughly 0.3–0.7), but really not much expansion of the share of countries that are at 0.7 of the US level of per capita GDP. At the bottom end, the share at 0.1 or less of US levels remains stuck near 40 per cent. Persistently, over 80 per cent of the countries in the world have GDP per capita levels that are half or less than half of the level in the United States.

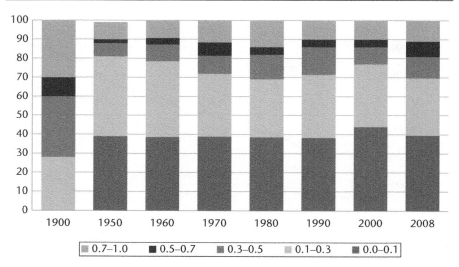

Figure 3.2 Distribution of Countries by (Relative) Income Classification, 1900–2008, %.
Source: Maddison (2010) data and World Bank for 2008 country thresholds.

There is also some 'churning' where countries not only converge up the ladder, but also diverge down the ladder. This is the case of some former colonies in Africa: many have gone from being lower MICs at independence to Low Income Countries (LICs) in 1980. Since then, some have climbed back up to MIC status. There are also countries at the High Income Country (HIC) end of the distribution that have, by this measure, fallen back to MIC status.

Many middle-income countries face the risk of falling into a middle-income trap. Even some previously high growth Asian economies, like Malaysia and Thailand,[6] experienced a substantial deceleration of growth following the Asian financial crisis. The Latin American and Caribbean region, however, probably provides the classic example of MICs failing to progress to high income country status. Figure 3.3 reveals the persistent lack of convergence of the Latin America region with the living standards in the United States. Periods of mild catch-up were followed by periods of declining relative incomes. More recently, most of the economies of Latin America have stabilized and there has been a strong upturn in growth, led by the largest economy of the region—Brazil. It remains to be seen whether the recent improved

---

[6] Post 1997 crisis GDP per capita growth rates were roughly half the level of pre-crisis growth rates. Malaysia's average growth of 6.4 per cent from 1988–1997 fell to 3 per cent from 1999–2010, and Thailand's average of 7.2 per cent over 1988–1997 fell to 3.4 per cent for 1999–2010. (GDP per capita growth rates are from *World Development Indicators*.) On the other hand, this would still imply convergence—albeit at a slower pace—given HIC per capita growth rates of around 2 per cent.

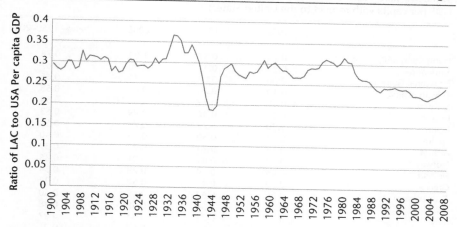

Figure 3.3 Latin American Economic Performance over the Last Century.
Source: Maddison (2010) database.

growth performance in Brazil and several other Latin American economies can be sustained into the future.

The net result is that during the twentieth century, very few countries managed to progress from low to middle and then to high income status. Table 3.1 summarizes how only a handful of developing countries have succeeded in reaching high levels of prosperity and many of them are in Western Europe. The few developing economy success stories—with the exception of a few small oil-rich countries[7]—are generally located in East Asia and achieved rapid industrialization (Lin 2009).

To make matters worse, there are over a dozen countries, displayed in Table 3.2, that suffered a greater than 0.10 decline in relative GDP per capita over the same period. Many of these are middle-income countries that failed to keep pace with the 2 per cent GDP per capita growth of the United States over this period. In addition, several oil-producing countries failed to diversify their economic base, and as a result, have experienced large declines in their relative income per capita.

3.3 Rethinking of Economic Development

The findings elaborated in the preceding section challenge the economics community to rethink the existing development theories. Why was there so

---

[7] This is the case for Equatorial Guinea, Trinidad and Tobago and Oman.

Table 3.1 Rare Cases of Catch-Up (Economies with a greater than 0.10 increase in relative GDP per capita with respect to the United States).

	1950	1980	2008	Change 1950–2008
Hong Kong SAR, China	0.23	0.57	1.02	0.78
Singapore	0.23	0.49	0.90	0.67
Equatorial Guinea	0.06	0.08	0.71	0.65
Taiwan, China	0.10	0.28	0.67	0.58
S. Korea	0.09	0.22	0.63	0.54
Ireland	0.36	0.46	0.89	0.53
Japan	0.20	0.72	0.73	0.53
Spain	0.23	0.50	0.63	0.40
Austria	0.39	0.74	0.77	0.39
Norway	0.57	0.81	0.91	0.35
Finland	0.44	0.70	0.78	0.34
Greece	0.20	0.48	0.52	0.32
T. & Tobago	0.38	0.67	0.68	0.30
Israel	0.29	0.59	0.58	0.28
Italy	0.37	0.71	0.64	0.27
Germany	0.41	0.76	0.67	0.26
Puerto Rico	0.22	0.44	0.48	0.26
Portugal	0.22	0.43	0.46	0.24
Mauritius	0.26	0.24	0.47	0.21
Oman	0.07	0.22	0.27	0.20
Thailand	0.09	0.14	0.28	0.20
Belgium	0.57	0.78	0.76	0.19
France	0.54	0.79	0.71	0.17
China	0.05	0.06	0.22	0.17
Malaysia	0.16	0.20	0.33	0.17
Netherlands	0.63	0.79	0.79	0.16
Botswana	0.04	0.09	0.15	0.12
Bulgaria	0.17	0.33	0.29	0.11

Memo/
Former Soviet Union/E. European countries with data only since 1990

	1990	2008	Change
Estonia	0.47	0.64	0.17
Slovenia	0.47	0.58	0.11
Armenia	0.26	0.37	0.11
Belarus	0.31	0.40	0.09
Slovakia	0.33	0.42	0.08
Bosnia	0.16	0.23	0.07
Azerbaijan	0.20	0.26	0.06
Latvia	0.43	0.48	0.05
Kazakhstan	0.32	0.36	0.04
Czech Rep.	0.38	0.41	0.03
Lithuania	0.37	0.36	−0.01
Uzbekistan	0.18	0.17	−0.01
Turkmenistan	0.16	0.14	−0.02
Croatia	0.32	0.29	−0.03
Macedonia	0.17	0.13	−0.04
Russia	0.34	0.29	−0.04
Kyrgyzstan	0.16	0.09	−0.06
Tajikistan	0.13	0.05	−0.08
Ukraine	0.26	0.16	−0.10
Serbia/Montenegro/Kosovo	0.22	0.12	−0.10
Georgia	0.33	0.19	−0.14
Moldova	0.27	0.11	−0.15

Source: Maddison (2010).

Table 3.2 Divergence 'leaders' (Countries suffering a 0.10 or greater decrease in relative GDP per capita with respect to the United States).

	1950	1980	2008	Change 1950–2008
Bolivia	0.20	0.14	0.09	−0.11
Iraq	0.14	0.34	0.03	−0.11
Lebanon	0.25	0.19	0.14	−0.11
South Africa	0.27	0.24	0.15	−0.11
Nicaragua	0.17	0.12	0.05	−0.12
Djibouti	0.16	0.09	0.04	−0.12
Switzerland	0.95	1.01	0.81	−0.14
Argentina	0.52	0.44	0.35	−0.17
Uruguay	0.49	0.35	0.32	−0.17
Gabon	0.33	0.36	0.12	−0.20
N. Zealand	0.88	0.66	0.60	−0.29
Venezuela	0.78	0.55	0.34	−0.44
UAE	1.65	1.49	0.50	−1.15
Kuwait	3.02	0.71	0.41	−2.61
Qatar	3.18	1.55	0.56	−2.62
Memo/				
Saudi Arabia	*0.23*	*__0.71__*	*0.27*	*0.04*

Source: Maddison (2010) dataset.

little convergence in the twentieth century in spite of the promise of the advantage of backwardness for the developing countries in their industrialization drives? What was special about the few countries that 'escaped' low and middle income status? Can their success be replicated in the laggard countries?

Development economics became a subfield of modern economics after World War II to guide the reconstruction of war-ravaged countries and the nation-building of newly independent former colonies. The first wave of development thinking was structuralism (Rosenstein-Rodan 1943, Prebisch 1950, Singer 1950). There may be a natural tendency in human nature to try to imitate success. The dominance of the few advanced countries that emerged from the industrial revolution was based on their advanced manufacturing industries. Many developing countries' economies, however, were still based on natural resources—intensive agriculture and mining—and these were seen as 'backward' rather than advanced sectors. The structuralists advised the developing countries to adopt an import substitution strategy with direct state intervention to create institutions, including financial repressions, distortions of resources prices and administrative allocation of resources, to mobilize capital to develop capital-intensive, large scale manufacturing industries similar to those in advanced countries (Lin 2009). These measures resembled those adopted by extreme backward continental European countries in their industrialization drives in the nineteenth century, summarized in Gerschenkron's six propositions.

Structuralism rejected the notion that the invisible hand of the free market could guide the process of development. The term 'structuralism' itself comes from the notion that structural rigidities are present in most economies, and in particular in countries at low levels of development. Structuralists believed that structural rigidities in developing countries would prevent the process of industrialization, and 'self-sustained' growth could not become a reality without more interventionist government policies, as Gershenkron had found based on his historical studies of 'moderate backward' and 'extreme backward' countries in continental Europe and the Soviet Union.

In structuralism, the underlying logic of state interventions was convincing. All socialist countries, as well as most capitalist countries followed the state-led, import substitution strategy advocated by structuralism in post World War II (Chenery 1961). But countries that adopted this strategy typically fell into a pattern of rapid growth driven by large-scale investments, similar to the experience of countries in Europe in the nineteenth century studied by Gershenkron, but followed by long periods of stagnation and frequent crises (Lin 2009). The overall results were universal development failure (Krueger and Tuncer 1982; Lal 1994; Pack and Saggi 2006).

The failures of the structuralist approach led to the second wave of development thinking—neoliberalism, encapsulated in the Washington Consensus policy package.[8] The original ten tenets of the Washington Consensus were: (i) fiscal discipline, (ii) reordering public expenditure priorities; (iii) tax reform (broad base with moderate rates); (iv) liberalizing interest rates; (v) competitive (not overvalued) exchange rates; (vi) trade liberalization; (vii) liberalization of inward foreign direct investment; (viii) privatization; (ix) deregulation; and (x) property rights (for the informal sector). In many ways, the Washington Consensus was a reaction to the complex web of distortions, summarized in Gerschenkron's fifth proposition, that had to be created to try to support competitive advantage defying import substitution. In fact, each of the ten items on the list responded to a particular distortion perceived to exist—particularly in Latin American countries.[9] For example, there was the perception that debt-financed overinvestment in low productivity activities had created fiscal sustainability problems and wasteful public expenditure patterns. There was the perception that complex tax breaks had led to an inefficient tax system with low revenue mobilization. There was the perception that interest rate caps lead to financial repression and low levels of financial intermediation, and that protectionism led to overvalued exchange rates. The Consensus critiqued public enterprises that had become inefficient

---

[8] See Williamson (1990, 2004).
[9] The original formulation was inspired by a meeting of high level Latin American policy makers in Washington.

and created a high cost for public services (as well as a fiscal drain). The Consensus also noted that restrictions on Foreign Direct Investment (FDI) had limited the potential for investment, and that a lack of property rights had locked out many poor people from access to formal credit markets.

The Washington Consensus was also a direct denial of the pervasive export pessimism that permeated the import substitution industrialization strategy. The focus was on liberalizing markets and balancing budgets—given that the end of the import substitution era coincided with sovereign debt defaults in a variety of developing countries. In the international development institutions, it became associated with structural adjustment lending where the multilateral development institutions provided financial support conditional on market-oriented reforms.

In the end, the Washington Consensus advised the developing countries to adopt the 'idealized' advanced countries' institutions, that is, establishing a strong system of property rights, opening the economy to trade, privatizing state-owned enterprises and establishing broadly free markets through deregulation, changing focus from trying to copy the industries to trying to copy the idealized market institutions of the high-income countries.[10] Again, the logic seemed sound. But growth rates of developing countries were lower and economic crises more frequent under Washington Consensus policies in the 1980s and 1990s than under the structuralist policies of the 1960s and 1970s. Some economists referred to this period as the 'lost decades' for developing countries (Easterly 2001).

The few countries that successfully accelerated their growth and closed the gap with developed countries did not follow the approaches proposed by the dominant development thinking of that time. In the 1950s and 1960s, Japan and the four Asian tigers—Korea, Taiwan, Singapore, and Hong Kong— were quietly catching up with developed countries. These newly industrializing economies grew rapidly from the 1950s to the 1970s by following an export-oriented development strategy based initially on labour-intensive, small-scale industries and gradually climbing the industrial ladder to larger, more capital-intensive industries (Amsden 1989; Chang 2003; Lin 2009; Wade 1990), contradicting the prevailing structuralism, which advocated import substitution to build up large heavy industries immediately.

In the 1980s and 1990s, under the sway of the Washington Consensus, economists branded planned economies as less efficient than market economies and called for transforming them into market economies through

---

[10] In fact, not all those policies recommended by the Washington Consensus were rigorously followed in the high-income countries. In the 1990s during the heyday of the Washington Consensus, many policy advisors for the high-income countries advised the developing countries to 'do as we say, not as we do.'

shock therapy: removing all economic distortions by ending government interventions and by leaping in a single bound from a planned to a market economy. The mainstream idea at that time believed that separating the transition into two or three steps, as China was doing, would only lead to failure. China's dual-track reform continued to protect and subsidize nonviable state-owned firms in the old prioritized capital-intensive industries while liberalizing the market for labour-intensive industries, which had been repressed. Many economists predicted rampant rent-seeking and deteriorating resource allocation (Murphy, Schleifer and Vishny 1992; Sachs, Woo and Yang 2000). In reality, however, economies that experienced stability and rapid growth in the transition, like Cambodia, China, Vietnam, and Mauritius all followed the gradual, dual-track reform approach.

The few success economies have something in common: they were market economies or transiting to a market economy, as emphasized by neoliberalism, while their governments also intervened actively in the economy, as emphasized by structuralism.

Policies based on structuralism and on neoliberalism failed to achieve their intended goals of helping developing countries achieve convergence and they also failed to explain the rare economic development successes. These failures suggest the need for a third wave of development thinking.

3.4 The New Structural Economics as the Third Wave of Development Thinking

When I started to promote the new structural economics as the third wave of development thinking (Lin 2011), I called for a return to Adam Smith, but not to *The Wealth of Nations*, a short-hand way of referring to the ideas advocated by Smith based on his research findings, but to Smith's methodology exemplified in the full title, *An Inquiry into the Nature and Causes of the Wealth of Nations*. I proposed following Smith in analyzing the nature and causes of economic development, asking: what is the nature of economic development, and what are its causes?

As discussed in the introduction, rapid, sustained economic growth is a modern phenomenon, emerging only in the eighteenth century. Before then, average annual growth of per capita income in Western Europe was just 0.05 per cent; at that rate it would take an economy 1,400 years to double per capita income. From the eighteenth to the mid-nineteenth century, annual growth in per capita income in Western European countries accelerated to 1 per cent, enabling per capita income to double in just 70 years. From the mid-nineteenth century to the present, per capita income growth accelerated to 2 per cent a year, shrinking the doubling time to 35 years (Maddison

2006). The impetus for accelerating growth was the industrial revolution of the mid-eighteenth century: continuous technological innovations and industrial upgrading made possible the acceleration of labour productivity and income growth that boosted per capita income.[11]

In other words, modern economic growth is a process of continuous technological innovation, which raises labour productivity, and industrial upgrading, which moves an economy from low value-added industries to higher value-added ones. But taking advantage of the potential of technologies and new industries requires well-functioning hard infrastructure to provide power, raw materials, and various inputs from domestic and foreign sources and to sell products to large domestic and foreign markets. As the scale of trade increases, market exchanges are at arm's length, thus requiring contracts and contract-enforcing legal systems. And as the scale and risk of investment increase with the upgrading of technology and industries, the financial structure has to adapt too. Thus, as argued by Marx in his voluminous writings, the entire soft infrastructure of institutions needs to improve accordingly (Kuznets 1966; Lin 1989; Lin and Nugent 1995; Harrison and Rodriguez-Clare 2010).

Therefore, while modern economic growth appears to be a process of ever increasing per capita income driven by rising labour productivity, it is actually a process of continuous structural changes in technologies, industries, and hard and soft infrastructure. The new structural economics uses a neoclassical approach to study why different countries have different structures in technologies, industries, soft and hard infrastructures, and what causes the structure in a country to change (Lin 2011). By convention such studies should be referred to as 'structural economics'. It is called 'new' structural economics to distinguish it from structuralism, the first wave of development thinking.

The new structural economics proposes that a country's economic structure at any specific time is endogenous to its given factor endowments, that is the amounts of capital, labour, and natural resources, at that time. Countries at different development stages differ in the relative abundance of factor endowments. In developing countries, capital is generally relatively scarce, while labour and natural resources are relatively abundant. In developed countries, capital is relatively abundant, while labour is relatively scarce. Though an economy's factor endowments are given at any particular time, they can change over time. The new structural economics posits an

---

[11] The industrial revolution was still in its infancy when Adam Smith was writing *An Inquiry into the Nature and Causes of the Wealth of Nations* Consequently, Smith paid little attention to technology innovation and industrial upgrading; rather, he focused on trade and specialization within given technologies and industries. Technological innovation is one of the main themes in Marxism, but it did not become a focus in mainstream economics until the notion of creative destruction made popular by Schumpeter (1942).

economy's factor endowments as the starting point for development analysis for two reasons: first, they are an economy's total budget at that time, and second, the structure of endowments determines the relative prices of factors: prices of relatively abundant factors are low, while prices of relatively scarce factors are high.

The relative factor prices determine a country's comparative advantages. Thus a prerequisite to achieving competitive advantage is for a country to develop its industries according to its comparative advantages (Porter 1990). For example, countries with relatively abundant labour and relatively scarce capital would have a comparative advantage in labour-intensive industries because factor costs of production will be lower than in countries with relatively scarce and more expensive labour.

In developed countries, income and labour productivity are high because their industries and technologies are capital intensive, which is in turn because of those countries' relative capital abundance. If a developing country wants to catch up to the income and industrial structure of developed countries, it first needs to increase the relative abundance of capital in its factor endowment structure to the level in advanced countries. The ultimate goal of economic development is to raise a country's income, the intermediate goal is to develop capital-intensive industries, and the immediate goal should be to accumulate capital quickly, so that the country's comparative advantage changes to more capital-intensive industries. In other words, boosting a country's income requires industrial upgrading, and industrial upgrading requires changing a country's endowment structure (Ju, Lin and Wang 2015).

How can a country accumulate capital quickly? Capital comes from saving economic surpluses. If a country's industries are all consistent with its comparative advantages, as determined by its endowment structure, the country will be competitive in both domestic and international markets and generate the largest possible surplus. If all investments are made in industries that are consistent with the comparative advantages determined by a country's endowment structure, the returns to investment will be maximized and the propensity to save will be at its highest. With the largest possible surplus and the highest incentives to save, capital will be accumulated in the fastest way possible. The changes in endowment structure and comparative advantages pave the way for upgrading industrial structure and the accompanying improvements in hard and soft industrial infrastructure. In the upgrading industrial structure, the developing countries can benefit from the advantage of backwardness as argued by Gershenkron.

But comparative advantage is an economic concept. How is it translated into the choices of technologies and industries made by entrepreneurs? Entrepreneurs care about profits. They will invest in industries in which a country has a comparative advantage if relative factor prices reflect the relative scarcities of factors in the country's endowments (Lin 2009; Lin and Chang 2009). If capital is relatively scarce, the price of capital will be relatively high; if labour is relatively scarce, the price of labour (wages) will be relatively high. Under an unfettered price system, profit-maximizing entrepreneurs will use a relatively inexpensive factor to substitute for a relatively expensive factor in their choice of production technologies, investing in industries that require more of a relatively inexpensive factor and less of a relatively expensive factor. A price system with these characteristics can arise only in a competitive market. And that is why successful economies are either market economies or on their way to becoming one.

If markets are so important, what is the government's role in economic development? Economic development is a process of structural change with continuous technological innovations, industrial upgrading, and improvement in infrastructure and institutions. When the factor endowment structure changes, economies need first-movers willing to enter new industries consistent with changing comparative advantages and who are eager to use the new technologies. The risks for first-movers are high. If they fail, they bear all the losses, and if they succeed, others will immediately follow them into the industry. The resulting competition will eliminate any monopoly profits (Aghion 2009; Romer 1990). There is an asymmetry between the losses of failures and the gains of successes for the first-movers (Hausmann and Rodrik 2003).

No matter whether the first-movers succeed or fail, they provide society with useful information. The government should encourage first-movers and compensate them for the information externality they generate. Otherwise, there will be little incentive for firms to be first-movers in technological innovation and industrial upgrading (Rodrik 2004; Lin 2009; Lin and Monga 2011; Harrison and Rodriguez-Clare 2010). In addition, the success or failure of first-movers also depends on whether improved hard and soft infrastructure match the needs of the new industries. Improving infrastructure and institutions is beyond the capacities of individual firms. Therefore, as argued by Gerschenkron and the structuralists, the government needs to play an enabling role to facilitate the industrial upgrading. The government may either coordinate firms' efforts to improve infrastructure and institutions or provide those improvements itself. By spontaneous market forces alone without the government taking a facilitating stand, the structural change will not happen at all or will happen very slowly.

The new structural economics helps in understanding why Gerschenkron's prediction of convergence did not occur and structuralism and neoliberalism did not work. Gerschenkron and structuralism failed to recognize the endogeneity of economic structure and sources of market failures. The import-substitution catch-up strategy required governments to give priority to capital- and technology-intensive industries, thus defying developing countries' comparative advantages. Firms in those industries were not viable in open and competitive markets. Entrepreneurs would not voluntarily invest in those industries, which were doomed to fail in competitive markets, without government protection and subsidies and help in mobilizing the required capital for investment. Structuralism mistakenly regarded market failures arising from structural rigidities as the cause of developing countries' inability to develop advanced, capital-intensive industries and called on the government to protect and subsidize non-viable firms in comparative advantage–defying industries. It is the violation of comparative advantage that caused the failure of structuralism despite governments being advised to implement the desirable interventions in line with Gerschenkron's six propositions to facilitate industrial upgrading.

The new structural economics also helps us understand why neoliberalism did not work. Washington Consensus policy failed to recognize the endogeneity of government interventions caused by structuralism and the need for governments to facilitate structural change. In developing countries, market distortions were endogenous to their government's need to protect and subsidize non-viable firms that had been promoted by the government's previous import-substitution strategies. Eliminating protections and subsidies would doom non-viable firms, resulting in large-scale unemployment, social and political unrest, and slow economic growth. To avoid those consequences and to continue to prop up non-viable capital-intensive industries that were still considered the cornerstone of modernization and national defence, governments often continued to protect them through new and less visible means after removing previous protections and subsidies in line with the precepts of the Washington Consensus. While the new protections and subsidies were necessary to avoid the collapse of non-viable firms in the old comparative advantage-defying industries, they are usually less efficient than the old ones, especially in the transition economies of the former Soviet Union and Eastern Europe (World Bank 2002). In addition, neoliberalism threw the baby out with the bath water, vehemently opposing any role for governments in facilitating structural change. Chile was a typical example. A model student of Washington Consensus reform, Chile diligently implemented the Washington Consensus reforms in the 1980s and then removed all government protections, subsidies, and interventions to facilitate industrial upgrading in spite of the previous success of Chilean government's supports to diversify the economy from mining to commercial agriculture and salmon farming. Chile ranks high among developing countries on the World Bank's Doing Business Index, based on indicators of the ease of doing business and investing. However, Chile has not seen dynamic structural change for more than thirty years after implementing the Washington

Consensus reform, and as a result unemployment is high, income gaps have widened, and Chile remains mired in 'the middle-income trap'.

The new structural economics also justifies the gradual, dual-track approach to reform that conventional economic thought labeled the wrong approach to transition. Dual-tracking calls for maintaining stability during the transition and stimulating dynamic and sustainable economic growth by continuing transitory protection of the non-viable firms in the old priority sectors while removing restrictions to entry and facilitating the development of previously repressed industries that are consistent with the country's comparative advantages. The dynamic growth of sectors consistent with comparative advantages helps the economy rapidly accumulate capital and changes the factor endowment structure. That makes some formerly non-viable firms in capital-intensive industries viable and creates jobs for workers who were unemployed because of the shut-down of non-viable firms. Once firms in the new sectors are viable, the transitory protection and subsidies can be eliminated, bringing the transition to a market economy to a smooth end (Naughton 1995; Lau, Qian and Roland 2000; Subramanian and Roy 2003; Lin 2009 and 2012a).

Lin (2009) derives five testable hypotheses related to the above discussions:

1. A country that adopted a structuralist comparative advantage defying (CAD) strategy will require various government interventions and distortions in its economy.

2. Over an extended period a country that adopts a CAD strategy will have poor growth performance.

3. Over an extended period a country that adopts a CAD strategy will have a volatile economy.

4. Over an extended period a country that adopts a CAD strategy will have less equitable income distribution.

5. In the transition to a market economy a country's overall economic performance will be improved if it creates conditions to facilitate the development of formerly repressed labour-intensive industries.

Lin uses a dataset of 102 countries over the period 1963–1999 to test the above hypotheses. The results are consistent with the prediction of the hypotheses.

3.5 Latent Comparative Advantage, Advantage of Backwardness and Industrial Policy

From the new structural economics point of view, to achieve dynamic structural change and economic growth in the economy the government needs to play a proactive role of externality compensation and coordination of infrastructure improvement, both of which require resources and are often industry specific. The government's resources are limited. To have the largest impact on economic growth, the government needs to use its limited resources strategically. That is, the government needs to have industrial policies which identify priority industries and improve infrastructure and institutions to facilitate their growth as encapsulated in Gerschenkron's propositions.

In practice, as discussed, industrial policies have largely failed in developing countries, tainting their reputation in mainstream economics. They failed not because the government's proactive facilitation is not necessary in industrial upgrading but because in many cases the developing country's government, with all the best intentions, tried to be too ambitious in supporting advanced industries similar to those in advanced countries, as stipulated by the structuralist viewpoint. Not understanding that a country's industrial structure is endogenous to its endowment structure, the targeted industries were inconsistent with the country's comparative advantages. That meant that the firms in priority industries were not viable in open and competitive markets, so governments had to protect and subsidize them, grant them monopoly rights, or provide low-price capital, raw material, and land. Such distortive interventions created economic rents that stimulated rent-seeking, embezzlement, and corruption (Krueger 1974; Krugman 1993). Haste makes waste. The backwardness became a disadvantage.

An effective industrial policy should aim instead to facilitate the growth of industries with latent comparative advantages, enabling them to become quickly the country's competitive advantage in the market. Latent comparative advantage in new structural economics refers to an industry in which firms have low factor costs of production because of the industry's congruence to the comparative advantage determined by the country's endowment structure. But the industry is not yet competitive in domestic and international markets because firms operating in the industry have high transaction costs due to the inadequacy of broadly defined hard or soft infrastructure. Such an industry will have difficult becoming the country's competitive advantage spontaneously without the government's facilitation, because of the innate coordination failures in required improvements in hard and soft infrastructure and the externality issue faced by pioneer firms. Externality compensation and improvements in hard and soft infrastructure are often industry specific and require resources. A government that wants to facilitate economic development through industrial policies must help industries with latent comparative advantage ease their specific bottlenecks of infrastructure, the financial constraint, the administrative red tape, and the legal system to reduce transaction costs. If the government does so, there will be the advantage of backwardness in industrial upgrading.

How can governments identify industries with latent comparative advantages? History offers many clues of what to do and what to avoid. Since the sixteenth and seventeenth centuries, countries succeeded in catching up have shared a common feature: first, they all adopted industrial policies to support industrial upgrading, and second, their industrial policies aimed to help firms enter industries that had flourished in dynamically growing countries that were slightly more developed than they were. Compared to the countries they wanted to catch up with they were 'moderately backward' instead of 'extremely backward' in Gerschenkron's category and the governments did not have to resort to serious distortions in the market to support the new industries. For example, the Netherlands was the most developed country in the world in the sixteenth and seventeenth centuries, with a highly developed wool textile industry. The British wool textile industry was immature by comparison. The British government implemented policies to encourage imports of machinery and skilled workers from the Netherlands. Those policies worked. At the time, per capita income in Great Britain was at 70 per cent of the Dutch level. That meant that their endowments and comparative advantages were not too different.

Following the Industrial Revolution, Great Britain became the most advanced economy in the world. In the late nineteenth century France, Germany, and the United States used similar policies to catch up with Great Britain. They were moderately backward compared to Britain as their per capita incomes at that time had already been about 60–75 per cent of the British level. In the 1950s and 1960s, Japan imitated industries in the United States at a time when its per capita income exceeded 40 per cent of the US level. Later, the four Asian tigers (Korea, Taiwan, Singapore, and Hong Kong) succeeded by imitating Japan's industries. Their per capita incomes were about 30–40 per cent of Japan's at the time (Akamatsu 1962; Chang 2003; Kim 1988; Ito 1980).

Most other countries also targeted and tried to imitate industries in the United States after the World War II but failed. One reason was that their income levels were less than twenty per cent of the US level and thus fell into Gerschenkron's category of extreme backwardness at the time of their attempted catching up. For example, in the 1950s China targeted and tried to imitate U.S. industries even though its per capita income was just five per cent of the US level. With the government's efforts to build up advanced industries, China was able to test atomic and the hydrogen bombs in the 1960s and launch satellites in the 1970s; the achievements came at a very high price to the economy. In 1979, when China began its transition to a market economy, its per capita income was less than one-third the average in Sub-Saharan African countries (Lin 2012a).

Drawing on the experience of successful economies and the idea of targeting latent comparative advantage so as to tap into the advantage of backwardness in industrial upgrading, the new structural economics proposes a Growth Identification and Facilitation framework as a new framework for industrial policy (Lin and Monga 2011). This framework has two tracks and six steps.

(1) The government in a developing country should identify a list of mature tradable goods and services that have been produced for about twenty years in dynamically growing countries with similar endowment structures and per capita income that is about 100 per cent higher than its own, or twenty years ago the country concerned and the dynamic growing countries had a similar per capita income level. That is, compared to the benchmark countries, the country attempting to catch up is moderately backward in Gerschenkron's terminology.

(2) If some private domestic firms are already present in those industries, the government should identify constraints to technological upgrading or further firm entry, and take actions, resembling those in Gerschenkorn's fifth proposition, to remove such constraints.

(3) In industries where no domestic firms are present or only a small number of domestic firms are exporting, the government may try to attract FDI from benchmark countries in step 1, or organize new firm-incubation programmes.

(4) In addition to the industries identified in step 1, the government should also pay attention to spontaneous self-discovery by private enterprises and support the scaling-up of the successful private innovations in new industries so as to benefit from the unique endowments in the country or opportunities made possible by rapid technological changes in the world.

(5) In countries with poor infrastructure and a bad business environment, special economic zones or industrial parks may be used to create in a pragmatic way a localized good environment to overcome barriers to firm entry and FDI and encourage the formation of industrial clusters.

(6) The government should be willing to compensate pioneer firms in the industries identified above with tax incentives for a limited period, co-financing for investments, or enabling access to foreign exchange to compensate for the externality.

The industries identified through the above process should be consistent with the country's latent comparative advantage. Once the pioneer firms come in successfully, many other firms will enter these industries as well. The government's facilitating role is mainly restricted to providing coordination of hard and soft infrastructure improvement, and compensation for externalities. Government facilitation through the above approach is likely to help developing countries tap into the potential of the advantage of backwardness in industrial upgrading, realize dynamic and sustained growth, and avoid backwardness becoming a disadvantage due to either over ambitious industrial policy or the inaction of the government in coordinating hard and soft infrastructure improvement and compensation for externalities in industrial upgrading.

3.6 Concluding Remarks

Modern economic growth is characterized by a continuous structural transformation in technology, industry, and hard and soft infrastructure as well. Gerschenkron is right to postulate that a developing country has an advantage of backwardness as they can access a large store of technological innovations from the advanced countries and can adopt the latest technology without facing resistance from users of old technologies. If a developing country uses that advantage right, they will have faster technological innovation, industrial upgrading, and economic growth than an advanced country and achieve convergence to that advanced country within one or two generations. The precondition for a country to use that advantage right is to follow the comparative advantage determined by its own factor endowment in the industrial upgrading and technological innovation. That is, they should borrow technologies from countries not too far ahead of them on development ladders. Unfortunately, most developing countries attempted to go counter to their comparative advantages and jump directly to developing the advanced industries prevailing in the high-income countries. Their economies became uncompetitive, growth was unsustainable and led to frequent crises. Rather than an advantage in achieving rapid, sustained growth, their backwardness became a disadvantage.

There was a fallacy in the development thinking that using high-income countries' industries and institutions as a reference for developing countries' development policy, focusing on what developing countries did not have and could not do well, and developing countries were advised to correct those shortcomings, for example, the development of advanced heavy industries in the import-substitution strategy as advocated by structuralism and the adoption of institutions prevailing in high-income countries as urged by the neo-liberal Washington Consensus. The results of various efforts based on that negative thinking by the developing countries themselves and by international development communities were disappointing. Instead of exploiting the potential from the advantage of backwardness to accelerate their growth, most developing countries encountered the disadvantage of backwardness and were trapped in low- or middle-income status.

The new structural economics proposes a change in the development mindset. The government in a developing country should identify and scale-up what they can do well (that is, their comparative advantages) based on what they have now (that is, their endowments). With this approach, they can benefit from the advantage of backwardness, as argued by Gerschenkron, in industrial upgrading, grow faster than the advanced countries, and achieve convergence.

If developing countries follow the approach offered by new structural economics, in the coming decades there will be a golden era for their industrialization. The pattern of flying geese is a useful metaphor to explain the idea of the advantage of backwardness. Beginning in the eighteenth century, the less-developed West European and East Asian countries followed their more successful neighbours, emulating a flying-geese pattern, benefiting from the leaders' tailwind as they first industrialized, and then became advanced countries themselves. Large emerging-market economies, especially China, have performed dynamically and industrialized quickly so they offer unprecedented opportunities for other developing economies that can emulate their success and jumpstart their industrialization process. China—once a 'follower goose'—is on the verge of becoming a leader, with the potential to relocate 85 million low-skilled manufacturing jobs in the coming decade. The scale of this shift is huge when compared with the 9.7 million jobs that Japan had in the modern sector in the 1960s, or South Korea's 2.3 million modern jobs in the 1980s (Lin 2012b). And a similar trend will arise in other emerging-market economies. If the governments in the low-income countries in the world play the right and desirable facilitating role recommended in new structural economics to incentivize industrial upgrading and to improve hard and soft infrastructure, the promise of Gershenkron's advantage of backwardness may finally be realized, helping backward countries to have a sustainable and dynamic industrialization and achieve convergence in the coming decades.

References

Aghion, P., 2009. *Some Thoughts on Industrial Policy and Growth*, Document de Travail 2009–09. Observatoire Français des conjonctures économiques, Sciences Po, Paris.

Akamatsu, K., 1962. 'A Historical Pattern of Economic Growth in Developing Countries'. *Journal of Developing Economies* vol. 1 number 1:3–25.

Amsden, A.H., 1989. *Asia's Next Giant*, New York and Oxford: Oxford University Press.

Azariadis, C. and J. Stachurski, 2005. 'Poverty Traps'. In *The Handbook of Economic Growth* edited by A. Phillipe and S. Durlauf, Elsevier.

Bourguignon, F. and C. Morrisson, 2002. 'Inequality among world citizens'. *American Economic Review* vol. 92 number 4:727–44.

Cameron, R., 1997. *A Concise Economic History of the World*, Oxford: Oxford University Press.

Cardoso, E. and A. Helwege, 1995. *Latin America's Economy*, Cambridge, MA: MIT Press.

Chang, H-J., 2003. *Kicking Away the Ladder: Development Strategy in Historical Perspective*, London: Anthem Press.

Chenery, H. B., 1961. 'Comparative Advantage and Development Policy'. *American Economic Review* vol.51 number 1:18–51.

Clark, G., 2007. *A Farewell to Alms*. Princeton, NJ: Princeton University Press.

Easterly, W., 2001. 'The Lost Decades: Explaining Developing Countries' Stagnation in Spite of Policy Reform 1980–1998'. *Journal of Economic Growth* vol. 6 number 2:135–57.

Gerschenkron, A., 1962. *Economic Backwardness in Historical Perspective: A Book of Essays*. Cambridge, MA: Belknap Press of Harvard University Press.

Harrison, A., and A. Rodríguez-Clare, 2010. 'Trade, Foreign Investment, and Industrial Policy for Developing Countries'. In *Handbook of Economic Growth, Vol. 5*, edited by D. Rodrik. Amsterdam: North-Holland: 4039–4213.

Hausmann, R., and D. Rodrik, 2003. 'Economic Development as Self-Discovery'. *Journal of Development Economics* vol. 72 (December).

Ito, T., 1980. 'Disequilibrium Growth Theory'. *Journal of Economic Theory* vol. 23 number 3:380–409.

Ju, J., J.Y. Lin, and Y. Wang, 2015. *Endowment Structures, Industrial Dynamics, and Economic Growth. Journal of Monetary Economics* (forthcoming).

Kim, Y.H., 1988. *Higashi Ajia Kogyoka to Sekai Shihonshugi (Industrialisation of East Asia and the World Capitalism)*, Tokyo: Toyo Keizai Shimpo-sha.

Krueger, A. O., 1974. 'The Political Economy of Rent-seeking Society'. *American Economic Review* vol. 64 number 3:291–303.

Krueger, A. and B. Tuncer, 1982. 'An Empirical Test of the Infant Industry Argument'. *American Economic Review* vol. 72 number 5:1142–52.

Krugman, P., 1993. 'Protection in Developing Countries'. In *Policymaking in the Open Economy: Concepts and Case Studies in Economic Performance*, edited by. R. Dornbusch. New York: Oxford University Press.

Kuznets, S., 1966. *Modern Economic Growth: Rate, Structure and Spread*, New Haven, CT: Yale University Press.

Lal, D., 1994. *Against Dirigisme: The Case for Unshackling Economic Markets*, San Francisco: International Center for Economic Growth, ICS Press.

Lau, L. J., Y. Qian, and G. Roland, 2000. 'Reform without Losers: An Interpretation of China's Dual-Track Approach to Transition'. *Journal of Political Economy*, vol. 108 number 1:120–43.

Lin, J. Y., 1989. 'An Economic Theory of Institutional Change: Induced and Imposed Change'. *Cato Journal*, vol. 9 number 1:1–33.

Lin, J. Y., 1995. 'The Needham Puzzle: Why the Industrial Revolution Did Not Originate in China' *Economic Development and Cultural Change*, vol. 41 number: January 1995: 269–92.

Lin, J. Y., 2009. *Economic Development and Transition: Thought, Strategy and Viability* (Marshall Lectures), Cambridge University Press.

Lin, J. Y., 2011. 'New Structural Economics: A Framework for Rethinking Economic Development'. *World Bank Research Observer*, vol. 26 number 2:193–221.

Lin, J. Y., 2012a. *Demystifying the Chinese Economy*, Cambridge University Press: Cambridge.

Lin, J. Y., 2012b. 'From Flying Geese to Leading Dragons: New Opportunities and Strategies for Structural Transformation in Developing Countries'. *Global Policy* vol. 3 number 4:397–409.

Lin, J. Y., and H. Chang, 2009. 'DPR Debate: Should Industrial Policy in Developing Countries Conform to Comparative Advantage or Defy It?' *Development Policy Review* vol. 27 number 5:483–502.

Lin, J. Y., and C. Monga, 2011. 'DPR Debate: Growth Identification and Facilitation: The Role of the State in the Dynamics of Structural Change'. *Development Policy Review* vol 29 number 3:259–310.

Lin, J. Y., and J. Nugent, 1995. 'Institutions and Economic Development.' In *Handbook of Development Economics, vol. 3, edited by*. T. N. Srinivasan and J. Behrman. Amsterdam: North Holland.

Lin, J. Y., and D. Rosenblatt, 2012. 'Shifting Patterns of Economic Growth and Rethinking Development'. *Journal of Economic Policy Reform*, vol. 15 number 3:71–94.

Maddison, A., 2006. *The World Economy*, Paris: Organization for Economic Cooperation and Development.

Maddison, A., 2010. *Historical Statistics of the World Economy: 1–2008 AD.* <http://www.ggdc.net/maddison/Historical_Statistics/horizontal-file_02-2010.xls>

Murphy, K., A. Schleifer, and R. Vishny, 1992. 'The Tradition to a Market Economy: Pitfall of Partial Reform'. *Quarterly Journal of Economics.* 107: 889–906.

Naughton, B. 1995, *Growing out of Plan: Chinese Economic Reform 1978–1993*. Cambridge: Cambridge University Press.

Pack, H., and K. Saggi, 2006. 'Is There a Case for Industrial Policy? A Critical Survey'. *World Bank Research Observer* vol. 21 number 2:267–97.

Porter, M.E., 1990. *The Competitive Advantage of Nations*, New York: Free Press.

Prebisch, R., 1950. *The Economic Development of Latin America and its Principal Problems*, New York: United Nations.

Pritchett, L.,1997. 'Divergence, Big Time'. *Journal of Economic Perspectives* vol. 11 number 3:3–17.

Rodrik, D., 2004. 'Industrial Policy for the Twenty-First Century'. Harvard University, Cambridge, MA.

Romer, P. M., 1990. 'Endogenous Technological Change'. *Journal of Political Economy* vol. 98, number 5: s71–s102.

Rosenstein-Rodan, P., 1943. 'Problems of Industrialization of Eastern and Southeastern Europe'. *Economic Journal* vol. 111 number 210–11:202–11.

Sachs, J. D., W.T. Woo, and X. Yang, 2000. 'Economic Reforms and Constitutional Transition'. *Annals of Economics and Finance*, 1, 435–91.

Schumpeter, J.A. 1942, 1994. *Capitalism, Socialism and Democracy*, London: Routledge.

Singer, H.W., 1950. 'The distribution of gains between investing and borrowing countries'. *American Economic Review* (Papers and Proceedings) 40:473–85.

Subramanian, A. D. and D. Roy, 2003. 'Who Can Explain the Mauritian Miracle? Meade, Romer, Sachs, or Rodrik?' In *In Search of Prosperity: Analytic Narratives on Economic Growth*, edited by D. Rodrik, [205–43], Princeton and Oxford: Princeton University Press.

Wade, R., 1990. *Governing the Market*, Princeton, NJ: Princeton University Press.

Williamson, J., 1990. 'What Washington Means by Policy Reform'. In *Latin American Adjustment: How Much Has Happened?* Edited by. J. Williamson. Washington, DC: Institute for International Economics.

Williamson, J., 2004. 'A Short History of the Washington Consensus'. Paper commissioned by Fundación CIDOB for a conference 'From the Washington Consensus towards a new Global Governance,' Barcelona, September 24–25, 2004.

World Bank, 2002. *Transition, the First Ten Years: Analysis and Lessons for Eastern Europe and the Former Soviet Union*. Washington, DC: World Bank.

4

The Role of Agriculture in 'Catching up'

A Gerschenkronian Perspective

C. Peter Timmer

4.1 Introduction

Professor Gerschenkron would have been perplexed, but possibly also bemused, by this chapter. His interest in agriculture extended only to its role in the backwardness of a country, where the sector sheltered a large share of the labour force from joining the spurt of industrialization that was the defining feature of modernization in Gerschenkron's world. In his most influential essay 'Economic Backwardness in Historical Perspective,' Gerschenkron mentioned agriculture only once, in a mild complaint that ready markets in the United Kingdom for Denmark's agricultural surpluses kept it from rapid industrialization (Gerschenkron 1962: 16).

The basic premise of this chapter is that agriculture has the potential (often not realized) to catalyze rapid economic growth in a backward economy. Through a series of market and non-market linkages, growth in agricultural productivity is transmitted to the rest of the economy. The resulting structural transformation has been the only sustainable pathway out of both rural and urban poverty. When stated as directly as this, Gerschenkron would almost certainly have agreed.

More to the point in terms of Gerschenkron's attitude toward agriculture, lessons about the critical importance of 'getting agriculture moving', to cite the title of Mosher's (1966) important volume, are drawn almost entirely from the historical record. Despite the modern emphasis on randomized controlled trials (RCTs) as the only legitimate way to design 'evidence-based policies' (Dercon and Gollin 2014), such trials are impossible to conduct on the big issues that face development policymakers. History is our only source of evidence. Of course, such evidence needs to be informed by theory and quantitative data. As an early and enthusiastic supporter of 'cliometrics', Gerschenkron would surely have been equally enthusiastic about using these tools to understand the role of agriculture in the 'catching up' process.

I was an avid student of Gerschenkron. Like all first-year economics PhD students at Harvard in the 1960s, I took his required year-long course in economic history. Many of my colleagues hated the course—it had a very long reading list, twice-weekly lectures that were incredibly erudite and chock-full of fascinating historical data, but often hard to follow from topic to topic. My lecture notes show just how hard it was to keep up with Gerschenkron's thinking out loud. The final exam each semester was renowned for its difficulty.

Finally, and most troubling to most of my classmates, Gerschenkron required a significant and original research paper each semester. His goal was that it would be publishable in a respected academic journal. The first year of graduate school in economics is daunting enough without that burden, and many students only finished their paper for Gerschenkron's class in time to graduate. By then (three or four years later), writing academic-quality papers was part of the drill, and Gerschenkron was generous with 'incompletes'. But to graduate they had to be made-up.

I struggled like everyone else with the readings, lectures, and final exam. But I thoroughly enjoyed writing the term paper. All topics had to be approved in advance, which required a half-hour appointment in Gerschenkron's office. This was a totally intimidating experience, as his office was piled full of books, leaving only a narrow path for him to get to his chair behind his desk, and for the trembling student to sit in the single chair in front of it.

At my appointment, half way through the fall semester, I explained that I wanted to write on the contribution of the turnip to the English agricultural revolution. He raised his eyebrow and puffed on his pipe for what seemed like an eternity. But then he said 'yes, there could be an interesting paper on that topic.' In response to his question 'why?', I explained my farm background in Southwestern Ohio, and my general interest in agriculture.[1]

I had also written a term paper the first semester of my freshman year at Harvard for a general education course on 'The Enterprise of Science,' taught by Leonard Nash, a professor of chemistry and a spellbinding lecturer. One of his lectures was on the use of the 'scientific method' by Jethro Tull in early seventeenth century England. Tull invented a seed drill to plant turnip seeds accurately, and he then carefully measured the yield from different spacing

---

[1] I had worked for two years on Wall Street, as a commodity analyst in the Business Economics Department of W.R. Grace and Company, where I followed agricultural prices quite closely.

(and treatment) of the seeds. My early paper, which was stimulated by my own farm experience operating a seed drill, was just a fuller description of what had been covered in the lecture (and did not get a particularly good grade), but my interest was piqued. Jethro Tull and turnip husbandry stuck in the back of my mind.

In Gerschenkron's course we read the standard references on the contribution of the English agricultural revolution to the first industrial revolution. It freed up labour to work in the new factories. Nurkse had put the historical lesson in front of the development profession early on:

> Consider what happened in the original home of industrial development, in England in the eighteenth century. Everyone knows that the spectacular industrial revolution would not have been possible without the agricultural revolution that preceded it. And what was this agricultural revolution? It was based mainly on the introduction of the turnip. The lowly turnip made possible a change in crop rotation which did not require much capital, but which brought about a tremendous rise in agricultural productivity. As a result, more food could be grown with much less manpower. Manpower was released for capital construction. The growth of industry would not have been possible without the turnip and other improvements in agriculture [Nurkse 1953: 52–3].

This story did not quite ring true. I had a sense that economic historians and early development economists were viewing the issue through an 'industrialization' lens rather than from what was actually happening on modernizing farms. The goal of my paper was to look at the agricultural revolution—and the subsequent industrial revolution—from the point of view of agriculture. It turned out to be quite an ambitious, but rewarding, project.

4.2 Understanding Agricultural Revolutions

As late as the mid-1960s, agricultural development was largely an ignored field, at least in the context of its broader contributions to economic growth.

> Most interpretations of the Lewis model (1954), especially the Fei-Ranis versions (1964) which became the main teaching paradigms, ignored the factors needed to modernize traditional agricultural sectors so that they could play positive contributory roles in the development of the rest of the economy. The structuralist views of Prebisch (1950) about declining terms of trade for traditional products and the importance Hirschman (1958) attached to linkages to "modern" economic activities further diminished any apparent rationale for actively investing in the modernization of agriculture itself. As Hirschman wrote in 1958, 'agriculture stands convicted on the count of its lack of direct stimulus to the setting up of new activities through linkage effect—the superiority of manufacturing in this respect is crushing (Hirschman 1958; 109–10)' [Timmer 1988: 288–9].

Exploring the origins and impacts of agricultural revolutions was virtually virgin territory.

Widener Library at Harvard is a marvellous resource for the curious student bent on such an exploration. I found the aisle with books on the economic history of England. One shelf had volumes from the early agricultural writers of the day—first editions in beautiful leather bindings by Arthur Young, Nathaniel Kent, and William Marshall dating from the late eighteenth and early nineteenth centuries. I remember checking them out and taking them home to my apartment (security was different in those days). They contained incredible details about visits to progressive farmers and their cultivation practices. Input costs, yields, prices, returns—'old husbandry' versus 'new husbandry'. Reading these volumes, with their quantitative data, virtually dictated the approach: build an input-output model of traditional agriculture and compare it with the new husbandry that incorporated turnips in the cultivation. What difference did it make?

A lot. Declining wheat yields from 'plough sick' lands in traditional rotations were converted to rising yields as turnips were fed to livestock during the winter months and their increased manure was turned back on the fields to increase fertility. The 'new husbandry' did increase agricultural productivity.

The paradox, however, was that 'turnip husbandry' was actually labour intensive. A careful analysis of monthly labour demands on a 'modern' farm practising turnip husbandry showed an increase in demand for labour, not an exodus to industrial mills. What was going on? The answer was complicated.

The English agricultural revolution fed the industrial workers, but did not provide a supply of many workers directly, at least in the early years. The new workers came from an increase in population growth (perhaps explaining a heavy reliance on child labour), which was fed mostly from English farms. Real wages rose as both farms and factories competed for labour, thus inducing the mechanization in both sectors that had been such an historical puzzle if there was so much surplus labour. The 'role of agriculture' in economic development turned out to be much more complex than the early literature had described. This was clearly an academic line of inquiry that was worth further pursuit.

Gerschenkron loved the paper I submitted for the first semester. Without naming me or the topic of the paper, he extolled its virtues in the first class of the second semester. I knew immediately who he was talking about, and I suddenly realized that maybe I had an academic future (my initial assumption when starting the PhD was that I would go back to Wall Street as a commodity analyst). It was heady stuff. At the end of the year, that paper and the second-semester extension into seasonal factors was nominated by Professor Gerschenkron for the Goldsmith Prize, which goes to the best paper

71

submitted in a Harvard economics course during the year. It won, and was published in the *Quarterly Journal of Economics*.[2]

I like to think that my paper led Gerschenkron to consider a more positive role for agriculture in economic development. He invited me to join his economic history seminar, which was a great honour. Although I did not do my dissertation in economic history, Gerschenkron remained nonetheless supportive. And a decade later, after time at Stanford, in Indonesia, and at Cornell, I was back at Harvard teaching the graduate development course, with Hollis Chenery, to PhD students in the Economics Department. A decade after that, Dwight Perkins, Jeff Williamson, and I were teaching a reincarnation of Gerschenkron's course.[3]

The course that Dwight, Jeff, and I co-taught was not just a reincarnation of Gerschenkron's required course in economic history, but it also counted as the introductory PhD course in development economics. Jeff did Latin America, Dwight did East Asia, and I took on the task of translating Gerschenkron's views on economic backwardness as a stimulus to development—views formed entirely from European experience—into a much broader understanding of the role of agriculture in that process.

Over more than a decade of teaching the course to a steady stream of economics PhD students, I came to realize how sharply my views were diverging from what Gerschenkron had taught. I think he would have approved—he loved modern economic modelling techniques and was a stickler for data.[4] My lectures examined the process of industrialization through the lens of the agricultural sector—what was the role of agriculture in stimulating broad-based economic growth, and how was it transformed in turn during this process? To answer these two-way questions, I was able to use computable general equilibrium models constructed by the economic history (and development) profession for an historically and geographically important set of countries—across two continents and three centuries:

[2] I received a nice note from the editor, Gottfried Habberler, saying that no changes would be needed as it was 'well written' (Timmer 1969). I was on my way.

[3] Gerschenkron was visibly disappointed when, midway through the second year of graduate school, I told him I could not do my PhD thesis in economic history because I did not read French, German or Russian (any two would have been OK in his mind, but all three would be important for my interest in agriculture). I was married, had a young child, and an offer from the Food Research Institute at Stanford University to be an assistant professor while writing my PhD thesis. That was an offer I could not refuse. But he remained very supportive, writing a job market letter and then one in support of my tenure at Stanford.

[4] A favourite phrase, used often in his seminar, was 'for example is not proof—but it does show that something is possible'. Good data could debunk a bad theory. Wally Falcon is fond of saying that 'In policy debates, three facts trump a theory. But a good story usually wins the day.'

— England, during the era of the Corn Laws from the late seventeenth to the early nineteenth century.[5] The Corn Laws protected English grain farmers from foreign competition and also stabilized domestic wheat prices. The result was arguably to stimulate the first agricultural revolution, which over two centuries provided food, labour and domestic markets for the first industrial revolution;

— France, which in the early nineteenth century fell behind a rapidly developing England in both rural and urban productivity. France only began to catch up in the latter half of the nineteenth century when it abandoned its long-held strategy of 'provisioning Paris' as cheaply as possible, and began to provide policy and investment support to the smallholder farmer who dominated French agriculture;

— Germany, with rapid industrialization as a 'conscious act of national policy', where Bismarck forged his 'pact of steel and rye' to stimulate productivity growth in German factories and on German farms;

— Russia, with its 'forced pace industrialization' directed by rigid, centralized plans, which would not have been possible without systematic and harsh extractions of agricultural surpluses from the peasantry. The failure to develop a modern agricultural economy was a major factor in the ultimate collapse of the Soviet Union;

— Japan, where very early investments in raising productivity on small farms paid high dividends in feeding a growing non-farm labour force, and providing the workers for it. There is an active historical debate over whether nascent industrialization stimulated this agricultural response or was stimulated by it, but the essential message is that both happened at more or less the same time;

— Thailand, where a land frontier made growth of extensive agriculture possible, in contrast to Japan, but also made universal education much more difficult to achieve for both supply reasons (a widely scattered rural population is hard to school efficiently) and demand reasons (farm labour was not surplus, children were needed to work the land, and thus they were not sent to school). Thailand fell systematically behind Japan in per capita incomes after 1880 as this education gap widened; and finally

— Indonesia, the country where I learned about modern development issues. Initially, this was from the point of view of an economic historian,

---

[5] In England, 'corn' has traditionally referred to the basic food grain, usually wheat, but also oats, barley and rye in some regions. Maize from the New World, now commonly called 'corn', did not feature in English diets.

as I had never studied development economics.[6] I was a 'participant/ observer' as a more than century long struggle to achieve food security at the national (macro) level was finally capped by an extraordinary spurt of rural-oriented, pro-poor growth that pulled more people out of poverty in a three decade period (1968–1998) than ever before (Timmer, 2004).[7] China ultimately topped that record, but Indonesia showed the way.[8]

In each of these countries, and many others, successful and sustained economic growth required active policy attention to food security at the national level. Even in the context of relatively open trade, achieving food security meant raising the productivity of domestic farmers (poor rural households have little access to imported food). No country has managed to get rich without generating significantly higher agricultural productivity than existed when the country was poor (Timmer 2002). There are two-way cause-and-effect relationships in this process, of course, but the historical evidence argues (controversially for some) for a fundamental (and probably prior) role for higher agricultural productivity as a driver of economic growth in the rest of the economy. A failure to modernize agriculture almost inevitably leads to a failed industrialization effort.[9]

My thinking about this critical role of raising agricultural productivity as a contributor to subsequent industrialization was clearly framed by putting together these lectures, and defending them in front of aggressive classes of dubious PhD students (none of whom had come to Harvard to study agricultural development). To my mind, history provided real evidence on the role of agricultural development in the broader development process, and how policy choices affected it. That sounds quaint when randomized controlled trials (RCTs) are now the 'gold standard' for evidence in policy debates, but most

---

[6] I was sent to Indonesia by the Harvard Advisory Group as a commodity specialist (drawing on my experience at W. R. Grace and Co.), assigned to study prospects for the country's major export commodities. Despite knowing nothing about the staple food economy, especially the role of rice, that is what I have worked on for more than 40 years. Quite ironically, I still know little about Indonesia's major export commodities.

[7] Although frequently confused, 'macro food security' is not the same as 'food self-sufficiency'. In the Indonesian context, macro food security meant stabilizing rice prices in major urban markets, a task that often incorporated imported rice, along with the serious effort to raise productivity of domestic rice farmers. Most of my advisory time in Indonesia was related to the food price stabilization program, not to agricultural development.

[8] Key references for the historical story summarized here would include Hayami and Ruttan (1985), Maddison, (1995), and Timmer (1969, 1988, 2002, 2009).

[9] The wording here is purposefully aggressive, but reflects experiences that are well within the historical record. Whether cause or effect, agricultural productivity has risen substantially in all successfully developing countries. Because so many of the inputs to higher agricultural productivity are public goods and need public sector investments with quite long time horizons, this dependence on higher agricultural productivity—whether cause or effect—to sustain economic growth requires an active public policy engagement with the process.

of the important questions in development economics cannot be answered by RCTs. History provides the only real evidence we have.[10]

4.3 Agriculture and Catching up

So, what is the role of agriculture in 'catching up' in a backward economy? Certainly, Gerschenkron's initial hypothesis would have been that it was part of the problem, not part of the solution. His analysis of Russia's failure to emancipate the serfs during Tsarist rule remains a classic example of agricultural backwardness holding back industrial modernization (Gerschenkron, 1968). An industrial spurt could not be maintained for long without a modernizing agriculture to provide food and labour. In such a world, the industrial sector leads and agriculture is brought along as necessary.

Whatever the historical record, by the late 1960s, experience from modern developing countries was beginning to show a high price for active discrimination against agriculture. Even benign neglect was not enough to stimulate rapid industrialization. Despite the esoteric title of my PhD thesis (*On Measuring Technical Efficiency*, see Timmer 1970; 1971), it was motivated by the desire to have a better understanding of why agriculture seemed to be so important to the development process. That remains a powerful motivation.

Putting this whole policy debate into historical context has turned out to be a real challenge, but a productive career. Clearly, 'valuing' the contribution of agriculture to economic development depends on what agricultural commodities are worth—what are the 'right prices?' (Timmer 1986). How can they be so volatile from year to year, if economic development is fundamentally a very long-run process? A focus on food price volatility is easy to understand from this perspective. I once described my career as 'stabilizing rice prices'. I became convinced that development is not possible without a sense of food security among the population, and in Asia, that means stable rice prices in the major urban markets (Timmer 1989).

Would Gerschenkron be perplexed by all this, as the opening paragraph suggests? Upon reflection, perhaps not. His mind encompassed, and comprehended, the most diverse experiences of modernizing Western and Eastern Europe (and he read, and wrote in, all of their languages—by his count, he could function in twenty different languages). It is a long time ago now, but my guess is that this entire debate over a positive role for agricultural modernization as a precursor to the industrial spurt that he studied so intensively would have been a welcome topic in the Economic History seminar, and

---

[10] It is slightly ironic that many of the leaders of the RCT movement were star students in this class, including Michael Kremer, Esther Duflo, and Abhijit Banerjee.

eventually would have found its way into his lectures. I am sure he would have been pleased that his legacy has persisted.

The rest of this chapter reviews the major lessons I have learned about the role of agriculture in the general development process, and in the 'catching up' process in particular. Three lessons stand out: (1) the heated contentiousness of the debate, reflecting sharply different ideological approaches to development strategies (witnessed early on in the debates between Ricardo and Malthus over the impact of the Corn Laws); (2) the critical importance to the poor of how the debates are resolved in actual development policies; and (3) the near irrelevance of most micro-based economic research into resolving the debates, designing effective 'pro-poor' growth policies, and helping them into implementation.

The first lesson is that the role of agriculture is highly contentious: even asking the question implies that market forces may not be producing the 'right' outcomes for broader development purposes and thus government interventions will be needed (Timmer 1995). The tension between market forces and government interventions remains a fundamental divide in economics and policy worlds. T.W. Schultz reflected the beliefs of many of his colleagues when he argued that economists should not become 'yes-men' in the halls of political economy (Schultz 1978). But the 'rational actor' model that underlies Chicago economics fails to appreciate the importance of market failures in the food sector. Consequently, free-market economists do not understand the political economy of food security because they do not appreciate the deep behavioural foundations that underpin a broad desire for stable food prices. An argument for free trade in the face of such political demands helps explain their irrelevance in many agricultural development and food security debates (Timmer 2012).

A second lesson is that the topic is incredibly important to the welfare of billions of individuals. Speeding the reduction in poverty through rapid growth in agricultural productivity has been one of the great success stories since the 1950s in East and Southeast Asia. However, that pathway out of poverty in South Asia and sub-Saharan Africa has not materialized to nearly the same extent. Understanding why is at the top of the agenda for most development agencies (Barrett 2014). Only macro- and sectoral- based historical analysis can hope to provide the answers. Only with these answers can we hope to understand the role of agriculture in the 'catching up' process.

The third lesson—the near irrelevance of modern micro-based economic analysis in helping to understand these issues—is also of long standing. Nearly half a century has passed since the general complaint in the early 1970s that the economics profession was 'busy designing the optimal location of deckchairs on the Titanic'. But the divergence has widened between modern empirical methodologies, with their insistence on identification strategies (hence the fondness for RCTs), and the messy real-world problems that policy makers must deal with on a regular basis. It is perverse pride, I suppose, that leads me to quote Dercon and Gollin's recent assertion in a prominent economics journal:

> We simply argue that there is little evidence that would support (or oppose) the claim that public investments in agriculture will generate greater improvements in social welfare than investments in other sectors (Dercon and Gollin 2014: 6).

They then cite my 1988 paper on 'The Agricultural Transformation' as the leading example of pro-agriculture analysts letting their enthusiasm get ahead of data and methodology (Timmer 1988).

> The Johnston-Mellor model provided a strong narrative and conceptual argument for agriculture's role in growth. The empirical roots of the paper were a (specific and highly contested) reading of historical experience, including from Europe and Japan, suggesting that growth success in these countries was closely linked to growth in agricultural productivity. Over the years, subsequent invocations of this theory became less nuanced, veering towards a more dramatic (and much less defensible) claim that all successful countries pass through a phase of fast agricultural growth as the engine for their growth process (e.g., Timmer 1988). This argument resonates still in policy narratives; for example the influential *World Development Report 2008* (World Bank 2007) highlighted the essential role of agriculture in early stages of development and made the case for a much stronger public policy focus on this sector from a growth perspective, not least in poor countries such as in sub-Saharan Africa (Dercon and Gollin 2014: 8).

What would 'evidence' look like to support public investments in agriculture? Nothing in the historical literature convinces Dercon and Gollin that the case has been made. Indeed, they seem to argue that the world is so complex that such a case can never be made to the satisfaction of serious economic analysts who might seek to offer advice on development strategies to policy makers. To be fair, they are concerned with sub-Saharan Africa, where heterogeneity is overwhelming and the historical record is short and unclear. But in dismissing the historical record of successful countries (or arguing that the historical interpretation is subject to challenge, which of course it is, but then that is the relevant debate), Dercon and Gollin have basically thrown out the only effective methodology that analysts have if they are to offer workable insights to policy makers. Such modesty is misplaced and even dangerous.

An earlier effort to understand the role of the Corn Laws in the development of English agriculture is used here to illuminate all of the three lessons just outlined (Timmer 2002). The debate over the impact of the Corn Laws in England provides a concrete example of how a public intervention into the agricultural sector had dramatic and surprising impact on English development broadly, including as a stimulus to the first Industrial

Revolution.[11] The following paragraphs draw on my discussion of this impact in the *Handbook of Agricultural Economics* edited by Gardner and Rausser (Timmer 2002: 1495–1506). An effort was made in that chapter to identify and even quantify the underlying mechanisms that drive the broad historical relationships between agricultural productivity and economic growth. A short summary should be sufficient to make the broad points.

4.4 Linkages between Agriculture and Economic Growth

The role of agriculture in economic development is complicated and controversial, despite a long historical literature examining the topic (Johnston and Mellor 1961; Hayami and Ruttan 1985; Timmer 2002; Dercon and Gollin 2014). Part of the controversy stems from the structural transformation itself, which is a general equilibrium process not easily understood from within the agricultural sector (Timmer, 1988). Part of the controversy stems from the heterogeneity of agricultural endowments and the vastly different cropping systems seen in Latin America, Africa and Asia. It is unrealistic to expect much of a common role in such diverse settings. And part of the controversy comes from the enormous differences around the world in stage of development, and accordingly the vastly different roles that agriculture plays in economies at different levels of economic maturity. Christiaensen et al. (2011) document clearly the different contributions of agriculture to national welfare across these various categories. The *World Development Report 2008* develops an analytical typology of countries (and appropriate policy approaches) according to where they are in the structural transformation (World Bank, 2007).

Three basic sets of linkages between growth in agricultural productivity and overall economic growth have been identified in the literature: direct, indirect and roundabout. The least controversial elements in the literature were first articulated to a general economics audience by Lewis (1954) (direct linkages through factor markets) and Johnston-Mellor (1961) (indirect linkages through product markets). These linkages have long been part of the core of modern development theory and practice (Timmer 1988; 2002; Dercon and Gollin 2014). The third set of linkages are more nebulous and hard to

---

[11] An influential review article by Robert Bates challenges the relevance of English agricultural experience for developing countries and argues for the relevance of 'historical France' (Bates 1988). His article includes a sobering reminder that historical lessons can be misconstrued when taken out of their context. The appropriate response, I would argue, is to identify (and quantify) the underlying economic (and political) mechanisms that generate the historical results, so that 'what if' questions can be asked about alternative situations. The 'New Economic History' movement that gave rise to the Cliometric Society was basically an effort to ask 'what if' questions about historical events. Gerschenkron was a keen supporter of the movement and a number of his students are active members of the Society.

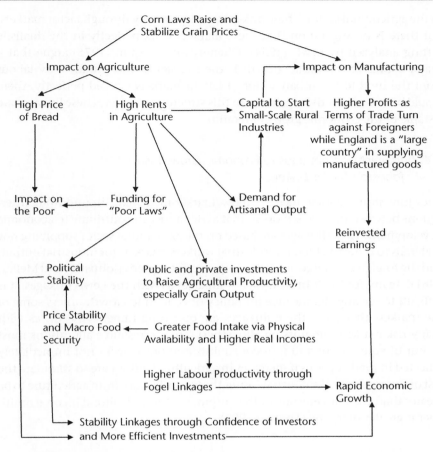

Figure 4.1 Impact of the English Corn Laws on the Industrial Revolution.
Source: Author.

measure, but may be important nonetheless: they include contributions of increased agricultural productivity to improved nutrition of workers that were highlighted by Fogel (1991, 1994) as partial explanation for earlier and more rapid economic growth in England compared with France (see Figure 4.1); spurts to economic growth that result from regime changes that lead to reductions in 'urban bias'. as described by Lipton (1977); and improvements in the efficiency of investments that stem from stable food prices and a political sense of food security (Timmer 1989; Dawe 1996).

4.4.1 *Direct Contribution to Economic Growth via Lewis Linkages*

The 'Lewis Linkages' between agriculture and economic growth provide the non-agricultural sector with labour and capital freed up by higher productivity in the agricultural sector. These linkages work primarily through factor markets, but there is no suggestion that these markets work perfectly in the dualistic setting analyzed by Lewis (1954). Chenery and Syrquin (1975) argue that a major source of economic growth is the transfer of low-productivity labour from the rural to the urban sector. If labour markets worked perfectly, there would be few productivity gains from this structural transfer. These linkages are a staple of the economic growth literature.

4.4.2 Indirect Contributions to Economic Growth via Johnston-Mellor Linkages

The 'Johnston-Mellor Linkages' allow market-mediated, input-output inter-actions between the two sectors so that agriculture can contribute to economic development. These linkages are based on the agricultural sector supplying raw materials to industry, food for industrial workers, markets for industrial output, and the foreign exchange needed to import capital goods (Johnston and Mellor, 1961). Again, for the Johnston-Mellor linkages as with the Lewis linkages, it is difficult to see any significance for policy or economic growth unless some of the markets that serve these linkages are operating imperfectly (or, as with many risk markets, are missing altogether). That is, resource allocations must be out of equilibrium and face constraints and bottlenecks not immediately reflected in market prices if increases in agricultural output are to stimulate the rest of the economy at a rate that causes the 'contribution' from agriculture to be greater than the market value of the output, i.e. the agricultural income multi-plier is greater than one (Timmer 1995).

4.4.3 Roundabout Contributions from Agriculture to Economic Growth via Fogel Linkages (Improved Nutrition), Lipton Linkages (Removing Urban Bias), and Stability Linkages (Improving Efficiency of Investment)

An additional set of linkages focuses on more nebulous and hard-to-measure connections between growth in agricultural productivity and growth in the rest of the economy. These linkages grow explicitly out of market failures, and, if they are quantitatively important, government interventions are required for the growth process to proceed as rapidly as possible. From this perspective, the contribution of agricultural growth to productivity growth in the non-agricultural economy stems from several sources: greater efficiency in decision making as rural enterprises claim a larger share of output and higher product-ivity of industrial capital as urban bias is reduced; higher productivity of labour as nutritional standards are improved; and a link between agricultural profitability (as distinct from agricultural *productivity*) and household investments in rural human capital, which thus raises labour productivity as well as facilitates rural-urban migration.

Several of these mechanisms stand out as likely to be important (and potentially measurable) because they draw on the efficiency of decision making in rural households, the low opportunity cost of their labour resources, the opportunity for farm investment without financial intermediaries, and the potential to earn high rates of return on public investments that correct for urban bias. Each of these factors alone, as public investments and favourable policy stimulate growth in the agricultural sector, should cause an increase in the efficiency of resource allocation. In combination, these mechanisms should translate faster agricultural growth into measurably faster economic growth in aggregate, after controlling for the direct contribution of the agricultural sector to growth in GDP itself.

The Fogel Linkages. Fogel (1991, 1994) calculates that increases in food intake among the British population since the late eighteenth century contributed substantially to increased productivity and income per capita. 'Thus, in combination, bringing the ultra poor into the labour force and raising the energy available for work by those in the labour force explains about thirty per cent of the British growth in per capita incomes over the past two centuries' (Fogel 1991: 47).

Where the food came from to 'fuel' this remarkable increase in labour productivity is crucial to the story. Grain production, the source of most of the calories of the poor, was significantly enhanced by the Corn Laws, but at the same time bread prices were kept high, contributing to the skewed distribution of income (Williamson 1985, 1990). In Fogel's judgment, only the Poor Laws, funded to a large extent from taxes on land rents that were enlarged by the Corn Laws themselves, prevented a French-style revolution (Fogel 1991: 47). By extension, the argument is that the Corn Laws caused the agricultural revolution instead, and they contributed in important ways to the Industrial Revolution.

The Lipton Linkages. In many countries of the developing world, a historically prolonged and deep urban bias led to a distorted pattern of investment. Too much public and private capital was invested in urban areas and too little in rural areas. Too much capital was held as liquid and non-productive investments that rural households use to manage risk. Too little capital was invested in raising rural productivity (Lipton 1977).

Such distortions resulted in strikingly different marginal productivities of capital in urban and rural areas. New growth strategies—such as those pursued in Indonesia after 1966, China after 1978, and Vietnam after 1989—altered investment priorities in favour of rural growth and benefited from this disequilibrium in rates of return, at least initially. For example, in Indonesia from the mid-1960s to the mid-1990s, farm GDP per capita increased by nearly half, whereas it had declined from 1900 to the mid-1960s. In China, the increase from 1978 to 1994 was nearly 70 per cent, whereas this measure had dropped by 20 per cent between 1935 and 1978 (Prasada Rao, Maddison and Lee, 2002). A switch in investment strategy and improved rates of return on capital increase factor productivity (and farm income) because efficiency in resource allocation is improved.

The Stability Linkages. Significant macroeconomic benefits in terms of investment and growth stem from a stable food economy, which for many countries is only possible when agricultural productivity is rising. These macroeconomic linkages arise for a number of reasons. Newbery and Stiglitz (1981: 441) conclude from their analysis that 'there are some significant macroeconomic benefits that might be derived from price stabilization'. Dawe (2001) shows how various market failures due to imperfect credit markets, partially irreversible investments, and signal extraction problems due to fluctuating prices under conditions of imperfect information provide a microeconomic foundation for macroeconomic benefits from stabilizing prices of staple foods.

Instability in food prices can lead to instability for other commodities in the economy because of the large share of food in consumer budgets. Changes in expenditures on food, due to price changes, spill over to changes in expenditures on other commodities. Dawe (1996) found that instability in export earnings has a large negative effect on the efficiency of investment and hence, on the rate of economic growth. The macroeconomic benefits from stability can be quantitatively significant. Timmer (2002) estimated that stabilization of rice prices added 0.5 to 1.0 percentage points of growth in GDP per year to the Indonesian economy in the 1970s, when rice was still a large share of the economy and the world rice market was particularly unstable. These estimates are consistent with the work of Rodrik (1999), who stresses the importance of macroeconomic stability for investment and growth, and Dawe (2001), who argues that food (rice) price stability is a key ingredient of macro stability in Asia. Thus, stabilization of food prices—as a policy measure—can bring about and sustain stable conditions for private investment and growth. Social and political stability can also be affected by food price volatility. Arezki and Bruckner (2011) have found that surges in international food prices lead to an increased frequency of anti-government riots and demonstrations, as well as a weakening of democratic institutions.

4.5 The Corn Laws as an Historical Example of Linkages between Growth in Agricultural Productivity and Rapid Economic Growth

It was not the intent of British parliamentarians in 1688 to provide an empirical test of the linkages between agricultural development and economic growth outlined above. But the passage of the Corn Laws, which provided protection to wheat growers in Great Britain from foreign imports, set in process a long-term, dynamic process of modernizing the agricultural sector, with attendant stimulus to what has become known as the first Industrial Revolution. Careful study of this example turns a theoretical discussion into an empirical one.

Most historical accounts of the 'Glorious Revolution' focus on Prince William's Protestant beliefs, in contrast to the Catholic religion of King James. Whatever the importance of the religious confrontation, a side effect of the revolution had large implications for agriculture. A slightly tongue-in-cheek account runs as follows: In 1688, a 'search committee' established by the English Parliament proposed that William and Mary of Holland be 'appointed' (with tenure) as reigning King and Queen of Great Britain (to replace King James, who was also Mary's older brother). Their conditions for accepting the position included guaranteed rents to English landlords so that sufficient revenue as land taxes could accrue to the crown. This clever response was a trade policy designed to raise profits for domestic grain producers, which did indeed raise grain prices (and hence incomes of landlords—the landed gentry), but which also stabilized domestic prices in relation to the prices from major ports of supply (mostly in the Baltic and Black Sea). The Corn Laws became an essential piece of English political economy for almost two centuries. Especially after 1815, the debate over their impact stimulated the evolution of modern analytical economics.

Ricardo was wrong about the Corn Laws, at least when he entered the debate with Malthus in 1815. By the time the Corn Laws were repealed in 1846, however, they had probably outlived their paradoxical (and unplanned) role as an optimal tariff that raised the profits of manufacturers by turning the terms of trade against cotton exporters and importers of British manufactured goods (McCloskey 1980; Irwin 1988; Williamson 1990). Although startling, this revisionist interpretation of the Corn Laws has its foundation firmly in neoclassical trade theory.

A second role of the Corn Laws, however, is less well appreciated. The much-praised English agricultural revolution had nearly all of its roots enriched by significant price protection for cereals, with prices stabilized by the Duke of Wellington's 'sliding scale'. With higher and more stable prices than those faced by farmers in France, Holland, or Germany, grain producers in England (and their local governments) invested heavily in new agricultural technology and rural infrastructure (Chambers and Mingay 1966; Timmer 1969).

Nearly all of the increases in average caloric intake per capita that Fogel sees driving up workers' heights and weights, and hence their potential for productive work, stemmed from food grown on English farms. France, with a 'provisioning' policy designed to keep food prices low, was unable to increase agricultural productivity (Kaplan 1984; Bates 1988). Imports were not sufficient to provide increases in caloric intake per capita, especially in rural areas where three-quarters of the labour force lived and worked. Hence, labour productivity in France lagged behind England by several decades (Fogel 1991; O'Brien and Keyder 1978).

The Corn Laws were connected to the Industrial Revolution and history's first sustained process of intensive economic growth by all of the linkages between agricultural productivity and economic growth just identified (see Figure 4.1). Although not all of the linkages shown in Figure 4.1 have been robustly quantified, the work of Fogel (1991), Williamson (1990), McCloskey (1980) and Irwin (1988), among other scholars of the Industrial Revolution, document clearly the importance of links between higher agricultural productivity, supplies of food available in domestic markets, impact on labour productivity, and stimulus to manufacturing activity.

Almost by definition, the Corn Laws dealt with how agriculture was valued, and Britain chose to 'overvalue' its agricultural sector at a time when the rest of Europe tried to keep food prices as cheap as possible. This is the 'British exceptionalism' to which Bates (1988) refers. And notwithstanding the relevance of the 'provisioning' approach used in historical France to understand the experience of modern developing countries, that does not make it a good strategic approach going forward.

Despite the positive lessons from providing active policy support to agriculture for over two centuries in Great Britain, the agricultural sector has been seriously undervalued by both the public and private sectors in many developing countries since the 1950s. The neglect has been particularly severe in those societies in which poverty has remained untouched or even deepened. In addition to an urban bias in domestic policies, the root cause of this undervaluation is a set of market failures. Commodity prices, by not valuing reduced hunger or progress against poverty, often do not send signals with appropriate incentives to decision makers. These inappropriate signals cause several problems.

First, low values for agricultural commodities in the marketplace are reflected in low political commitments. But political commitments to rural growth are needed to generate a more balanced political economy, with less urban bias than has been seen in most developing countries historically (Lipton 1977; Timmer 1993). The developing world has already seen a notable reduction in the macroeconomic biases against agriculture, such as overvalued currencies, repression of financial systems, and exploitive terms of trade (Westphal and Robinson 2002). Further progress might be expected as democracy spreads and empowers the rural population in poor countries (although agricultural policies in most democracies make economists cringe).

The world food crisis of 2007/2008 was also a wake-up call to political leaders to provide more resources to agricultural development. Major new investments in the CGIAR system for basic research on improved agricultural technologies have been led by the Bill and Melinda Gates Foundation, many countries have revisited domestic policies for food security, with an emphasis on increasing food production, and the United Nations just incorporated ambitious goals for increasing agricultural productivity into the Post-2015 Sustainable Development Goals, which were finalized in October, 2015.

The second problem with low valuation of agricultural commodities is that rural labour is also undervalued. This weakens the link between urban and rural labour markets, which is often manifested in the form of seasonal migration and remittances. There is no hope of reducing rural poverty without rising real wages for rural workers. Rising wages have a demand and a supply dimension, and migration can affect both in ways that support higher living standards in both parts of the economy. Migration of workers from rural to urban areas raises other issues, of course, but those issues depend fundamentally on whether this migration is driven by the push of rural poverty or the pull of urban jobs (Larson and Mundlak 1997).

Either way, the food security dimensions of rural-urban migration are clear. Indeed, this is the basic message of a successful structural transformation. Urban markets become relatively more important in supplying food needs for the population. Whether the country's own rural economy or the world market is the best source of this supply will be one of the prime strategic issues facing economic policy makers for the next several decades.

4.6 Concluding Reflections on the Role of Agriculture in 'Catching up'

The societies in Europe that framed Gerschenkron's basic hypothesis about the 'advantages of backwardness' and the role of substitutes for meeting 'prerequisites' to rapid industrialization showed a reasonably clear gradation on the scale of industrial modernization—from Britain to France to Germany to Russia as a rough generalization. No similarly clear pattern existed for agriculture. To be sure, British agriculture was more productive in its use of land and labour than most regions on the Continent, but once there—where Gerschenkron's views were formed—the same patterns of backwardness (and any advantages) were not nearly so clear for agriculture as they were for industry. It is no wonder that Gerschenkron was little concerned with how to modernize agriculture and its potential to serve as a stimulus to economic growth.

Contrast that pattern with those in developing countries since the 1950s. The differences in both land and labour productivity in agriculture were, and

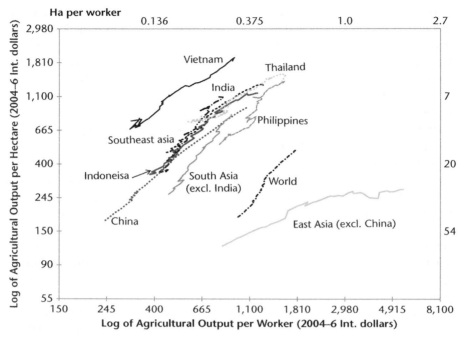

Figure 4.2 Land and Labour Productivity in Agriculture, 1961–2010.
Source: FAOSTAT (<http://faostat.fao.org>).

are, at least as stark as in the industrial sectors of these countries (see Figure 4.2). In the initial enthusiasm of decolonization and economic independence, it seemed agriculture could be ignored, even taxed heavily, on behalf of catching up industrially with rich countries. There was no understanding that agricultural productivity was linked to industrial productivity in ways that made investing in agriculture critical to overall economic growth.

Ignoring, or heavily taxing, agriculture was not feasible in much of Asia because of dense populations and severe pressure on land resources. Especially in East Asia, concerns for food security pressed countries to invest in raising agricultural productivity. Japan first showed how to do this by investing heavily in agricultural research, rural infrastructure and human capital, but most of East and Southeast Asia learned the lessons quickly. At least in the context of a new Green Revolution technology that offered sharply higher agricultural productivity in conditions where it could be adopted, there were advantages to backwardness in agriculture as well as in industry.

Coming to grips with this Asian experience would almost certainly have led Gerschenkron to extend his framework to agricultural modernization as well as to industrial spurts. He would have insisted, I am sure, that substitutes for any particular approach to agricultural modernization might be possible and should be part of the historical analysis. The wide array of linkages between agriculture and the rest of the economy invite such a search. It is particularly relevant to ask whether there are substitutes for stability of the food system, which played such an important role in East and Southeast Asia. If not, Africa will face serious difficulties in developing a modern urban economy.

Thus, the big question for the development profession in the middle of the second decade of the twenty-first century is whether either the European experience or the East and Southeast Asian experience can be the basis for growth strategies in sub-Saharan Africa and South Asia. The evidence suggests that being 'backward' in agricultural productivity in 2015 conveys little advantage in a highly competitive global economy. The reasons for that continuing backwardness, after decades of more or less well-intentioned efforts to fix it, have no easy rationale. Complex interactions among natural resource bases, local tenure arrangements, poor institutions subject to the constraint of small state size, and unstable political regimes unable to commit to the lengthy investment horizons required to build rural infrastructure, all argue for local approaches rather than grand visions.

That said, strategic direction is critical. Such long-term processes need guidance in the short run. From this perspective, a grand vision of successful structural transformation is likely to be needed to support and stimulate the necessary local policies and investments in rural productivity that will bring about rapid reductions in poverty and broad-based economic growth.

The historical record remains abundantly clear in this regard. It will be difficult, perhaps impossible, to sustain modernization in the urban economy unless productivity rises in the rural economy. Scholars can debate which sector needs to come first, whether small-scale farming is the right approach to raising agricultural productivity, and how the ingredients for modern agriculture will reach farmers—through private or public initiatives.[12] But the need for all of this to happen in Africa and South Asia if poverty is to be reduced quickly is obvious. And I am pretty sure that Gerschenkron would have agreed that careful historical analysis in each context, based on theory and examination of the relevant historical data, would be a key ingredient in understanding how to go about these tasks.[13]

---

[12] And perhaps there is scope for using randomized controlled trials (RCTs) to identify the most efficient approaches to addressing these debates. But the overall strategic approach will remain firmly grounded in historical analysis.

[13] There is clear evidence that such an approach is possible. The PhD dissertation by Lopez Jerez (2014) explicitly and successfully uses a Gerschenkronian methodological approach to understand the very different paths of agricultural development in the Red River and Mekong River Deltas of Vietnam.

Acknowledgements

I would like to thank participants at a seminar at Lund University on 17 December, 2014, where we talked through many of the ideas in this chapter. I am also indebted to a biography of Gerschenkron by his grandson for insights into 'the Great Gerschenkron's' intellectual background and approach to scholarship (Dawidoff, 2002). The memories and observations reported in this chapter, however, are personal.

References

Arezki, R. and M. Bruckner, 2011. *Food prices and political instability*, International Monetary Fund Working Paper 11/62. Washington, DC, International Monetary Fund.

Barrett, Christopher B., 2014. *Accelerating the Structural Transformation of Rural Africa*, Draft paper prepared for the African Development Bank, August. Ithaca, NY: Cornell University.

Bates, R.H., 1988. 'Lessons from History, or the Perfidy of English Exceptionalism and the Significance of Historical France'. *World Politics* (review article) vol. XL, number 4:499–516.

Chambers, J.D., and G.E. Mingay, 1966. *The Agricultural Revolution, 1750–1880*, Schocken: New York.

Chenery, H.B., and M. Syrquin, 1975. *Patterns of Development, 1950–1970*, London: Oxford University Press.

Christiaensen, L., L. Demery and J. Kuhl, 2011. 'The (evolving) role of agriculture in poverty reduction—an empirical perspective'. *Journal of Development Economics* vol. 96 number 2: 239–54.

Dawe, D., 1996. 'A New Look at the Effects of Export Instability on Investment and Growth'. *World Development* vol 24 number 12:1905–14.

Dawe, D., 2001. 'How far down the path to free trade? The importance of rice price stabilization in developing Asia'. *Food Policy* vol 26:163–75.

Dercon, S. and D. Gollin, 2014. 'Agriculture in African Development: Theories and Strategies'. *Annual Review of Resource Economics*. Vol. 6 (October), pp. 471–492.

Fei, J.C.H., and G. Ranis, 1964. *Development of the Labor Surplus Economy: Theory and Policy*, Homewood, NJ: Irwin.

Fogel, R.W., 1991. 'The Conquest of High Mortality and Hunger in Europe and America: Timing and Mechanisms'. In *Favorites of Fortune: Technology, Growth, and Economic Development since the Industrial Revolution*, edited by P. Higonnet, D.S. Landes, and H. Rosovsky, [35–71], Cambridge, MA: Harvard University Press.

Fogel, R.W., 1994. 'Economic Growth, Population Theory, and Physiology: The Bearing of Long-Term Processes on the Making of Economic Policy'. [Nobel Prize Lecture] *American Economic Review* vol. 84 number 3:369–95.

Gerschenkron, A., 1962. *Economic Backwardness in Historical Perspective*, Cambridge, MA: Harvard University Press.

Gerschenkron, A., 1968. *Continuity in History and Other Essays*, Cambridge, MA: Harvard University Press.

Hayami, Y., and V. Ruttan, 1985. *Agricultural Development: An International Perspective*. Revised and expanded edition. Baltimore: Johns Hopkins University Press.

Hirschman, A.O., 1958. *The Strategy of Economic Development*, New Haven: CT. Yale University Press.

Irwin, D.A., 1988. 'Welfare effects of British free trade: Debate and evidence from the 1840s'. *Journal of Political Economy* vol. 96 number 6:1142–64.

Johnston, B.F., and J.W. Mellor, 1961. 'The Role of Agriculture in Economic Development'. *American Economic Review* vol. 51 number 4:566–93.

Kaplan, S.L., 1984. *Provisioning Paris: Merchants and Millers in the Grain and Flour Trade during the Eighteenth Century*. Ithaca, NY: Cornell University Press.

Larson, D., and Y. Mundlak, 1997. 'On the Intersectoral Migration of Agricultural Labor' *Economic Development and Cultural Change*, Vol. 45, no. 2, pp. 295–319.

Lewis, W.A., 1954. 'Economic Development with Unlimited Supplies of Labor'. *The Manchester School* Vol. 22: 3–42.

Lipton, M., 1977. *Why Poor People Stay Poor: Urban Bias in World Development*, Cambridge, MA: Harvard University Press.

Lopez Jerez, M., 2014. *Deltas Apart: Factor Endowments, Colonial Extraction and Pathways of Agricultural Development in Vietnam*, Doctoral Dissertation defended December 19, Department of Economic History, Lund University, Sweden.

Maddison, A., 1995. *Monitoring the World Economy: 1820–1992*, Development Centre of the Organisation for Economic Co-operation and Development (OECD). Paris, France.

McCloskey, D.N., 1980. 'Magnanimous Albion: Free Trade and British National Income, 1841–1881'. *Explorations in Economic History* vol. 17 number 3:303–20.

Mosher, A.T., 1966. *Getting Agriculture Moving: Essentials for Development and Modernization*, New York: Praeger.

Newbery, D.M.G., and J.E. Stiglitz, 1981. *The Theory of Commodity Price Stabilization: A Study in the Economics of Risk*, New York: Oxford University Press.

Nurkse, R., 1953. *Problems of Capital Formation in Underdeveloped Countries*, Oxford, England: Blackwell.

O'Brien, P., and C. Keyder, 1978. *Economic Growth in Britain and France, 1780–1914: Two Paths to the Twentieth Century*, London: Allen and Unwin.

Pardey, P., 2011. *African Agricultural Productivity Growth and R&D in a Global Setting*, Stanford Symposium Series on Global Food Policy and Food Security in the 21st Century, (October 6), Stanford University.

Prasada R.D.S., A. Maddison, and B. Lee, 2002. 'International Comparison of Farm Sector Performance: Methodological Options and Empirical Findings for Asia-Pacific Economies, 1900–94'. In *The Asian Economies in the Twentieth Century*, edited by A. Maddison, D.S. Prasada Rao and W.F. Shepherd, [27–52] England: Edward Elgar.

Prebish, R., 1950. *The Economic Development of Latin America and its Principal Problems*. U.N. Lake Success, NY: Department of Economic Affairs.

Rodrik, D., 1999. *The New Global Economy and the Developing Countries: Making Openness Work*, Washington, D.C: Overseas Development Council.

Schultz, T.W., (ed.), 1978. *Distortions of Agricultural Incentives,* Bloomington, IN: University of Indiana Press.

Timmer, C.P., 1969. 'The Turnip, the New Husbandry, and the English Agricultural Revolution'. *Quarterly Journal of Economics* vol. 83 number 3:375–95.

Timmer, C.P., 1970. 'On Measuring Technical Efficiency'. *Food Research Institute Studies in Agricultural Economics, Trade, and Development* vol. 9 Number 2:98–171.

Timmer, C.P., 1971. 'Using a Probabilistic Frontier Production Function to Measure Technical Efficiency'. *Journal of Political Economy* vol. 79 number. 4:776–94.

Timmer, C.P., 1986. *Getting Prices Right: The Scope and Limits of Agricultural Price Policy,* Ithaca, NY: Cornell University Press.

Timmer, C.P., 1988. 'The Agricultural Transformation'. In *Handbook of Development Economics. Vol. 1,* edited by H. Chenery and T.N. Srinivasan, [275–331], Amsterdam: North-Holland.

Timmer, C.P., 1989. 'Food Price Policy: The Rationale for Government Intervention'. *Food Policy* vol. 14 number 1:17–27.

Timmer, C.P., 1993. 'Rural Bias in the East and Southeast Asian Rice Economy: Indonesia in Comparative Perspective'. *Journal of Development Studies* Vol. 29 number 4:149–76.

Timmer, C.P., 1995. 'Getting Agriculture Moving: Do Markets Provide the Right Signals?' *Food Policy* vol. 20, number 5:455–72.

Timmer, C.P., 2002. 'Agriculture and Economic Growth'. In *Handbook of Agricultural Economics, Vol. IIA,* edited by B. Gardner and G. Rausser, [1487–1546], Amsterdam: North-Holland.

Timmer, C.P., 2004. 'The Road to Pro-Poor Growth: The Indonesian Experience in Regional Perspective'. *Bulletin of Indonesian Economic Studies* vol. 40, number 2:177–207.

Timmer, C.P., 2009. *A World without Agriculture: The Structural Transformation in Historical Perspective.* Wendt Distinguished Lecture. Washington, DC: American Enterprise Institute.

Timmer, C.P., 2012. 'Behavioral Dimensions of Food Security'. *Proceedings of the National Academy of Sciences (PNAS),* Agricultural Development and Nutrition Security Special Feature, vol. 109 number 31: 12315–20.

Westphal, L. and S. Robinson, 2002. *The State of Industrial Competitiveness in Developing Countries,* New York: UNDP.

Williamson, J.G., 1985. *Did British Capitalism Breed Inequality?* London: Allen and Unwin.

Williamson, J.G., 1990. 'The impact of the Corn Laws just prior to repeal'. *Explorations in Economic History* vol. 27:123–56.

World Bank, 2007. *World Development Report 2008: Agriculture for Development.* Washington, DC: The World Bank.

Part 2
Diversity in Development

5

Misinterpreting the East Asian Miracle—a Gerschenkronian Perspective on Substitution and Advantages of Backwardness in the Industrialization of Eastern Asia

Christer Gunnarsson

5.1 The Miracle Explained—or Not?

Hardly anything has contributed more to changing the pathway of global economic development over the past half century than the unprecedented economic and social transformation of Eastern Asia. More than half of the world's economic output is today produced in Asia, and intra-Asian trade reaches higher volumes than all other intraregional trade relations. Hundreds of millions of people have been lifted out of extreme poverty and the rise of a new global middle class is largely due to income growth and wealth accumulation in Eastern Asia (Milanovic 2013). The way in which the living conditions of millions of Japanese, Chinese, Koreans, Malaysians, and other Asians have been transformed and enhanced is astonishing in itself. To this should be added the great promise, i.e. that the success stories of Eastern Asia may display to people in less developed countries an image of their own future; what can be achieved and, at least imaginably, how it can be done.[1]

The emergence of an alleged 'East Asian model' has challenged and, some would say, shattered conventional development thinking, policy and theory alike. Many suggestions have been made about what lessons to draw from this 'East Asian miracle'. While in policy circles the East Asian success story is

[1] The term Eastern Asia used here refers to Northeast Asian countries China, Japan, South Korea and Taiwan, and Southeast Asian countries Indonesia, Malaysia, Philippines, Singapore, Thailand, and Vietnam.

conceived as a role model, a good example for how to design development policy, it has also greatly impacted on theory, on the ways we seek to understand the causes and dynamics of sustained modern economic growth and development. A major theoretical divide has arisen on whether East Asian economic growth conforms to a professed conventional 'Western' model or represents a distinctively new prototype for development. A core question is then if East Asian growth has been following a pattern of imitation of a presumed Western model of industrialization, or whether it is best described as a web of substitutions for supposedly Western practices by Eastern-style adjustments. In the latter sense diversity in development would mean that an Asian mode of industrialization differs from a Western path but also that there might be diversity in development paths between Asian countries.

Export-led growth is an overarching concept used to describe and explain the transformation. In a Western-style, almost textbook-like explanation, free markets combined with prudent macroeconomic management, non-distorted prices and public investments in education, infrastructure and institutional arrangements have done the job (Westphal 1978; World Bank 1983, 1993; Balassa 1988; Kreuger 1984, 1991; Kuznets 1988; ADB 1997). In a market-critical 'revisionist' account it is rather intervention by strong East Asian states promoting certain sectors that has made the difference. Industrial policy and other direct interventions have distorted the market and guided or directed incentives and investments in favour of the export sector (Wade 1990; Amsden 1989, 2001; Chang 2002; Rodrik 1994; Woo-Cumings 1991, 1999; Kohli 2004). The bottom line is a familiar state versus market polemic, often with a strong ideological bias, in which the East Asian example is held up by either side to provide supposedly convincing stories about the preeminence of a particular dogma.

More recently a third approach that emphasizes East Asian specificity and in large degree, uniqueness, has gained prominence. This is the so-called 'labour-intensive' or 'industrious' path to industrialization. As opposed to an alleged 'Western path' associated with capital- and energy-intensive industry the 'East Asian path' is taken to have been a labour-intensive industrialization built on quality labour resources cultivated in the traditional sector (Sugihara 2000, 2007; Arrighi 2007).[2] This was the path, so the story goes, that transformed Japan from the mid nineteenth century onwards, and it was by following this very pathway that the entire region could begin its drive to modern economic growth from the 1950s.

---

[2] This is not the same as a comparative cost approach, which holds that East Asia has had its comparative advantage in a large pool of low-paid but semi-skilled labour that could be transferred to the manufacturing sector. The industrious approach argues against this dualistic approach and holds that the East Asian road to industrialization is characterized by a continuity and complementarity between traditional and modern sectors.

It is not that these approaches get their facts all wrong, they do not! Although conflicting on several accounts, they raise important aspects that cannot be ignored. All three approaches are part of 'grand' narratives that have a higher aim than to be correct in all detail. Policymakers with an unwavering conviction to pursue a certain political agenda will tend to use scholarly explanations to legitimize their claims, with the aim to build support and coalitions, and win battles. This is why the Washington Consensus claim about East Asia as a role model for development in terms of deregulation, privatization, central bank independence, independent judiciary, and small public sector could live on long after its factual base had been shattered (World Bank 1993; ADB 1997). But theory per se often serves as a narrative, especially if the problem at hand is to explain longitudinal change such as the industrialization of Eastern Asia. Such a narrative, or story, is made up by a sequence of connected events or assumed causal linkages and mechanisms aimed at providing a coherent and logical explanation of the process of change.

A theory of export-led growth signals that trade is good for growth and that too little trade is a major source of economic backwardness. A market-friendly approach to export-led growth aims at telling a story that unfettered markets accompanied by proper institutional arrangements (or 'good governance') will be a formula for success. A state-oriented approach aims at attesting that the East Asian success story demonstrates that markets need to be harnessed. In both cases the claims are high but as testable hypotheses the yields from such approaches would be dismal. Both approaches aim at explaining the mechanisms of long-term change by referring to alternate policy choices rather than structural characteristics and dynamics of transformation. It is in this context that the labour-intensive industrialization tale becomes relevant since it purports to tell a story according to which East Asia stands out as distinctively different from the West by representing a diverging, and largely more sustainable, model of industrialization. The credibility of these approaches is difficult to assess by means of quantitative estimation techniques. What we can expect is that each one of the approaches can offer a coherent and plausible story that fundamentally enhances our understanding of the East Asian miracle. Such a story should be undistorted by biases, errors, omissions, flaws, and mistaken deductions. If not, some other approach has to be tried out.

The first two approaches are decidedly policy oriented. They both exploit the case of East Asian development with a purpose to demonstrate superiority of a specific development policy and theory. As is often the case today history is used to test, and with the aim to prove correct, a specific economic theory or hypothesis, and to legitimize a choice of policy. Only those facts that give support to the predetermined theory will be considered while there is no real search for a deeper understanding of the complexities involved in processes of industrialization and long-run economic growth. Given that, it is hardly surprising that an approach focusing on Asian specificity has gained prominence since it is likely to do more justice to historical detail in the real economy. Whether continuity and complementarity between modern and traditional activities is the best way to characterize such complexities is more doubtful.

5.2 An Alternative Interpretation

In the present chapter an attempt is made to review the concepts of export-led growth, state-directed development, and labour intensive industrialization by exposing them to Alexander Gerschenkron's methodology for the study of industrialization. It is argued that all three approaches, although accurate in many respects, in different ways miss out on identifying fundamental aspects of the industrialization process of Eastern Asia. Gerschenkron's concepts of 'types' to account for variety as opposed to one single development path, 'the 'advantage of backwardness', which signals that a poor and non-industrial country can jump-start industrialization by importing technology, and 'substitution' as a mode to compensate for missing growth prerequisites in less developed economies, are particularly useful analytical categories in this respect.

The aim is to take Gerschenkron's methodology one step further by revisiting the concept of substitution. In Gerschenkron's thinking backwardness does encourage substitutions, but different types of substitution would also reflect different levels of backwardness, since they are, in Gerschenkron's words, 'part and parcel of a system of gradations of backwardness' (Gerschenkron 1962:41). So, when substitutive forms of industrialization are identified they will indicate different levels and types of 'backwardness' manifest in the form of retarded or delayed structural change. In this perspective not only extensive state intervention but also extreme export dependence of the industrial sector would be forms of substitution, and thus be expressions of different degrees of underdevelopment. Since for Gerschenkron the degree of backwardness is related to the extent to which agriculture can play a dynamic role in industrialization it can be argued that the countries in which the roots of backwardness, which is fundamentally proxied by low labour productivity and retarding institutions in agriculture, have been combatted and eradicated, are the real success stories. In contrast, substitutive models exist when agricultural productivity has remained low as industry advances, which may be due to persistence of retarding institutional arrangements. This does not mean that substitutive models are always undesirable although their persistence might be detrimental in the long run. It is indeed possible that foundations for long-term and less substitutive development can be created under substitutive industrialization regimes.

The building of technological capacities in interwar Japan and agricultural reforms in China under Mao are cases in point.

The purpose here is not to present new data and 'evidence' about the East Asian miracle. Instead, what follows is an account that aims to represent variety and substitution in the development story. In one sense this is by no means an original proposition. Booth (2002), Jomo (1997) Amsden (2001) and others have demonstrated that the late industrializing countries of Southeast Asia have been more market-led and export-dependent than their predecessors in Northeast Asia. Technology has been acquired by reliance on Foreign Direct Investments (FDI) and industrial policy has clearly been less imperative. Nonetheless, the argument here is that they are also more substitutive and industrially unbalanced, and within the ASEAN region there is a strong association between the level of development on the one hand and previous institutional change and productivity growth in agriculture on the other. For the Northeast Asian countries—Japan, Taiwan and South Korea—it can be argued that their industrialization models were less substitutive, in spite of the fact that state involvement at times has been extensive and export promotion a key feature of trade and industrial policy. Japan in the 1950s and Taiwan and South Korea about one decade later underwent fundamental structural changes in which improvements in agricultural productivity coincided with and initially drove the process of industrialization. Similar mechanisms appear to have been at work in China during the first decade of growth after the reforms beginning in 1978. Agricultural change thus appears to have been a major factor explaining the timing of East Asia's industrializations also key to overcoming bottlenecks and weaknesses in previously more substitutive models.

The present approach does not give support to a suggestion that the East Asian road to industrialization is characterized by a continuity and complementarity between traditional and modern sectors, as argued in the literature on the industrious or labour-intensive path to industrialization (Sugihara 2007; Francks 2000, 2005). Japan's industrialization before World War II was largely substitutive and unbalanced and driven by export dependence and increasing state dominance. Industrialization after World War II was decidedly different; it was initially led by transforming agriculture which made possible a sectoral shift out to non-agricultural employment. In South Korea and Taiwan industrialization took off in the early 1960s. In both countries industrialization was preceded by agricultural transformations encompassing technological and institutional reforms. In both countries industrialization resembled the Japanese path, although South Korea retained more substitutive elements than Taiwan which is evidenced by a faster mounting productivity gap between manufacturing and agriculture. The Chinese path logically contains ample substitution given the strong role retained by the state-owned enterprises and the control over the banking system. Nonetheless, the rise of labour-intensive manufacturing coincided with the institutional reform process in agriculture around 1980. Some doubt can be cast on China's current development path with its great dependence on a largely state supported or guided export industry while large parts of the agricultural economy have remained low in productivity with low incomes and, increasingly, a redundant and jobless low-skilled labour force.

Thus, the argument made in this chapter is that the role of agricultural transformation becomes imperative for initiating and sustaining industrialization and structural change. Paradoxically, this might appear to be contradictory to Gerschenkron's own proposition that agriculture is unlikely to play an important role in late industrializing countries and that industrialization can happen without structural change. It can indeed, but such cases are commonly referred to as failures, as 'growth without development'. It comes out clearly in inter-sectoral imbalances of output and employment, but can also be seen directly in human development indicators, such as infant and child mortality and life expectancy. In fact, by employing Gerschenkron's methodology it is possible to argue that in the case of Eastern Asia there appears to be a direct link between the degree of agricultural transformation and the process of sustained and successful industrialization.

5.3 Gerschenkron's Methodology

In Gerschenkron's classification low productivity and retarding institutional arrangements in agriculture appear as major indicators of backwardness. A key assumption made by Gerschenkron was that European industrialization did not follow one uniform development path, but that several types of development patterns emerged. In his thinking there was no such thing as a single possible road to industrialization, but a variety of ways in which an 'ideal' precondition for growth could be interchanged or substituted. The lesson is that one should not expect to find 'the' recipe or blueprint for development. Bringing that perspective back in would be an important corrective to a current development discourse that is hopping from one explanation or theory to another, each one with claims to tell the one and only truthful story. The East Asian miracle discourse is no exception; it is dominated by a search for a unified model, one type, instead of a unified process comprising a variety of types. This is unfortunate since, after all, it is well understood that the countries of Eastern Asia differ greatly among themselves with respect to factor endowments, institutions, and timing of the industrialization spurt, and, of course, also in terms of success rate.

Gerschenkron's approach to the study of economic development is today either essentially forgotten or largely misrepresented and his grand typology of nineteenth century European industrialization is nowadays much contested (For a review of the Russian debate see Nafziger 2006). When cited in present-day development literature it is mostly with reference to an alleged proposition that in less developed economies the state will have to step in and act as the main vehicle of economic growth (Weiss & Hobson 1995). Such a view is meant to give support to an agenda for active government intervention and industrial policy. For advocates of such an agenda the East Asian case appears to fit in nicely. But this is a superficial conclusion for which there would be difficulty in finding much support in Gerschenkron's thinking on industrialization.

Revisiting Gerschenkron's research approach brings to life some largely neglected aspects of the study of economic development. His typology is a tool of analysis for providing an interpretive understanding of industrialization and modern economic growth. It is not a hypothesis to be tested in a strict sense, but rather a device for telling a coherent story about dynamics and patterns of industrialization in a given context. In this framework 'historical research consists essentially in application to empirical material of various sets of empirically derived hypothetical generalizations and in testing the closeness in the resulting fit' (Gerschenkron 1962:34). This is an attempt to understand the complexities involved in industrialization processes, an attempt to understand history in its own right instead of testing hypotheses by making commando raids into history in search of supportive evidence.

With Gerschenkron's approach economic theory enters by providing a systematic framework for theorizing by which it may be possible to ascertain certain uniformities, regularities, and relationships in how industrialization occurs among countries. The emerging patters are, however, delimited in time and space; they are mainly relevant within one and the same coherent process as in the case of European industrialization. Gerschenkron's story was about Europe from around 1830–50 up until the World War I. It offers no theory that can, or should, be tested on other historical processes and no claim is made about universal applicability of the typology. On the basis of Gerschenkron's approach other typologies are possible for other processes at other times. So, it makes little or no sense to make a strict comparison between Gerschenkron's specific typology for Europe and the processes of industrialization in Eastern Asia. The variety in the unified process will be different, and so will be the advantages, and disadvantages, of backwardness and the modes of substitution at work.

Gerschenkron's typology rests upon two key concepts—'advantage of backwardness' and 'substitution'. The first denotes opportunity for development; change can be achieved if proper policy choices are made. The second concept accounts for the different ways in which missing prerequisites, or initial conditions, can be compensated for under differing circumstances. Disadvantageous initial conditions of access to capital could be overcome through new institutional arrangements. But diversity is not infinite and if we wish to arrive at a higher level of understanding it should be possible to identify regularities, combinations, and general patterns. The industrial history of Europe is conceived as comprising several types within 'a unified, and yet graduated pattern'. If there is regularity, there should be some organizing principle, some underlying determinant that shapes the ways in which backwardness can be turned into an advantage and how substitutions are applied and types may appear.

Industrializations in Eastern Asia after 1950 and Europe in the late nineteenth century have in common that both are coherent processes involving interdependence between changes going on in a number of countries over long periods of time, spanning over two or three generations. These processes need not be identical, in fact they are not, and the combination of the characteristics of the countries involved differs greatly between Europe and Asia. However, Gerschenkron's approach involves a set of key assumptions and concepts that can be applied to assessing stories told about the East Asian miracle countries, the stories of export-led growth, state-led growth, and labour-intensive industrialization. Seen from this perspective those stories, although pointing to important aspects of the East Asian transformation, are weakened not so much by errors, omissions, and flaws, but by recurrent biases, some of which are suspiciously ideological, and by dubious deductions.

Following Gerschenkron, the focus is on the drive to modern economic growth in the Kuznetsian sense, i.e. industrialization, the application of science-based technologies in the production process, which involves mechanization and economies of scale. Sustained industrialization encompasses structural change. It is true that industrialization can take place without structural change from an agriculture-based to an industrially-driven economy, but in Gerschenkron's framework a persistence of such conditions would be signifying failed industrialization as exemplified by Bulgaria. Structural change is also what distinguishes today those countries that have made the journey to high income from those that have been less successful. In addition, emphasis is on change rather than continuity. Instead of searching for very long historical roots of economic growth, the focus is on identifying preconditions, mechanisms, dynamics, patterns, and drivers of change as the process of industrialization actually unfolds. In the case of Eastern Asia it makes little sense to search for the origins of development (or backwardness) way back in a remote past if the task is to identify different types and patterns of industrialization. The time perspective chosen will, however, differ. For Japan and China, and perhaps also Thailand, it would be relevant to look at initial conditions by the mid-nineteenth century; how these countries which were not colonized at that time coped with the challenges and threats posed by the rise of Western industrialist powers. For all the other countries that gained independence after World War II the relevant conditions and challenges are the ones emerging from the 1950s onwards when industrialization was placed on the agenda.

In Gerschenkron's terminology it is clear how missing prerequisites can be substituted by a gradual escalation in the application of institutional arrangements that are not of market origin, such as banks and the state, or a combination thereof. Less clear is what it is to be substituted for. The case of England's industrialization is always somehow used to set the stage but its characteristics are seldom or never spelled out. When specifically referred to, the emphasis is on financing of industrialization from private sources and the emergence of a class of entrepreneurs. But it is also, although rarely ever quoted, clearly stated that agricultural reforms, such as enclosures, had a strong role to play. Industrial progress was aided 'by the growth of productivity in English agriculture that took place in the eighteenth century' (Gerschenkron 1962:49). So, the more backward the economy, the less likely that the agricultural sector would provide a growing market to industry, and the more dependent industry was to become for its expansion upon growing productivity and inter-industrial sales. Obviously then, the degree of backwardness is directly related to, and probably determined by, the level of productivity in agriculture.

To Gerschenkron, substitution meant that industrial spurts could occur in the less developed countries of Europe under conditions of relative agricultural stagnation or even exploitation of the agrarian sector. Surpluses could be appropriated without previous productivity improvements. In such cases agriculture could function as a source of capital formation, but did not play a significant role as a market for manufactured goods since real incomes in agriculture were depressed. This in turn motivated the forced type of industrialization Gerschenkron thought was typical in the most backward countries. While in England the growth of entrepreneurship was a bottom-up process led by productivity improvements in agriculture, which raised incomes and savings and thereby induced the growth of an internal market, two distinctly different models transpired in Europe, a German bank-driven industrialization and a Russian state-led or forced type.

The German type rested on the rise of a large land-owning class (*junkers*) in symbiosis with the state. Since income growth potential among the peasantry was limited, market growth was slow and capital accumulation was concentrated in banks. In Russia, agricultural productivity growth came later and was slower, which called for extensive state involvement in capital accumulation. The higher the degree of backwardness, i.e. the more absent the market institutions, the more likely that the state would step in and act as the vehicle of growth. In a high degree of forced industrialization one would not only find relative agricultural stagnation and depressed purchasing power in the agrarian sector, but also high capital intensity and investments in heavy industry. Gerschenkron inferred that as the industrial spurt materializes, capital intensive rather than labour intensive methods of production will be used, large scale production will be dominant and production of producers' goods would have priority over consumers' goods. All this relates back to backwardness in agriculture.

Backwardness is the organizing principle in Gerschenkron's scheme and retarding institutions and low productivity in agriculture the fundamental roots of backwardness. The higher the degree of backwardness the greater the extent of substitution as expressed in a lesser reliance on home market mechanisms and institutions. Obviously then, substitutive forms of industrialization are indications of initial backwardness. But if substitutive forms of industrial development persist without inducing broad-based entrepreneurship and market development as well as sustained consumption growth, it would indicate enduring backwardness since the more persistent the substitutive form of industrialization the higher the likelihood of the structural backwardness of the economy remaining. If the manufacturing sector advances while productivity remains low in agriculture the industrialization model is substitutive, reflecting a manifest level of backwardness. That Russia appears to fit Gerschenkron's substitution-backwardness scheme goes without saying. Germany is more problematic given that it had reached industrial dominance and scientific leadership in Europe by World War I. But Gerschenkron points to another problem, namely that the substitutive form of industrialization, conditioned as it were by unequal land ownership endured, obstructing democratization and fostering authoritarianism, fascism, and militarism, and thereby logically also large-scale capital-intensive industry (Gerschenkron 1946; See also Moore 1966). Japan before World War II appears to fit even better. Although landlordism of a German *junker* type was absent in Japan there seems to have been a link between an unresolved agrarian question and the rise of authoritarianism, fascism and militarism. There is also certainly a link to the type of industrialization that emerged and became dominant in the 1930s.[3] In contrast, Japan's industrial development after World War II is clearly the least substitutive of all East and Southeast Asian cases of industrializations. Rather than continuity this would indicate a weak link between the development paths before and after World War II.

---

[3] Productivity and institutions in agriculture appear to have been fundamental for Gerschenkron's definition of backwardness and decisive for structuring substitutions. Barrington Moore's (Moore 1966) identification of a link between social structure in agriculture and the subsequent political developments in Europe and Asia appears to be based on the same type of thinking.

5.4 Gerschenkron's Relevance for Asian Industrialization

How relevant is this for understanding industrialization in Eastern Asia? For Japan and China the relevance is straightforward since these two countries were directly affected, and thereby also part of the process of global industrialization of the latter half of the nineteenth century. They represent two different models, Japan a relatively successful case and China a case of failure. For the rest of Asia the relevance is indirect and conditional on trends and forces in the post-World War II global economy. Industrialization might happen spontaneously, but ever since the rise of Britain as an industrial power, and even more so after World War II, national projects focused on industrial development. Relative backwardness creates a tension between the promise of economic development, as observed among friends and foes, and existing obstacles to such development. Tension takes political form and motivates initiatives from above, the state, to induce institutional innovation. Measures taken for this purpose include efforts to regulate consumption, mobilize savings, and earmark investments. Alexander Eckstein has formulated the same urge as 'the more backward the economy in relative terms the greater will tend to be the urge, push, and pressure for massive state intervention and initiative in the process of industrialization, and at the same time, the greater will be the need for such intervention if a breakthrough, rather than a breakdown, is to be attained' (Eckstein 1958: 84).[4]

That strong political tension caused by relative backwardness has played a motivating role in East Asian industrialization, from the Meiji Restoration to Deng Xiaoping's Chinese reforms, goes without saying. Eastern Asia was the most turbulent and politically explosive region of the world during the 1950s and 1960s. Given the rise of communist China, the wars in Korea and Vietnam, the political insurgencies in Indonesia and Malaysia, and the recurrent instabilities in Thailand and the Philippines the tension between the need for change and obstacles to such change has been exceptionally strong at times. This is an important element and determinant of the urge for economic growth and development in the region. But it does not explain the Asian success stories. There is no apparent causal link from political tension to economic achievement.

When in the 1950s and early 1960s Gerschenkron was developing his typology, industrialization was top of the agenda for governments all over the developing world. Regimes of different colours were deeply involved in industrial projects and in doing so they were replacing, and often suppressing,

---

[4] Eckstein's proposal is in fact more far-reaching than Gerschenkron's. Interestingly, Eckstein did his most important empirical research on Asian, particularly Chinese, economic development. See in particular his *China's Economic Revolution* (1977).

market institutions. A proposition that the higher the degree of backwardness, the more encompassing state intervention would be, was quite realistic at the time. That state-led industrialization efforts were the norm in the developing world from the 1950s was a sign of relative backwardness as much as socialist ideology. Governments assumed the task of development planning and capital accumulation. Private corporations were nationalized and state-owned enterprises established. In the least developed countries, notably in Africa, statutory buying monopolies and monopoly pricing became key instruments for accumulating capital by appropriating the surplus from and, as it were, gradually suffocating agriculture. China under Mao represented an extreme type of forced industrialization by extracting the surplus from agriculture. Extraction was extensive, and sometimes excessive as during the Great Leap Forward, while industrialization gained momentum. In a UNIDO study (United Nations 1979) China's share of world manufacturing value added in 1976 was estimated in a range between 4.96 and 7.28 per cent depending on the method of estimation. These are questionable figures of course, but nonetheless indications are that China before 1978 was an outstanding case of substitutive industrialization even in the developing world. A large heavy industry sector developed while 80 per cent of the workforce remained in a largely low productive agriculture. Any consumer goods industry was inferior and market development by definition non-existent. The model was conspicuously untenable and had to be reformed.[5]

If substitution was the rule in the developing world and obviously most often closely connected to eventual failure in industrialization, a relevant question would be if there is a lower bound of backwardness, a level below which industrialization is unlikely to occur. Gerschenkron is not very clear about this. As he settles for the level of GNP as the best indicator he argues in passing that the economy shouldn't be 'too backward' and that a preparatory period would perhaps be required. Post-independence African cases, specifically but not solely, seem to indicate that not even substitutive types of industrialization would be possible since they could hardly be sustained over one single generation. In a simplistic sense it is understandable that societies in which property rights are badly protected, systems of conflict resolution largely absent, and social insurance systems rudimentary, are too backward to have a comparative advantage in industrialization. Retarding arrangements

---

[5] Ka and Selden (1986) argue that China's industrialization under Mao resembles the early phases of industrialization in Taiwan in that 'developmentalist states launched agrarian centered domestic accumulation in the service of urban-based industrialization. The state, not private entrepreneurs working through the market shaped the contours of the industrial fabric during original accumulation' (1986:1293–4). This misses out on the important difference that in Taiwan surplus transfer went through, admittedly regulated, market mechanisms while surplus extraction in China was done through taxation until the introduction of the Household Responsibility System.

can also be found in the labour process, in corporate structures, in predatory state policies, in land tenure arrangements, and in shortages in human skills. Apparently, Eastern Asia was not 'too backward', which seems to have been the case in some African attempts towards industrialization. This challenges some commonly held views that by the early 1960s development levels in Eastern Asia (except Japan) were on par with African countries such as Kenya and Ghana as is indicated by GNP/capita figures.

Since both state-led and the market-friendly policy models have been tried out without much success outside a handful of developing countries it can be argued that certain preconditions have to be in place before industrialization can be expected to take off. Even more substitutive forms would need to transcend some fundamental obstacles before they can move ahead. Gerschenkron saw Russia as the most substitutive form of industrialization in Europe, but he considered only developments after the abolition of serfdom in 1861, before which time Russia was obviously too backward. For Eastern Asia (except for Japan and China) it is not realistic to expect industrialization to have happened before independence. In terms of GDP per capita Malaysia was the most developed economy by the late 1950s followed by a catching-up Taiwan and a falling-behind Philippines. Per capita income in a war-torn South Korea was much lower and in fact on par with Ghana. Thailand's per capita equalled that of Kenya. From then onwards, Taiwan and South Korea forged ahead to join the ranks of high income countries. Malaysia fell slightly behind but is now next in line to move up to high income level.

In 1960 Thailand's and Indonesia's income levels were on a par with Kenya's while in China per capita income was about the same as in India. The rise of Eastern Asia in the subsequent decades stands in glaring contrast to the dismal growth performance of Kenya and Ghana. The only country underperforming, but only in relative terms, is the Philippines. So, what did the Asians do right that the Africans did not, or could not, do? Or was it simply that Ghana and Kenya were not ready for industrialization whereas the Asian countries were? GNP per capita estimates for Taiwan and South Korea might be misleading and understate both actual development levels and capabilities for industrialization. In colonial Korea the average living standard was much lower than in Japan and also considerably lower than in Taiwan. Nonetheless, in some parts of the country living standards were probably as high as in the most developed parts of the Asian mainland at the end of the colonial period and before much of the capital stock had been destroyed by devastating wars. Colonial Taiwan was less industrial but agricultural productivity growth was overall higher in the colony than in reigning Japan (Oshima 1987; Nasu 1941). Obviously, some preconditions for industrialization had been created under Japanese colonial rule.

5.5 Export-led Growth—a Substitutive Form

What distinguishes Eastern Asia generally, including China after the reform, is that industrial breakthrough has been attained, not breakdown, as in a majority of developing countries where industrialization has been attempted. The rise of successful export-oriented manufacturing industries is part and parcel of the breakthrough. But the theory (or story) of an East Asian export-led growth is questionable for many reasons. One reason is that causality between exports and GNP growth is anticipated rather than investigated to which should be added that we can be even less certain about the impact of export-policy on GNP growth (Rodrik 1998). Another is that export-led growth far from always represents a formula for sustained industrial growth and structural change. It can just as well be a form of industrialization that substitutes for missing growth prerequisites in the domestic market.

A major vulnerability of an export-led growth process is that it might signify a substitutive form of industrialization with development of a modern enclave-like export-oriented sector that coexists with a backward traditional economy. Not all countries in Eastern Asia have entirely escaped that type of setup. Southeast Asia is generally more export-dependent but also more unbalanced than East Asia. How can export-led growth be a substitutive form of industrialization? The important connection is the ways in which inter-sectoral shifts in production factors emerge. Fundamentally, and again relating to Gerschenkron, it has to do with the growth dynamics within agriculture. Although industrial development might be founded on exploit-ation of the agricultural sector, it is highly unlikely that a process of sustained growth in the manufacturing sector will be sustained over a long period of time if the agricultural sector is constantly suppressed in terms of productivity and per capita incomes. Exploitation is efficient in the short run only; in the long run the labour force will be locked up in low productive activities, capital transfers will decline and the development of the internal market will be impeded. An alternative, yet to be proven sustainable, model is the command economy, in which all market mechanisms are ruled out and the state takes almighty decisions about production and consumption.

Export-led growth is often seen as typical of industrial late-industrializers, especially for countries with smaller domestic markets. It is thought to have been typical in the late industrializing nations of the European periphery towards the end of the nineteenth century.[6] Therefore, it is not surprising that the model is thought to apply at least to the relatively smaller countries of Asia. The assumption is that the home market is too small to function as an

---

[6] Gerschenkron saw Denmark as a typical case of export-led or, as he called it derived, industrialization since its development was contingent on access to the English market.

engine of growth. The size and dynamics of the home market are, however, not only determined by the size of the population, but also by the dynamics of intra- and inter-sectoral change. Without productivity and per capita income growth in the agricultural sector, weak market development and substitutive industrialization become logical outcomes. In the Lewis model (Lewis 1954) the agricultural sector functions as a source of capital accumulation and as a supplier of redundant labour. The modern sector grows by attracting under-employed low-cost labour from agriculture thereby inducing profit accumulation in the manufacturing sector. No institutional or technological change in agriculture is required. In the Fei-Ranis (Ranis and Fei 1961) model of the dual economy a large scale exodus of labour from agriculture occurs only after technological change in agriculture. Most importantly, the dynamics that will unfold from there onwards will be dependent on the surplus productive capacity and the pre-existing distribution of income and assets within the agricultural sector (Adelman 1984). This is by no means unique for Eastern Asia. North (1961) has argued the same for nineteenth century industrialization in the United States.[7] If the initial distribution of assets in agriculture (land and capital) is uneven, income inequality within agriculture will tend to increase because of the productivity gap between different types and sizes of land holdings. In extremely bimodal systems a minority will gain non-proportionately and the income gap between industry and agriculture will tend to widen more in initially more unequal societies. If a majority of rural households are faced with slow or no income growth, the surplus capacity of agriculture will shrink over time and the total income-generating capacity of agriculture will be insufficient for the sector to serve as a market for manufactured consumption goods. In such a scenario it is logical that the export sector functions as the engine of industrial growth. Growth of domestic demand will occur only indirectly via accelerators and multiplier effects on investment and consumption from manufacturing exports.

For industrialization to be export-led it should be expected that the growth of manufacturing exports precedes growth of production for the home market, the development of the manufacturing sector precedes the growth of the

---

[7] North (1961:4) writes: 'If the export commodity is a plantation type which is relatively labor intensive, with significant increasing returns to scale, then its development will be in marked contrast to one where the export commodity may be most efficiently produced on a family-size farm with relatively smaller absolute amounts of labor required. In the first case, extremely unequal distribution of income will result in the bulk of the population devoting most its income to foodstuffs and simple production. At the other end of the income scale, the plantation owners will tend to spend most of their income on imported luxury goods. There will be slight encouragement of residentiary types of economic activity. With more equitable distribution of incomes, there is a demand for a broad range of goods and services, part of which will be residentiary, thus inducing investment in other types of economic activities.'

agricultural sector, agriculture serves as a source of capital accumulation and labour supply, whereas its role as a market for consumption goods will be limited. This is clearly a form of substitutive industrialization in a Gerschenkronian sense. Industrialization is highly unlikely to occur without access to welcoming foreign markets and foreign capital. The internal forces at work are on the supply side, i.e. improvements which make the economy apt to respond to foreign technology and demand. The obvious vulnerability of such a model is that the sectoral duality will become permanent so that the manufacturing sector keeps expanding while agriculture becomes relatively more backward. Then, export-led growth has enticed a substitutive form of industrialization, one that is likely to become contingent on government intervention or FDI, or both in combination. If rural incomes remain low it will exert downward pressure on the average national wage level. This might benefit the export industry but will be detrimental to the long-term growth of domestic consumption.

If the home market functions as an important driver of industrialization the mechanisms of growth will derive from a different type of agricultural modernization, one in which productivity improvements in agriculture are widespread and involve a broad cross-section of the farming households. Since incomes may be rising, the sector could be competing for labour with the industrial sector and the terms of trade will not necessarily develop in favour of the industrial sector. Due to the competition for labour, industrial wages will tend to rise and put pressure on industry to advance technology and alter forms of organization. As a consequence, the purchasing power increases in both agriculture and industry, and the home market is both enlarged (more people involved) and deepened (they have more money). In this model industrial development does not precede or exclude modernization of agriculture and the growth of exports does not precede or preclude the growth of the home market.

How do these models apply to Eastern Asia? Undoubtedly, productivity improvements in agriculture are part and parcel of the modernization process. The Meiji reforms in Japan were essential for the first stage of industrialization. Feudal land taxes in kind were replaced by monetary payments to the central government. Taxes were levied directly on the landowners and the Tokugawa prohibition on land sales was lifted. The result was the private property rights in land and the rise of a class of owner-cultivators (Rosovsky 1966). Up until the start of the twentieth century land taxes and revenues from agriculture constituted a major source of financing for industrial development. There was also a noticeable outflow of labour to industry. However, later on, and especially from the 1920s onwards, structural change was halted. Manufacturing industry, especially export production of textiles, kept expanding but agricultural incomes remained relatively unchanged.

Sometimes the Japanese development is compared to the *junker*-led modernization of agriculture in Germany. This is partly incorrect since holdings in Japan remained small and a class of very large landowners never came into being. But the rural population remained very big and there was no visible large-scale continuous exodus to industry. One characteristic of this development was the combination of industrial and traditional agricultural activities. A large part of the workforce consisted of young men and women working part-time or on temporary contracts in manufacturing while really not making the complete shift from agriculture to industry. This has led some scholars (Sugihara 2007) to the conclusion that Japan's industrialization, instead of being of dualistic type, is characterized by complementarity between sectors and pluriactivity in employment rather that a sectoral shift out of agriculture. Correct as this may be it also illustrates the vulnerability and substitutive form of Japan's industrialization before World War II. Japan had developed a very strong and competitive export industry in textile products. While Japan was challenging Britain's hegemony in the global textile trade, its home market development remained weak, mainly because incomes in agriculture remained low. On the other hand, surplus labour in an agriculture offering low incomes and wages provided a competitive advantage to Japan's export industries. According to agricultural economist Shiroshi Nasu, the 'existence of up-to-date factories with high technical efficiency side by side with millions of small farms amply supplying these factories with skillful but low-waged man-power constitutes the backbone of the national economy' (Nasu 1941:8).

Whether this portrays a surplus-labour economy of a Lewis type or a well-balanced and sustainable economy based on a 'pluriactive' workforce that moves back and forth between sectors is of fundamental importance. In the 1930s about half of the rural population consisted of tenants paying rents in kind to landlords. Household incomes were maintained by the part-time off-farm employment of farmers' sons and daughters, but since labour productivity in agriculture proper improved only slowly, living standards remained low. In the 1930s the rural population was clearly becoming unsustainably large (Nasu 1941). Some surplus population could be released by migration to occupied Manchuria but it was obvious to contemporary analysts that the situation was becoming untenable. Tenancy conditions constituted a recurrent matter of political controversy. Most tenants lived under the old system of paying rent in kind while the landowner payed monetary taxes. This made it difficult for tenants to respond to price incentives. In the 1930s the government introduced price regulation with the intention of sheltering agricultural producers from the effects of the global crisis. While having little impact on tenants, regulation appears to have had the effect of taking away price incentives also for landowners. This was a policy that combined nicely with the state-driven industrialization project that was initiated at that time.

A renowned (some would say notorious) contemporary was Freda Utley. Her verdict on the state of development in Japanese agriculture (Utley 1937) is perhaps not the most widely appreciated view in a recent literature that lays emphasis on the efficiency and sustainability of a system of complementarity between small-scale agriculture and manufacturing industry (Francks 2000; Sugihara 2007).[8] However, few of Utley's contemporaries seem to have disagreed with her argument that Japanese agricultural development was retarded by lack of institutional reform and technological advance. On institutions, Utley writes: 'the continuation of rent payments in kind, combined with heavy taxation by the State for an artificial fostering of urban industry for armaments, have prevented a capitalist organization of agriculture and the introduction of modern technology' (Utley 1937:101). On the pluriactive workforce, she infers that a large part comes from 'the homes of the peasantry whose women and children are sweated in domestic industry in the hours they are free from labour in the fields' (Utley 1937:65). She goes on to argue: 'the more miserable the condition of the peasantry the lower the wages in the cotton and rayon industries, the cheaper the price of textiles and the larger the export' (Utley 1937:177). The limited home market is of little concern for the larger industries since they work for export 'which is a natural consequence of the backwardness and poverty of Japanese agriculture' (Utley 1937:163). Most Western observers of the time, e.g. Hubbard (1937, 1938) appear to have agreed with the analysis.[9]

In the 1930s Japan entered into its fascist and militaristic phase in which heavy industry and large-scale state involvement became dominant features. Few would disagree that this is a typical Gerschenkronian substitution model of industrialization (Pomeranz 2001).[10] It can also be argued however that the previous model with an expanding export industry alongside a slow-growing agriculture was already a substitutive form of development. Although industry grew strong, rural incomes were low and in terms of human development indicators Japan ranked on a par with the poorest countries of Europe and far worse that the industrial North (League of Nations 1939/40). The choice was

---

[8] Freda Utley's best-known book *Japan's Feet of Clay* (1937) was criticized for factual inaccuracies, an exaggerated negative view of the Japanese people. The book was banned in Japan and Utley herself banned from entering Japan.

[9] Hubbard writes: 'In the spate of writings on Japan of the last twelve months, it would be hardly too much to say that the high-water mark has been reached by *Japan's Feet of Clay* in spite of the fact that it suffers from having been written with a strong political bias. This thorough, competent and up-to-date survey of the present state of Japan is the work of a trained student of economics who writes for the expressed purpose of "debunking" popular notions about the invincibility of Japan' (Hubbard 1937:165). What most commentators did not agree on was Utley's urge that the West needed to stand up against an upcoming Japanese aggression.

[10] Pomerantz who agrees with the idea of a sustainable 'industrious' Asian path describes Japan's development in the 1930s as 'Gerschenkronian' but he offers no analysis or explanation that relates to conditions in agriculture.

between reforming agriculture, removing retarding institutions and implementing machine-driven technology or building a state-driven heavy industry. The choice fell on the latter alternative. Militarism and imperialist aggression followed logically. Sugihara argues that Japan's outward aggression was caused by Western 'imperialistic' protection that sought to impede further expansion of Japan's flourishing textiles export and that thereby Japan had to adopt a more resource intensive model, and thus had to become aggressive (Sugihara 2007). From the analysis in the present paper there follows instead that, although increasing protectionism was indeed characteristic for the 1930s, Japan's switch to heavy industry should rather be seen as a replacement of one substitutive industrialization model by another.

Another side of the pluriactivity story is how to interpret the so-called Ishikawa curve (see Figure 5.1). Ishikawa (1978) inferred that while the rice yield of land had increased in the Tokugawa period, it was accompanied by an increasing labour intensity until about the turn of the nineteenth century. Labour-saving technologies gained increasing importance from the early twentieth century when labour was beginning to be released to activities other than agricultural production.

This Ishikawa curve stops moving to the right and crawls upwards after the Meiji Restoration but turns decisively to the left only after World War II when the big movement out of agriculture began. Ishikawa envisages also another curve, which depicts the changing relations between labour input in rice cultivation and the total labour input by household members (for a comment see Saito 2005). This indicates that when labour was released from working in the rice fields it was still kept within the family, and incomes generated from other activities remained within the rural household. Part-time incomes from

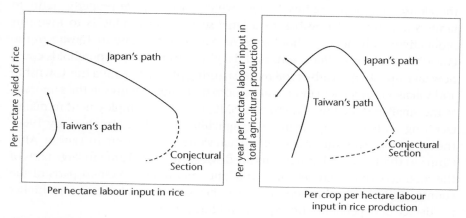

Figure 5.1 The Ishikawa curves.
Source: Ishikawa 1978.

manufacturing were to play an increasingly important role. So, while it was beneficial for manufacturing industry to have access to a large pool of low-waged labour from rural households it was also beneficial for the rural households to have access to additional incomes generated from sources outside agriculture. This was typical for Japan up until World War II. It was only after that War that Japan could escape its substitutive path of industrialization when institutional reforms and technological change paved the way for a broad-based productivity improvement during the 1950s. It is difficult to detect much continuity from the past.

Agriculture played an important role in the modernization process after independence in both South Korea and Taiwan. In Taiwan the growth impetus from agriculture was extremely strong up until around 1965. In the early phase agriculture expanded rapidly which necessitated more labour input, i.e. the Ishikawa curve moved to the right as the labour input per hectare ratio increased. By the early 1960s the curve started moving upwards and then turned rapidly backwards when the big outflow of agricultural labour to manufacturing began after 1965. During this phase agricultural income growth contributed more to the growth of demand than the export sector. Rodrik (1995) has argued that that almost 90 per cent of South Korea's and Taiwan's growth experience between 1960 and 1995 can be related to the initial equal income distribution. In both countries land reforms paved the way for a broad-based transformation of agriculture although the Korean model was somewhat shakier. The enormous export drive in the 1960s threatened to create a big sectoral income gap as agriculture was increasingly left relatively less modernized. The capital goods and heavy industry projects implemented around 1970 coincided with a growing sectoral imbalance.

In China the reform process began in agriculture with the implementation of the Household Responsibility System which gave *de facto* property rights to farmers and made it possible for a large segment of producers to invest in productivity-enhancing technologies. As had been the case in Taiwan in the late 1950s and early 1960s, sons and daughters in the rural households could now take up jobs in nearby rural manufacturing plants. In China the Township and Villages Enterprises (TVE) could absorb household savings in the same way as the Small and Medium Enterprises (SME) of Taiwan. Employment in manufacturing started as supplementary to agricultural work but by the early 1960s the big sectoral shift out of agriculture had gained momentum in Taiwan. After China in the 1990s had initiated its big drive to export-led growth large parts of the rural economy were left behind in the interior and Western parts of the country. Industrialization appears to have become more substitutive the higher the degree of dependence on exports and foreign capital.

In Southeast Asia progress has been more erratic and uneven. Although progress in agriculture has been achieved in most countries, sectoral imbalances have remained or worsened. The industrialization model that was tried out in the 1960s was decisively substitutive with its emphasis on import substitution and large government involvement while progress in agriculture remained slow or absent. Although much progress has been made in agriculture since then, most notably in Thailand, Malaysia and Vietnam, a new form of substitutive model has developed, one that builds on reliance on FDI and, in some countries, active industrial policy to promote export manufacturing.

5.6 Substitutions and the Developmental State

State involvement has been extensive in many East Asian economies as is well-known. The question is whether the successful export-oriented industrialization indicates that government intervention has been supporting rather than substituting for market institutions (see the debate between Lin and Chang 2009)? While in the real world, market mechanisms have become increasingly influential—even in Eastern Asia—development thinking has moved from stressing 'prices right' to getting 'institutions right'. To identify the institutions underpinning East Asian industrialization would therefore be of interest. The problem is then that it is clearly questionable how far the existing institutions conform to the standard recommendations of a favourable macroeconomic policy environment: clear and transparent property rights, open market access, and non-distorted prices. Instead we observe distorted prices, selective government intervention and active industrial policy. It is certainly not clear that property rights protection has been prioritized, and this applies not only to China.

Gerschenkron's typology of European industrialization held that the greater the degree of backwardness of the national economy, the higher was the likelihood that banks or the state would take on a leading role in the process of industrialization. Reliance on banks can be seen as a substitute for undeveloped capital markets—meaning stock markets—but it would of course be unrealistic to expect capital markets to be developed before industrialization got underway. Bank funding has become important because of the size of the operations. While smaller firms have had to rely on informal credit channels, large companies have had access to bank loans. Fundamentally, this means that large corporations have entered the stage early in the process. It also means that bank funding, with Japan as an exception, is closely connected to the state and that the state had a large stake in creating big corporations. But this has little to do with any degree of backwardness. What matters is that political motives for industrialization have been strong. This would also prove

Gerschenkron right, political motives are strong in late industrializers. Laissez-faire is not a politically rational option.

This seems to lend support to a theory of state-led development and to go hand in hand with Chalmers Johnson's famed story about the developmental state and its application to Japan and other industrializing countries in Asia (Johnson 1982). In contrast, the World Bank's *East Asian Miracle* study from 1993 (World Bank 1993) recognized the importance of state involvement for explaining Asian development, but maintained that developments in Southeast Asia were even more promising since state involvement was less.

The concept of the developmental state is problematic since it tends to be a measure of state performance, whether interventionist policies have been successful or not. This excludes all policy mistakes and failures from being deemed developmental.[11] If, instead of sampling by outcome, we measure by type of activity, a workable definition of a developmental state can be a state that is in control of the financial system and uses it to direct resources to industries and branches that are deemed advancing. This is based on the assumption that the state by this intervention leads the structural transformation from agricultural society to industry-based economy. For this to materialize there should be some kind of surplus mobilization and reallocation to the industrial sector either directly by taxation or regulated agricultural markets or indirectly by an exodus of redundant labour à la Lewis. Industrial policy is the core of the developmental state's policy actions and resources are directed towards industry while agriculture is neglected in relative and sometimes even in absolute terms.

The Asian developmental state is defined and explained in a variety of ways. Amsden argues that South Korea differs from most other late industrializing countries in the discipline the state exercised over private firms (Amsden 1989:14). Wade contends that Taiwanese development was based on 'an authoritarian, executive-based political structure' that can guard 'the feebleness of the legislature' (Wade 1988:159). In Amsden's and Wade's thinking economic decision making bodies were insulated from political and other pressure groups. Johnson, in contrast, emphasizes that in Japan there was a close and mutually beneficial symbiotic relationship between state agencies and key industrial capitalists (Johnson 1982). Ministry of International Trade and Industry in Japan (MITI), Economic Planning Board in Korea (EPB) and

---

[11] In a prominent study of industrialization in Asia and Latin America, Evans (1995) introduced the concept 'embedded autonomy' to account for state-business relations. A developmental state is one that is 'sufficiently embedded 'in society so that it can attain development goals without being too close to business interests and the risk of being captured. A major problem with such a definition is that developmental states are defined by success, not by institutions and agency. Success is the proof of their existence.

Council on International Economic Cooperation and Development in Taiwan (CIECD) are key agencies which supposedly represent different varieties of developmental states. These agencies were given high executive powers and enjoyed high degrees of prestige and legitimacy which would warrant that they were not only setting up development policies but also powerful enough to implement them.

Whether this conforms to Gerschenkron's typology is a matter of definition. For obvious reasons the administrative capacities of these Asian governments are likely to have been considerably more developed than those in nineteenth century Europe. According to Johnson (1982) the industrial policy undertaken by a Japanese developmental state consisted of two basic components: industrial rationalization policy and industrial policy. Industrial rationalization policy contains detailed measures for the operation of specific industrial sectors or individual firms. Industrial policy, comprising selective and strategic interventions, concerns the identification of the strategic sectors and arranging the transfer of resources to strategic industries. When it comes to actual interventions, Johnson argues that the Japanese state deliberately orchestrated a capital transfer to selected industrial sectors while transfers to agriculture were neglected. This would fit with Gerschenkron but, alas, it is hardly consistent with realities. George Mulgan (2005) argues in a critical assessment that Johnson's thesis both over- and under-generalizes key features of Japan's political economy. It over-generalizes by building a model of Japanese political economy focussing only on government-business relations in a number of large-scale, export-oriented manufacturing industries. More importantly, it under-generalizes Japanese political economy because types and modes of bureaucratic intervention were consistent across different sectors of the economy, and even more prevalent in weaker sectors, such as agriculture. In all probability the support to agriculture was instrumental in setting in motion the large-scale transformation of agriculture in the 1950s. At any rate, an argument that state allocation towards manufacturing took place at the expense of agriculture is not consistent with historical evidence. So, Chalmers Johnson's Japanese developmental state was not substitutive in Gerschenkron's sense. In fact, it was the opposite, agriculture was not neglected; it was promoted.

The *zaibatsu* in Japan, and the *chaebol* in Korea were in large degree creations in partnerships with the state. The South Korean economy is the one which comes closest to the description of forced development. Allocation was administered by a state controlled banking sector. Also in Taiwan banks were state controlled and remained so even after those in South Korea had been privatized in 1983. Woo argues that state control over the banking sector was decisive for the success of the Korean developmental state (Woo 1991). On the other hand, state owned, or controlled, banks played no developmental role in Japan. Thus, state control over the financial system was not characteristic of a Japanese developmental state and the system for capital mobilization and financing of industrial enterprises was not substitutive in the gerschenkronian sense. The Korean system of accumulation and allocation was more state directed and more substitutive also in the sense of being driven by manufacturing exports while agriculture was trailing. In the initial stages of industrialization in both Taiwan and South Korea, however, industrialization did not occur at the expense of agriculture. On the contrary, massive resources were pumped into agriculture, not least via US development assistance.

When Southeast Asian countries entered the path to industrialization it was decidedly substitutive and characterized by different combinations of export promotion policies by attracting FDI and industrial policies. Singapore developed a particular form of state intervention with the state monitoring capital formation via policies for attracting FDI, a model which is quite contrary to the Northeastern countries in which FDI initially played a marginal role (Huff 1999: 229). Malaysia launched an industrial master plan in 1985 that was thought to replicate the Korean model for industrial upgrading. This can of course be seen as a type of substitutive development but before that, comprehensive rural development programmes (e.g. the, at the time, much criticized FELDA settlement schemes) had been implemented. At the same time as the master plan the large-scale influx of FDI had begun and in the coming decades reliance on FDI and export markets was to become more important than industrial policy. Malaysia has indeed been successful, in fact more so than expected, in its industrial upgrading, but its main achievement is the eradication of rural poverty. Poverty incidence in Malaysia fell from 52.4 per cent in 1970 to 5.5 per cent in 2000 (Abhayaratne 2003). The reduction in poverty was accompanied by rising living standards with a relatively equal distribution of income. Thus, Malaysia may well have been more successful in pursuing its industrial pathway than other countries, but a reduction in poverty of such magnitude can hardly be ascribed primarily either to more openness to FDI or to superior industrial policy. It is more plausible that productivity growth in agriculture plays a bigger role. This would hold also for Thailand as compared to Indonesia and the Philippines. In Southern Vietnam where manufacturing industry is booming, agricultural productivity is several times higher than in the North where land plots are small, productivity low, incomes meagre and the industrial structure clearly more substitutive than in the South (Lopez Jerez 2014).

In Gerschenkron's thinking the most substitutive forms of industrialization with extensive state involvement would be necessary due to institutional obstacles in the agricultural economy. A familiar problem with that is that the state can become the problem rather that being the solution. A strong, insulated state would, consciously or not, risk to implement extractive policies that obstruct and retard development rather than promoting it. A less insulated state would instead risk becoming captured by the forces it aims at fostering. Russia became a communist commando economy and Germany, as did Japan, developed into fascism with the state in symbiosis with big business interest. Was this not the case in Eastern Asia after World War II? Here the relatively equal distribution of land and incomes may be a factor impacting on institutional quality. Japan, South Korea, and Taiwan all launched encompassing land reforms after World War II (Kuznets 1988). Wade and Amsden both cite Taiwan's land reform as very important in the initial stages of industrialization (Wade 1990:241; Amsden 1979). Wade argues that the land reform in Taiwan was important for limiting wealth concentration in addition to diffusing opportunities for improvements in agricultural productivity (Wade 1988). So it can be argued that while Southeast Asian countries in varying degree inherited 'extractive colonial institutions' (Acemoglu, Johnson and Robinson 2002) that preserved income inequality, Japan, South Korea and Taiwan were able to ensure that a broad cross-section of society had effective property rights. Wade and Amsden see this initial income equality as fundamental constituencies of the developmental state by prohibiting elite capture of the state. In retrospect we know that rent capture by business elites was quite considerable, at least after the political authoritarian regimes had given way to democratic governance. Perhaps this would indicate that in Taiwan and South Korea authoritarian political rule was more important for effective state performance than formal rules and a competent bureaucracy. It is more than probable that a sudden shift to democratic rule in China would risk giving leeway to powerful business interests, or oligarchs as we call them nowadays.

We have already argued that income and asset equality was crucial for the possibility of avoiding substitutive forms of industrialization. Those were the Northeast Asian countries in which developmental states are assumed to have been most prominent. It may very well be that Japan, South Korea, and Taiwan were characterized by both efficient states and less substitutive forms of development. That has nothing to do with the Gerschenkronian link between retarding agricultural institutions and the necessity of state intervention. It does not seem as if promotion of industry took the form of exploiting or bypassing agriculture. The process of industrialization was thus less substitutive in the most successful economies. This lends no support to an idea that strong state intervention can be a means to overcome and substitute for high degrees of underdevelopment. Instead, combatting the roots of backwardness was a key to successful industrialization. Nor does it, however, lend support to a conclusion that successful and non-substitutive development can occur without active state involvement and institutional change, in particular in the agricultural sector.

5.7 The Advantage of Backwardness—Catching up or Another Form of Substitution?

Does a Gerschenkronian approach to industrialization actually lend support to an openness paradigm? One fundamental assumption in Gerschenkron's framework is that backwardness involves a potential advantage in that it might be possible for a less developed country to learn from the experience of predecessors. This so-called Veblen-Gerschenkron hypothesis holds that technologically disadvantaged countries or regions may enjoy faster product-ivity growth relative to advanced countries or regions by relying on borrowed or imported technology (Findlay 1978). This is measured as the positive effect of the original productivity gap on subsequent productivity growth in the more backward economy.

This idea is often mostly referred to in relation to spillover effects from FDI. Reliance on openness to foreign trade and FDI would then be a way to bring about institutional adjustments. This conforms nicely with an idea of openness as the driver of East Asian industrialization. The idea of catching up as a story of technological transfer in the regional context of East and South-east Asia was coined by Akamatsu in terms of the theory of the 'flying geese' pattern (Akamatsu 1961, 1962). Modern versions of the model (inspired by Vernon 1966), which identify differences in factor proportions as structuring comparative advantages, regard Asian industrialization as a neatly organized transfer of industrial activities throughout the region according to a techno-logical hierarchy headed by Japan (Kimura 2006). Thereby a high degree of imitation of leaders is assumed and that such imitation is feasible largely without a process of initial learning, i.e. without state intervention.

Ozawa (2009) calls this a mechanism of recycling comparative advantage. The developmental task of the state is taken over by the market, and state actions that defy the market should be minimized. But there are others who argue that state initiatives should defy its present comparative advantage in order to upgrade its industry (see, for instance, the debate in Lin and Chang 2009). An empirical problem is that FDI played a marginal role among the East Asian pioneers, which were more characterized by heavy emphasis on skill-building, R&D, and pervasive use of industrial policy. The big movement of intra-regional FDI did not take off until after 1985 when Japanese and Taiwanese investments were becoming important in Indonesia, Thailand, Malaysia, and, after 1990 also in China. Taiwan and Singapore relied more on FDI but with use of selective industrial policy to direct investments into high value activities.

In a revision of Gerschenkron, Alice Amsden has proposed that the later a country industrializes the farther away it will be from the technological frontier. Thereby, reliance on FDI will increase and 'the greater the probability that its major manufacturing firms will be foreign-owned' (Amsden 2001:286). A passive reliance on FDI would then represent a kind of substitution since it is based on the premise that skills can be 'bought'. Backwardness involves a potential catching up advantage through imported technology, but real catching up can hardly be achieved by technological spillovers alone. Late developers that are FDI dependent and relying greatly on welcoming policies, stable macro environment, low wages, and access to a semi-skilled labour force, tend to have problems developing competencies necessary in order for the economy to climb the technology ladder. Abramovitz (1986:390) and Ohkawa and Rosovsky (1973) have argued that countries that are technologically backward have a potentiality for generating rapid growth only if their social capabilities are sufficiently developed to permit successful exploitation of already employed technologies. The pace at which the potential for catch-up can be realized will depend on factors limiting the diffusion of knowledge, the rate of structural change, the accumulation of capital and the expansion of demand (Abramovitz, 1986:390). Skills cannot be bought, they have to be created.

Social capabilities might include educational levels, quality of institutions, state capacity and social unity. In that sense, the flying geese model might be contradictory since it is likely to work effectively only in combination with such institutional qualities. As argued by Kasahara (2013) replicating the flying geese paradigm may turn out to be self-contradictory. In the East Asian context this complies well with the revisionist story (Amsden 1989, 2001; Wade 1990; Rodrik 1994) that emphasizes the importance of learning as against standard policy recommendations such as dismantling of quantitative restrictions on imports, reduction of import tariffs and their dispersion, making the currency convertible for current account transactions, elimination of bureaucratic red tape and establishment of the rule of law.

Rodrik (1994) has suggested that the investment boom of the 1960s is the core explanation behind the East Asian miracle. This was launched by a successful co-ordination of investment decisions by the state and facilitated through a combination of a well-educated population and the relative equality of income. So, the social capability to emulate productivity differences is conditional on a complex of institutional arrangements and factors. In another study Rodrik (2008) has argued that appropriate institutions for developing countries are 'second-best' institutions—those that take into account context-specific market and government failures that cannot be removed in the short run. Rodrik uses examples from four areas as illustrations: contract enforcement, entrepreneurship, trade openness, and macro-economic stability.

It is possible to find examples of relatively high levels of social capability in countries that score low in terms of per capita income levels if institutions are 'right' and human skills well developed. For instance, Sandberg has argued for Sweden, one of Europe's poorest countries by 1850, that 'Sweden had a stock of human capital wildly disproportionate to its very low income level' (Sandberg 1979:225). A comparatively high literacy rate, low infant mortality, and efficient institutional arrangements constituted a pool of social capabilities that could be transformed into productive activity as industrialization gained momentum. In East Asia it appears sensible to attribute similar characteristics to Japan just before the Meiji Restoration. That Sweden had such social capabilities was a factor that was to make Swedish industrialization less substitutive in a Gerschenkronian sense. A relevant question is whether the same applied to Japan in the decades before World War II when the industrial pattern was becoming increasingly substitutive. That the social capabilities revealed in East Asia have roots back in the pre-industrial economy is quite evident in the case of Japan. The human skills developed in the traditional economy apparently gave Japan a competitive advantage vis-à-vis the rest of the non-Western world once the urge to industrialize began after 1850. But human capabilities can be fraught by institutional obstacles as demonstrated by the case of China both before and under communist rule. That such obstacles remained also in pre-war Japan is evidenced by its gradual development of a substitutive form of industrial economy. So, in case there is continuity in industrial development, as argued by the proponents of labour-intensive industrialization, it will have to be sought in the large supply of human skills that was released after 1950 rather than in historically rooted institutional and organizational arrangements.

5.8 Implications

In an article published three decades ago Patrick O'Brien raised the provocative question 'Do we have a typology for the study of European industrialization in the nineteenth century?' (O'Brien 1986). O'Brien undertook a major critique of Gerschenkron's typology and questioned its value for making generalizations about Europe's great industrial transformation. In the years to come he was largely proven right. In spite of a now voluminous literature in European economic history few scholars have ventured to take on the task to generalize and create a typology that could help enhance our knowledge about the complexities involved in the European industrialization process. Instead, what we get is one book after another about 'the Western model', which almost always deals specifically, and sometimes exclusively, with the rise of Britain with occasional reference to European cases. A European pattern of industrialization is yet to be agreed upon. So, in contrast to Gerschenkron's agenda, we now appear to be back to the idea of a single, and unique, Western model. It should therefore come as no surprise that attempts to understand and explain the great transformation of our time, the rise of Eastern Asia, have been framed in contrast to this largely imaginary Western model. It should also come as no surprise that the idea of one single East Asian model has proven to have little validity for explaining the Asian economic transformation.[12]

So, although granted that Gerschenkron's typology has failed to materialize for Europe, can we pretend to have a typology of industrialization in Eastern Asia? It seems clear that a strict application of Gerschenkron's basic sequence of types (market-banks-state) has little bearing in Asia. Bank funding has been distinctive all over Asia, but its presence is hardly related to a certain degree of backwardness. Nor is the existence of strong state involvement. Where Gerschenkron was to be proven particularly wrong was in his assumption that late industrialization would occur without productivity improvements in agriculture. In fact, if it is possible to come close to anything resembling a typology of industrialization for Eastern Asia the organizing principle of such a typology should be the pace and type of agricultural modernization. The more encompassing the rate of technological and institutional progress in agriculture the more sustainable the industrial growth process. Conversely, feeble progress and large initial inequality in agriculture encourage substitutive forms of industrialization.

Three forms of substitution have been singled out: export-led growth, state-driven growth, and FDI-led growth, of which only the second has resemblance to Gerschenkron's types. Eastern Asian industrialization had its early beginning in the second half of the nineteenth century with Japan as a successful case and China as a failure.[13] Still, it is apparent that industrialization involving large-scale structural transformation is a relatively modern phenomenon, even if we include Japan. Although Japan began its industrialization around 1880, the process was becoming increasingly substitutive and largely unbalanced before 1950. A majority of the workforce had remained tied to agriculture, and a large proportion of the workers in the manufacturing sector had not shifted completely out of agriculture but remained part-time workers. Substitution was evident in the duality between an expanding manufacturing export sector on the one hand and the slow growth of the home market on the other. It was not until the 1950s that the real, and indeed very dramatic, structural transformation began, when the agricultural workforce was shifted

---

[12] Acemoglu and Robinson in their celebrated book *Why Nations Fail* (2012) tell story after story about why developing countries fail to live up to Western development requirements, but they have conspicuously little to say about the industrialization 'miracle' of Eastern Asia.

[13] The Shanghai region experienced fast and sustained economic growth from the 1860s up until World War II. However, Shanghai's growth was exclusively derived from its attachment to the global economy and had few lasting bonds to the Chinese economy at large.

over permanently to industry on a large-scale and a sustained growth of the domestic market achieved.

Perhaps South Korea is the case where a stricter application of Gerschenkron's types would have a chance to fit. Korea was initially poorer and with stronger feudal institutions than both Japan and Taiwan and made extensive use of a state-controlled banking sector for accumulation and allocation of investment capital. Taiwan was less substitutive due to the extremely fast transformation of an initially highly egalitarian agriculture which induced the growth of small-scale manufacturing industries. In China industrialization was unquestionably substitutive under the communist command economy. China's metamorphosis began with the transformation of agriculture in the 1980s, which was instrumental for the rise of the TVEs that initially drove the new type of industrial economy. Since the mid-1990s China has become extremely export-dependent given its size. Agriculture in the interior and western parts holding some 200 million people has largely been left behind. If there is an aggregate consumption deficit in China's modern economy it can be seen as a consequence of a high degree of substitution in the growth model. Southeast Asia is in varying degrees more substitutive than East Asia, mainly because of the region's high dependence on FDI and access to foreign demand. This is in accordance with Alice Amsden's proposal that the later a country industrializes the greater the probability that its major manufacturing firms will be foreign-owned (Amsden 2001:286). So, in some sense there is a 'big typology' with East Asia as a whole being less substitutive than Southeast Asia. But within the regions there are 'little typologies'; in East Asia South Korea and China stand out as more unbalanced and substitutive than Japan and Taiwan and in Southeast Asia the countries with stronger agricultural growth, e.g. Malaysia and Thailand, are less unbalanced than Indonesia and the Philippines. For the same reason industrialization in Southern Vietnam is less substitutive than in Northern Vietnam.

Gerschenkron's typology focused on change as opposed to continuity. Also in the present study change has been the focal point and no attempt has been made to trace the origins of an Asian miracle back to a remote past in search of preconditions for industrial growth. A few words should be said about creation of preconditions. An important issue is whether in the more substitutive types and phases of industrialization, preconditions for market led-growth may not only have been substituted for but also created. One question yet to be studied is whether the substitutive forms of industrialization in Japan before World War II contained some seeds for later growth. It can be argued that the industrial drive in the 1930s, which spurred capital intensification and technological upgrading, contributed to building capacities that after the war could be fully released under different forms. Many companies that were later to become successful exporters saw their beginnings under the state-driven substitutive regime. Chalmers Johnson also traces the origins of his Developmental State back to institutional arrangements that were set up under this regime. A parallel could perhaps be drawn with the long-term effects of rural collect-ives in China. That the rural economy responded to market mechanisms after the 1978 reform was due to the Household Responsibility System but success was also contingent on previous investments in infrastructure, technology and education; investments that had been done under completely different circumstances and with utterly different intentions.

Another and perhaps even more important factor is the endowment of human skills. In this study not much tribute has been paid to the labour-intensive industrialization story which emphasizes continuity and balance between sectors in contrast to discontinuity and sectoral shifts of labour. However, one fundamental aspect deserves to be highlighted; the role of human skills, the high quality of the labour force which is so typical for Japan. There is little doubt that its origins ought to be sought for in the traditional labour intensive economy. Whether the high level of skills should be primarily attributed to formal education or to a special type of work organization in extremely labour-intensive agriculture remains a question for further research.

Eastern Asia does not stand out as distinctively different from the West by representing an alternative, and largely more sustainable, model of industri-alization. Applying Gerschenkron's methodology reveals that a typology for industrialization in Eastern Asia would be decidedly different from a European one. The combination of types is different and the ways of substitution divergent from the European pattern. Within the region, the Northeast Asian pioneering industrializers employed less substitutive modes of industri-alization. After World War II the roots of backwardness, which Gerschenkron identifies in retarding institutions and low productivity in agriculture, were eradicated from the start while in the less developed countries substitution became more prevalent.

The creation of conditions of relative equal income distribution played a decisive role in the successful initiation of a broad-based agricultural transformation—the initial engine of growth. Since the promotion of industry did not occur in combination with the exploitation of agriculture, the process of industrialization was not substitutive in the most successful economies. In contrast to Gerschenkron this lends no support to an idea that state-driven industrialization can be a means to overcome and substitute for high levels of underdevelopment. Nor does it support a conclusion that successful and non-substitutive development can occur without institutional change, which implicitly involves state agency. It was more substitutive in economies relying on FDI and export markets. This follows a Gerschenkronian perspective in that the organizing principle, the degree of backwardness in agriculture, will determine the extent of substitution employed. This also complies with Gerschenkron by helping to identify 'a unified, and yet graduated pattern' of industrialization in Eastern Asia.

References

Abhayaratne, A., 2003. *Poverty reduction strategies in Malaysia 1970–2000: Some lessons.* University of Peradeniya, Sri Lanka.

Abramovitz, M., 1986. 'Catching up, forging ahead, and falling behind'. *The Journal of Economic History*, vol. 46 number 02:385–406.

Acemoglu, D., S. Johnson, and J. Robinson, 2002. 'Reversal of Fortune: Geography and Institutions in the Making of the Modern World Income Distribution'. *The Quarterly Journal of Economics,* vol. 117 number 4:1231–94.

Acemoglu, D., and J. Robinson 2012. *Why Nations Fail. The Origins of Power, Prosperity, and Poverty*. New York: Crown.

Adelman, I., 1984. 'Beyond export-led growth'. *World Development,* vol. 12 number 9:937–49.

Akamatsu, K., 1961. 'A Theory of Unbalanced Growth in the World Economy'. *Welt-wirtschaftliches Archiv*, vol. 82 number 2:196–217.

Akamatsu, K., 1962. 'A Historical Pattern of Economic Growth in Developing Coun-tries'. *Journal of Developing Economies*, vol. 1 number 1:3–25.

Amsden, A.H., 1979. 'Taiwan's Economic History: A Case of Etatisme and a Challenge to Dependency Theory'. *Modern China*, vol. 5 number 3:341–79.

Amsden, A.H., 1989. *Asia's Next Giant*. Oxford: Oxford University Press.

Amsden, A.H., 2001. *The Rise of the Rest: Challenges to the West from Late-Industrializing Economies*. New York: Oxford University Press.

Arrighi, G., 2007. *Adam Smith in Beijing: Lineages of the Twenty-first Century*. London and New York: Verso.

Asian Development Bank, 1997. *Emerging Asia: Changes and Challenges*. Manila: Asian Development Bank.

Balassa, B., 1988. 'The Lessons of East Asian Development: An Overview'. *Economic Development and Cultural Change*, Vol. 36, No. 3, Supplement: Why Does Over-crowded, Resource-Poor East Asia Succeed: Lessons for the LDCs? (April 1988), pp. 273–290.

Booth, A., 2002. 'Rethinking the Role of Agriculture in the "East Asian" Model: Why Is Southeast Asia Different from Northeast Asia?' *ASEAN Economic Bulletin* vol. 19 number 1: 40–51.

Chang, Ha-Joon, 2002. *Kicking Away the Ladder. Development Strategy in Historical per-spective*. London, New York, Dehli: Anthem Press.

Eckstein, A., 1958. 'Individualism and the Role of the State in Economic Growth'. *Economic Development and Cultural Change,* vol. 6 issue 2:81–7.

Eckstein, A., 1977. *China's Economic Revolution*. Cambridge: Cambridge University Press.

Evans, P., 1995. *Embedded Autonomy: States and Industrial Transformation*. Princeton: Princeton University Press.

Findlay, R., 1978. 'Relative Backwardness, Direct Foreign Investment, and the Transfer of Technology: A Simple Dynamic Model'. *Quarterly Journal of Economics*, 92:1–16.

Francks, P., 2000. 'Japan and the East Asian Model of Agriculture's Role in Industrialisation'. *Japan Forum* vol. 12 number 1:43–54.

Francks, P., 2005. 'Multiple Choices: Rural Household Diversification and Japan's Path to Industrialization'. *Journal of Agrarian Change* vol. 5 number 4:451–75.

George Mulgan, A., 2005. 'Japan's Interventionist State: Bringing Agriculture Back In'. *Japanese Journal of Political Science* vol. 6 number 1:29–61.

Gerschenkron, A., 1946. *Bread and Democracy in Germany*. Ithaca, NY: Cornell University Press.

Gerschenkron, A., 1962. *Economic Backwardness in Historical Perspective. A book of essays.* New York: Fredrick A.Praeger.

Hubbard, G.E., 1937. 'Review of *Japan's Feet of Clay* by Freda Utley'. *International Affairs (Royal Institute of International Affairs 1931–1939)* vol. 16 number 1:165–7.

Hubbard, G. E., 1938. *Eastern Industrialization and its Effect on the West*. Oxford: Oxford University Press.

Huff, W.G., 1999. 'Turning the Corner in Singapore's Developmental State?'. *Asian Survey* vol. 39 number 2:214–42.

Ishikawa, S., 1978. *Labour Absorption in Asian Agriculture—An Issue Paper*. ILO, ARTEP Publication.

Johnson, C., 1982. *MITI and the Japanese Miracle: the Growth of Japanese Industrial Policy, 1925–1975*. Stanford: Stanford University Press.

Jomo K.S., 1997. *Southeast Asia's Misunderstood Miracle: Industrial Policy and Economic Development in Thailand, Malaysia and Indonesia*. Singapore: Cambridge University Press.

Ka, Chih-Ming and M. Selden, 1986. 'Original Accumulation, Equity and Late Industrialization: The Cases of Socialist China and Capitalist Taiwan'. *World Development* vol. 14 number 10/11:1293–310.

Kasahara, S., 2013. *The Flying Geese Paradigm: A critical study of its application to East Asia*, UNCTAD Discussion Paper 213. United Nations Conference on Trade and Development (UNCTAD), Geneva.

Kimura, F., 2006. 'International Production and Distribution Networks in East Asia: Eighteen facts, mechanics, and policy implications'. *Asian Economic Policy Review* vol. 1 number 1:326–44.

Kohli, A., 2004. *State-Directed Development: Political Power and Industrialization in the Global Periphery*. Cambridge: Cambridge University Press.

Kreuger, A.O., 1984. 'Comparative Advantage and Development Policy 20 Years Later'. In *Economic Structure and Performance*, edited by M. Syrquin, L. Taylor, and L.E. Westphal. London: Academic Press.

Kreuger, A.O., 1991. 'Industrial Development and Liberalisation'. In *Liberalisation in the Process of Economic Development*, edited by L. B. Krause and K. Kim. Berkeley: University of California Press.

Kuznets, P.W., 1988. 'An East Asian Model of Economic Development: Japan, Taiwan, and South Korea'. *Economic Development and Cultural Change* vol. 36 number 3:11–43.

League of Nations, 1940. Statistical Yearbook of the League of Nations. Geneva: Série de Publications e la Société des Nations.

Lewis, W.A., 1954. 'Economic development with unlimited supplies of labour'. *Manchester School* vol. 22 number 2:139–91.

Lin, J. and Chang, H-J., 2009. 'DPR Debate: Should industrial policy in developing countries conform to comparative advantage or defy it? A debate between Justin Lin and Ha-Joon Chang'. *Development Policy Review* vol. 27 number 5:483–502.

López Jerez, M., 2014. *Deltas Apart. Factor Endowments, Colonial Extraction and Pathways of Agricultural Development in Vietnam.* Lund studies in economic history (69).

Milanovic, B., 2013. 'Global Income Inequality in Numbers: in History and Now'. *Global Policy*, vol. 4 number 2:198–208.

Moore, Barrington Jr., 1966. *Social Origins of Dictatorship and Democracy: Lord and Peasant in the Making of the Modern World.* Boston: Beacon Press.

Nafziger, S.E., 2006. *Communal Institutions, Resource Allocation, and Russian Economic Development: 1861–1905.* PhD. Dissertation, Yale University.

Nasu, S., 1941. *Aspects of Japanese Agriculture—A Preliminary Survey.* Institute of Pacific Relations. New York.

North, D.C., 1961. *The Economic Growth of the United States, 1790–1860.* Englewood Cliffs, N. J.: Prentice-Hall.

O'Brien, P. K., 1986. 'Do We Have a Typology for the Study of European Industrialization in the Nineteenth Century?' *Journal of European Economic History*, 15 (2):291–333.

Ohkawa, K. and H. Rosovsky, 1973. *Japanese Economic Growth. Trend Acceleration in the Twentieth Century.* Stanford: Stanford University Press.

Oshima, H., 1987. *Economic Growth in Monsoon Asia. A Comparative Survey.* University of Tokyo Press.

Ozawa, T., 2009. *The Rise of Asia: The flying-geese theory of tandem growth and regional agglomeration.* Cheltenham, UK, and Northampton, MA: Edward Elgar.

Pomeranz, K., 2001. Is There an East Asian Development Path? Long-Term Comparisons, Constraints, and Continuities. *Journal of the Economic and Social History of the Orient* vol. 44 number 3:322–62.

Ranis, G. and John C.H. Fei, 1961. 'A Theory of Economic Development'. *The American Economic Review,* vol. 51 number 4:533–65.

Rodrik, D., 1994. 'King Kong Meets Godzilla: The World Bank and the East Asian Miracle', in *Miracle or Design?: Lessons from the East Asian Experience*, edited by Albert Fishlow et al.. Washington: Overseas Development Council.

Rodrik, D., 1995. 'Getting Interventions Right: How South Korea and Taiwan Grew Rich'. *Economic Policy* 20:55–107. Previously published as Rodrik, D., 1994. *Getting Interventions Right: How South Korea and Taiwan Grew Rich.* NBER Working Paper No. 4964.

Rodrik, D., 1998. *Trade Policy and Economic Performance in Sub-Saharan Africa.* EGDI Discussion Paper Series. Stockholm: Swedish Ministry of Foreign Affairs.

Rodrik, D., 2008. 'Second-Best Institutions'. *American Economic Review,* Papers and Proceedings vol. 98 number 2:100–4.

Rosovsky, H., 1966. 'Japan's Transition to Economic Growth, 1868–1885'. In *Industrialization in Two Systems: Essays in Honor of Alexander Gerschenkron*, edited by Henry Rosovsky, [91–139], New York: Wiley.

Saito, O., 2005. *Pre-Modern Economic Growth Revisited: Japan and The West*. Working Paper No. 16/05, Department of Economic History, London School of Economics.

Sandberg, L.G., 1979. 'The Case of the Impoverished Sophisticate: Human Capital and Swedish Economic Growth before World War I'. *The Journal of Economic History* vol. 39 number 1:225–41.

Sugihara, K., 2000. *The East Asian Path of Economic Development: A Long-Term Perspective. Discussion Paper 00–17*. Graduate School of Economics and Osaka School of International Public Policy, Osaka University.

Sugihara, K., 2007. 'The Second Noel Butlin Lecture: Labour-Intensive Industrialisation in Global History'. *Australian Economic History Review* vol. 47 number 2:121–54.

United Nations, 1979. *World Industry since 1960: Progress and Prospects*. Special issue of the Industrial Development Survey for the Third General Conference of UNIDO. New York: United Nations Publications.

Utley, F., 1937. *Japan's Feet of Clay*, London: Faber & Faber.

Vernon, R., 1966. 'International Investment and International Trade in the Product Cycles'. *Quarterly Journal of Economics* vol. 80 number 2:190–207.

Wade, R., 1988. 'The Role of Government in Overcoming Market Failure: Taiwan, Republic of Korea and Japan'. In *Achieving Industrialization in East Asia*, edited by H. Hughes, Cambridge: Cambridge University Press.

Wade, R., 1990. *Governing the Market: Economic Theory and the Role of Government in East Asian Industrialisation*, Princeton: Princeton University Press.

Weiss, L. and J.M. Hobson, 1995. *States and Economic Development: A Comparative Historical Analysis*. Cambridge: Polity Press.

Westphal, L.E., 1978. 'The Republic of Korea's Experience with Export-Led Industrial Development'. *World Development* vol. 6 number 3:347–82.

Woo, J. [M.Woo-Cumings], 1991. *Race to the Swift: State and Finance in Korean Industrialization*. New York: Colombia University Press.

Woo-Cumings, M. (ed.), 1999. *The Developmental State*. Ithaca: Cornell University Press.

World Bank, 1983. *World Development Report*. Oxford: Oxford University Press.

World Bank, 1993. *The East Asian Miracle: Economic Growth and Public Policy*. Oxford: Oxford University Press.

6

Southeast Asia

The Half-way Miracle?

Anne Booth

6.1 The Abramovitz Argument

In a well-known paper originally published in 1986, Abramovitz argued that all countries which are relatively backward in terms of levels of productivity had the potential for rapid advance, and indeed could catch up quickly with the leading economies if they could realize this potential. Their ability to catch up was to a large extent determined by their social capabilities, a term he borrowed from the Japanese literature (Abramovitz 1986: 222). These capabilities included the educational level of the labour force, and institutional arrangements which facilitated their openness to the adoption of new technologies, and to competition from both the home and the international economies. Using the data assembled by Maddison (1982) he examined catch-up among fifteen countries, mainly in Europe and Japan, with GDP per worker hour in the USA. He found a significant degree of convergence in the decades after 1945. The poorer countries had grown faster, and the gap between the rich and poor had narrowed.

In a later paper, Abramovitz addressed the issue of catch-up growth in a broader context. In particular he addressed the problem of what he termed the 'erratic' growth pattern of the developing countries in Asia, Africa and Latin America. He argued that, if all the developing countries are considered, 'there was no simple relation between national levels of per capita income and their growth rates' (Abramovitz 1995: 44). Many of the poorest countries grew slowly and some had negative growth in per capita terms. This result was contrary to his earlier findings, and required a more searching examination of both the economic characteristics of the laggard countries and also of their social capabilities. Abramovitz argued that many of the world's poorest countries have failed to develop the set of attitudinal and institutional characteristics which are needed for accelerated economic growth. Governments have neglected education and infrastructure, and they have often failed to build institutions which facilitate the peaceful resolution of conflict, and the evolution of a market economy. As a result, many countries have failed to produce business people and administrators who can manage large-scale business organizations. Nor have they developed capital markets which can provide efficient financial intermediation.

Abramovitz (1995: 45) stressed that social capabilities as he defines them develop 'in an interactive and cumulative process in which social capability supports economic development and development supports the further advance of social capability'. In another paper, Abramovitz and David (1996: 33) argued that over time, 'there is a two-way interaction between the evolution of a nation's social capabilities and the articulation of societal conditions required for the mastery of production technologies' which are close to the best practice frontier. On the one hand, a country which has inadequate capabilities, compared to the economic leader, and fails to develop them is unlikely to embark on a process of sustained growth, and may succumb to ethnic or religious conflict, which leads to further economic decline. On the other hand, those countries which have managed to achieve some economic growth and structural change are more likely to develop the institutions and social capabilities which facilitate further growth. Abramovitz and David (1996: 57) pointed out that many features of the social structure and outlook that delayed catch-up in parts of Europe and Japan in the nineteenth century weakened in the early part of the twentieth, and in the post-1945 era, with its emphasis on both political and economic reconstruction, these features 'crumbled altogether'.

But nothing can be taken for granted. Although economic growth is now pursued as a major policy goal by most countries in the world, it is clear that many countries have had at best partial success in achieving sustained growth in per capita terms over a long enough period to eliminate the gap between them and the world leaders. Japan, once the economy which most other Asian countries regarded as the model of successful catch-up, has had very little growth in per capita GDP since 1990. The current discussion about the middle income trap reflects a worry that countries in Asia and elsewhere which have achieved some measure of economic growth might slow down, or even cease to grow at all, long before they have caught up with the economic leaders. In this paper, I explore some of the issues relating to catch-up in the context of Southeast Asia.

6.2 Thinking about Growth and Development in Southeast Asia

In the extensive literature on growth and development across the world since the 1950s, the countries of Southeast Asia often play a smaller part than their size and importance in the global economy would appear to justify. They are frequently included in broad categories, along with the economies of Northeast Asia, or South Asia, although the ten economies which are members of the Association of Southeast Asian Nations (ASEAN) have had very different economic, political and demographic histories compared with the two Asian giants, India and China, or with Japan and the two former colonies of Japan, Taiwan and the Republic of Korea. They also vary widely among themselves. Only two of the ten, Singapore and Brunei, are included in the 'very high human development' category in the UNDP Human Development Index rankings. The other eight are spread across the spectrum of development from high to low (Table 6.1).

While most of the ten have experienced some improvement in the indicators which make up the Human Development Index (GDP per capita, literacy, educational enrollments and life expectancy) there are very considerable variations in each of these indicators between the ten countries. They also vary in their positions in other well-known rankings including those published by the World Economic Forum, Transparency International and the World Bank (Table 6.1). If we just focus on GDP per capita, for which we have comparable data over at least four decades, two facts emerge clearly. First, there was already wide variation in 1960, by which time all had achieved a large measure of self-government and most full political independence (Table 6.2).

Second, growth rates have varied considerably over the fifty years from 1960 to 2010.

Of the five original founding member states of ASEAN, Singapore had the highest per capita GDP in 1960 and has sustained high rates of growth until 2010 (Table 6.3). Malaysia and the Philippines had roughly the same per capita GDP in 1960, but very different rates of growth over the next fifty years, so that by 2010 Malaysia's GDP was almost four times that of the Philippines, although still much lower than Singapore's. Thailand, which had a lower per capita GDP than either Malaysia or the Philippines in 1960 experienced rapid growth until 1996, in which year it had overtaken the Philippines by a considerable margin, but not caught up with Malaysia. Indonesia which had the lowest per capita GDP of the five in 1960, also experienced quite rapid growth up to 1996, by which year it had overtaken the Philippines but was still below the other four.

Table 6.1 Rankings of Southeast Asian Countries According to Five League Tables, c.2014.

Country	HDI	T.I.	WB	WEF (1)	WEF(2)
Singapore	9	7	1	2	59
Brunei	30	n.a	101	n.a	98
Malaysia	62	50	18	20	107
Thailand	89	85	26	31	61
Indonesia	108	107	114	34	97
Philippines	117	85	95	52	9
Vietnam	121	119	78	68	76
Laos	139	145	148	93	60
Cambodia	136	156	135	95	108
Myanmar	150	156	177	134	n.a
China	91	100	90	28	87
India	135	85	142	71	114
Number of Countries ranked	187	174	189	144	142

Notes: HDI is the Human Development Index, prepared by the UNDP (Data refer to 2013). T.I. is the Corruption Perceptions Index, prepared by Transparency International; WB refers to the Ease of Doing Business Index prepared by the World Bank; WEF (1) refers to the Global Competitiveness Index prepared by the World Economic Forum and published in Schwab (2014); WEF (2) refers to the Global Gender Gap Index prepared by the World Economic Forum. Unless otherwise stated, all figures refer to 2014.

Sources: WEF (1) from Schwab (2014), Table 4; other indexes can be obtained from the websites of the organizations which prepare them.

Table 6.2 Per Capita GDP (2005 prices): Southeast Asia, India, and China, 1960–2010 (US$'000).

Country	1960	1970	1996	2010
Singapore	4.5	7.14	31.6	54.8
Brunei	n.a	51.8	54.4	44.3
Malaysia	1.5	2.1	8.7	11.9
Thailand	1.0	1.6	6.3	8.1
Indonesia	0.7	0.8	3.1	4.0
Philippines	1.5	1.8	2.5	3.2
Vietnam	n.a	0.5	1.3	2.8
Laos	n.a	0.5	1.2	2.5
Cambodia	n.a	1.1	0.8	1.9
(Myanmar	0.6	0.6	1.1	n.a)*
China (v.1)	0.3	0.4	2.1	7.2
India	0.7	0.9	1.6	3.5

* Data for Myanmar are not given in the source document; the figures for 1960, 1970 and 1996 are taken from Maddison (2003: 184–5).

Source: Heston, Summers and Aten (2012).

Over the 1980s and 1990s, membership of the ASEAN club expanded from five to ten members with the accession of Brunei, Vietnam, Laos, Cambodia and Myanmar (formerly Burma). Brunei, a small sultanate which exports oil and gas, had a per capita GDP which was much higher than the other nine in 1970, but has experienced some decline since 1996, and in 2010 had fallen behind Singapore (Table 6.2). Vietnam, Laos and Cambodia, all part of the

Table 6.3 Annual Average Growth Rates of Per Capita GDP (2005 dollars): 1960–96 and 1996–2010 (%).

Country	1960–96	1996–2010
Singapore	5.6	4.0
Brunei	0.2	−1.5
Malaysia	5.0	2.3
Thailand	5.3	1.8
Indonesia	4.5	1.7
Philippines	1.4	1.9
Vietnam	3.4	5.9
Laos	3.0	5.7
Cambodia	−0.9	6.0
Myanmar	2.0	n.a
China	5.2	9.1
India	2.3	5.7

Sources: As for Table 6.2.

colony known as French Indochina, had low growth until the 1990s, but much faster growth in the years from 1996 to 2010 (Table 6.3). But the growth was from a low base and by 2010 all three countries still had a lower per capita GDP than the original five, although Vietnam had almost caught up with the Philippines. The Myanmar economy almost certainly had a lower per capita GDP than the other nine in 2010, with the possible exception of Cambodia, but its statistics are considered unreliable, and the country is not included in the PWT data base.

When viewed in the light of the Abramovitz hypothesis, the growth experience of the ten Southeast Asian economies since 1960 raises a number of questions. First, two countries which already had relatively high GDP in 1960, Singapore and Malaysia, have both forged ahead over the fifty years until 2010, albeit with some slowdown after 1996. Both Singapore and Malaysia inherited economies from the colonial era which were relatively advanced by Asian standards, and both have managed to sustain growth in spite of several shocks, including the financial crisis which hit the region in 1997/98. How were they able to build on their relatively favourable colonial legacy and sustain growth over five decades?

A second question concerns Thailand and Indonesia, two countries which were considerably poorer than either Singapore or Malaysia in 1960, but which both managed to grow rapidly between 1960 and 1996. The acceleration in Thailand's growth rate after 1960 was surprising as the country had not managed to achieve much growth in per capita terms between 1870 and 1940 (Manarungsan 1989). This was in spite of being the only Southeast Asian state which had escaped direct colonial control in the nineteenth century. What determined the sudden growth acceleration after 1960, and the slowdown after 1996? Indonesia, which had been a Dutch colony until 1942, did experience some growth in per capita terms especially in the years from 1900 to 1930. But for over three decades from 1930 to 1965, per capita GDP hardly grew at all. Then in the three decades from 1967 to 1997, growth accelerated, and in spite of the slowdown after 1997, by 2010 per capita GDP was well above the level achieved in 1990. What caused this reversal of fortune?

The third question concerns the Philippines, a country which achieved some economic growth in the four decades of American control, and where there was considerable progress in educational development and in public health. The country was granted full independence in 1946, and to many observers appeared to have inherited a favourable institutional legacy from the American colonial era, including a political system modeled on the American one. In the 1950s, it seemed set to achieve rapid economic and social development. But by 2010, the Philippines was the only Asian colony not to have achieved some measure of catch-up with the former colonizing power; per capita GDP was around thirteen per cent of American GDP in 1960 and had fallen to ten per cent in 2010 (Table 6.4). Per capita GDP in 2010 was also below that in Indonesia and Thailand. What went wrong?

The Philippine performance can be contrasted with that of the three countries which were part of French Indochina until the creation of four states in the mid-1950s. The poor growth performance of these countries, which

Table 6.4 Per Capita GDP (2005 dollars) as Percentage of the Former Colonial Power, Southeast Asia, China, and India.

Country	1960	1970	1996	2010
As percentage of the UK				
Singapore	26.7	41.2	106.2	122.1
Malaysia	17.7	19.3	42.2	42.5
India	8.7	8.1	9.1	14.2
As percentage of the USA*				
Thailand	9.5	11.3	27.0	30.7
China	5.8	5.2	11.4	26.3
Philippines	13.0	11.7	9.0	9.9
As percentage of the Netherlands				
Indonesia	12.2	10.3	18.6	19.4
As percentage of France				
Vietnam	10.8	6.4	8.1	17.5
Laos	9.2	6.6	5.9	n.a
Cambodia	9.1	5.7	5.7	13.3
As percentage of Japan				
Taiwan	33.9	26.1	69.1	106.2
Republic of Korea	30.8	22.3	63.2	98.9

* China and Thailand were not colonies of the USA, but in recent decades both countries tend to benchmark their progress against the USA.

Source: The Maddison Project data, downloaded from <http://www.ggdc/maddison/maddison-project/home.htm>, 2013 version.

became three after the unification of Vietnam in 1975, can be explained in terms of outside military interventions which led to considerable devastation and loss of life. After 1975, rigid central planning was imposed in Vietnam, while in Cambodia the political faction which took control in 1975 pushed the entire population into agricultural communes. Many educated Cambodians were killed or fled the country. Between 1968 and 1991, there was only very slow growth in per capita GDP. The important question in these three countries concerns the dramatic increase in growth rates which occurred from the 1990s onwards.

Last there is the case of Myanmar, a country which appears to have been dogged by slow growth ever since it achieved independence in 1948. The economic literature is sparse compared with much of the rest of the region, but recent surveys have stressed the devastation of the war years from 1942 to 1945, the slow recovery and the determination of its military rulers to turn away from engagement with the regional and global economies (Brown 2013). A change of policy took place in 2011, but it is far from clear to what extent Myanmar can close the very wide gap which now exists with its neighbours, particularly China and Thailand.

The rest of this chapter will try to answer these questions, drawing on the Abramovitz arguments about catch up. But before looking at how different countries in the region have responded to the challenges of the post-1960 era, it is necessary to say something about the legacies from earlier periods in their economic histories. The recent revival of interest in the 'deep causes' of economic backwardness, while it can be criticized on several grounds, at least has pushed economists and historians working in Asia, Africa and Latin America into looking more carefully at the pre-colonial characteristics of these countries, as well as at the impact of colonialism. To the extent that there are useful lessons to be learnt from history, it is now acknowledged that these lessons come not just from the economic history of the high income countries in Asia, Europe and North America, but also from the economic, social and demographic pasts of those countries now classified as middle or low income.

6.3 Pre-colonial Southeast Asia and the Colonial Impact

In recent years the study of pre-colonial Southeast Asia has made considerable progress with scholars such as Reid and Liebermann producing important works of synthesis. Reid (1993: 70) argued that Southeast Asia reached a commercial peak in the six decades from 1570 to 1630, 'with some established cities growing and new ones appearing'. He estimated that at least five per cent of the total population would have lived in cities of more than 30,000 people, which was a larger proportion than in Northern Europe at the time, although

Table 6.5 Population of Southeast Asia and China: 1820–2030 (millions).

Country	1820	1930	2014	2030*
China	381	489	1364	1400
Southeast Asia	43	131	621	733
As % of China	11	27	46	52

* Projections made by the Population Reference Bureau.

Sources: 1820 and 1930: Boomgaard (2014: 133); Maddison (2003: 160–163). 2014 and 2030: Population Reference Bureau (2014).

lower than Mughal India or China. He also argues that urbanization was 'spectacularly high' for the most commercialized areas along the Straits of Malacca. These high rates of urbanization were made possible by the large marketed surplus of rice, which in most cases could be easily transported to urban markets on waterways. The cities paid for their food using profits from trade, which flourished in much of the region.

In 1600, the population of Southeast Asia was probably around 25 million and had increased to around 35 million by 1800 (Boomgaard 2014: 133). This was a low rate of growth compared with most of Europe and China over these two centuries. In 1820, it is likely that the population of the region was only about eleven per cent of China's (Table 6.5).

Boomgaard suggested that high mortality was a major cause of the slow growth. This was the result of disease, constant low-level warfare and famine, which in turn was due to recurring droughts. Crude birth rates were also rather low. In most parts of the region population densities were low and much land was still under forest. All these factors probably held back economic growth across the region in the seventeenth and eighteenth centuries. European colonialism was probably not a major factor in economic stagnation, at least until the nineteenth century. Although the major European powers had established trading posts in the region from the sixteenth century onwards, by the early nineteenth the main European-controlled possessions in the region were those of the Spanish in the Philippines, especially Luzon, and the Dutch in Java.

Some aspects of Southeast Asian society appear to have diverged early from both China and India. Reid (1988: 146–72) put forward a strong argument that women had a high degree of economic and social autonomy in pre-modern Southeast Asia. He stresses the absence of the dowry system; payment of a bride price seems to have been much more common even in Vietnam where Confucian traditions were stronger than elsewhere.[1] Newly married

---

[1] Lieberman (2003: 448–9) contrasts Burmese with Vietnamese elite norms of behaviour. He argues that in Burma, there were no dramatic differences between the administrative class and

couples often resided in the bride's village rather than that of the husband. The tyranny of the mother-in-law over the young bride, so common in India and China, appears to have been a less prominent feature of married life across the region, with the exception of Vietnam (Marr 1981: 193–4). Monogamy was the dominant marriage pattern, except among rulers. Most striking was the tendency for women to work outside the home, especially in trade. Both European and Chinese visitors noted the involvement of women not just in the bazaar economy but also in large-scale trade and transport enterprises, as well as in public entertainment, and even in diplomacy and government. Even where Islam gained more adherents, West Asian and North Indian customs such as face veils and *purdah* never really took hold. Chinese customs such as feet binding were unknown, even in Vietnam.

Rapid changes took place from the middle years of the nineteenth century. First, the British and French began to assert more territorial control over Burma, the Malayan peninsula, and Indochina, while the Dutch extended their control over the vast Indonesian archipelago from the northern tip of Sumatra to West New Guinea. After the defeat of Spain by the USA in the Spanish-American war at the end of the nineteenth century, America took control of the Philippines. Only Thailand remained an independent kingdom, but was forced from the 1850s onwards to sign a series of treaties with the major western powers, which limited the government's action in trade and fiscal policy. Partly as a result of more intensive colonial control, which curbed local warfare, population growth accelerated to over one per cent per annum in most parts of the region (Boomgaard 2014: 133).

This was a higher rate of population growth than in most other parts of Asia. It was facilitated by increased food production, particularly of crops such as corn and cassava which were imported from the Americas, and by the middle decades of the nineteenth century were widely grown across the region. At the same time, growing involvement in international trade led to increased cultivation of crops such as coffee, pepper, spices, tropical fruits, and sugar. By the closing years of the century, colonial governments were encouraging the establishment of large estates, usually owned by companies based in Europe or the USA, which grew crops such as sugar and tobacco for which there was a growing demand in western markets. In the early twentieth century, new crops were introduced, including rubber and palm oil, demand for which resulted from rapid industrialization in Britain, France, Germany, and the USA. Exports of tin grew rapidly from both British Malaya and Indonesia,

---

commoners regarding female roles. In Vietnam the peasants tended to resemble other Southeast Asians but the higher classes adopted Chinese patterns of behaviour. He also argues that in the eighteenth and nineteenth centuries, Sinic models of behaviour penetrated into the villages.

and from the late nineteenth century petroleum production grew in both Sumatra and Borneo.

The growing trade and investment links with Europe, the USA, and after 1920 with Japan, demonstrated that Southeast Asia was increasingly engaged with the international economy in what has been termed the first phase of globalization, from 1870 to 1913. Perhaps, given the involvement of the region in trade with both China and the Indian sub-continent in the Age of Commerce, it should be thought of as the second phase of globalization in the region. All the evidence indicates that exports from Southeast Asia grew as a proportion of global trade; in 1912, Southeast Asia accounted for thirty per cent of all commodity exports from Asia, excluding Japan. The region also accounted for around half of the total stock of foreign direct investment in Asia (Booth 2004: Tables 4 and 6).

In addition to trade and capital flows, Southeast Asia also experienced considerable inward migration from India and China. The proportion of 'foreign Asians' to indigenous populations varied widely; in British Malaya, including Singapore, migrants from China and India accounted for more than half the population by the early 1930s, but elsewhere migrants were a much lower proportion. In Thailand, migration from China had been taking place for many decades; Bangkok and its environs had attracted most of the migration and Chinese merchants dominated trade and commerce. In Indonesia the 1930 census found that Chinese were only two per cent of the population, but Chinese merchants were well established in most coastal cities. Migrants from China provided labour in the plantation sector in both Sumatra and British Malaya although after 1900, government policy in Indonesia was to move Javanese to agricultural settlements outside Java, and as indentured workers, especially to North Sumatra. These migration patterns left a legacy of the plural economy, which will be discussed further below.

In the first three decades of the twentieth century, GDP per capita grew in all those parts of Southeast Asia for which we have estimates. Population for the entire region was also growing, and was estimated to be around 130 million in 1930. Although most people still relied on agriculture for the bulk of their income, a considerable part of the labour force, over thirty per cent in several colonies, was employed in non-agricultural activities (Table 6.6).

Across much of Southeast Asia, both men and women were becoming more involved in the market economy, selling part of their output, purchasing food and other household needs, hiring in or out labour and borrowing or lending money. This involvement alarmed some colonial officials, but the more far-sighted realized that it was inevitable, and it was the responsibility of the colonial power to provide indigenous populations with modern education, to equip them for life in an increasingly commercialized world.

Table 6.6 Occupational Distribution of the Employed Population in Asian Colonies and Thailand, c.1930.

Country/Year	Agriculture	Industry	Other	Total
Taiwan (1930)	73.0	8.6	18.3	100.0
Korea (1930)	79.6	6.3	14.1	100.0
Thailand (1929)	84.2	2.2	13.6	100.0
Burma (1931)	69.6	11.0	19.4	100.0
British Malaya (1930)	60.8	12.3	26.9	100.0
Philippines (1939)	69.0	12.2	18.8	100.0
Indonesia (1930)	68.0	10.4	19.6	100.0

Sources: Korea: Suh 1978: Table 2; Taiwan: Grajdanzev 1944: 33; British Malaya: Vlieland 1932: 99; Burma: Saito and Lee 1999: Table 1.6; Indonesia: Mertens 1978: Appendix Table 1.5; Philippines: Kurihara 1945: 16; Thailand: Ingram 1971: 57,144.

By 1930, there was also concern about what colonial officials saw as the problem of 'over-population', especially in the inner islands of Indonesia, and in northern Vietnam. The Dutch had launched the ethical policy at the beginning of the twentieth century, which was intended to improve living standards in Java through investment in irrigation, and increased provision of education to allow more Javanese to take jobs in the non-agricultural economy. In addition, an ambitious programme of land settlement outside Java was launched, and Javanese were encouraged to move to the east coast of Sumatra to take waged work in the rapidly expanding estate sector. But in spite of these initiatives, Indonesia performed rather badly on health and education indicators compared with most other colonies in Southeast Asia (Booth 2012: Table 4). Infant mortality rates in Java were higher than in the Philippines or British Malaya, and the proportion of the population in school was low.

No other colony in Southeast Asia could compare with the Philippines in educational achievement. Not only did the American administration expand access to primary education, but they also greatly increased numbers in secondary and tertiary institutions. The implications of this for Philippine economic development after 1950 will be examined further below. In British Malaya, which comprised the Straits Settlements, and the Federated and Unfederated States of Malaya, there was some progress in the provision of education but it was very skewed towards the Chinese and Indian communities. Singapore was the main port not just for the Malayan peninsula but also served as an entrepôt for much of Indonesia, especially for the processing and shipment of rubber (Huff 1994: Chapter 7). It became an important educational centre, with a number of high schools, and a university teaching in English.

The decade of the 1940s was a bad one for much of Asia. In 1942, the armies of Japan swept through Southeast Asia, inflicting humiliating defeats on the colonial powers. Some Southeast Asians welcomed the Japanese as liberators,

Table 6.7 Per capita GDP in Pre-war Peak, 1950, 1955, and 1960 (1990 international dollars).

Country	c.1940	1950	1955	1960
Singapore (1937)	2524	2219	2358	2310
Malaysia (1941)	1673	1559	1460	1530
Philippines (1940)	1507	1070	1358	1476
Indonesia (1941)	1154	817	948	1015
Thailand (1938)	826	817	945	1078
Burma (1938)	740	396	467	564
China (1936)	597	448	577	662
India (1943)	698	619	676	753
Taiwan (1940)	1250	916	1189	1353
South Korea (1938)	904	854	1169	1226

Source: The Maddison Project data, downloaded from http://www.ggdc.net/maddison/maddison-project/home.htm, 2013 version.

but disillusion rapidly set in as the Japanese military conscripted indigenous workers and confiscated rice to feed their troops. By early 1944, food shortages were causing serious hardship; in Java and Northern Vietnam shortages were turning into famines. By 1945, output per capita in most parts of Southeast Asia had fallen below the levels reached in the late 1930s, and in several cases recovery was slow. By 1960, per capita GDP in most parts of Southeast Asia had still not recovered to pre-1942 levels (Table 6.7).

The main exception was Thailand, which had experienced less war damage than most other parts of the region; per capita GDP recovered to pre-war levels by the early 1950s.

6.4 Singapore and Malaysia

Although per capita GDP in British Malaya was higher than elsewhere in Southeast Asia in the 1950s, the decade was a troubled one for what had become the Malayan Federation, and for Singapore, with slow economic recovery and considerable political unrest. The Malayan Emergency which pitted British and Commonwealth troops against Communist rebels rumbled on until 1957, when self-government was conceded to the Malayan Federation. The British proposed to grant independence to a new state to be called Malaysia, which comprised all the territories in Southeast Asia controlled by the British except Burma (which had been granted independence in 1948) and Brunei. Singapore joined Malaysia in 1963, but after two years differences between the governments of Singapore and Malaysia became irreconcilable, and in 1965 Singapore broke away to become an independent republic.

The Singapore government had to fashion a new development strategy for the island economy, which had developed over the past century as a port and financial centre serving what were now the independent states of Malaysia and Indonesia. Neither of these states was sympathetic to Singapore's problems in 1965; Indonesia was openly hostile even after Suharto wrested power from Sukarno in 1966. The development model crafted after 1965 relied on advice from a range of sources, including the Netherlands and Israel (Peebles and Wilson 2002: 34–5). A Dutch adviser, Dr Winsemius, grasped Singapore's potential as the main port for the region using the new container technology, which was already leading to considerable productivity increases in ports in Europe and elsewhere. He also was quick to appreciate Singapore's potential role as the leading financial centre in the region (Peebles and Wilson 2002: 108–17). Foreign advisers also stressed that Singapore, which lacked a robust entrepreneurial class, would have to rely on foreign investment to develop modern manufacturing and services. By the late 1980s, thirty per cent of gross domestic capital formation in Singapore came from Foreign Direct Investment (FDI), a very high proportion by world standards[2].

The remarkable growth performance of Singapore after 1965 has influenced development strategies in small economies around the world, not just in Asia but as far away as Ireland and Malta. But there were flaws in the model which became more obvious in the 1980s when a new generation of leaders were taking over, and were aware that sustaining high rates of growth would not be easy in a changing global economy. Influenced by the Taiwanese and Korean experiences, the Singapore government understood that Singapore could no longer rely on low wages to attract foreign investment, and would have to move up the technological ladder. But this needed skilled workers, and compared with Taiwan and South Korea Singapore had neglected post-primary education (Booth 2003). After the mid-1980s, Singapore's development strategy changed gear, with much more emphasis on improving the skills of the local labour force through education and training. Where these were lacking, the government imported skilled workers from other parts of the world, in both industry and services. Unskilled workers were also brought in from neighbouring countries, to work in construction and other occupations which Singaporeans were increasingly unwilling to fill.

In 1957, the British granted self-government to the Malayan Federation. Although per capita GDP was still below the pre-1942 peak, the economy was relatively prosperous compared with most other former colonies in Asia, including Taiwan and South Korea. But the economy was still largely dependent on a narrow range of commodity exports, whose prices were subject to considerable fluctuations on world markets. In addition, the British had left behind a more extreme plural economy than elsewhere in the region.

---

[2] Yoshida, Akimune, Nohara, and Sato (1994: 72).

According to the 1931 census, Chinese and other Asian (mainly Indian) migrants comprised the majority of the population, and Malays and other indigenous races only 45 per cent (Booth 2007: Table 2.2). The Chinese and Indians dominated modern business and commerce, while the Malays were largely confined to farming and fishing. Little changed in the immediate post-1945 years.

After Singapore left Malaysia in 1965, the demographic balance shifted in favour of ethnic Malays; by 1970 they comprised 53 per cent of the population (Government of Malaysia 1976: 142). But Chinese and Indians still dominated the non-agricultural economy; they comprised 65 per cent of the labour force in manufacturing and commerce. Chinese and Indians also comprised the majority of students in urban schools and universities. These persistent disparities had unfortunate political consequences; in 1969 serious race riots broke out after disputed election results, and forced a change in government policy in education and employment. The Malay majority was overtly favoured in terms of educational places, especially at the secondary and tertiary levels, and in terms of government employment. Private enterprises were also expected to employ a certain proportion of ethnic Malays in managerial and technical positions.

The New Economic Policy, as the government termed it, was controversial from the outset. Many Malaysian citizens of Chinese and Indian descent with skills in demand in other parts of the world decided that they had no future in Malaysia and left the country. There was a rapid growth in public expenditures from around 31 per cent of GDP in 1971 to over 50 per cent a decade later. In addition there was a considerable growth in off-budget spending on public enterprises (Jomo 1990: Table 8.3). In 1981, Dr Mahathir Mohammad took over as Prime Minister, and initiated an ambitious series of policies aimed at transforming Malaysia into a newly industrializing economy. Although the post-1950 Japanese economic miracle was an important inspiration, the example of South Korea was probably more important. South Korean advisers played an important role in drawing up the Industrial Master Plan published in 1986. This plan set ambitious targets for industrial growth in Malaysia, but also stressed the weaknesses of the industrial sector including high dependence on foreign technology, a lack of skilled workers, excessive protection against foreign imports and a neglect of small and medium enterprises.

Over the 1980s and 1990s, export-oriented manufacturing industries grew rapidly. Most exports came from foreign-invested firms, many of which were located in special economic zones. After the Singapore government raised wages as part of its industrial upgrading policy in the early 1980s, manufacturing industries in sectors such as textiles, garments, footwear and electronics moved to Malaysia. By the early 1990s, the old dependence on a few commodity exports was changing rapidly; manufactured exports accounted for well over half of total export revenues. Poverty was also falling and there was a marked increase in numbers of ethnic Malays in professional, technical and administrative occupations (Gomez and Jomo 1997: 167). By the mid-1990s the government relaxed certain aspects of the NEP, especially in the education sector. It allowed the entry of private and foreign universities, and modified ethnic quotas, in order to increase the supply of scientists, technicians and engineers.

The Malaysian government claimed that the policy of affirmative action was necessary to correct the severe ethnic imbalances inherited from the colonial era while at the same time allowing the economy to achieve impressive rates of economic growth. But critics have argued that much of the industrial growth was in low-technology sectors employing mainly unskilled or semi-skilled workers. Technology transfer was limited. In addition, the pro-Malay policies built up powerful vested interests among the Malay elite, which have resisted reform down to the present day. The privatization policies of the 1980s were often used as a means of transferring valuable assets to politicians connected with the ruling party, while at the same time a broader class of Malay capitalists emerged which relied heavily on state patronage.[3] The export-oriented manufacturing sector has remained dependent on foreign capital and technology, and Malaysian industry has had little success in developing 'national champions' such as those which have emerged in Taiwan and South Korea. As will be discussed further below, debates about Malaysia's economic future became more contentious after the financial crisis of 1997/98.

6.5 Thailand and Indonesia

Perhaps the most remarkable example of catch-up in Southeast Asia after 1960 from unpromising beginnings was to be found in Thailand. The Thai economy experienced little growth in per capita terms in the early decades of the twentieth century. The government of Phibunsongkram, the pro-Japanese leader who was removed in 1944 but returned to power in 1947, was hostile to both foreign investment and the local Chinese, who dominated industry and commerce in Bangkok and the larger towns. Most indigenous Thais worked in agriculture. In the immediate post-1945 years, the industrialization strategy was based on state enterprises, which were frequently managed by former military officers who lacked managerial experience (Yoshihara 1994: 32–5).

---

[3] On these issues see Gomez and Jomo (1997).

But the change of government in 1957/8 brought new military leaders into power who favoured more open trade and investment policies. They gave considerable autonomy in economic policymaking to a group of technocrats led by Dr Puey Ungphakorn, the Governor of the Bank of Thailand from 1959 to 1971. Dr Puey built up the 'four agency' system, comprising the Bank of Thailand, the National Economic and Social Development Board (NESDB), the Ministry of Finance and the Bureau of the Budget.[4] These four arms of the bureaucracy exchanged staff, and were able to maintain control over the levers of economic policy even when governments changed. Promising graduates from Thai schools and universities were sent abroad on government scholarships and returned to work in one of the four agencies.

Beginning in the late 1970s, export-oriented manufacturing replaced export-oriented agriculture as the main engine of growth in the Thai economy. The modern service sector also grew rapidly, and in the decade from 1985 to 1995 Thailand was one of the fastest growing economies in the world. There was also a sharp decline in the headcount measure of poverty (Warr 2004). But a conservative approach to fiscal policy, inherited from the pre-1940 era, led to underinvestment in education and infrastructure. By the late 1980s, it was widely appreciated in policy circles that the percentage of Thai children going on to secondary and tertiary education was very low compared with South Korea and Taiwan at similar levels of per capita GDP (Booth 2003: 153). In 1989 only about 35 per cent of the age cohort was in lower secondary school, and less than a quarter in upper secondary school.

The neglect of education might not have mattered when the demand in manufacturing and the service sector was mainly for unskilled workers performing routine tasks. But by the early 1990s it was becoming clear that wages were rising, and many labour-intensive industries in Thailand could no longer compete with those in China, Vietnam and South Asia. Thai industry and services would have to upgrade to higher value added sectors, but were held back by skills shortages. The sharp decline in fertility meant that growth in the labour force was slowing, which pushed up real wages. These problems were aggravated by the government's policy of maintaining a fixed rate of exchange against the dollar. In 1993 the government decided to remove most controls on capital inflows and outflows in the expectation that Bangkok would become a regional banking centre to rival Singapore. Foreign borrowing by the private sector increased rapidly, but most went into non-traded sectors, especially urban property. By 1996, the Thai economy faced an appreciating real exchange rate, a sharp slowdown in export growth, and increasing excess capacity in the property sector. Although it seemed clear to many observers

[4] Good discussions of the four agency system can be found in Yoshihara (1994: 138–40), Warr and Nidhipradha (1996) and Suehiro (2005).

that Thailand could not sustain the growth rates of the previous decade, few predicted the magnitude of the crisis which would hit in 1997/98, or its consequences for Thailand's subsequent economic performance.

Indonesia's economic performance between 1966 and 1996 had much in common with that of Thailand, with the important difference that Indonesia had an exportable surplus of oil and gas. When Suharto took over in 1966, the economic situation was dire. Inflation was out of control, and per capita GDP was still below the level reached in 1941. Malnutrition and poverty were widespread, and the majority of children did not complete primary school. Like the Thai generals, Suharto realized that he would need advice on economic policy. He recruited a team of economists from the University of Indonesia, and several were given key cabinet positions in the late 1960s. Most were educated in the USA, and proved valuable in dealing with foreign donors and potential investors.[5] Helped by flows of foreign aid and increased oil revenues the economy recovered quickly after 1968; even before world oil prices began to rise in 1973, Indonesia was already achieving rates of growth of six to seven per cent per annum. These growth rates were sustained, with only a few fluctuations until 1997.

The oil boom in Indonesia led to a rapid increase in government revenues after 1973. Part of the revenues were used to pay down foreign debts including those incurred by the state oil enterprise, *Pertamina*, in its flawed attempt to establish various enterprises, including an iron and steel plant in West Java. The rest was used to expand central government grants to regional governments, which were intended to rehabilitate and extend rural infrastructure, including roads and irrigation. In addition grants were given to build schools and health clinics in rural areas. By the early 1980s health indicators were improving, more children were enrolling in schools and per capita food consumption was increasing. After world oil prices fell in the early 1980s, the government implemented a series of policy reforms, including two devaluations of the *rupiah* which led to a growth in non-oil exports, including manufactures. Growth was sustained through until the crisis of 1997/98.

6.6 The Miracle Collapses: The Crisis and Recovery

By the early 1990s, there was considerable optimism about Southeast Asia's economic prospects. The 'Asian Miracle' report, published with considerable fanfare by the World Bank in 1993, examined the economic record of eight economies in East and Southeast Asia since the 1960s. The four selected from

---

[5] On the role of the technocrats in Indonesia see in particular Bresnan (1993: Chapter 3).

Southeast Asia were those which had experienced rapid growth of GDP since the 1960s (Singapore, Malaysia, Thailand and Indonesia). Also included were Taiwan, the Republic of Korea, Hong Kong and Japan (World Bank 1993). While acknowledging that these eight countries differed widely in terms of natural resource endowment, population, culture and economic policies, the report argued that they had all managed to achieve not just sustained economic growth but also considerable improvement in living standards. The key to their success was to encourage private investment from both domestic and foreign sources, and promote human capital formation while implementing fiscal, monetary and exchange rate policies which achieved domestic price stability, and facilitated rapid export growth.

The main message of the 1993 report was that these eight countries had succeeded through implementing a policy package which was replicable in other parts of the world. What the report ignored or underplayed were the vulnerabilities which were already evident by the early 1990s.[6] Financial sectors had been liberalized, but in Indonesia this had led to the rapid growth of private banks, many of which were owned by large conglomerates and lent mainly to other firms within the conglomerate. Both Thailand and Indonesia had experienced a massive increase in foreign borrowing by domestic corporations and, in the case of Thailand, non-bank financial companies which were not regulated by the central bank. Both countries had also seen a sharp decline in the influence of economic technocrats, which had damaged the capacity of central banks, planning agencies and finance ministries to influence policy.

In the early months of 1997, the Thai authorities struggled to maintain the baht-dollar peg in the face of increasing capital outflows. By early July, with foreign exchange reserves exhausted, a decision was taken to float the baht, and seek a loan from the International Monetary Fund (IMF). The conditions which the IMF attached to the loan, especially regarding tight fiscal and monetary policies, attracted considerable criticism. There was universal agreement that the problems in Thailand were not brought about by large fiscal deficits; successive governments in Thailand had pursued balanced budgets, and government debt was low relative to GDP and exports. But the IMF insisted on even larger budget surpluses, together with tight monetary policies in order to attract back funds which had been remitted abroad and to strengthen the currency. The baht did appreciate against the dollar in 1998/99, but the tight monetary and fiscal policies brought about a severe contraction in real GDP, which fell by ten per cent in 1998, and only recovered to 1996 levels in 2001. Even export-oriented firms which had not borrowed abroad and which were generating most of their revenues in foreign

---

[6] The literature on the vulnerabilities which led to the crisis of 1997/98 is now very large; a good survey can be found in Sheng (2009).

currencies experienced difficulties due to a reluctance on the part of banks to lend, even for working capital.

The slow economic recovery in Thailand caused considerable resentment not just in the business community but among the broader population in both urban and rural areas. This was an important factor in the election of Thaksin Shinawatra in 2001. He had built up a power base in the north of the country, and promised populist policies aimed at farmers and small businesses. In addition he introduced low cost medical care to the entire population. The economy did experience some growth between 2001 and 2006, but his policies were increasingly resented in both Bangkok and the south of the country. Thaksin was deposed in a military-led coup in 2006, and left the country, but his political supporters still achieved a majority in subsequent elections. In 2014 another army coup removed a government led by his sister, and installed a military regime. The political instability had serious economic consequences; between 2007 and 2013, Thailand's GDP grew more slowly than in Malaysia, Indonesia, Vietnam, and the Philippines, and Thailand has become a net exporter of capital. At the end of 2014 its medium term economic prospects were uncertain.

When Thailand was forced to float the baht, it was widely considered that there was little likelihood of contagion to other parts of the region. But in the final months of 1997, it was clear that problems were emerging in neighbouring countries, especially Indonesia and Malaysia. In Indonesia, the government led by Suharto, who had been in power for over three decades, was reluctant to tackle the problems in the financial sector, or indeed to take any measures which might imperil the business interests of the Suharto family and their associates.[7] He was determined to seek a further term as president in 1998, in spite of health problems and opposition from various non-government groups, both religious and secular. By early 1998, he appeared to be in complete denial about the seriousness of the economic problems facing the country as capital flight accelerated and the rupiah fell to less than twenty per cent of its value against the dollar in early 1997. Only after serious riots in May 1998 did Suharto lose the confidence of his cabinet, and was forced to resign in favour of his vice-president, Dr B.J. Habibie.

Malaysia also suffered from capital outflow and a decline in the value of its currency in late 1997 and early 1998. Although not forced to seek assistance from the IMF, the deputy prime minister began to introduce austerity measures, and several expensive government projects promoted by the prime minister were scaled back or cancelled. Tensions within the government mounted, and in September 1998 the prime minister sacked his deputy,

---

[7] A good overview of events in Indonesia in the final phase of the Suharto era can be found in Borsuk and Chng (2014), especially Chapters 15–17.

pegged the currency to the dollar at the depreciated rate to which it had fallen, and imposed capital controls. These measures contrasted with those imposed by the IMF on both Indonesia and Thailand, and although the Malaysian economy suffered a decline in real GDP in 1998, recovery was faster.[8] In Singapore, GDP fell only slightly in 1998, and the economy returned to growth in 1999.

Thus the four Southeast Asian countries which featured in the 1993 World Bank report all experienced either zero growth or growth contractions in 1998. In per capita terms, Indonesia and Thailand only returned to pre-crisis levels of GDP in 2003/4. Apart from the impact of the 1997/98 crisis, Singapore, Malaysia and Thailand were also hit by falling world demand for exports of electronics and IT equipment in the wake of the dotcom crash in 2001. By the early 2000s it was clear that new competitors for a range of manufactured products had emerged in other parts of the region, especially China. Malaysia and Singapore managed to maintain quite robust rates of growth until 2009 through export diversification, but GDP contracted in both economies in that year as a result of the global crisis.

After 2004, economic growth began to accelerate in Indonesia, spurred on by an increase in demand for commodity exports including gas, coal and vegetable oils. Between 2007 and 2013, GDP growth was faster in Indonesia than in either Thailand or Malaysia (Table 6.8).

But serious problems were emerging. Infrastructure had been neglected since the latter part of the Suharto era, and by 2010 was a serious impediment to further economic growth.[9] In addition it was clear that the quantitative expansion in education had not led to an improvement in quality, and skills

Table 6.8 Growth in GDP: Indonesia, Vietnam, Philippines, Malaysia, and Thailand (2007 =100).

	Indonesia	Vietnam	Philippines	Malaysia	Thailand
2007	100	100	100	100	100
2008	106	106	104	105	102
2009	111	111	105	103	101
2010	118	119	113	111	108
2011	125	126	118	117	109
2012	133	133	126	123	117
2013	141	140	135	129	120

Sources: Indonesia: www.bps.go.id; Other countries from Asian Development Bank, *Key Indicators for Asia and the Pacific*, *2014* (www.abd.org).

[8] See Athukorola (2001) for an analysis of the 1998 policies in Malaysia.
[9] A useful discussion of the infrastructure problems in Indonesia can be found in Suleman and Iqbal (2012).

shortages were emerging in technical, administrative and managerial occupations. Indonesia escaped quite lightly from the global crisis of 2008/9, because it was less reliant on manufactured exports, and benefited from high commodity prices, and growing trade with other parts of Asia, especially China. But Chinese, and global demand for coal and gas were weakening in 2014 when elections were held to replace Susilo Bambang Yudhoyono as president. The successful candidate, Joko Widodo, was committed to further policy reform but his party did not have a parliamentary majority and faced opposition from powerful factions both in the parliament and in the wider community.

6.7 The Philippines Puzzle

The Philippine economy suffered serious damage in 1944/45, and although economic growth was quite robust after 1950, in 1960, per capita GDP had not recovered to pre-1940 levels. As a result of the American emphasis on secondary and tertiary education, its labour force was better educated than in most other Asian countries, and English was quite widely spoken. To many observers in the 1950s, its economic prospects seemed better than those in the former Japanese or European colonies. But there were problems. After independence, the manufacturing sector was granted protection against imports through tariffs and quantitative restrictions, and the exchange rate was overvalued. Elections were often violent and corrupt and the congress was dominated by conservative landed families who opposed agrarian reforms. Between 1950 and 1965 successive presidents failed to tackle the country's economic problems. When Marcos was elected in 1965 he was at first viewed as a tough reformer, and his 1972 declaration of martial law was greeted with quiet approval by the USA and Japan.

It was hoped that by removing the conservative and often venal congress and governing through presidential decrees he would be able to circumvent powerful vested interests and push through economy-wide reforms in both agriculture and industry. But Marcos grew increasingly corrupt and his business cronies more powerful. Several were granted lucrative monopolies which damaged business confidence, and capital outflow accelerated. After the assassination of a key opposition leader, Benigno Aquino, in 1983 per capita GDP fell rapidly, and by 1986 it was only 83 per cent of the 1981 level. A massive display of popular discontent in 1986 led to the fall of Marcos and his flight to the USA, but economic recovery was slow. Already in the early 1970s, per capita GDP had fallen behind Thailand and by 1996 it was below Indonesia (Table 6.2). But in the decade after 1986 reforms were implemented in the financial sector and the trade regime was liberalized. The Philippines was less affected by the 1997/98 crisis than Thailand, Indonesia and Malaysia, with only a slight contraction in GDP in 1998. Growth in per capita GDP in the years from 1996 to 2010 was faster than in Thailand or Indonesia, although in 2010 per capita GDP was still below both these countries. But in spite of the country's improved economic performance in recent years, especially relative to Thailand, the catch-up will be slow.

In his comparison of the economic performance of Thailand and the Philippines from 1950 to 1990, Yoshihara (1994: 234–38) stressed three crucial differences between the two countries. First, since 1960 Thailand pursued more open policies to foreign investment; indeed he argued that only after 1986 did the Philippine government actively encourage foreign investment from Japan, the USA and Europe. Successive Thai governments, whether military or civilian, were also more supportive of the Chinese minority and tolerated their dominant role in industry and commerce. Second, the Thai government was less interventionist in crucial markets such as that for foreign exchange, and Thai industry was subject to greater import competition. Third, the Thai government, at least until the early 1990s, did a better job in terms of maintaining law and order, and preventing the rise of insurgencies inspired either by Communism or Islam.

A further important difference concerned population growth. The Philippines experienced rapid population growth for most of the twentieth century, and although fertility declined after 1960, the rate of decline was much slower than in Thailand or in most other parts of Southeast Asia. The census conducted in 1939 found that the population was a little above 16 million; in 2014 it reached 100 million. The fast growth in population exceeded the economy's capacity to create employment in either industry or modern services, while in rural areas many did not have access to land and were employed either as agricultural labourers or in low-productivity service occupations. In 2012 the Philippines had a very high percentage of the labour force in services compared with other Asian countries when they had achieved broadly similar levels of GDP (Table 6.9).

Recent estimates indicate that in 2010 the Philippines had a much higher incidence of poverty than Thailand and higher even than Vietnam, in spite of the fact that per capita GDP was higher (Asian Development Bank 2014: 11) In Thailand, landlessness was historically not such a serious problem, and since 1960 population growth has been much slower than in the Philippines. The two countries had roughly similar populations in 1950; by 2014 the population of Thailand was 66.4 million or two thirds of that in the Philippines.

From the 1960s onwards, increasing numbers of workers from the Philippines sought employment abroad; in 2012 the Commission on Overseas Filipinos estimated that 10.5 million Filipinos were working outside the country. This was over eleven per cent of the total resident population. The largest

Table 6.9 Percentage Breakdown of the Labour Force: Various Years.*

	Agriculture	Manufacturing	Industry**	Services
Taiwan (1971)	35.2	21.6	30.2	34.6
Korea (1974)	48.8	16.2	21.5	29.6
Malaysia (1978)	43.9	13.1	20.1	36.0
Thailand (1989)	66.6	9.0	11.9	21.5
Indonesia (2010)	40.5	10.8	17.5	42.0
Philippines (2012)	32.3	8.3	15.1	52.6

* Per capita GDP in the years shown was between $3,700 and $3,900 except the Philippines which was slightly lower (from Penn World Tables, v. 7.1, 2005 constant prices; data are derived from the growth rates of domestic absorption)
** Includes mining, manufacturing, utilities and construction.

Sources: GDP data: Heston, Summers and Aten (2012); Labour force data: Taiwan: Taiwan Statistical Data Book, 1974, (Taipei: Executive Yuan), Korea: 1974 Special Labor Force Survey Report (Seoul: Bureau of Statistics), Malaysia: Mid-Term Review of the Third Malaysia Plan, 1976-80 (KualaLumpur: Government Printing Office), Thailand: Statistical Yearbook of Thailand No. 39, 1992 (Bangkok: National Statistical Office), Indonesia: Population of Indonesia: Results of Indonesia Population Census 2010 (Jakarta: Statistics Indonesia), Philippines: Philippine Statistical Yearbook 2013 (Makati: National Statistical Coordination Board).

number, around 3.5 million, were in the USA which as the former colonial power, and a high income economy, has always been a favoured destination for both skilled and unskilled migrants. In addition large numbers were in Saudi Arabia and the UAE, around 2.3 million. On the plus side, their remittances were an important contribution to the balance of payments, but on the negative side their skills have left the country.

6.8 Vietnam, Laos, and Cambodia

The three countries which emerged in 1975 from the carnage of the wars against the French and the Americans were slow to recover from the devastation wrought by three decades of conflict. Cambodia was the worst affected; in 1996 per capita GDP was still below the 1970 level (Table 6.2). In Vietnam and Laos, a reform process, influenced by the Deng Xiao Peng reforms in China, began in the late 1980s. Vietnam promulgated a new foreign investment law, moved to a market-determined exchange rate and reduced the budget deficit which was the main cause of inflation. The process of policy reform was largely internally driven, and attracted support from both the Communist Party, and the wider community. After 1990, GDP growth accelerated as policy reforms took hold. The decision to join ASEAN probably did not have much immediate impact on trade or investment flows but it did give Vietnam exposure to economic policy debates in other parts of the region.

Between 1996 and 2010, these three economies grew more rapidly than the other ASEAN economies, albeit from a much lower level of per capita GDP (Table 6.3). They were far less affected by the financial crisis of 1997/98, mainly because their financial sectors were still small, and heavily dominated by state-owned banks. Controls on inward and outward flows of capital were also in force. Both Vietnam and Cambodia attracted foreign investment into labour-intensive manufacturing including garments and footwear. They also successfully applied the green revolution technologies in rice which led to increases in yields per hectare; by the early 2000s, Vietnam had re-emerged as a major exporter of rice. Laos developed several hydroelectric projects along the Mekong River, selling much of the electricity to Thailand. The accelerated growth had led to an improvement in living standards in these countries, and some decline in poverty, although recent figures show that the headcount measure of poverty varied between 22 per cent in Vietnam and 38 per cent in Laos in 2010 (Asian Development Bank 2014: 11).

6.9 Myanmar

It is widely acknowledged that Burma, as the country was then called, emerged into independence in 1948 with huge economic problems. The destruction of infrastructure and industrial plant was massive and in 1948 the state was barely functioning (Brown 2013: 203). With the assassination of Aung San, the government lost the one leader who might have been able to bring together the country's disparate ethnic and religious groups. Brown (2013: 205) also stressed the 'ferocious rejection of the colonial economic structure' which dominated the economic thinking of both military and civilian leaders. Whether the rejection was more complete than in North Vietnam after partition, or indeed in Indonesia after 1949 can be debated, but there can be little doubt that, as Myint (1967) later argued, Burma was one of the Southeast Asian countries which rejected the open, export-oriented policies of the colonial era, and chose an inward-looking strategy of economic development.

When the military under Ne Win achieved power in the early 1960s, they adopted a policy of autarky, under the rubric of the 'Burmese path to socialism'. The economy disengaged from trade and investment links with the outside world, and economic growth was slow. In spite of poor economic performance, the government resisted comprehensive reform until the student-led protests of 1988. After Ne Win was deposed in that year, the new military government appeared to be changing course, and opening the economy up to foreign investment in both the mining and manufacturing sectors. But after the election of 1990 which produced a massive victory for the National League for Democracy, the military reacted by jailing most of its leadership. This led to international sanctions and growing dependence on China. Only in 2011 did the military-led government adopt a more accommodating policy towards the opposition, in return for the removal of sanctions and increased economic aid. The economic reforms implemented since then have given some reason for hope that finally Myanmar is on the path to faster growth and improved living standards for its people.

One of the casualties of long years of economic isolation has been the statistical system; Myanmar is now excluded from many international data sets, and is ranked very low on the Human Development Index, as well as on the Transparency International Index and the World Bank Ease of Doing Business Index (Table 6.1). It seems probable that by 1996, per capita GDP had already fallen behind Vietnam, and was about the same, or lower than Laos (Table 6.2). In 2014, the country was almost certainly well behind all its neighbours in ASEAN, and even with faster growth, the catch-up process will take decades, if it occurs at all.

6.10 Are the Countries of Southeast Asia Catching Up? If Not, Why Not?

This chapter has examined the very mixed growth records of the ten Southeast Asian nations using the catch-up hypothesis formulated by Abramovitz (1986, 1995). It is clear that there has been only a limited degree of convergence between the ten countries in the five decades from 1960 to 2010, whether we look at per capita GDP or more broadly based indicators of development such as the Human Development Index. The three parts of British Malaya before 1942, together with the British territories of North Borneo and Sarawak, emerged as three separate nations after 1965. These three countries, Singapore, Malaysia and Brunei were ahead of other parts of the region in the 1960s, and the gap had not narrowed much by 2010. Thailand, which grew rapidly from rather unpromising beginnings between 1960 and 1996, was in fact further behind Singapore in terms of per capita GDP in 2010 than in 1960, and the gap between Thailand and Malaysia has changed little over these decades.

This is not to deny that all the countries of Southeast Asia have seen some growth in per capita GDP since 1960, and some improvement in non-monetary indicators of development including literacy, educational enrollments and infant and child mortality rates. In most countries there has been some catch-up with the former colonial power, although only in Singapore and Brunei has per capita GDP surpassed that of the United Kingdom. In the Philippines, per capita GDP fell behind that of the USA between 1960 and 1990; although growth rates in the Philippines accelerated after 1990, per capita GDP in 2010 was still less than ten per cent of the US figure, which was lower than in 1960. With the exception of Singapore and Brunei, no country in Southeast Asia caught up with the former colonial power to the same extent as Taiwan and the Republic of Korea. In 2010, per capita GDP in Taiwan was slightly above Japan, and in Korea it was almost equal to that of Japan (Table 6.4).

To what extent can the relative failure of the poorer countries in Southeast Asia to forge ahead be blamed on a failure to develop social capabilities, as Abramovitz defined them? Many among the early post-independence leaders were inclined to blame the colonial powers for failing to develop infrastructure and education, and for preventing the emergence of an indigenous class of political leaders. The faster catch-up in the Japanese colonies has been attributed to the Japanese colonial legacy which is often considered to have been more developmental than that of the European colonial powers. But the evidence for this is not entirely convincing; in secondary and tertiary education the Japanese certainly achieved less than the Americans in the Philippines, and the Americans were unique in their determination to give their colony self-government, which they did in 1935. But in spite of these advantages, the Philippines has been a spectacular example of failure to catch-up, either with the former colonial power, or with regional neighbours.

The failure of the Philippines to forge ahead raises questions about the form of government which is most likely to support rapid economic growth, an issue which Abramovitz did not directly address.[10] The Taiwan, Korean, and Singaporean cases have often been used to support the argument that strong leadership is essential. Taiwan and the Republic of Korea moved towards a more open democracy over the 1980s, while Singapore has remained a one party state with little open political opposition. Malaysian politics have also been dominated by the United Malay National Organisation since 1957, and in recent years the leadership of the main opposition movement has been subject to intimidation and worse. Thailand has oscillated between periods of army rule and parliamentary government since the end of the absolute monarchy in 1932. The political disturbances, some violent, which became more frequent after 2006 were, in part at least, the result of perceived inequalities between regions and social classes, and a perception on the part of many outside Bangkok that they had not had a fair share of the fruits of rapid growth.[11] The coup in 2014 was triggered in part at least by a perception among the Bangkok elite that democracy was bringing about social conflict

---

[10] It could also be argued that the combination of rapid population growth and sluggish economic growth, which has led to the very high proportion of the labour force in the service sector in the Philippines implies that the country is not following the 'East Asian' model of economic development, as outlined by Austin and Suguhara (2013: 7). According to these authors, the 'East Asian model' is characterized by an absence of proletarianization, or large numbers of people in rural areas who do not control land. In both the Philippines and Indonesia, growing landlessness has been a feature of the rural economy for several decades.

[11] A perceptive discussion of the problems facing Thailand since the 1997/98 crisis can be found in Phongpaichit and Benyaapikul (2012).

which was incompatible with a return to rapid economic growth. How these different views can be reconciled remains to be seen.

Vietnam, Laos and Cambodia, which had fallen well behind the ASEAN six by the early 1990s, have all grown rapidly since then, although given the gap between them and the leading economies, the catch-up process will take time, and might not occur at all. Vietnam is still a one party state where little open political dissent is tolerated; political opposition groups have also been harshly treated in Cambodia. Will rapid economic growth produce political and social conflict, as in Thailand, which negatively affects further growth? Or will it lead to a more open and democratic system which is still compatible with reasonable rates of growth, as occurred in Indonesia after 2004? The concept of social capabilities, as developed by Abramovitz does not provide us with easy answers to these questions.

The countries of Southeast Asia have demonstrated since 1960 that catch-up growth is possible given appropriate domestic policies and favourable external circumstances. But for most countries in the region, catch-up has been a slow process and liable to sudden reversals. Some of these reversals have been the result of declining terms of trade and other external shocks about which these countries can do very little in the short-run. Others were the result of domestic policy mistakes, or failures to remedy long-standing grievances about the distribution of income and assets between regions, ethnic groups and social classes. Given political will, the domestic problems which hold back growth can be remedied. But if they are not, it is likely that substantial gaps in output per capita both within Southeast Asia, and between most of these countries and other parts of the global economy will persist. The concept of social capabilities, developed by Abramovitz and others writing in the 'catch-up' tradition can be criticized for failing to take into account the many traps which lie in the path of even the more successful countries. A country which has forged ahead for several decades can slow down, stagnate or even go into reverse. In the growth game, little can be taken for granted.

References

Abramovitz, M., 1986. 'Catching up, forging ahead and falling behind', *Journal of Economic History* vol. 46 (2), as reprinted in M. Abramovitz, 1989. *Thinking About Growth*, Cambridge: Cambridge University Press: 220–42.

Abramovitz, M., 1995. 'The Elements of Social Capability'. In *Social Capability and Long-Term Economic Growth,* edited by B.H. Koo and D.H. Perkins, Basingstoke: Macmillan Press: 19–47.

Abramovitz, M. and P.A. David, 1996. 'Convergence and deferred catch-up: productivity leadership and the waning of American exceptionalism'. In *The Mosaic of Economic*

Growth, edited by R. Landau, T. Taylor, and G. Wright, Stanford: Stanford University Press: 21–62.

Asian Development Bank, 2014. 'Poverty in Asia: A Deeper Look'. In *Key Indicators for Asia and the Pacific 2014*, Manila: Asian Development Bank.

Athukorola, P., 2001. *Crisis and Recovery in Malaysia: The Role of Capital Controls*, Cheltenham: Edward Elgar.

Austin, G. and K. Suguhara, 2013. 'Introduction'. In *Labour-Intensive Industrialization in Global History*, edited by Gareth Austin and Kaoru Sugihara, Abingdon: Routledge.

Boomgaard, P., 2014. 'Population Growth and Environmental Change: A two-track model'. In *Routledge Handbook of Southeast Asian History*, edited by N. G. Owen, Abingdon: Routledge: 133–43.

Booth, A., 2003. 'Education, equality and economic development in Asia-Pacific economies'. In *Development and Structural Change in the Asia-Pacific: Globalising miracles or end of a model?* edited by M. Andersson and C. Gunnarsson, London: Routledge Curzon.

Booth, A., 2004. 'Linking, de-linking and re-linking: Southeast Asia in the global economy in the 20th century' *Australian Economic History Review* vol. 44 number 1:35–51.

Booth., A, 2007. *Colonial Legacies: Economic and Social Development in East and Southeast Asia*, Honolulu: University of Hawaii Press.

Booth, A., 2012. 'Measuring Living Standards in Different Colonial Systems: Some evidence from South East Asia, 1900–1942'. *Modern Asian Studies* vol. 46 number 5:1145–81.

Borsuk, R. and N. Chng, 2014. *Liem Sioe Liong's Salim Group: The Business Pillar of Suharto's Indonesia*, Singapore: Institute of Southeast Asian Studies.

Bresnan, J., 1993. *Managing Indonesia: The Modern Political Economy*, New York: Columbia University Press.

Brown, I., 2013. *Burma's Economy in the Twentieth Century*, Cambridge: Cambridge University Press.

Gomez, E.T. and K.S. Jomo, 1997. *Malaysia's Political Economy: Politics, Patronage and Profits*, Cambridge: Cambridge University Press.

Government of Malaysia, 1976. *Third Malaysia Plan 1976–80*, Kuala Lumpur: Government Press.

Grajdanzev, A.J., 1944. *Modern Korea*, New York: Institute of Pacific Relations.

Heston, A., R. Summers, and Bettina Aten, 2012. *Penn World Tables version 7.1*, Philadelphia: Center for International Comparisons of Production, Income and Prices at the University of Pennsylvania, July 2012.

Huff, W.G., 1994. *The Economic Growth of Singapore: Trade and development in the Twentieth Century*, Cambridge: Cambridge University Press.

Ingram, J.C., 1971. *Economic Change in Thailand, 1850–1970*, Kuala Lumpur: Oxford University Press.

Jomo, K.S., 1990. *Growth and Structural Change in the Malaysian Economy*, Basingstoke: Macmillan Press.

Kurihara, K, 1945. *Labor in the Philippine Economy*, Stanford: Stanford University Press.

Lieberman, V., 2003. *Strange Parallels: Southeast Asia in Global Context, c. 800–1830*, Cambridge: Cambridge University Press.

Maddison, A., 1982. *Phases of Capitalist Development*, Oxford: Oxford University Press.

Maddison, A., 2003. *The World Economy: Historical Statistics*, Paris: OECD Development Centre Studies.

Manarungsan, Sompop., 1989. *Economic Development of Thailand, 1850–1950*, PhD Dissertation, State University of Groningen.

Marr, D., 1981. *Vietnamese Tradition on Trial, 1920–1945*, Berkeley: University of California Press.

Mertens, W., 1978. 'Population Census Data on Agricultural Activities in Indonesia', *Majalah Demografi Indonesia*, Number 9: 9–53.

Myint, H., 1967. 'The inward and outward looking countries of Southeast Asia', *Malayan Economic Review* Vol. 12 number 1:1–13.

Peebles, G. and P. Wilson, 2002. *Economic Growth and Development in Singapore: Past and Future*, Cheltenham: Edward Elgar.

Phongpaichit, P. and P. Benyaapikul, 2012. *Locked in the Middle-Income Trap: Thailand's economy between resilience and future challenges*, Bangkok: Friedrich Ebert Stiftung.

Population Reference Bureau, 2014. *World Population Data Sheet*, Washington: Population Reference Bureau.

Reid, A., 1988. *Southeast Asia in the Age of Commerce 1450–1680, Volume 1: The Lands Below the Wind*, New Haven: Yale University Press.

Reid, A.,1993. *Southeast Asia in the Age of Commerce 1450–1680: Volume 2: Expansion and Crisis*, New Haven: Yale University Press.

Saito, T. and Lee K.K., 1999. *Statistics on the Burmese Economy: The Nineteenth and Twentieth Centuries*, Singapore: Institute of Southeast Asian Studies.

Schwab, K. (Editor), 2014. *The Global Competitiveness Report, 2014–2015*, Geneva: World Economic Forum.

Sheng, A., 2009. *From Asian to Global Financial Crisis: An Asian Regulator's View of Unfettered Finance in the 1990s and the 2000s*, Cambridge: Cambridge University Press.

Suehiro, A., 2005. 'Who Manages and Who Damages the Thai Economy? The Technocracy and the Four Core Agency System and Dr Puey's Networks'. In *After the Crisis: Hegemony, Technocracy and Governance in Southeast Asia*, edited by S. Takahashi and P. Abinales, Kyoto, Kyoto University Press.

Suh, S-C., 1978. *Growth and Structural Changes in the Korean Economy, 1910–1940*, Cambridge: Harvard University Press.

Suleman, A. and Zafar Iqbal, 2012. 'Infrastructure Development: Challenges and the Way Forward'. In *Diagnosing the Indonesian Economy: Towards Inclusive and Green Growth*, edited by H. Hill, M.E. Khan, and J. Zhuang, London: Asian Development Bank and Anthem Press.

Vlieland, C.A., 1932. *British Malaya: A Report on the 1931 Census and on Certain Problems of Vital Statistics*, London: Crown Agents.

Warr, P.G., 2004. 'Globalization, Growth and Poverty Reduction in Thailand', ASEAN Economic Bulletin vol. 21 number 1:1–18.

Warr, P.G. and B. Nidhiprabha, 1996. *Thailand's Macroeconomic Miracle: Stable Adjustment and Sustained Growth*, Washington: World Bank.

World Bank, 1993. *The East Asian Miracle: Economic Growth and Public Policy*, New York: Oxford University Press Inc.

Yoshida, M., I. Akimune, M. Nohara, and Kimitoshi Sato, 1994. 'Regional Economic Integration in East Asia: Special Features and Policy Implications'. In, *Trade Blocs? The Future of Regional Integration*, edited by V. Cable and D. Henderson London: Royal Institute of International Affairs.

Yoshihara, K., 1994. *The Nation and Economic Growth: The Philippines and Thailand*, Kuala Lumpur: Oxford University Press.

7

Has Latin America Changed Tracks?

Catching up: Now and Then. An essay

Luis Bértola

7.1 Introduction

Latin America has been performing rather well during the last decade: high per capita GDP growth, diminishing poverty and inequality, and a rather stable democratic climate. This combination of good news, in a context of a world economy facing deep economic crisis and many regions dealing with hot political and ethnic conflicts, is challenging the observers' credulity and raises many different questions.

What is going on in Latin America? Is this performance sustainable? How endogenous are these trends and how much do they depend on external factors? How stable is the external environment?

While I am thinking about and writing this chapter, historical times seem to have returned and the OECD and ECLAC let us know that, in 2014, Latin America, on average, grew less than the average of the OECD countries (OCDE/United Nations/CAF (2014). Is this just an accident or the end of a relatively short process of convergence? The prospects for the next five years are not very bright at the moment, with estimated growth rates below two per cent a year.

In this chapter I will first present the long term development of Latin America, in a comparative perspective, trying to identify general features as well as national and regional differences. Second, I will present what I think are decisive long-term determinants of Latin American performance. Third, I will discuss the current expansive cycle and conclude with some prospects for future development.

The main argument is that Latin America has not yet been able to transform the structural features that explain its long-run divergent trend with the leaders of the world economy. While achievements in the consolidation of democratic institutions and the reduction of poverty and inequality may be a basis on which these transformations can be set in motion, the risk exists that, with changing external conditions, these achievements could be reversed, or even contribute to a transition to a new phase of slow growth and relative backwardness.

7.2 Development Without Convergence: is that Possible? A Long-run View of Latin America's Convergence and Divergence Trends since Independence

The main stylized facts about Latin American long-run development are rather well-known by now, in spite of the relatively low quality of quantitative sources.[1] Let's limit our study to the period since Independence, about 200 years ago. This does not mean that colonial, or even pre-conquest, times, do not play an unimportant role in this development.

And let us make a difference between absolute and relative performance. This distinction is quite important. Absolute performance is what really matters, i.e., the concrete improvements in income, education, life expectancy, rights, or whatever we want to use as a measure of well-being. Nevertheless, relative performance is crucial in many ways. First, because development and performance are historical concepts: a particular growth rate may be high in some context but low in another. Absolute performance is good or bad in relation to a particular state of the art, to particular scientific, technological, institutional, and organizational environments. Then, even if we could agree that more is better than less, the question here is how the rest is performing, which are the potentials of a particular time. Development is not just a stage or a level, but is circumstantial and is about being able to use and reproduce the best practices (scientific, technological, social, institutional, and organizational) of a time. Moreover, the reproduction of best practices always implies innovation and social transformation. Then, performance is a relative concept. Second, we are dealing with economies and societies that are, more and more, interrelated. No matter how asymmetric the relation between different countries and regions are, the fact is that we are dealing with a world economy with increasing interaction, through migration, trade, capital movements, information, technology transfer, war, culture, and more. At the core of this

---

[1] If no other reference is mentioned, the data referred to in what follows is taken from Bertola and Ocampo (2012).

volume, and of this chapter in particular, are the concerns about how these interactions impact on relative performance.

7.2.1 Development

In absolute terms, population growth in Latin America was amazing. This is important: Latin America has been able to feed a population that, in bold terms, increased from 22 to almost 600 million between 1820 and 2010. During a similar period, GDP increased about 300 times, and per capita GDP became 10 times bigger. If we happen to be sceptical about per capita GDP as a measure of development, we could also add that life expectancy at birth in Latin America was twenty-nine years in 1900, and seventy-five by 2010. Similarly, in 1900 Latin Americans had, on average, one-and-a-half years of education, while by 2010 they had more than eight years.

In terms of democratic development, progress has been amazing. From being, even at the beginning of the twentieth century, a region almost exclusively ruled by authoritarian and oligarchic regimes, almost all Latin America now enjoys rather stable democratic regimes, with important levels of political participation. While democracy did not become the dominant political regime in Western Europe until the post World War II period, Latin America was very backward in the development of democratic institutions. Until the 1980s we could see the prevalence of pre-democratic dictatorships (of the banana republic kind, tightly controlled by powerful economic elites, as in the case of Paraguay and Central America) and post-democratic dictatorships, such as Argentina, Brazil, Chile and Uruguay (where democratic regimes collapsed following processes of strong social transformation and the growth of conflicts that were finally dealt with under authoritarian rule with the heavy involvement of the US government). Nowadays we are experiencing what can be labeled as a new wave of democratic expansion, á la Huntington, and seemingly, we can see neither clouds on the political horizon, nor incipient armed international conflicts. Quite the contrary, the longest-lasting armed political conflict on the continent, the Colombian guerilla war, is coming to an end, as well as the USA's blockade of Cuba, where, paradoxically, the Colombian negotiations are taking place.

Achievements in terms of the reduction of inequality are ambiguous. Inequality in Latin America has been structurally high, but subject to significant fluctuations, depending on the level of economic activity and different political economy environments around periods of expansion and crisis. Changes in distribution and on the level of activity and employment have important impacts on poverty, as a large share of the population lives either below or slightly above the poverty line. While the recent per capita income growth implies that the proportion of the poor must have been reduced, changes in distribution and fluctuations in economic activity ensure that poverty has remained a hot topic. According to ECLAC (2014), still twenty per cent of the Latin American population, or 127 million, lives in poverty. And many of those who managed to leave poverty behind are vulnerable to the possibility of reverting back to poverty in the future, if some critical situations turn negative.

In spite of some common features, differences among the Latin American countries are strong and have shown to be long-lasting. Still today, no matter which variable we choose, we will find significant variation.

The continent, running mainly from North to South, and being segmented by huge geographical accidents, such as forests, mountains, and deserts, exhibits huge climatic and environmental variation. Ethnic diversity changes accordingly and was reinforced by strong migration movements from Africa, Asia and Europe.

Inequality between the Latin American regions was already present at the eve of the fight for Independence, and increased during the first decades after that. Unequal development deepened during the so called first globalization period, until World War I, or maybe until the 1929 world financial crisis. During the so-called State Led Industrialization, the relatively poorer Latin American countries grew more than the richer ones, so differences became smaller. Since the 1980s a new trend can be noticed, in which the medium and large Latin American countries, as well as the richer ones (Argentina, Chile and Uruguay), tend to grow more than the small countries of South America (Ecuador, Bolivia, Paraguay) and of Central America.

In short, while significant progress took place everywhere, the levels of development among the Latin American countries remained unequal. Even if the differences tended to be somewhat reduced, hardly any change in the Latin American ranking could be noticed over these two centuries of economic life.

7.2.2 Convergence and Divergence Trends

Four main stylized facts can be found in terms of the convergence-divergence trends of Latin America in relation to other regions.

i. In the long run, Latin America has diverged from world leaders

In the very long run, Latin American per capita GDP has been growing at world average. But during the last two centuries a huge divergence in per capita GDP appeared and widened among world regions. The Latin American experience is thus difficult to interpret. It has performed better than Africa and some parts of Asia, but it has diverged in relation to world leaders and was not able to replicate the miracles experienced by South Korea, Finland, Singapore and other previously peripheral regions. No single Latin American country has joined the club of the world leaders. In other words, Latin America has been able to grow and take advantage of the international development, but at a much slower pace than the world leaders.

ii. Three main periods can be found: during the first decades of independence in most countries—divergence; between 1870–1980— similar growth rates to those of the leaders, and since the 1980s (the recent decade is discussed later on)—clear divergence.

There is an ongoing debate on how Latin America performed during the decades after Independence. A traditional view states that the decades after Independence were a long delay, in which the advantages of independence and free trade could not yield good economic results due to the institutional chaos and lack of economic integration. A revisionist point of view (Gelman 2011, for instance) has it that economic performance was varied and was mainly determined by geographical, rather than institutional factors. For example, the coastal regions of what was becoming the Argentine Republic had a very good performance, while that of the interior showed as very bad. These features were present almost all over the continent. Recently, Bértola and Ocampo (2012) supported the original point of view, in an attempt to weight the contribution to growth of the different regions. All in all, while different performances could be noticed, the most populated areas were those that grew the less (Brazil, Perú, Mexico), while the dynamic ones were very small in terms of population (Argentina, Chile, and Uruguay).

The whole period 1870–1980 was one of rapid growth, but not one of convergence. It took place under two very different patterns of development: export-led growth until 1913–1929, and State-led growth during the 1930s through to the 1970s. Export-led growth was driven by a demand and price boom, which started to reverse at the beginning of the twentieth century. A shorter boom could be noticed in the aftermath of World War II. The first half of this period was characterized by the exploitation of natural resources, a very active role for international trade and capital flows, and important inflows of labour from different regions. The second half was one in which the State took an active role in redirecting investment towards the manufacturing industry and services. While import substitution was a source of economic growth in some countries and periods, as well as external demand, the main source of growth was, by far, the expansion of domestic demand.

Since the 1970s and to the turn of the century, with the combination of foreign forces (as the changes in international capital flows), and domestic ones (as the exhaustion of the expansion of domestic demand and the limits imposed by poor innovative activity), the region started a process of deep divergence with world leaders. During this time, on the contrary, other peripheral regions started powerful catching-up processes. While Latin America opened up its economy and exports grew very fast, the domestic sector showed disappointing performance. At the same time, the destruction of many productive capabilities and the dismantling of many social policies went hand in hand with increasing volatility, poverty, and inequality.

iii.   These trends are blurred by profound cyclical movements

A structural feature of the Latin American economies has been the high volatility of the pattern of growth and the strong cyclical pattern. The Latin American economies are not stagnating ones, they are not societies that rest on traditional structures that do not show important movement. Quite on the contrary, the story of Latin America is one of changing dynamics, of ups and downs, of social and political conflicts following periods of fast growth, that most of the time end in deep crisis. The Latin American countries showed periods of fast economic growth, during which they seemed to join the club of the developed countries. However, sooner or later, the growth trend was transformed into deep divergent periods. During these periods of fast growth and catching-up, very optimistic views tend to develop, hindering the perception of the cyclical character of these economies. Empirical analysis shows that this pattern of high volatility and cyclical fluctuations is highly correlated with the strong concentration of Latin American exports in a very few raw materials, whose demand and prices are very volatile.

iv.   There are important differences among the Latin American countries: different groups showed different trends

Diversity is huge among the Latin American countries, notwithstanding the common features.

There are many ways to approach these differences. A powerful typology takes into consideration the different ethnic compositions. This is not because of ethnicity itself, but because different ethnic groups are associated with different cultures and economic and social backgrounds.

The most populated areas since colonial times, and up to the first decades of the twentieth century, were the so-called Indo-American societies (Peru, Bolivia, Paraguay, Ecuador, Colombia, Mexico, El Salvador, Guatemala, Honduras, and Nicaragua). Dominated by natives, and mainly in the highlands of South and Central America, these cultures had developed complex and hierarchical social structures, and economic systems which covered very large territories and ecological environments. These structures interacted with economic, social and political institutions brought in by the colonial powers, creating a new mix of extraction of natural resources and native work by mainly coercive institutions. These were the countries with the lowest per capita income throughout Latin American independent history. They were the most developed regions in pre-Columbian times, with high density and an advanced division of labour. These were the richest regions during the colonial times, due to the existence of mainly gold and silver, as well as of a large labour force to be exploited. However, measured by modern standards, and after the exhaustion of the large reserves of gold and silver, these countries were characterized by a large poor peasant population. These societies also remained socially fragmented: ethnic differences there being a very good proxy for economic inequality.

This group of countries, the core of the colonial economy, suffered the most in the wars of independence, as the royalist forces there were very strong. They suffered the most from the collapse of the colonial economy. The fragmentation of the economic space into small national unities, not very well defined in geographical and political terms, contributed to the destruction of the colonial economic systems. This group of countries could benefit from the great expansion of trade during the export-led period, without being able to shorten the distance between themselves and world leaders. Most of these countries were small ones and, due to size and the limited transformation of their economy during the export-led period, they were not able to apply any countercyclical policy during the 1930s and 1940s. Only the medium-sized and large countries, like Peru, Colombia and Mexico, were able to set in motion industrial policies with at least limited results. The size of the countries became an important explanatory factor when the pattern of growth was more oriented towards the expansion of domestic demand in the middle decades of the twentieth century. In different ways, they benefitted from the price boom of the post-World War II period, and of the continued expansion of world trade up to the 1970s. As in most of the countries, they suffered the collapse of capital flows in the 1970s, which was followed by radical changes in the pattern of growth. While exports boomed in most of the countries, the domestic economies contracted significantly.

The Afro-American economies (Brazil, Venezuela, Cuba, for instance), had evolved helped by a massive introduction of slaves from Africa for the production of tropical agricultural commodities (cacao, sugar, coffee, and more). They had, on average, similar low levels of per capita income than those of the Indo-American group. However, they did not suffer the collapse of their economies after Independence, as much as the Indo-American group did. They showed similar trends during the independent period, except for post-World War II. This group of countries benefitted from the expansion of demand from the industrialized world for tropical products it could not produce itself. Then, a gap appeared between the Indo-Americans and the Afro-Americans, which remains until now. The gap was reduced during the last decades of the twentieth century, when the Afro-American group joined the divergent trend of the whole continent. This is a group that shows high inequality levels, as a result of the long-lasting effects of the slave economy, and the powerful expansion of some dynamic sectors.

A third group is the Euro-American one, composed mainly by Argentina, Uruguay, and with less clear similarities, Chile. This is the group of countries that enjoyed the highest per capita income throughout the whole period under study. Some regions of other countries share these features, as Antioquia in Colombia, and Southern Brazil. These were less populated areas during the colonial times, and they lacked mineral products of high value. They were marginal regions of the colonial economy, and their role was mainly determined by their location for trade, or by military considerations. This is the case of the harbour cities of Buenos Aires, Montevideo, Valparaíso and even Porto Alegre. These regions of temperate climate could produce agricultural goods similar to those produced in Europe, which is why their production was attractive only for domestic consumption. They also produced jerked beef for the slave population of the Afro-American countries. Their marginal role in the colonial economy made it easier for the forces of independence to meet with success, and why the domestic economies suffered less from these struggles. Also because of their location, they could more easily take advantage of trade liberalization after independence. Nevertheless, and in spite of an important growth of exports, the domestic economy could not stabilize due to steady and sometimes long-lasting national and international military conflicts and a painful process of state building. During the so-called first globalization boom, a combination of very favourable external conditions (expansion of demand and prices for foodstuffs and raw materials, and the availability of foreign capital willing to invest in infrastructure, trade, and industries), made it possible for these regions to achieve very high growth rates and levels of income. Argentina and Uruguay had, as the nineteenth became the twentieth century, similar levels of per capita income to those of the leading European countries. Chile, owing to its superior military forces and State consolidation, incorporated large amounts of natural resources (mainly nitrates in the North and land in the South) after its successful war against Bolivia and Peru, and against the native Mapuche population in the South. The gap between this group and the two others increased during the whole of the nineteenth century.

When export-led growth collapsed during the 1930s, these countries had relatively developed and diversified domestic economies, as well as significant State capabilities. They were thus able to apply defensive economic measures to promote the growth of industries and services, making use of the resources left idle by the world crisis. Later on, these defensive policies were transformed into more systematic industrial and welfare policies. While the economy was diversified, social policy developed, and inequality significantly reduced, these economies had huge problems in sustaining high growth rates. Volatility was somewhat reduced, but these economies grew less than in other Latin American countries, and much less than in the leading world economies that were going through the Golden Age up to the 1970s. Changing trends in the terms of trade, the difficulties in accessing the European market (more and more protectionist of its own agrarian production), and the exhaustion of the expansion of domestic demand for a too much inward-looking industrial production, led to a crisis of the pattern of development, which, differently from other regions, preceded the debt crisis of the 1980s. Post-democratic dictatorships prevailed in the region, in an attempt to dismantle industrial and welfare policies, to open up the economies and produce a significant shift in the distribution of income in favour of financial capital and different economic sectors linked to the exploitation of natural resources and infrastructure. Volatility increased once again and the process of divergence was deepened, in spite of the existence of short growth periods during which the illusion of convergence was fueled. Based on a profound process of liberalization and backed by a steadily high copper price, Chile was the most successful and stable economy. However, the catching-up process ended far from the levels of the developed countries (50 per cent), and inequality remained as a strong structural feature of its economy and society.

Size matters when we consider long-run development. Given the limited success of the different processes of integration in Latin America, the size of the countries became an important factor explaining performance. This does not mean that size per se is a limit on growth. Some of the countries with higher levels of development are small ones, as Uruguay, Costa Rica, or even Chile. Nevertheless, the size of the country was particularly important during state-led industrialization. Large and medium size countries, as Brazil, Mexico, Colombia, Peru, and Venezuela, shared many structural problems with small countries as Paraguay, Bolivia, Ecuador, and the Central American ones. Nevertheless, it seems that size was important in order to diversify the economies and achieve higher levels of per capita income. The gap between the small countries, on one side, and the rest remained high in favour of the latter, and divergence between them increased again in the late twentieth century.

7.3 The Underlying Forces

The way in which we interpret long-run Latin American development is crucial for our understanding of what happened during the last decade and for looking into the future.

The main question to be answered is why Latin America as a whole, or any single Latin American country, has not been able to join the group of the core countries in the world economy. Besides Africa, Latin America is the only world region that has so far failed as a whole. A following question is whether it will be possible for any Latin American country or group of countries to make it in the future.

In what follows, an attempt is made to briefly present the main explanations for that. The point of departure is a sceptical view about models that try to discover a single explanation, whether institutions, geography, culture, or any other single factor. On the contrary, complex systems evolve as the result of many inter- and counter-acting forces that overlap from one period to another, in a sometimes confusing sequence of continuity and change. This combination of continuity and change is what often makes it difficult to analyze recent historical periods and to detect the persistent factors and the seeds for change. So if the reader is expecting a simple explanation, I am afraid I will disappoint her/him.

7.3.1 Pre-Columbian Development

Diamond's (2005) illustrative description of the level of development of two different civilizations in the context of the conquest saves us a lot of words. In spite of being empires able to organize strong states covering large territories and achieving certain degrees of technical development, there was a huge technological and institutional advantage in favour of the European colonizers. In terms of per capita level, Maddison guessed it was 2 to 1. In terms of military outcomes, the distance was wider by far. Latin America had always to fight with this original relative backwardness. The devastating effect of conquest, due to military destruction, resource plundering, social exploitation, cultural domination, and the dissemination of germs, have produced a reaction in favour of the rights of the indigenous population which is completely legitimated. Nevertheless, a naïve view about the prospects for development of the pre-Columbian societies is, in terms of modern outcomes, not sustainable. The idea that today's backwardness is to be simply related to dependency relations started by the European colonization is clearly misleading. Similarly, the idea that the conquerors only brought progress with them is nothing but wishful thinking. If we were able to construct a Human Development Index for the two centuries after the conquest, introducing education, life-expectancy at birth, and income, the result would be catastrophic, even if the optimistic assumption is made that the surviving population achieved higher per capita income levels. In short, pre-Columbian civilizations were not composed by neutral 'endowments': they were economies with values, culture, and hierarchies far distant from European standards, and many of their features in terms of what we now can call low productivity, were to remain present for centuries, until now.

This relative backwardness cannot be related to the disposal of draft animals, as cows and horses, as even the availability of these and other more advanced technologies have not led to significant increases in productivity in vast areas of the agrarian Latin American economy. A more detailed analysis of the reasons of this pre-Columbian backwardness is beyond the reach of this chapter.

7.3.2 *The Colonial Heritage*

This is an ambiguous concept. No doubt, the colonizers brought with them new technologies and institutions that, in the very long-run, were able to put the Latin American countries in a growth trend superior to the one that could have been expected, had the colonizers not arrived. However, the societies that arose after the first period of collapse and plundering were very complex and diverse.

While many authors, with some reason, stress that the endowments of the different societies were decisive for the pattern of social and economic organization established (Sokoloff and Robinson in de Ferranti et al. 2004, chapter 4), the type of colonial power is not to be neglected. While many British colonies did not develop as the USA, Canada, Australia and New Zealand did, it was very difficult to expect that colonial Latin America should have experienced an agrarian revolution when Spain and Portugal did not, and we could not expect a process of industrialization to have taken place in Latin America when the Iberian Peninsula did not take part in the European industrial revolution.

Even worse, the Iberian colonial powers exerted a monopoly in trade and supply of manufactured goods, which weakened the development of such industries and capabilities in the continent. The so-called Pombaline and Bourbon reforms of the late eighteenth century, rather than changing the pattern of colonial production, rationalized and deepened the main features of the traditional pattern. The sources and geographic spread of revenues were diversified, without changing its nature. One outcome of the colonial heritage was the weakness of the local elite, in relation to the crown and the peninsular traders established in the colonies.

Among the many heritages of the colonial rule that were to hinder development, it is possible to count the important spread of slavery in the tropical regions, the persistence of a huge variety of dependent labour relations, particularly in the Indo-American region, and the lack of a real land market, due to the large extensions of land owned by the church, as well as to the legal system ruling land use by the indigenous population. The latter had the right to use the land, but not to own, buy or sell it. The liberal reforms were to wait until the nineteenth century was well advanced.

7.3.3 Independence and State Building

The nature of the national state in Latin America has been a subject of hot debate. As almost everywhere else, the boundaries of the States that emerged after independence were, with some exceptions, not clear. The process of state building lasted at least for about half a century, during which significant civil and international wars were fought. The wars of independence and the collapse of the colonial economy led to the disintegration of productive spaces developed during colonial times, which did not square with the boundaries of the new republics. The weakness of the domestic elites was another side of this same situation: no clear hegemonic forces could lead the construction of the national state; at the time the military forces were a way for upward mobility and one of the most important power factors, but badly prepared for war, and even less for government. The fiscal basis for the construction of the new states was very weak and governments relied to a high extent on a similar tax structure as during colonial times, with the tenth still playing an important role. Most national states were finally consolidated during the export-led boom, thanks to the strengthened economic position of the elites, the access to new military technology and infrastructure (including the telegraph and railways), and the support given by foreign capital and foreign nations to institutional stability. The state, led by powerful and enriched elites, promoted a radical redistribution and concentration of wealth and income, basically derived from natural resources. Given the lack of state capabilities and the mentioned weaknesses of state bureaucracy, the new nations became an easy capture for the elites. This was a feature that was to remain as a structural one, even during the central decades of the twentieth century, when the states developed important capabilities and promoted radical changes of the productive structure and the distribution of power and income. Export-led growth had created some diversification of the productive and social structure. The new sectors were marginalized from the power circles. That is why, here and there, populist movements arose, with varied authoritarian features, which expressed a need to meet the demands of these groups. The new alliances, however, seldom implied radical changes and the traditional elites kept important spheres of power, now shared with other organized groups, as peasants, unions and populist parties.

As state-led growth weakened, either because of domestic or external forces, the wave of structural reforms of neoliberal inspiration that came to prevail during the last decades of the twentieth century, produced a significant reduction of the spheres in which the state was expected to be active, and consequently reduced its capabilities. First at the beginning of the twenty-first century, in the last wave of economic growth that took place together with a predominant shift to the left of the region's governments, the state recovered the initiative in fields such as an active macroeconomic management, industrial and social policy.

In any case, the long-run feature of a weak state is far from being overcome. And this is paradoxical, as one of the most important interpretations of Latin American backwardness, the one that lay behind the neo-liberal structural reforms, was that the Latin American states were too strong and inhibited private initiative in many ways. However, not even during the periods of the most aggressive state-led industrialization was private entrepreneurship denied the hegemonic role in economic activity. Latin American industrialization was clearly market oriented.

7.3.4 *The Pattern of Specialization*

The importance of the pattern of specialization of Latin America has been intensively debated. Latin America was always integrated into the world economy through exports of primary goods. Plundered first, produced later on, the productive system was about controlling the land and the mines and mobilizing, in different forms and with different intensity, labour to produce these goods. Much has been discussed about whether the resources were a blessing or a curse. There is no clear-cut answer to that, and the resources themselves can hardly have been responsible for success or failure. There are always different social and institutional possible outcomes for each technological and natural environment. Those who succeed or perform well are the societies; they are responsible for what is achieved with the help of natural resources.

Natural resources may be a good and inevitable point of departure. However, economic development is about adding value to resources, is about diversification, and about the development of new technologies, products, processes, and forms of social organization.

Many countries succeeded in transforming their economies departing from an important specialization in natural resources. However, all developed economies have succeeded with a process of development that implied different levels of transformation of the productive structure.

Latin America has succeeded only partially with that. Still today a very large part of Latin American exports is concentrated on very few families of products, most of them natural resources. When industrialization made huge progress, it was mainly orientated towards the domestic market and with productivity levels significantly lower than those of competitors in the developed countries. It could be said that the more the natural basis was industrialized, the less competitive the process. Industrial growth had important deficits, both because of the sluggish process of innovation behind them in terms of R&D activities, and because the induced dynamics of exports was lost in inward-looking production. Latin America developed economic structures that were labelled as heterogeneous, as contrary to the relative homogeneity of the productive structure in developed countries. Thus, a few high-tech/high productivity sectors, often linked to the exploitation of natural resources, were to be found lost in an ocean of low productivity activities. When manufacturing activities succeeded in going global, more often than not they were *maquila* industries, where cheap labour assembles high-tech products, whose design and technology-intensive activities were performed somewhere else.

The reasons why Latin America has not been able to break with this long term feature are many and complex. They are related to the different aspects discussed so far: weakness of the state, power of the elites, backward social environment, huge technological gaps with world leaders, ethnic diversity as a basis for social marginalization, very low human capital formation. In spite of all of that, and thanks to the existence of natural resources, Latin Americans have been able to achieve much higher levels of per capita income than the one that should be achieved with the given levels of human capital formation.

These features were counteracted, not always successfully, during state-led growth. The neo-liberal reforms implied a step backwards in that direction. While exports grew very much during the last decades of the twentieth century, the domestic market did not keep pace with that growth, overall performance was bad, and divergence in relation to the world leaders deepened.

7.3.5 *The Link between the Productive Structure and Volatility*

As mentioned, high volatility is an outstanding characteristic of the Latin American economies. There are no signs that volatility has been reduced through time. On the contrary, a slight reduction could be noticed in the central decades of the twentieth century, but it increased later on. Latin American volatility has nothing to do with the level of per capita income, or the speed of economic growth. The main explanation for volatility seems to be the high concentration on exports of a limited variety of goods, which, besides, are themselves subject to strong fluctuations in supply, demand, and prices. The impact of such shifts in the purchasing power of exports is very high. This has been clearly shown as a long-term structural feature by Williamson (2012), among others.

There is a well-known pattern in Latin America, which looks like this. An export boom occurs when demand for certain commodities expands, with the following increases in prices. This boom permeates to different sectors of the domestic economy: state revenues and expenditures, related infrastructural investment, logistics, banking, insurances, trade, and more. More often than not, export booms attract foreign capital, and the wealth of the economy allows governments to receive financial credits for different activities. With some lag, imports start to grow. As the domestic productive structure is competitive in a limited number of sectors, the growth of consumption and investment induces a high income elasticity of demand for imports of goods and services. This process is also fueled by the strengthening of the domestic currency. The cycle starts to change when demand and/or prices diminish, or start to grow more slowly or when the current account starts to show serious imbalances. This process may take many different forms, depending on the macroeconomic policy environment, the international factors affecting financial capital flows, and even the domestic social and political environment. A very common way out from the imbalances is a radical reduction of the level of activity, the devaluation of the domestic currency and a drastic reduction of imports. During the crisis, obviously, capital starts to flow out of the country, mainly in the form of service of external debt. This really stark description of the pattern has been present in Latin America since the late nineteenth century until very recently and has been summarized with the words: 'goodbye Dutch disease, hello balance of payments constraint'. The question is whether it has been possible to tame the cycle more recently.

In short, the concentration of exports in a few families of products subject to strong price and demand fluctuations, the high and related propensity to import as income grows, and the co-evolution of exports and capital inflows constitute an explosive environment with high propensity to high volatility, unless macroeconomic policy devotes important efforts to counteract this pattern. However, while macroeconomic policy may counteract high volatility, industrial policy promoting structural change is the only way out in order to sustainably change the growth trend.

7.3.6 *The Link between the Productive Structure and Inequality*

Why Latin America is the continent with the highest inequality, closely followed in recent times by sub-Saharan Africa, has been a topic of much debate.

The principal pattern followed by Latin America was to combine the access to natural resources with different forms of 'non-economic' mechanisms to subordinate the labour force. With the exception of low density regions to which free labour was attracted, both slave labour and other forms of coercion were applied in the Indo-American regions. The labour market of both kinds of regions tended to converge as the liberal reforms advanced, creating a market for land and spreading wage labour. Nevertheless, the pattern of development remained as one of employment of unskilled labour with very low wages in most parts of the region.

Besides these forms of inequality in what we can define as the more formal export-oriented sector, another source of inequality is the persistence of a wide sector of subsistence agriculture and traditional low productivity services. The transition towards wage labour was completed during the last decades of the nineteenth century, during which an increase in inequality has been documented in these three different ways: within the export-led sector, between the export-led sector and others, and between different regions and countries.

There are different stories about inequality during state-led industrialization. The evidence suggests that inequality was significantly reduced in the Euro-American countries. There, free labour and strong union activities, introduced mainly by immigrants, were combined with a more aggressive industrial and social policy. During a first stage, after World War I, inequality was reduced because of the drop of export prices which affected the high income sector more. Later on, institutional factors played the decisive role. Even during periods in which export prices rocketed, the equilibrium of forces led to a significant redistribution of incomes.

Different situations can be noticed in the large countries, like Mexico and Brazil. In spite of going through important social and structural transformations, the process there can be better approached in terms of the classical Lewis model of economic growth with unlimited supply of labour. There industrialization produced important concentrations of income, and inequality could have increased, even within wage earners, due to the relative power of skilled workers and the elite of the unionized labour movement in the large manufacturing industries. In these countries, the outcome of social and structural change may have been that of a dynamic stability of high inequality levels.

During the period of the so-called 'structural reforms', in the last decades of the twentieth century, inequality increased significantly, due to the reversal of social policy and to the dismantling of industrial policy. In the countries where social transformation had advanced more, military dictatorships were the main instrument for introducing the structural reforms and generating a profound process of regressive redistribution of income.

7.3.7 The Link between the Productive Structure and the Welfare State

The development of the Welfare State (WS) in advanced countries went hand in hand with the changes of the productive structure, with urbanization, with the appearance of new social risks, as well as with the political changes associated with those. Strengthened unions, labour parties, democracy, were the socio-political companions of structural change. The way in which the WS developed in these countries showed many variations, depending on many differentiating features. The Latin American WS has been an incomplete one, partly because of the limited process of structural change underlying it. The Latin American WS, in the best of the cases, was similar to the corporative model according to the well-known typology proposed by Esping-Andersen. Nonetheless, the coverage of these Welfare States was much more limited than in advanced countries and the differences in the quality and extent of the coverage was very radical among the Latin American countries. While the Euro-American countries were those who came closer to the corporative model, in most Afro- and Indo-American countries the welfare policies reached a very small proportion of the population. The important advance of the informal sector during the last decades of the twentieth century, together with the structural reforms, exerted huge pressure on social policy, similar to the one exerted by globalization in developed countries, but with much more dramatic impact, as large parts of the population were very close to the poverty line.

7.3.8 *The Link between the Productive Structure and Regional Integration*

Two important examples of development opposite to the Latin American experience may be considered in this respect: the USA and the European Union.

In the USA the process of independence created a large market which was undoubtedly one of the preconditions for the large-scale industrialization there. To the contrary, the independence process in Latin America created a large number of relatively small republics. The reasons for that are many: geographic obstacles; the limited exchange between regions due to trade controls; constraints on the diversification of the productive structure, even if, by that time, the diversity in natural resources was very important; the role played by the European nations, blocking regional hegemonic powers; the already mentioned weakness of the national states and of the local elites; the lack of adequate technology that could create more incentives for unification, and the strong divide between Portuguese and Hispanic Latin America. Regardless how we weight these factors and how we explain their interrelation, the fact is that Latin America failed to integrate its large domestic market, and this failure became even greater as the patterns of specialization became more and more oriented towards a few export products.

One of the most frustrating aspects of this story is related to the process of state-led growth. Obviously, industrialization could have benefitted from economic integration and the exploitation of economies of scale and different complementarities. The defensive way in which industrial policy started, worked against integration. When the pragmatic first stage of industrialization gave place to a more planned and conceptualized industrialization strategy, the first voices were raised against inward-looking growth. ECLA, the most important think-tank promoting industrialization, warned at early stages about the limits of inward-looking growth and strongly advocated different initiatives for regional integration, which also should have in mind competition in world markets. This was a strategy quite different to the dominant character of industrialization ideas in Latin America.

In spite of that, and in spite of some progress made since the 1960s in the promotion of regional trade and integration, the result so far has been really disappointing. The process of European integration, which led to the European Union, started more or less at the same time as the Latin American efforts. The results do not invite any comparison. In spite of much progress that must be acknowledged, the results are really short-lived and during the last decade of fast growth the general belief is that integration has been a failure.

The process may be tackled from many different approaches, but the one I want to stress is that related to the productive structure. In Europe, structural change preceded integration, it was a pre-condition. A way to avoid war was to find ways in which the European nations could cooperate through the division of labour, rather than compete for markets and natural resources. The strong growth of intra-industrial trade was the result of industrialization. On the contrary, industrialization in Latin America was a defensive reaction to the collapse of the world trade in commodities. While regional integration was a wise recommendation by technicians, the political economy of industrialization in which national states were easily captured by corporate elites, led to the refuge within the walls of each domestic market.

During the process of structural reforms and trade liberalization, regional trade made important progress. Still the share of regional trade in Latin American exports is really low compared to other world regions. During commodity booms, when the market is in Asia, the incentives for home industrial production are low and there is tough competition from Chinese manufactures, regional integration does not have the best environment to make progress, given the lack of leadership within the national States.

7.4 The Recent Expansive Cycle

During the last decade Latin America experienced very high growth rates that, once again, seemed to be promising in the sense that Latin America could finally break with history and set in motion a process of continuous growth and convergence. Moreover, fast growth was combined with other positive and reinforcing phenomena: macroeconomic stability expressed in the reduction of inflation and clear progress in the monitoring of the economic cycle, a new democratic wave that now covered almost all the continent, an important reduction of inequality, a likewise very important reduction of poverty, some progress in the construction of supranational institutions, as the UNASUR. Some particular countries achieved important international recognition, expressed, for example, in Chile and Mexico joining the OECD, and Brazil playing a global role as a member of the BRICS countries.

As many times before, during the expansive phases of the economic cycles that Latin America went through, some kind of euphoria appeared. Governments, and the social groups linked to the successful sprint, tend to construct discourses about how we finally broke with historical trends and how we finally found the road to development. The last time we saw something similar was when, during the 1990s, Argentina discovered stability thanks to the 1=1 exchange rate, privatized a large part of its service sector and opened up the economy. The end of this story was a very deep economic, social, and political crisis, the aftermath of which still fills the front pages of the newspapers in relation to Argentine debt management. In the small neighbouring country, Uruguay, that was growing more modestly but fast, the liberal president liked to congratulate himself and his citizens for being so outstanding. Two years later, Uruguay also entered a deep crisis, and its citizens voted for a leftist government for the first time in the history of the country.

The question is whether we are in a different position right now, and whether, contrary to previous experiences, the lessons have been learned and we really could lay the basis for sustainable and stable growth and catching-up.

No doubt, many lessons have been learned. In terms of industrial policy, the dark 1980s and 1990s are behind. Almost all countries have tried to reconstruct capabilities; the systemic approach to innovation has been more widely adopted (leaving behind both the linear model that assumed that everything started with science and ended in innovation, as well as the demand-driven model without sectorial selectivity).

The results of these policies cannot be viewed in the short run. Precisely as we are now seeing how many industries created during the period of State-led growth are successful enterprises that have been transformed into multinational businesses (the so-called *multilatinas*), entrepreneurial capabilities that were fostered during this recent period may flourish in the years to come.

I will concentrate on a few indicators that show a less optimistic view of recent achievements.

An important debate arose during the last decades on whether commodity prices had gone into a new historical phase characterized by strong constraints on the availability of raw materials and foodstuffs, due both to the exhaustion of oil and its substitution by renewable sources of energy linked to agrarian production and to the increase in the living standards of large sections of the world population, particularly in Asia. The sceptical view about this new price trend emphasizes that there were many speculative forces behind the later price rise. Besides, it is argued, if demand is expanding, some low elasticity of supply may give place to a price rise in the short run, but if prices remain high, technological change, the exploitation of new reserves and the expansion of the frontier should give place to a downward adjustment of prices in the medium and long run. This has been the story of capitalism so far, and nothing is telling us that the rate of technical change will diminish. On the contrary, the limits to output growth tend to be more institutional than technological, and with high prices, incentives to change are likely to prevail.

According to many observers, the wave of rising prices is gone. The last year has shown a sudden shift in the trend and a sharp decline in prices. Of course, a new change in the trend does not have to be discarded. In any case, what is once again clearly shown is that commodity prices are highly volatile, and planning the future relying on the price levels during the booms is not recommended.

The downward trend in commodity prices does not necessarily have to be expressed in worsened terms of trade. In the case of commodity exporters that are not oil producers, the terms of trade may not change that much with varying commodity prices, but the export sector will suffer the price fall, because its demand for oil is not necessarily high.

While it is very difficult to predict the future development of prices, it is nonetheless difficult to believe that commodity prices will show the same trend in the future as in the last decade.

Commodity prices really are an important force behind the growth of the last decades. These prices created rents clearly above productivity growth. It is possible to say that Latin America experienced some kind of price-driven, rather than a productivity-driven growth.

According to many different measures, productivity growth in Latin America was quite modest in the last decade. According to these measures, Latin America not only did not catch-up, but continued to fall behind the USA, while other countries, like China and Korea (even if from very different levels) reduced the productivity gap with the USA.

Another important aspect is whether Latin America was able to go through a process of structural change that could prove that a new basis was laid for future development.

The well-known typology of Lall (2000) has been the object of many criticisms, because it assumes that the agricultural sector is a low technology one. Obviously, this is not always true. In order to study structural change, other measures have been developed. Departing from the idea that you become what you export and that rich countries export products that only rich countries export, and that poor countries specialize in products that only poor countries export, an index is produced to check whether there has been some change in the index and in the ranking (Hausmann, Hwang and Rodrik, 2005; Hausmann and Klinger, 2006). Using data provided by Bértola, Isabella and Saavedra (2014), between 1997–9 and 2009–11, the Latin American countries fell on average from 57th to 59th place. That means that the position is a bad one, and that there was no catching up in spite of fast growth.

Another way to approach the problem is to use the Reflex Method (Hausmann and Hidalgo, 2009), which measures how diverse the export basket of each country is, and how exclusive this country is in exporting this product. The index also takes into consideration whether exports are directed to countries which rank high in these two respects. Again, with data provided by Bértola, Isabella and Saavedra (2014), we learn that on average the Latin American countries fell from 61st to 64th, among 98 countries.

Finally, a method called successive steps (Isabella 2012) is used, combining the space product approach and a sophistication of exports index. Using data from the same source as previously, we learn that the fall was, on average, from 66th to 68th position.

A special case is that of Mexico. This is the country that ranks best in all these indices, due to the important role of its manufacturing industry and the much less important role played by the exports of commodities. Nevertheless, it is often noticed that the *maquila* industry is specialized in high-tech products, but the activities developed in Mexico are not the ones that add more value in the productive process. The Global Value Chains approach is powerful in order to detect these problems. In any case, Mexico does not escape the general trends, and its position was worsened or remained stable during this period. Mexico's comparative advantage has been the access to cheap labour rather than its good performance in developing competitive advantage.

7.5 Conclusions: How does the Future Look?

To find a path of development and convergence is not a matter of luck or something that happens within a short period of time. The several and complex forces that have inhibited all the Latin American countries from joining the club of developed countries, will not be overcome suddenly.

The comparatively limited development of Latin America has many overlapping and interacting explanatory factors. The relative development of pre-Colombian societies; the pattern of development established by colonial powers that were marginal in the profound transformation that led to the Industrial Revolution and the Great Divergence; the very heterogeneous ethnic composition of the Latin American society, which was a vehicle for segregation, exploitation and inequality; the weakness of the local elites and of the national states, together with very low capital formation; the scarcely diversified economic structure, which left Latin America exposed to large swings in demand and prices the impact of which was particularly powerful because of the very concentrated structures of exports in a few products and a few markets. In spite of strengthened states, institutional learning, human capital accumulation, capital inflows, technology transfers, opportunities for trade, and many other positive forces for development, the outcome has been disappointing and Latin America, as a whole, has not been able to catch up with world leaders.

During the last decade different factors combined to result in a process of relatively fast growth and some convergence. Nevertheless, the gap between Latin America and the world leaders, both in terms of per capita income and productivity, is still too large.

Some of the factors that contributed to this catching-up were the result of a process of learning and accumulation of capabilities: improved human development, recovery of some State capabilities, more mature and stable political systems, a better institutional environment for investment, macroeconomic stability, stronger interaction with foreign investment, and a better understanding of the role played by technical change, innovation and investment in research and development. In some sectors, new entrepreneurship has been quite successful, giving place to multinational enterprises of Latin American origin.

The good outcomes were, however, also the result of particularly favourable external conditions, increasing commodity prices and strong capital inflows, an important share of which took the form of Foreign Direct Investment, especially for the exploitation of natural resources and the sectors of infrastructure and services linked to them. The important rents of the natural resources created by the high international prices, stimulated new investment and an important productivity growth in some sectors.

The prospects for the future are not as bright as during the last decade. Commodity prices are receding, the growth of demand has been slowing down, the Latin American countries did not go through any significant change of their productive structures, and in spite of the favourable conditions, no catching-up in productivity was achieved. While the links between Latin America and commodity importers were significantly strengthened, regional integration made less progress. The Latin American market may still play an important role in terms of demand for a more diversified production, if commodity exports show low dynamics, but progress in regional integration was far more limited than the progress made, for instance, in the European Union.

The most likely development for Latin America in the next decade is not that of a deep crisis like the ones experienced before. What we can instead expect is a transition to a slow growth trend which will not make it possible to converge, even conditionally, to the levels of the world leaders.

References

Bértola, L. and J.A. Ocampo, 2012. *The Economic Development of Latin America since Independence*, Oxford: Oxford University Press.

Bértola, L., F. Isabella, and C. Saavedra, 2014. *El ciclo económico en Uruguay, 1998–2012. Serie Estudios y Perspectivas, Oficina de CEPAL de Montevideo*, Santiago de Chile.

Bértola, L. and P. Gerchunoff, 2011. Dos Siglos de Transformación Productiva y Social en América Hispana. Santiago de Chile: CEPAL.

De Ferranti, D., G. Perry, F. Ferreira, and M. Walton, (eds.), 2004. *Inequality in Latin America and the Caribbean: Breaking with History?* Washington DC: World Bank.

Diamond, J., 2005. *Guns, Germs, and Steel: The Fates of Human Societies*, London: W.W: Norton & Company Inc.

ECLAC 2014. *Social Panorama of Latin America*, Santiago de Chile.

Gelman, J., 2011. 'Senderos que se bifurcan. Las economías de América Latina luego de las Independencias'. In *Institucionalidad y desarrollo económico en América Latina* edited by Bértola, L. and P. Gerchunoff. CEPAL

Hausmann, R. and Hidalgo, C., 2009. 'The building blocks of economic complexity'. *Center for International Development*, Harvard Kennedy School, Harvard University, Cambridge.

Hausmann, R. and Klinger, B., 2006. *Structural Transformation and Patterns of Comparative Advantage in the Product Space, Center for International Development Working Paper,* 128, Harvard University.

Hausmann, R., J. Hwang, Rodrik, D, 2005. *What you Export Matters* Center for International Development Working Paper, 123, Harvard University.

Isabella, F., 2012. *'Senderos Productivos para el Cambio Estructural; Una propuesta para evaluar caminos de transformación productiva y su aplicación a Uruguay'.* Magister Thesis in Economics, Facultad de Ciencias Económicas y de Administración, Universidad de la República.

Lall, S., 2000. *The technological structure and performance of developing country manufactures exports, 1985–1998*, Queen Elizabeth House; Working Paper Series, 44, Oxford University.

OCDE/United Nations/CAF, 2014. *Latin American Economic Outlook 2015. Education, Skills and Innovation for Development.*

Williamson, J.G., 2012. 'Commodity Prices over Two Centuries: Trends, Volatility, and Impact'. *Annual Review of Resource Economics* vol. 4, number 6 pp. 1–22.

8

Economic Backwardness and Catching up

Brazilian Agriculture, 1964–2014

Lee Alston and Bernardo Mueller

> What can be derived from a historical review is a strong sense for the
> *significance of the native elements* in the industrialization of backward
> countries.
>
> —Alexander Gerschenkron ([1962] 1965: 26; emphasis added)

8.1 Introduction

In the nineteenth century and through much of the twentieth, modernization
or economic development was equated with industrialization. Gerschenkron,
one of the titans of economic history, assessed the industrialization of France,
Germany, and Russia in a comparative fashion. He does not dispute the role of
industrialization in catching up with economies that had already industrialized, but he was ahead of his time by noting the contextual nature of development. France, Germany, and Russia all industrialized in different ways. It
seems almost part of human nature to presume that there is a template for
economic development. The notions of 'leading sectors', 'Import Substitution', and the 'Washington Consensus' have all had their day in the sun.

Industrialization seemed a likely candidate for imitation because it was technology that could be reverse engineered and backward countries could borrow
from the already industrialized world and leap forward.[1] Gerschenkron notes
that countries that industrialized did so rapidly, but they needed certain

---

[1] We hear the same argument invoked about China today.

prerequisites. First, industrialization needs to be financed. In France and Germany, banks played a role, though in Germany banks were more directly involved with the industries that they financed rather than simply lending. In contrast, in Russia, banking in the late nineteenth century was primitive, so the state played a big role by directly or indirectly taxing its citizens to finance rapid industrialization. All three countries industrialized, though only France and Germany fully developed.[2] Gerschenkron was ahead of his time in recognizing that to industrialize (or modernize), countries had to have the right ideology of entrepreneurship, whether state or privately led:

> To break through the barriers of stagnation in a backward country, to ignite the imaginations of men to place their energies in the service of economic development a stronger medicine is needed than the promise of a better allocation of resources. . . . Or the prospect of profits. What is needed to remove the mountains of routine and prejudice is faith—faith, . . . that the golden age lies not behind but ahead of mankind.   (Gerschenkron [1962] 1965: 24)

Gerschenkron's argument presages the pathbreaking work of Joel Mokyr (2009), who argued that it was the internalization in Britain of the enlightenment ideals that man could change nature that led to Britain being the first to industrialize. Similarly, Deirdre McCloskey (2006, 2010) maintains that the ideas are paramount to institutions for development. For McCloskey, the idea that work had dignity allowed Britain to be the first to industrialize. Beliefs form an umbrella over the dominant network in society when they choose which institutions to put in place to achieve desired economic or political outcomes. This is the underlying premise of Alston et al. (forthcoming). Of course, desired outcomes do not always mean economic or political development. Many in the dominant network of power prefer the status quo because of the rents that they derive.

The notion that industrialization is still a sufficient condition has been abandoned for a more nuanced view that institutions matter.[3] Some still come close to presuming that there is an institutional template.[4] To say that institutions matter does not give much insight into just which institutions mattered, where, and how. In addition, institutions cannot be transplanted, as Gerschenkron well understood.

---

[2] At the time of Gerschenkron's writing, the West vastly overestimated the GDP of the Soviet Union and its satellites.

[3] If industrialization was sufficient, Brazil would have begun its developmental trajectory in the 1930s when the state supported industry and unions.

[4] See, for example, Acemoglu and Robinson (2012), who come close with the notion that societies cannot be extractive to develop, but rather need to be inclusive. We agree, but there are many shades of inclusiveness and hence not a recipe.

8.2 Fitness Landscapes as a Heuristic to Understand Economic Development

In this section, we explore fitness landscapes as a different way of looking at Gerschenkron's approach to economic backwardness. Fitness landscapes are a useful heuristic for understanding development as a search process. A backward country that seeks to develop must choose a set of institutions that it believes will provide the rules and constraints on economic, political, and social life that will, in turn, induce the desired outcomes.[5] But there is an extremely large variety of institutions that can be put in place, and considerable uncertainty as to the effect that each specific set will yield. That is, the country knows what results it wants to achieve and knows the set of possible institutions, but it does not have full information on the mapping from one to the other. The country can look at the example of other countries, but that will only partially help, as each country's experience is, to a large extent, idiosyncratic. So inevitably, each nation has to induce the relationship it expects to exist between institutions and outcomes, that is, it forms and relies on beliefs of how the world works. Fitness landscapes provide a useful way to portray and analyze the process of forming beliefs and searching through a large design space of institutions for appropriate development strategies for backward countries.[6]

Assume that a set of institutions can be described as a series of N dimensions, each related to a specific characteristic of the institutions. These dimensions could be things like economic inclusion, political inclusion, role of state vs. market, rate of time preference, role of religion, the individual vs. the collective, social capital and trust, globalization vs. inwardness, racial discrimination, attitude toward the environment, and so on. In order to simplify, consider that each dimension can be either present or absent (e.g., the institutions are either inclusive or extractive) so that a specific set of institutions can be described as a string of N zeros or ones. There are thus 2^N different combinations of possible institutions from which a country can choose. As N becomes larger, the number of possibilities grows very fast; with $N=10$ there are 1,024 combinations. If the dimensions were more finely gradated instead of being binary, the number of combinations would equal A^N (where A is the number of values the dimension can take), which could easily reach an astronomical number of possible institutions. The process of searching for combinations that promote good results, that is, the search for a development

---

[5] We use institutions rather than proximate conditions of development familiar at Gerschenkron's time of writing (e.g., industrialization or financial intermediation).

[6] Fitness landscapes (or adaptive landscapes) were originally devised by Sewall Wright (1932) in order to provide a visual method to understand how evolution searches for fit genotype design. Kauffman (1993, 1995) extended and gave more rigour to the treatment of fitness landscapes.

strategy, is therefore not a trivial task. A country cannot simply try every combination and choose that which works best. On the other hand, it is not totally blind, as there are the examples of other countries as well as theory and logic, which can serve as guides. The process of development can therefore be conceptualized as a search strategy that can be analyzed using the heuristic of fitness landscapes.

In order to construct a fitness landscape, it is first necessary to create the design space of all possible institutions, which arrays along a plane the possible combinations of institutions. To do this, start out with a given configuration of institutions, that is, a N-dimensional bit-string of zeros and ones, and place surrounding it each one-bit mutation that flips a single 1 to a 0 (or vice versa). The resulting plane (the design space) contains every possible combination of institutions.[7] For each element in the plane, we can then plot the fitness of those institutions on the third (vertical) axis. In the case of biology, the fitness of a genotype is clear. It represents the ability of that design to replicate in the given environment.[8] Designs with higher fitness will thus tend to dominate over time in the population. For institutions and other social substrates, the notion of fitness is not as direct. Fitness still involves the notion that the specific design is able to perpetuate itself in the future, but it is easier to think of this as being the case because that design is achieving the desired and expected outcomes and so is not being radically changed by that society. In this perspective, the height of the landscape represents the success of that specific development strategy. Because the bit-strings are arrayed alongside other very similar bit-strings, they will not usually have very different levels of fitness, so the resulting landscapes will tend to be relatively smooth, though, as we shall see, this may not always be the case.

Figure 8.1 shows three different classes of fitness landscapes. Panel A shows a smooth (Mount Fuji) landscape where there is a single superior development strategy. In these circumstances, it is relatively easy to find the best solution as simple search strategies, such as a hill-climbing algorithm, will easily reach the best design. The rugged landscape in panel B presents a more difficult challenge, as there are many local optima where a hill-climbing strategy might get stuck. Furthermore, if the landscape is large, it is difficult to even know which is the best design, as there are too many peaks to compare. In panel C, there is

---

[7] There are some mathematical limitations of this approach as it seeks to plot multiple dimensions into a low dimension space, but it is useful because it facilitates visualization. A more rigorous approach uses Boolean hypercubes (see Kauffman 1993). For more discussion on this point and a different approach, see McCandlish (2011).

[8] Note that it is the phenotype—the actual rendered design—that reproduces or fails to do so. Nevertheless, it is ultimately the genotype, that is, the set of instructions on how to design the phenotype, that is being evolved.

A. Smooth landscape

B. Rugged landscape

C. Random landscape

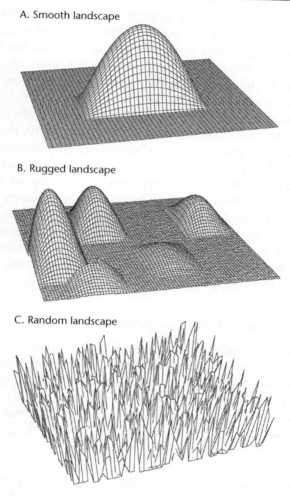

Figure 8.1 Smooth, rugged, and random fitness landscapes.
Source: Figures produced by the authors using QtiPlot.

no relation between the fitness of neighbouring designs, so the landscape is essentially random and even more difficult to search.

What determines the shape of a given landscape is the degree to which there are interrelationships among the different dimensions, that is, complementarities and substitutability among, say, the economic and political inclusion.[9] If the dimensions are all independent, then the search process can tune each

---

[9] In genetics, these interrelationships are called epistatic links between the individual genes. They exist when, for example, the fitness contribution of a gene for beak length affects the fitness contribution of the gene for wing shape.

dimension without setting back optimal designs already found for other dimensions, and the result is a smooth landscape. Furthermore, the single peak will exhibit high levels of fitness because there are few limiting constraints. But, if every single dimension is connected to every other dimension, then every minute change in design has repercussions on every other dimension leading to a random landscape. Because there are so many internal constraints, there is not only an unwieldy number of peaks but they reach only relatively low levels of fitness. If, on the other hand, there are only a moderate number of interconnected dimensions, the landscape will be rugged, with more than one peak, but not a chaotic configuration. In this scenario, a simple hill-climbing search process risks getting trapped on suboptimal solutions, even when there are better designs nearby. A search process based on variation, selection, and replication—that is, Darwinian evolution—turns out to be particularly well-suited for searching rugged landscapes. The variation that takes place due to recombination or mutation allows for experimentation of non-contiguous designs, thus permitting jumps across nearby valleys to other potentially higher peaks.

8.2.1 *Coevolution and Dancing Landscapes*

Besides the internal configuration of each design, its fitness level also depends on the design of other entities that inhabit the same environment, competing or cooperating for resources. Thus, the fitness of a given design of a frog is contingent on the designs of its predators, preys, symbionts, and parasites. When a variation gives a fly better wings, the fitness of that frog's current design goes down. This means the frog's landscape has shifted. Coevolution thus causes linked landscapes to dance over time, which means that the search process is never over, but rather requires constant adaptation. In this sense, the ability to constantly adapt to changing circumstances is more important than the actual current design.

For a country's institutions, the level of fitness is linked to changes in physical and social technologies as well as the institutions adopted by competing and cooperating countries. When a new disruptive technology emerges, or when a competing country becomes fitter, the current institutions of a given country lose fitness, causing the landscape to dance.

When landscapes dance, there is a perpetual need for adaption to new circumstances. In smooth landscapes, this adaptation is difficult because when the single peak recedes and pops up unexpectedly elsewhere, the new optimal design may be far away, and by the time it is reached the landscape will have danced again. Thus, the average level of fitness will be low over time. In random landscapes, the dancing involves the (already low fitness) spikes thrusting up and down chaotically, making it impossible to adapt. Once again, the average level of fitness over time is low, half the time you are on a low peak and the other half in an even lower trough. In rugged landscapes, however, when the peak you are on recedes, a new different peak is bound to pop up relatively nearby, allowing the design to adapt reasonably quickly to the dancing landscape. Even if it does not adapt to the global optimum, the average level of fitness over time will be relatively high, as you spend much time on or near reasonably high peaks. Because rugged landscapes maintain higher levels of fitness than smooth or random landscapes, it is believed that most coevolutionary processes tend to evolve toward this type of configuration, that is, an evolution of evolution (Kauffman 1995). We therefore assume, when applying these concepts to economic development, that in this substrate too, rugged landscapes best represent the problem faced by developmental strategies.

8.2.2 *Economic Backwardness and Stages of Growth as Fitness Landscapes*

From the above, a fitness landscape can be viewed as portraying the problem that a country faces in choosing the institutions that will constrain and shape its development. Let us see how these concepts can give us a different way to understand Gerschenkron's approach to economic backwardness.[10] Although institutions change incrementally all the time, this takes place under a stable set of beliefs of how the world works. While the outcomes match the beliefs, there will not be much pressure for change. But often the beliefs are not good descriptions of how things really work, and outcomes will eventually deviate from what is expected. When this happens, there will be a window of opportunity or a critical juncture where elites, beliefs, and institutions may be replaced (see Alston et al. forthcoming for a detailed description of these relationships). It is at this point, when new beliefs are emerging, that the landscapes are most useful as an analytical device.

The new dominant coalition is faced with the immense plane of possible institutional designs and must choose a single specific set that it deems most conducive to its desired objectives. It does not view the landscape that contains the information on the fitness of each design. The actual landscape is invisible to them. Also, there are too many possibilities to go by trial and error, so they cannot reveal the actual landscape by experimentation. They therefore

[10] Fitness landscapes have had a deep impact in the study of evolutionary biology. Nevertheless, there is wide disagreement on how useful they actually are. It is very common to see fitness landscapes referred to as a 'metaphor' and the debate then centres on how useful or misleading is the metaphor (see, e.g., Pigliucci 2012 and Skipper and Dietrich 2012 for different sides in the debate). McCloskey 1991 argues at length that the strength of Gerschenkron's approach was the recognition that social theories are metaphors, that is, 'tales constrained by facts'. So even if one chooses to see fitness landscapes as metaphors, they can nevertheless provide a different way to understand Gerschenkron's approach.

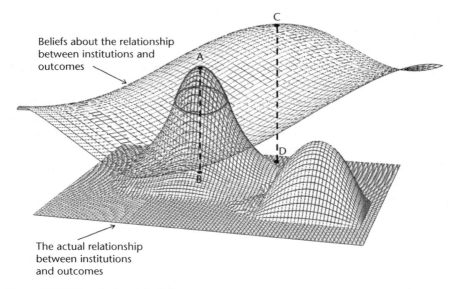

Beliefs about the relationship
between institutions and
outcomes

The actual relationship
between institutions
and outcomes

Figure 8.2 The actual and beliefs.
Source: Figures produced by the authors using QtiPlot.

have to conjure up a notion, an estimate, a guess, of what would be the consequence of each combination they might consider. This is what we are calling a 'belief'. They use their own past experience, that of other countries, theory, instinct, and any other means at their disposal to create a mental map of the fitness of each possible set of institutions. Thus, although they do not see the actual landscape, they see a landscape informed by their beliefs.

An example of the problem of choosing institutions in terms of fitness landscapes is given in Figure 8.2.

The actual relationship between institutions and outcomes is the lower landscape with two humps. This tells us that the best course of action would be to choose institutions represented by point *B*, which would yield the highest level of fitness possible in this environment, that is, *AB*. But the actual relationship is not observed, and the country has to rely on its beliefs, which are represented by the higher plane. As drawn, these beliefs are quite far from the actual, they are not really a good guide for a development strategy. Based on these beliefs, institutions at point *D* will be chosen, with an expectation of outcomes corresponding to *CD*. But the actual fitness will be much lower than expected. This distance between the expected and the actual will eventually emerge in the form of poor outcomes along several measures, bringing with it disappointment and frustration, inducing a new window of opportunity for change, though it might take some time for the society to admit its beliefs are mistaken.

Let us now use these concepts to characterize Gerschenkron's theory of economic backwardness. This theory is often contrasted with Rostow's *The Stages of Economic Growth* (1960), which postulates that economic modernization follows a series of universal predefined stages. As noted by McCloskey (1991), Gerschenkron was going against a much more unified and prevalent view:

> Gerschenkron's chief scientific accomplishment was to undermine the metaphor of social stages which had dominated nineteenth-century and much twentieth-century thought. Henry Maine, Auguste Comte, Friedrich List, Karl Marx, Werner Sombart, Bruno Hildebrand, and lately Walt Rostow, thought of a nation as a person, with predictable stages of development from birth to maturity. If the stage theorists viewed the child as the father of the man, Gerschenkron was a new Freud, noting the pathologies arising from retarded growth. (McCloskey 1991: 95)

Similarly, Fenoaltea (2014) stresses the contraposition between views of development that expect a single universal path versus another where development can take many different and unexpected paths:

> The analysis developed by Alexander Gerschenkron is less widely known, but far richer than Rostow's one-dimensional scheme. To Gerschenkron's mind the most interesting aspect of the industrialization of backward countries is that it does not await the fullness of time: the take-off (or 'great spurt' as he prefers to call it) begins even before all the canonical prerequisites are in place, thanks to innovative solutions that create *substitutes* for the missing prerequisites.
> (Fenoaltea 2014: 9)

This contrast is illustrated in Figure 8.3.

The top panel portrays a world where there is a clear single set of institutions that best induces development.[11] It is a view of the world beset by universal propositions. This was a powerful view in the mid-twentieth century because most developed countries at that time could, at least weakly, have their development trajectories portrayed as having followed a similar path. But Gerschenkron, looking at the problem faced by backward countries in a world where the pioneers had already developed, realized that there were actually several different contextual paths with different consequences depending on which prerequisites were present or absent. That is:

> In this area the first conclusion that Gerschenkron arrived at was that Marx's generalization—that 'the industrially more developed country presents to the less developed country a picture of the latter's future'—was only partially true,

---

[11] Both the Stages of Economic Growth and the Economic Backwardness theories overwhelmingly discuss development as being affected by policies and not in terms of institutions. We adapt the discussion to fit the current consensus that institutions are the fundamental determinants of the policies, which have a more proximate effect.

and possibly trivially so. What was more relevant for him was that most often, the industrialization process in a backward country was substantially different—not just in terms of speed, but also in nature—from that in an advanced country. This obviously meant that countries that were different—in terms of the degree of their backwardness—would also be characterized by different processes of industrialization. (Chandrasekhar 2005: 182)

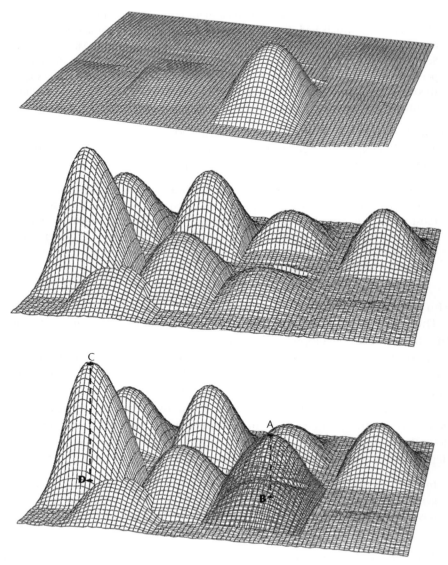

Figure 8.3 Stages of economic growth vs. economic backwardness.
Source: Figures produced by the authors using QtiPlot.

Such a world is portrayed in terms of fitness landscapes in the middle panel of Figure 8.3. It is important to bear in mind that each country faces its own individual landscape that depends on its own specific circumstance, that is, there are few, if any, universal propositions. At the very least, the fact that backward countries have templates to learn from (or to be misled by) already assures that their context is different from that of the pioneer countries that had no such guides. But also, there are many different development strategies that yield relatively high fitness. Because of the rugged nature of the landscape, there is a risk of being trapped in relatively low local peaks. Furthermore, the actual landscape is not observed, so it is not the case of simply tweaking the institutions until you reach the highest peak. Instead, a country will often be faced with disappointing and unexpected results, and it may not be obvious how to set things right.

One way or another, the country will have to form beliefs of what the landscape looks like and use those as a guide to pursue better outcomes. A natural strategy is to follow Rostow's notion of universal stages and presume that the development problem that is being faced is similar to that faced by the countries that have already successfully developed. In the lower panel in Figure 8.3, the backward country is facing the unobserved rugged landscape from the middle panel and has formed beliefs based on the perceived experience of the developed countries in the upper panel. These beliefs induce the choice of institutions at point B and create an expectation of fitness commensurate with AB, which will not be realized. The best development strategy would have been institutions at point D, which would induce a fitness level of CD. Thus, a country can go through an endless series of development strategies never reaching the desired outcomes, which seems to be a good description of the trajectory of a large number of countries in the past centuries.

Besides the empirical evidence of multiple paths to development that the world has witnessed since the time of Gerschenkron and Rostow, the mathematical structure of landscapes also indicates that development is best portrayed as a hard problem with many competing solutions, rather than one with a clear winning path. Any reasonable definition of the dimensions that make up a country's institutions is bound to have many interrelationships among those dimensions. Institutions composed of perfectly orthogonal dimensions would not be very realistic. Since the number of interrelationships mathematically determines the ruggedness of the fitness surface, this implies that development is probably best characterized as a search along a rugged landscape, as in the middle panel of Figure 8.3, instead of the single-peaked landscape of the upper figure.

Development is an even harder problem than this. As noted earlier, due to coevolution with technologies and other countries, the landscape actually changes over time, with tectonic shifts making what were good solutions in the past no longer fit for the backward countries of the present. Although we do not explore this issue here, this propensity for shifting landscapes probably means that more so than specific development strategies, what is most important is the capability to adapt to the ever-changing problems that are thrown in a country's way. For example, the lack of authoritarian governments among currently developed countries may be an indication that the higher ability of democracies to adapt is a crucial characteristic of a successful development strategy.

8.2.3 *The Hiding Hand Principle—That Which does not Destroy Me, Makes Me Stronger*

A related use of fitness landscapes is to illustrate the Hiding Hand Principle. Although this was put forward by Albert Hirschman and not by Alexander Gerschenkron, the idea is highly compatible with the theory of economic backwardness. Gerschenkron and Hirschman had a long and intertwined relationship.[12] Malcolm Gladwell recently described Hirschman's Hiding Hand Principle as follows:

> People don't seek out challenges. They are "apt to take on and plunge into new tasks because of the erroneously presumed *absence* of a challenge—because the task looks easier and more manageable than it will turn out to be." This was the Hiding Hand principle—a play on Adam Smith's Invisible Hand. The entrepreneur takes risks but does not see himself as a risk-taker, because he operates under the useful delusion that what he's attempting is not risky. Then, trapped in mid-mountain, people discover the truth—and, because it is too late to turn back, they're forced to finish the job.   (Gladwell 2013; original emphasis)

Note that when Gladwell uses the term 'trapped mid-mountain', it conjures up the image of fitness landscapes, which we will use below to illustrate Hirschman's idea.

Cass Sunstein (2014), in a preface to a new edition of Hirschman's 1967 *Development Projects Observed*, discusses the two reasons that Hirschman offers to explain why planners are so prone to underestimating obstacles and

---

[12] For an outstanding biography of Hirschman, see Adelman (2013), upon whom we draw. Hirschman's first position in the United States in 1941 was under a Rockefeller Fellowship working on a project on trade regulation headed by Professors Condriffe and Ellis at the University of California, Berkeley. Gerschenkron was also hired to work on the project, and he and Hirschman shared an office. After Pearl Harbor, the fellowships ran out. A hiatus between the two followed, but coincidentally, Professor Ellis (who was now at the Federal Reserve Board) hired Gerschenkron, who quickly rose up the ranks to become head of the international section. Following Hirschman's return from the war in Europe, Gerschenkron hired Hirschman and they became colleagues again. They parted ways in 1948, when Harvard hired Gerschenkron. Over the next decade and a half, they corresponded on their overlapping work. In 1964, Gerschenkron was the force behind Harvard hiring Hirschman. Ten years later, Gerschenkron was instrumental once again by championing Hirschman for a position at the Institute for Advanced Studies at Princeton.

challenges. Both of these explanations are directly relevant to the discussion above about Gerschenkron's approach of economic backwardness.

He calls the first the "pseudo-imitation" technique, which means that planners pretend, or think, "that a project is nothing but a straightforward application of a well-known technique that has been successfully used elsewhere." The devastating problem, of course, is that situations and circumstances are different, so a project that is sold as if it were pure imitation usually has a large component of "indigenous initiative and execution".   (Sunstein 2014)

This is a near-perfect restatement of Gerschenkron's critique of viewing development as composed of universal propositions.

The second explanation given by Sunstein for why planners are so often deluded is that:

planners dismiss previous efforts as piecemeal, and portray their own effort as a comprehensive program. With this technique, policymakers give, and are given, the illusion "that the 'experts' have already found all the answers", and all that is needed is faithful implementation. Those who enlist the pseudo-comprehensive-program technique end up underplaying the need for "imagination, insight, and the application of creative energies", thus covering up "the ignorance of the experts about the real cure of the malady they have been summoned to examine".

(Sunstein 2014)

Here again, the notion of development strategies requiring only 'faithful implementation', rather than creativity and imagination to make the most of unexpected opportunities to deal with unexpected problems, is reminiscent of Gerschenkron's critique.

Figure 8.4 illustrates how Hirschman's Hiding Hand Principle can be conceptualized through fitness landscapes.

The upper panel shows a country's belief regarding the fitness of different institutions as a developmental strategy. Possibly the country is following the example of other countries that have already been successful with the strategy indicated by point A, and, as drawn, it believes that is basically the only way forward. The expectation is that this will induce outcomes with a high fitness level equal to AB. But things do not really turn out as expected by those beliefs, and the actual outcome is a fitness of only AC. This is an inferior outcome that undermines the previously held beliefs; things turn out not to work as the overly optimistic planners expected. But now that the country is already at point A and with the information gleaned from failure, the country may sometimes find itself in an unexpected vantage point to adopt a different developmental strategy that it had not perceived before. Being at A has revealed the true landscape (or new beliefs closer to the true landscape), as portrayed in the lower panel of Figure 8.4. The old mistaken belief is superimposed on the new, more accurate belief. From its failure the country can, with

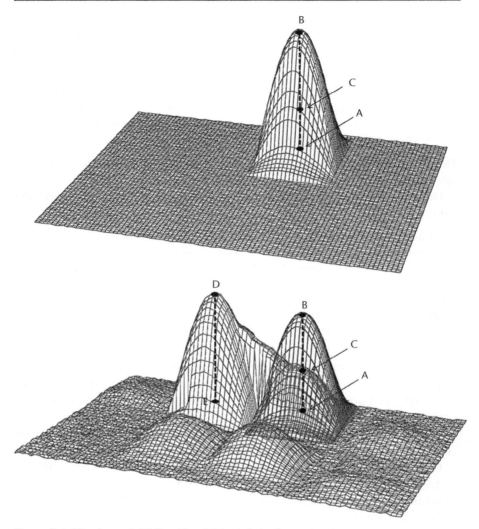

Figure 8.4 Hirschman's Hiding Hand Principle in fitness landscapes.
Source: Figures produced by the authors using QtiPlot.

newfound creativity and imagination, find the ridge that allows a transition from its low-level current peak to a new development strategy at *E*, that might be even better than what they had initially expected at *A*, that is, it may be that $DE > AB$.[13] Hirschman suggests that in many cases, had the country not made the mistake, it would not have achieved those good outcomes.

---

[13] These ridges are common in biological examples of evolution. They allow an evolution of the genotype from one peak to a more distant peak without going into the perilous regions of low fitness, which might lead to extinction before reaching the second peak.

8.3 From the Abstract to the Concrete: Brazilian Agriculture; Backward to Cutting Edge

The fitness landscapes illustrated the difficulty with development strategies. But we can learn a great deal from case studies chronicling success cases. Over time, we may be able to develop some generalizations. In this section, we analyze the remarkable transformation of agriculture in Brazil, which could be characterized as backward in the 1960s to today's characterization of a world agricultural powerhouse.

By any standards, Brazil in 2014 was a global agricultural powerhouse, both in terms of absolute production as well as recent changes in productivity. Figure 8.5 shows the evolution of production, input use, and total factor productivity (TFP) for Brazilian agriculture since 1975.

In three and a half decades, production increased fourfold using the same amount of land and slightly less labour. This impressive result was achieved by the growth of total factor productivity spurred mostly by agricultural research. Figure 8.6 compares the change in agricultural productivity in Brazil with the United States and with the average value for Europe, Asia, Africa, and Latin America.

The comparison shows that the improvements in Brazil were in fact quite exceptional (although it must be taken into account that some countries, such

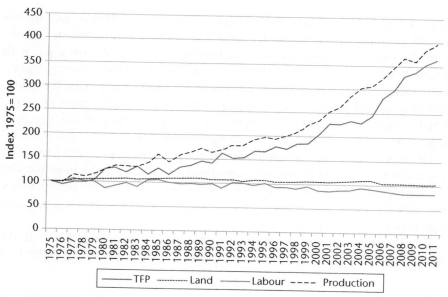

Figure 8.5 The evolution of production, land, labour, and TFP in Brazilian agriculture. *Source:* Data from Gasques et al. (2012).

195

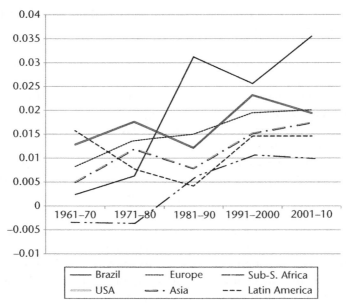

Figure 8.6 The evolution of TFP across countries.

Source: Compiled with data from USDA—Economic Research Service: International Agricultural Productivity. <http://www.ers.usda.gov/data-products/international-agricultural-productivity. aspx#.UsVs67SzSJQ>.

as the United States, already had higher levels at the start of the series and thus would naturally find it harder to achieve additional improvements). In the past decades only China has achieved levels of TFP growth on a par with Brazil. But importantly, Brazil still has, more than any other country, significant areas of unused or degraded land in which to expand production (without counting the Amazon), as well as a favourable endowment of water. Finally, Figure 8.7 shows how Brazil's rank in production of the ten most important crops and livestock has changed from 1970 to 2012.[14]

The first thing to note is that Brazil was already a major producer of most of the major products. Still, over four decades, it increased its rank in all but two (coffee remained first and rice fell one notch). Because all other countries were also simultaneously striving to increase their production, improving the rankings is not a trivial accomplishment.

How did they achieve this? It was certainly not preordained or planned. We assess Brazil's rise in agricultural development using Gerschenkron's criteria of

[14] The list of the world's ten highest value products in 2012 was taken from <http://en. wikipedia.org/wiki/List_of_most_valuable_crops_and_livestock_products>.

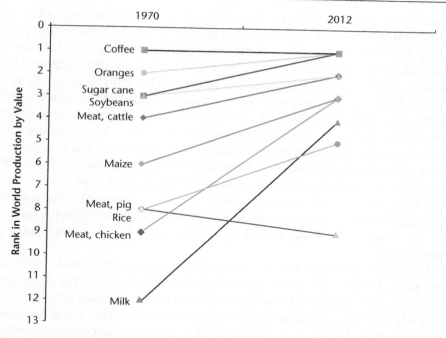

Figure 8.7 Brazil's rank in 1970 and 2012 as a producer of the top-ten most valuable crops and livestock products of 2012.
Source: FAOSTAT (<http://faostat.fao.org>).

the necessary supporting conditions for industrialization: financial intermediation, the role of the state, and ideology (beliefs). Gerschenkron suggested that if backward countries have these supporting conditions, industrialization would be rapid. We agree that for rapid growth in agriculture you need these conditions, but they are not sufficient. In addition to entrepreneurship at the farm level, you also need the right set of beliefs in the government to establish institutions that will generate modernization in agriculture. Furthermore, agricultural techniques cannot be reversed, engineered, or transplanted from other advanced agricultural areas (e.g., the United States or Europe). Productivity for agriculture is location specific. Soils, climate, precipitation, topography, and temperature, inter alia, matter. We will come back to this point under the role of the state.

8.3.1 *The Military Years: 1964–1984*

We treat the twenty years of military rule as one period because throughout this time, the military could rule by decree. A belief in 'developmentalism' shaped the policies of the military government throughout their reign. By developmentalism, we mean state-led growth driven by technocratic planning. The military also held to the strategy in the preceding period of Import Substitution Industrialization (ISI). As a result, the industrialists supported the military regime as long as it produced growth. What did this mean for agriculture? Overall, the belief system had a negative impact at the farm level for promoting entrepreneurship. The government relied on agriculture to generate foreign exchange, especially from coffee and sugar. An overvalued currency was part of the strategy, which was a tax on agriculture. The government provided sufficient subsidized credit in the 1970s to ensure that Brazil was self-sufficient in foodstuff while also earning dear foreign exchange. Over time, it did establish a set of minimum prices to ensure continued expansion in production on the extensive margin, which were the savannahs in the middle of the country. This also served as a safety valve for an ever-expanding population.

Within the set of developmentalist beliefs, the government had a conflicting set of beliefs that overall negatively affected agriculture. The dominant network in the technocratic military regime believed that rural elites were an obstacle to progress because land brought status and the elite was impervious to technological change in agriculture but instead wished to be viewed as *Coronels*.[15] The belief that farmers were immune to economics was part of the reasoning behind the military land reform based on forceful expropriations. Land reform per se was at odds with the developmentalist belief, but the military believed it was necessary because this was the only way to modernize agriculture. Also at odds with the military mentality was its support of rural unions, but only those that supported the military regime.

The dominant network in the military regime also believed that the United States and the rest of the world wanted to take away the Amazon. This belief prompted much of the disastrous colonization and subsidies to promote occupation of the Amazon. Though the Amazon was far away from the rest of settled Brazil, the military falsely thought that they could control the process, but it turned out incredibly harder and more complex than expected. They started colonization of small farmers, mostly from the southeast of Brazil. Most of the projects turned out to be non-profitable in the short run because of the lack of infrastructure and distance from markets. When the colonization strategy failed, Brazil turned to subsidies to large firms. In the 1970s, the military turned to subsidizing large-scale cattle ranching in the

---

[15] The belief was sufficiently strong, even among academics, that it led to a debate as to whether farmers responded to prices or were motivated by power in semi-feudal fashion. A classic paper in the 1960s (Pastore 1968) showed that farmers do respond to prices so that taxes and incentives could be used in agricultural policy.

Amazon with tax credits. The result was a mixture of some settlement, along with 'phantom' ranches just to receive the tax credits. Landless peasants subsequently initiated land invasions and land conflict, which would dampen the motivation to invest in modernizing agriculture. As such, productivity in agriculture remained flat, and expansion was only on the extensive margin.

On the plus side, the military regime supplied abundant credit at subsidized rates to the rural sector through the National System of Rural Credit. It aimed at promoting modern inputs (e.g., fertilizers, pesticides, and insecticides). Credit supply soared from US$6.2 billion in 1970 to US$12.8 billion in 1973 to a maximum of US$26.8 billion in 1979. Throughout the 1970s, credit came at negative rates of interest from a low of –1.4 per cent (1973) to a high of –37.7 per cent (1980). The credit boom expanded output and hectares cultivated considerably, but overall productivity remained flat.

Throughout the military regime, they relied on minimum prices, but in a haphazard fashion. The goal of minimum prices was twofold: promote production and promote settlement, especially of the *Cerrado*, the semi-tropical savannahs. Minimum prices achieved their goals, but they did not promote productivity. Much of the output ended up in government inventories, especially the output in frontier areas that were too far from markets.

Overall, because everyone knew that the military's priority was industrialization, it did not release entrepreneurial zeal among the potential agribusiness community. In terms of Gerschenkron's three conditions—financial intermediation, state support, and ideology—the military provided enough finance, but agribusiness felt constrained because of the limited opportunities under the umbrella of ISI. Agribusiness also felt threatened by rural unions and the uptick in land conflict and expropriations. On the plus side, the military laid the groundwork for future productivity increases through the initiation of EMBRAPA, a decentralized research organization. In its early years, EMBRAPA appeared more a political boondoggle than a coordinated research strategy. But later, it developed collaborations with universities, much like the USDA. But it would take years before EMBRAPA paid technological dividends.

Overall, the twenty years of the military regime sent an erratic set of signals to the farmers. Despite the mixed set of signals, the supply of credit and the establishment of minimum prices persuaded a small but increasingly important agribusiness sector that money could be made in agriculture. Significant non-subsidized investment by agribusiness awaited a more consistent set of policies along with a stable macroeconomic environment.

8.3.2 *Reopening to Democracy and Social Inclusion: 1985–1994*

Unlike most military regimes, Brazil's planned its exit from governing society. Opening up proceeded in stages, with first elections at the state and local level followed by an indirect election for president in 1984. Tancredo Neves won the election amid incredible popular support. Tragically, Tancredo died before assuming office. His death shocked society, and brought uncertainty to the future of Brazil in part because the vice president, Jose Sarney, had been allied with the former military regime.

After the repressive years of military government, society yearned for and demanded inclusion. Sarney had no choice but to become more inclusive. As an early signal of inclusion, illiterates were given the right to vote simply because the dominant network felt that it was the right thing to do. During the first ten years of redemocratization, the dominant network was large—every interest group had a seat at the table. Rather than forming a coherent economic plan, including agricultural policy, the first order of business was a new constitution formed in 1988. The process was long and protracted, but importantly codified the belief in social inclusion. The constitution was highly aspirational in that it sought reform and redistribution as part and parcel of its *raison d'être*.

As a result of: the dominant network being large; no leadership among the dominant leaders; and an overarching societal desire for inclusion, every interest group received something. Businesses initially retained high tariff barriers. Rural workers would receive the same benefits as urban workers. Unions gained increasing recognition and labour law favoured labour over business. The nascent rising agribusiness sector retained minimum prices and credit, though this was relatively short-lived and as in the military years, policies were erratic. On the downside for agriculture was a new emphasis on land reform. The constitution stated that land should be put into beneficial use, and, if not, the government could expropriate it. This led to an increased incentive for land invasions, which forced the government to act and expropriate in order to limit violence.[16] The overall impact of social inclusion without a budget constraint was mounting inflation. By the late 1980s until 1993, inflation roared ahead at more than 1,000 per cent per annum.

What was the impact on agricultural entrepreneurs and agribusiness? Not as bad as one might have expected. This suggests that agriculture had begun to modernize, though the percentage of farms in the modern sector was small. As is generally the case, there is a large stasis in most government policies because interest groups lobby to retain benefits. For agriculture, this meant that credit continued to be available, though now through different channels, and minimum prices were retained for part of the period. With hyperinflation roaring,

---

[16] See Alston, Libecap, and Mueller (2013) for a discussion of land conflict generated by misguided federal policies. See Alston and Mueller (2013) for a discussion of the negative impact of land reform on tenancy and crop choices.

the government attempted several plans to quell inflation, but each plan failed because of a lack of commitment and leadership to weather the storm. The main obstacle inhibiting the modernization of agriculture in the late 1980s and early 1990s was uncertainty over prices and policies. Uncertainty over policies, particularly inflation, causes investments to fall. Political scandal added to uncertainty. In 1990 and 1991, markets reacted favourably to the election of Fernando Collor, the first directly-elected president since redemocratization. Collor embarked on a series of liberal policies that favoured markets that would favour agriculture. But Collor resigned in 1992 rather than be impeached. Itamar Franco, as vice president, took over, but uncertainty remained. Throughout the first ten years of democracy, the agricultural sector was poised to expand because market forces increasingly mattered, but the macroeconomic and political instability caused would-be investors to wait out the storm.

8.3.3 *Fiscally Sustainable Social Inclusion: 1994–2014*

Brazil finally tamed hyperinflation with the *Plano Real* in 1993. Given the numerous plans to stop inflation, the expectations were low for the success of the *Plano Real*. It was largely the brainchild of a group of US-trained economists brought into policy by the Finance Minister Fernando Henrique Cardoso. The beauty of the plan was twofold: the nuts and bolts; and the messenger. The economists understood technically how to reduce inflation, and Cardoso understood the importance of transparency. In the *Plano Real*, there were no surprises and it succeeded faster than anticipated. From the success of the *Plano Real*, Cardoso ran for president and succeeded. He brought two of the architects of the *Plano Real* on board: Pedro Malan as finance minister, and Gustavo Franco as head of the Central Bank.

The taming of inflation was a punctuated change for Brazil, but it alone would not have been sufficient to modernize Brazilian agriculture or Brazil at large. Under the leadership of Cardoso, Brazil adopted a new belief in the importance of fiscal and monetary orthodoxy wedded to social inclusion— together fiscally sound social inclusion. It took time for Cardoso to convince the dominant network of the importance of sustaining macroeconomic stability, but it took hold with his re-election and was cemented with the election of Lula, who continued to maintain the same beliefs system. After her recent close contest to gain re-election, Dilma has also reaffirmed the belief in fiscally sound social inclusion.

Why is the new belief important for the modernization of agriculture? A stable macroeconomic climate is a necessary condition to prompt long-term investments. Agriculture is no exception. Though land can and was used as a hedge against inflation, entrepreneurs prefer clear and stable policies to better assess investment prospects. Government subsidies for agriculture declined, but the government policies toward exports became more favourable and Brazil became a more open economy.

Two other factors importantly aided the modernization of Brazilian agriculture: research and high commodity prices. Agricultural productivity is site-specific, and EMBRAPA transformed itself from a sleepy bureaucracy under the military government and early years of the opening-up into a dynamic collaborative research institute. EMBRAPA can best be thought of as a focal node of a research network tying together research at universities and other research entities tied to farming on the ground. The dividends in research productivity really paid off around 2000. Sustained high commodity prices over the first decade of the twenty-first century further fueled modernization. Both domestic and foreign direct investment flooded into agriculture. Though commodity prices have fallen, Brazil is now an infra-marginal producer so that while profits may be lower, they are sufficient to reward the modern sector of Brazilian agriculture.

Modernization has started, but it has a long way to go. More than 50 per cent of Brazilian agriculture comes from less than 1 per cent of the farms. What is holding back the sector? Agricultural land reform still hampers investment. With the credible threat of an expropriation, frequently the result of a violent land conflict, many farmers do not rent to would-be productive tenants but instead turn land into a less productive use (e.g., pasture). Not only do deaths result but many would-be tenants remain landless. This is particularly harmful to career advancement because agricultural tenancy has been shown to be a step on the way to ownership (Alston and Ferrie 2005). The increase in the landless also leads some would-be tenants to migrate to the Amazon, turning to subsistence agriculture (an extremely low-valued use of land). Migration and subsistence farming also lead to increased deforestation—not an intended outcome of land reform.

Alston and Mueller (2013) show that not only is tenancy too low but land reform policies alter crop mix. The aggregate effects on the amount of hectares in non-optimal use are very large, the size of small countries (e.g., Greece or Portugal). Given that both landowners and the majority of landless peasants would win from a more sensible land reform (e.g., subsidized mortgages), what are the impediments to change? We conjecture that the urban electorate, who favours redistribution of agricultural land and increased ownership by peasants, is unaware of the link between land reform and the unintended consequences of land conflicts, reduced tenancy, inefficient farm sizes, and inefficient crop mixes. Politicians respond to votes. Moreover, many politicians too are likely unaware of the consequences of extant land reform policies.

8.4 Back to Gerschenkron

Did being backward enable Brazilian agriculture to modernize faster? Of course, if you are backward, the only way is up. Also, what does faster mean? Mueller and Mueller (2014) date early modernization with the military regime. In this case, it took 36 years for modernization to begin. If we date it from Cardoso, the speed was quite rapid—six years. The slowness can be attributed to the wrong set of beliefs (ideology) held by the dominant network for many years of the impact of institutions on outcomes.

The belief during the military regime in developmentalism led to agricultural policies where the role for agriculture was a means to help industrialization and later to fight inflation. From the mid-1980s, under the new belief umbrella of social inclusion, agriculture should be used to achieve social justice. Under both periods, land reform was seen as the key ingredient for agricultural policy but with different rationales. Only with the belief of socially sound fiscal inclusion from the mid-1990s onward did policymakers begin to interfere less with agriculture. This was the beginning of the boom. With hyperinflation tamed and policy stability, private investment took off in some regions. Yet, the modernization reached only a very small part of Brazilian agriculture, in terms of hectares or farms. In addition, though the military established EMBRAPA in the early 1970s, it did not function properly until around 2000. High commodity prices also added fuel to the speed of modernization once it had been set in motion.

The important insight to retain from Gerschenkron and Hirschman is the role of beliefs and absence of template for development. In Gerschenkron's mind, it was the belief of the entrepreneurial spirit that drives development. This matters, as shown by the robust agribusiness in Brazil. Gerschenkron neglected to stress the importance of macro policy stability that sets the incentives for the private sector to invest. For Hirschman, the key message for development is adaptability and the readiness to abandon failure. Brazil experimented with agricultural policy and still continues to do so. They appear to have followed the text of Hirschman's message with lags, but it was not experimentation *ex-ante* but rather by default.

References

Acemoglu, D. and J.A. Robinson, 2012. *Why Nations Fail: The Origins of Power, Prosperity, and Poverty*. New York: Random House.

Adelman, J., 2013. *Worldly Philosopher*. Princeton, NJ: Princeton University Press.

Alston, L. J., and J. Ferrie, 2005. 'Time on the Ladder: Career Mobility in Agriculture, 1890–1938'. *Journal of Economic History* vol. 65 number 4:1058–81.

Alston, L.J., G. Libecap, and B. Mueller, 2013. *Interest Groups, Information Manipulation in the Media, and Public Policy: The Case of the Landless Peasants Movement in Brazil.* NBER Working Paper No. 15865, March.

Alston, L.J., M. Melo, B. Mueller, and C. Pereira, Forthcoming 2015. *Beliefs, Leadership, and Critical Transitions: Brazil, 1964–2014.* Princeton, NJ: Princeton University Press.

Alston, L.J., and B. Mueller, 2013. *Tenancy, Conflict and Priests in Brazil.* Working Paper, January, University of Colorado. NBER Working Paper No. 15771 (June).

Chandrasekhar, C.P., 2005. 'Alexander Gerschenkron and Late Industrialization'. In *The Pioneers of Development Economics: Great Economists on Development*, edited by K.S. Jomo. New Delhi: Tulika Books.

Fenoaltea, S., 2014. *The Reinterpretation of Italian Economic History.* Cambridge, MA: Cambridge University Press.

Gasques, J., E.T. Bastos, C. Valdes, and M. Bacchi, 2012. 'Total Factor Productivity in Brazilian Agriculture'. In *Productivity Growth in Agriculture: An International Perspective*, edited by O. F. Keith, S.L. Wang, and E. Ball. Oxfordshire, UK: CAB International.

Gerschenkron, A., [1962] 1965. *Economic Backwardness in Historical Perspective: A Book of Essays.* New York: F. Praeger.

Gladwell, M., 2013. 'The Gift of Doubt: Albert O. Hirschman and the Power of Failure'. *The New Yorker*, Books, June 24.

Hirschman, Albert O. 1967. *Development Projects Observed.* Washington, DC: Brookings Institution Press.

Kauffman, S., 1993. *The Origins of Order: Self-Organization and Selection in Evolution.* New York: Oxford University Press.

Kauffman, S., 1995. *At Home in the Universe.* New York: Oxford University Press.

McCandlish, D.M., 2011. 'Visualizing Fitness Landscapes'. *Evolution* vol. 65 number 6:1544–58.

McCloskey, D., 1991. 'Kinks, Tools, Spurts, and Substitutes: Gerschenkron's Rhetoric of Relative Backwardness'. In *Patterns of European Industrialization: The Nineteenth Century*, edited by Richard Sylla and Gianni Toniolo. London: Routledge.

McCloskey, D., 2006. *Bourgeois Virtues: Ethics for an Age of Commerce.* Vol. 1 of 4 on 'The Bourgeois Era.' Chicago, IL: University of Chicago Press.

McCloskey, D., 2010. *Bourgeois Dignity: Why Economics Can't Explain the Modern World.* Vol. 2 of 4 on 'The Bourgeois Era.' Chicago, IL: University of Chicago Press.

Mokyr, J., 2009. *The Enlightened Economy: An Economic History of Britain, 1700–1850.* New Haven, CT: Yale University Press.

Mueller, B., and C. Mueller, 2014.*The Economics of the Brazilian Model of Agricultural Development. International Research Initiative on Brazil and Africa (IRIBA).* IRIBA Working Paper 01. Manchester, UK: University of Manchester.

Pastore, A.C., 1968. 'A Resposta da Produção aos Preços no Brasil.' Boletim 55, FCEA-USP.

Pigliucci, M., 2012. 'Landscapes, Surfaces, and Morphospaces? What are They Good For?' In *The Adaptive Landscape in Evolutionary Biology*, edited by E. Svensson and R. Calsbeek. New York: Oxford University Press.

Rostow, W., 1960. *The Stages of Economic Growth.* New York: Cambridge University Press.

Skipper, R.A., and M.R. Dietrich. 2012. 'Sewall Wright's Adaptive Landscape? Philosophical Reflections on Heuristic Value'. In *The Adaptive Landscape in Evolutionary Biology*, edited by E. Svensson and R. Calsbeek. New York: Oxford University Press.

Sunstein, C., 2014. 'Albert Hirschman's Hiding Hand'. Foreword to a reissued edition of Albert Hirschman's *Development Projects Observed*. Washington, DC: Brookings Institution Press.

Wright, S., 1932. 'The Roles of Mutation, Inbreeding, Crossbreeding, and Selection in Evolution.' In *Proceedings of the Sixth International Congress of Genetics*, vol. I, edited by Donald F. Jones, 356–66. Ithaca.

9

Is Africa Too Late for 'Late Development'? Gerschenkron South of the Sahara

Gareth Austin

9.1 Introduction

Alexander Gerschenkron's fundamental insight was the concept of 'late development', or (as Alice Amsden put it, more precisely) 'late industrialization', albeit without using either term himself (Gerschenkron 1962; Amsden 1992). He was not the first to notice the existence of late-comer advantages (Van der Linden 2012: 561–2). But he was perhaps the first to consider systematically how the industrialization of even one country altered the circumstances affecting possible future industrializations elsewhere: not only by creating a competitive challenge and, on the other hand, the opportunity to borrow industrial technology, but also by changing the incentives to rulers. The military risks of not industrializing were frightening for empires facing the possible loss of great-power status (Russia) or even independence (Japan) in the late nineteenth century. The general conclusion of Gerschenkron's work was that the process of industrialization—its motors, form and timing—would be different in late-comers. The policy implication was that late-comers did not need to wait until they had spontaneously accumulated all the prerequisites for *ab initio* industrialization; nor could they afford to do so. Rather, they could and should find 'substitutes' for any missing prerequisites. Elaborating his approach, Gerschenkron (1962) coined the term 'relative backwardness', as the key to a framework for analysing later industrializations as calibrated deviations from the requirements of spontaneous industrialization.

Those requirements included, for instance, 'an expanded' market for manufactures based 'on the rising productivity of agricultural labor' (Gerschenkron 1962: 354). The more a country lacked such requirements, the greater was its need to 'substitute' for them in the course of a deliberate industrialization. A key aspect of this was that, the more backward the economy, the more likely it was that its industrialization would 'proceed under some organized direction', to supply more 'capital to the nascent industries' and 'provide them with less decentralized and better informed entrepreneurial guidance' (Gerschenkron 1962: 44, 354). Further, the greater the extent of deviations from a spontaneous industrialization, the greater the likelihood that the organizational substitute for the market as the coordinator of industrialization would be, not a group of private actors (cartelistic investment banks, in his interpretation of the German case) but, rather, the state (Gerschenkron 1962).

Defining late industrialization simply as industrialization with borrowed technology, Amsden sought to adjust Gerschenkron's insight to the twentieth century. As the spread of industrialization proceeded, the technological gap between the industrialized countries and the rest had become bigger, and was now increasingly protected by the construction of an international law of intellectual property (Amsden 1992). She enlarged on the guiding role of the state in late industrialization, which required 'getting prices wrong' (Amsden 1989; also Wade 1990).

Gerschenkron did not try to apply his analysis beyond Europe, because it was outside his own comparative advantage (Gerschenkron 1962: 7n). Amsden, following her influential study of 'late industrialization' in South Korea (Amsden 1989), went on to present arguments that appeared to leave little prospect of Africa joining the otherwise growing industrial and developmental catch-up club. Specifically, she maintained that the possibilities for successful 'substitution' were limited to countries which, while 'relatively backward' in Gerschenkron's terms, were so only up to a point. In Amsden's view, countries that lacked relatively high levels of education, and therefore 'human capital', would be unable to take-off industrially in a world in which the advantage of cheap labour had been neutralized by a combination of labour-saving technology and segmented labour markets, the latter allowing rich countries to exploit pools of cheap (typically immigrant) labour within their own economies (Amsden 1992, 2001). There is also an argument that African industrialists are much too late to be able to exploit labour in the harsh ways open to earlier industrializers—with unions repressed, voting rights restricted or absent, and no sick pay or overtime, let alone pensions (O. F. Onoge in 1974).[1] What happened for a time during the industrializations of Britain, Germany and the USA, and indeed in segregationist and

---

[1] O. F. Onoge, 'The indigenisation decree and economic independence: another piece of bourgeois utopianism', in Nigerian Economic Society, *Nigeria's Indigenisation Policy: Proceedings of the November 1974 Symposium* (Ibadan, n.d.), quoted in Iliffe 1983: 85.

apartheid South Africa (Trapido 1971), may now be unacceptable to consumers and lenders from some of those same countries, and to African electorates. Meanwhile, recent national-accounting work in comparative economic history has shown that countries that develop manufacturing sectors have generally experienced faster growth in manufacturing output than the early industrializers: Agustín Bénétrix, Kevin O'Rourke and Jeffrey Williamson (2014) report 'unconditional convergence' of followers on leaders since the 1870s. But this has yet to be replicated south of the Sahara (Austin, Frankema and Jerven 2014). Even with the recent economic GDP growth, averaging about 2 per cent per year since 1995, there has been no industrial breakthrough. According to World Bank data, the percentage share of manufacturing value-added in GDP actually declined in sub-Saharan Africa from 17.6 in 1990 to 15.0 in 2000, 12.5 in 2010 and 10.0 in 2013.[2]

This essay asks whether Africa is too late to catch up the existing industrialized countries: whether because, as Amsden might have said, it lacks the conditions necessary to adopt and use borrowed technology to its full potential; or because, to use Gerschenkron's terminology with more explicit pessimism than he did, the 'substitutions' that African countries can now make for missing prerequisites of spontaneous industrialization are insufficient for catching up the industrialized countries when the technological gap seems so wide and apparently so unfavourable for bridging by the means available in Africa.

The discussion that follows is organized in five sections. The first, 9.2, draws attention to some of the other historical perspectives on the dynamics of contemporary developing economies, besides the Gerschenkronian tradition. Particularly important among these is the notion of very long-term paths of technical and institutional choice, responding to—and gradually changing— particular kinds of factor endowments. Section 9.3 is devoted to clarifying the problem, in that I argue that African 'late development' does indeed require industrialization, at least of several of the larger African economies. Section 9.4 outlines the main path of economic development pursued in Africa during *c*.1500–*c*.1900, which, for most of the continent, was the last four centuries before colonization. I describe this path as 'land-extensive', and seek to specify the major reasons, economic *and* political-economic, why it was unlikely to lead to industrialization. Section 9.5 considers the colonial and post-colonial periods, focussing on the eventual, if so far incomplete and continuing, transition towards land scarcity and, in response, to a path of development that is more intensive in labour, capital, and human capital terms. The conclusion,

---

[2] <http://www.tradingeconomics.com/sub-saharan-africa/manufacturing-value-added-percent-of-gdp-wb-data.html>, accessed 6 September 2015.

Section 9.6, reflects on the possibilities for 'substitution' strategies and practices in the pursuit of 'late development' over the next generation.

9.2 Long-term 'Paths' and Other Historical Perspectives

The historical perspectives pertinent to the analysis of contemporary late-development are not limited to substitution and the state, important as they are. Three other issues seem to me particularly pertinent.[3] One is the role of institutions, the rules surrounding economic activity, which in recent decades have received particular emphasis within the rational-choice tradition (cf. North 1990). Because this has received huge attention in relation to economic development on a global scale, and because I have expressed elsewhere some major reservations about aspects of rational-choice institutionalism in economic history (Austin 2008b; following a mixed verdict in Austin 2005), I will keep the present discussion of this very important perspective brief. There is a very influential argument that the kind of rules about political power and individual property rights which obtain in the richest of the industrialized countries today are optimal for the economic development of the rest of the world. Not only are such views strongly put in the academy (Acemoglu, Johnson and Robinson 2001, 2002; Acemoglu and Johnson 2012), they are also frequently (if, understandably, more crudely) stated when politicians in rich democracies speak on world development. Briefly, in my view, this confuses process and (frequent, though not inevitable) outcome. Democracy as it is understood today (based on one person one vote and freedom of speech and protest) has simply not been the norm during industrializations to date (Trapido 1971; Chang 2002). Again, that secure private property rights is essential for economic take-off is contradicted by the experience of the USSR and, more recently, China (Clarke, Murrell, and Whiting 2008).

The second issue is the lessons, if any, to be learned for 'late development' in Asia, Africa, and Latin America from the experience of 'catch-up growth' within the 'First World'. This discussion is not about initial industrial take-off, as had either happened or was well under way in most of western Europe and in North America and Japan by the late nineteenth century. Rather, it is about the jockeying among the club of leading industrial countries since then, focussing on how the USA, after overtaking the UK by the World War I, established a very strong lead in total factor productivity (TFP), and how far,

---

[3] My approach is from economic history. For an important assessment from economic sociology, bearing particularly on the first two issues identified here, see Schrank 2015.

when, and why, countries in western Europe—as well as Japan—eroded that lead after the World War II. This debate has produced ideas pertinent to the rest of the world, such as the notion of 'technological congruence', denoting the extent to which a particular technology fits both the supply and demand sides of the economic context in which it is introduced (Abramovitz and David 1996). Historians of industrialized economies have also provided growth economists with much to inspire them concerning models of endogenous economic growth, especially those which seek directly to explain growth in TFP, rather than subsuming it under increased investment, whether narrow (physical capital) or broad (including human capital) (Crafts 1997). This is useful for the analysis of how late-developing economies sustain, or fail to sustain, economic expansion from 'extensive' growth (based on increased factor inputs) to 'intensive' growth (based on rising TFP). But it is not so relevant to the problem of how an economy takes off in the first place, in a world in which others have already done so, creating a context in which take-off requires adoption and adaptation, but not necessarily invention.

The third issue is factor endowments, and especially human reactions to them. Recently, Kaoru Sugihara (2003, 2007, 2013) has developed a framework for analysing the dynamics of economic development that differs fundamentally from Gerschenkron and Amsden. Rather than seeing the British Industrial Revolution as the original pattern from which later industrializations deviate, Sugihara distinguished different 'paths' of long-term development, each defined by a distinctive factor-bias in choices of technique and institution, and followed as far as possible before and during industrialization. Thus, whereas British industrialization was part of a 'capital-intensive path', Japan industrialized within a 'labour-intensive path'. Whereas Gerschenkron thought late-industrialization more capital-intensive than early-industrialization, in Meiji Japan the textile industry responded to the comparatively high cost of capital and low cost of labour by opting for second-hand machines, with wooden rather than metal frames, and worked twenty-four hours a day (Sugihara 2003, 2007). Compared to (or alongside) the 'late development' tradition initiated by Gerschenkron, Sugihara's 'paths' framework has the attractions for historians of taking a longer view, of recognizing the polycentric character of global economic history before the nineteenth century, and of highlighting the distinctiveness of technical and institutional responses in different societies to relatively persistent differences in resource endowments: a pattern of dynamic difference that formed the context in which they faced the political threat and the total challenge (economic, technical, social, cultural) of the beginning of industrialization elsewhere.[4] Africa, however, did not fit either

---

[4] I discuss Sugihara's 'paths' thesis, in the light of further work by himself and others, in Austin 2013b.

of Sugihara's original two paths, 'capital-intensive' and 'labour-intensive': not only was and is it short of capital, but historically it has been short of labour in relation to land (Hopkins 1973, Austin 2008a). But the 'plural paths' framework is flexible enough to accommodate a 'land-extensive' path (Austin 2013a, b) which, as we will see later, is much more congruent with African history.

9.3 The Place of Manufacturing in African 'Late Development'

Despite the generally disappointing contribution of manufacturing to Africa's economic expansion over the last twenty years, it seems inconceivable that Africa can catch up the OECD members in average living standards without major growth in this sector, including the industrialization of at least some of the larger African countries. The spatial distribution of manufacturing is often very uneven within a region, which may reflect specialization by comparative advantage. Conversely, the lack of such specialization within Africa to date is itself a major symptom of 'under-development'. The United Nations Economic Commission for Africa states that intra-African trade is already 'dominated by industrial products', but notes that such trade is still only ten to twelve per cent of the trade of the African continent (UNECA 2013: 46). Again, the need to turn commodity-based growth into what policy-makers currently call 'structural transformation', notably including manufacturing, is not only because of the familiar observations that productivity tends to be higher in manufacturing than in agriculture, that mineral deposits are finite, and that demand for beverage crops is not very elastic.

Africa needs more manufacturing also—paradoxical as this may seem—because of environmental constraints on extraction and agriculture. These are multiple. If the major fossil-fuel-using world regions eventually act to mitigate climate change, the market for oil and gas will be reduced and part of Africa's potential fossil-fuel exports would almost certainly remain underground. More fundamentally, Africa needs a 'Green Revolution', but the reason why (with a few exceptions) it has not happened already is partly because many soils in Sub-Saharan Africa are either low in fertility or fertile but easily eroded (Vanlauwe et al. 2002, especially Mokwunye and Bationo 2002: 209–11; Breman 2012). Agriculture is necessarily water-intensive, and high-yielding varieties of seed are even more so. Africa is the most arid of the continents, and with the Intergovernmental Panel on Climate Change forecasting greater aridity for Africa in future (IPCC 2014), this is a major problem, making it all the more doubtful that Africa's future comparative advantage lies in agriculture, some countries probably excepted. Desalination is fossil-fuel intensive; as are chemical fertilisers, and more experimentation and additional investments in the soils are needed before fertilisers become as effective in Africa as they have been in some other areas (Breman 2012; further, Vanlauwe et al. 2002).[5] Services will play a part, but largely as a function of the growth of manufacturing. For example, without such growth, Africa—in the same time zones as London and Frankfurt—is literally not well placed to export financial services, though Johannesburg and younger financial centres in Africa may be expected to increase their share of the African market(s). In this context, ironically but not perversely, there is a stronger case for more manufacturing south of the Sahara, especially if it takes advantage of the region's existing—and warming—environment to power it in large part by solar energy. Moreover, with Africa's historic share in greenhouse gas emissions having been relatively tiny, its governments can justly argue that it is the responsibility of the existing industrialized countries to make a little space for the late-comers. So, while individual countries may join the club of 'developed' economies without industrializing, a general African catch-up will surely involve—and require—the industrialization of enough countries within the region to provide a motor for the rest.

Given the pessimism of Amsden and others, however, the question is whether such an ambition is even remotely realistic: is the technological gap between the current industrial leaders and the poorest region on earth now too great to be closed, do political conditions internationally and domestically fatally inhibit the required 'substitutions' anyway, and does Africa have sufficient late-comer or other advantages to give it a real chance? The starting-point for any plausible answer must be an examination of why there has not been an industrial revolution in Africa already, and whether economic and political circumstances have been changing in ways that make an African 'late industrialization' more or less feasible.

9.4 The 'Land-extensive' Path of Development in Late Pre-colonial Africa, c.1500–c.1890

The speed and extent to which African countries could participate in the global spread of industrialization since the late eighteenth century depended on both economic and political conditions. In Gerschenkronian terms, their economic situations would determine the extent and form of 'substitutions' for the 'prerequisites' of spontaneous industrialization that would be needed for 'late industrialization'; while political, and political economic, conditions would greatly affect the capacity and willingness of the state to do whatever was necessary to bring the substitutions about. Vast and varied as Africa is, certain generalizations may be made, with appropriate qualifications.

---

[5] I discuss this in historical context, and in more detail, in Austin forthcoming, 2016b.

Until the twentieth century, at least, at any given time most of the continent south of the Sahara was relatively short of labour as well as capital, at least in agriculture (as of 1800, the kingdom of Abyssinia—northern Ethiopia—was the biggest exception). However, land abundance did not mean resource wealth. Many of the mineral deposits that have contributed to export growth in recent decades were not valuable until markets for them were created by inventions during industrialization elsewhere: from rubber tyres to mobile phones. Transport costs were high because of the relative rarity of navigable rivers and the prevalence, in the forests and much of the savannahs of tropical Africa, of sleeping sickness, whose principal economic effect was to kill large animals, thereby preventing their use in transport or farming over wide areas. Exploitation of the land surplus was further constrained by other features of the environment, such as soils that were often infertile and, where fertile, thin and easily leached; and extreme seasonality in the distribution of rainfall, which in many areas precluded productive use of the land during the heart of the dry season. In this setting, agricultural methods were aimed at maximizing returns to labour rather than yield per hectare. Land-extensiveness was the characteristic approach both in arable and pastoral economies: in the former, extended forms of land rotation plus avoidance of clear felling; in the latter, transhumance. Over centuries, despite local histories of irrigation, terracing and ploughing where necessary or possible, the main source of higher productivity and improved food security was the selective adoption of new crops and crop varieties, from Asia and (from the sixteenth century onwards) the Americas. Some of these adoptions also permitted more efficient use of the dry season, where they could be used to extend the agricultural year, via irrigation or in harvesting. Otherwise, the opportunity cost of dry season labour was often very low, with the paradoxical effect—in an otherwise labour-scarce region—of facilitating low labour-productivity activities such as narrow-loom weaving (by choice) as well as head-loading (by necessity) (Austin 2008a).

Considering the incentives to self-sufficiency presented by land abundance and high transport costs, responsiveness to market incentives was remarkably high, notably in early modern West Africa (Hopkins 1973; Austin 2012). There a major component of imports from the Atlantic trade was currency materials such as cowries. As Joseph Inikori has pointed out, these were not accepted back by European merchants, so it must be assumed that they were imported to lubricate intra-African trade (Inikori 2007). The gradual adoption of cowries plus (for high-value exchanges) gold dust as the currency system over much of West Africa can be seen as a process of institutional reform that reduced transaction costs. The initiative for this apparently came from African merchant networks, rather than from states (Austin, forthcoming 2016c).

In these settings, it was generally difficult to secure the fiscal foundations for state building. Abyssinia was founded on an agricultural surplus, extracted via tribute from peasants (Crummey 1980). Elsewhere states were more commonly based on locational rents (taxing trade), or resource rents (control of gold mines). As with intensive agriculture, state-building is ancient in Africa, but stateless societies and mini-states remained common on the eve of the European partition of the continent, which occurred between 1879 and about 1900 (Goody 1971; Law 1978; Herbst 2000).

Another institutional response to the abundance of (usually not very fertile) land was inheritance systems that tended not to concentrate but rather to spread wealth, favouring the accumulation of allies and clients (Goody 1976), though in some cases these systems were to become narrower where and when land became scarce in the twentieth century (Bates 1990). Another response was the use of coercion to reduce the supply cost of labour. For instance, a growth of commodity production for internal and external markets stimulated a major increase in the importation of slaves by many societies in East and West Africa in the nineteenth century. While no economic explanation for any form of forced labour can ever be sufficient, the private profitability of labour coercion is indispensable to accounting for the growth of slavery within Africa, especially in the nineteenth century (Austin, forthcoming 2016a).

Throughout this era, slaves were exported from Sub-Saharan Africa on a scale which can only have reinforced the structural problem of low population density. Some 13 million captives were embarked in the Atlantic trade, from the fifteenth century to 1867; guesstimates put the Saharan, Red Sea and Indian Ocean trades at a combined total of over 5.8 million for 1500–1900 (Lovejoy 2012: 46, 138). The durability and scale of the trade suggest that the labour productivity of enslaved Africans was higher in the regions to which they were forcibly taken than in those from which they were exported (rather than sold to African slave-owners, which also happened, and increasingly from the late eighteenth century). Part of the difference may be exchange value (proximity to the markets for slave-produced goods and services), but part of it presumably reflected constraints on labour productivity within sub-Saharan Africa, which can indeed be accounted for by the environmental obstacles (Manning 1990: 33–4; Austin 2008a, 2008b). Again, an economic explanation is insufficient, in this case for an activity which, however profitable for the sellers as well as the buyers, involved immense external costs for the wider region including collateral deaths and injuries, destruction of property, and general insecurity within a political economy that rewarded militarism. This extreme free-riding was encouraged by the rarity of huge states and the widespread political fragmentation (Inikori 2003). Whether or not the external slave trades produced an aggregate fall in the population south of the

Sahara, or simply slowed its growth, the loss of so many people can only have reinforced the underlying problems of labour scarcity and small markets.

In these circumstances, despite certain economic advances during the sixteenth to nineteenth centuries, African economies in the eighteenth and nineteenth centuries lacked many of Gerschenkron's 'prerequisites' for spontaneous industrialization, such as expanding markets for industrial goods based on rising labour productivity in agriculture, not to mention very low rates of modern schooling. Moreover, African states were in an extremely weak position in the face of the existential threat from European imperialism towards the end of the nineteenth century, strengthened as it was in both logistics and military technology by industrialization. One of the reasons why most of Africa was finally colonized then—so late in the history of European overseas expansion—was that industrialization, plus the adoption of quinine against malaria, had greatly reduced the cost of conquest in Africa for European states. Some of the stronger African states tried to import specific industrial technologies, including the telegraph, while mission-educated African elites on the west coast vainly sought a modernization under European overrule but with some sort of African autonomy. But only the most fiscally powerful African polity, Abyssinia, was able not only to defeat a full-scale invasion, but also to expand its own empire (to incorporate what is now southern Ethiopia) and establish itself, at least pre-Mussolini, as a political and business partner for Europe. Even Abyssinia/Ethiopia—with its long indigenous history of agricultural surpluses and Christianity, the latter entailing at least elite literacy—did not set out to match Meiji Japan's feat of 'late industrialization' in the face of Western imperialism.

9.5 From Land-extensiveness to Modern Manufacturing? The Colonial Period, c.1890–c.1960

The incoming colonial administrations, established mainly during the 1880s–1900s, promoted primary product exports, not manufacturing. This was partly out of necessity: their political masters in Europe generally demanded that they make the colonies fiscally self-sufficient as soon as possible. To this end they needed to raise revenue, and the obvious way to do this was to induce higher export earnings, which they could tax, directly or indirectly, more easily than any other potentially sizable source of income. Agriculture and mining were the only sectors in which this seemed feasible. As before colonization, revenue-raising in Africa was largely a function of access to locational and resource rents (Austin 2006; Frankema and van Waijenburg 2014): having soils suitable for growing export crops in an area from which railway or road-distance to the coast was relatively small was a huge help (Ghana, to a lesser extent Senegal), as was the presence of mineral wealth (South Africa, to a lesser extent the Belgian Congo with its copper-rich province of Katanga). Colonial officials were also aware of calls from manufacturing interests back home that the colonies should generate raw materials, notably cotton, to reduce metro-politan manufacturers' costs, and to secure their supplies. Such calls were given organized amplification by lobby groups such as the British Cotton Growers' Association (founded in 1902). But the boot was often on the other foot: colonial administrators also sought buyers, and in some cases (notably Kenya) settlers, from the metropole in the hope that they would increase the taxable output of the economy. In the event, colonial governments in Africa, like the African states that preceded them, managed to extract only relatively meagre tax revenues from their subjects (Gardner 2012). Ewout Frankema calculated that, excluding customs duties, on average, the number of days of unskilled wage work required to match the government revenue per capita was 1 day a year in Nigeria in 1911, and still 1 day in 1929 and 1937. Nigeria was an extreme case, but was also the most populous colony on the continent. At the opposite extreme, among British colonies, was the quasi-settler colony of Kenya, where the figure rose from 5 days in 1911 to 11 in 1929 and 13 in 1937 (Frankema 2010: 465–6). As a result, colonial states in tropical Africa could afford only modest bureaucracies. In the 1930s, the ratio of whites employed by the colonial administration to the population they sought to rule was 1: 27,000 in French West Africa, 1: 35,000 in the Congo, and 1: 54,000 in Nigeria, 1: 27,000 in French West Africa, and 1: 19,000 in Kenya (Kirk-Greene 1980: 35, 39). Actually, the ratios were even lower than that, because the population censuses were usually significantly under-counted, precisely because of the limited administrative capacity (Manning 2010; Frankema and Jerven 2014).

Thus colonial regimes in Africa were generally lacking in the capacities to be ambitious 'developmental states' on the Gerschenkron-Amsden model, even had they wished to be. The biggest financial advantage the colonial regimes had over the African polities they had annexed was their ability to borrow on the European bond markets, often specifically to finance the construction of railways and ports, thus deepening the infrastructure of the export-import economies. But this did not mean that they had the option of using loans to finance infant industries, had they wished to do so. Their ability to borrow was subject to control from the imperial treasuries, who expected loans to be repaid with interest and on time: which would have been unlikely in a sector in which African economies lacked comparative advantage, and would no doubt have elicited outrage from metropolitan manufacturers with whom colonial industries would be competing (cf. Brett 1973). Colonial administra-tions in Africa lacked the political legitimacy and economic opportunity that enabled the elected governments of Australia, Canada, and New Zealand to tax and borrow on the kind of scale required for the state to make a really powerful and sustained difference to human capital formation and other investments in long-term economic development (Accominotti, Flandreau, Rezzik and Zumer 2010; Frankema 2010; Frankema and van Waijenburg 2014).

But three major qualifications or complications should be added about manufacturing and colonial rule.

9.5.1 *Sources of Specialization in Primary-product Exports*

First, in Africa, the colonial-era specialization in farming and digging for export was not simply imposed by the alien rulers. Even in West Africa, which had the most substantial indigenous cotton textiles industry, the factor endowment of the time, by favouring land-extensive activities, meant that a direct transition from artisanal handicrafts to modern manufacturing (defined by reliance on inanimate sources of energy) was unlikely even without colonial rule. It was much more probable that any industrialization would be preceded by a phase of specialization in the kind of products suited to a labour-scarce environment in which cultivable land was relatively abundant but also relatively highly susceptible to over-use. Such a phase occurred when the industrial revolution created new markets for agricultural products that could be profitably grown by land-extensive methods in African conditions (Austin 2013a). This had already begun before colonial rule, on the west coast during the early nineteenth century, following the beginning of the abolition of the Atlantic slave trade, with peanuts and palm oil becoming the major exports (Hopkins 1973: 124–35; Law 1995). Even under European occupation, Africans retained much of the initiative in the development of agricultural exporting, being responsible for the origins of cocoa-growing in Nigeria, and having the main role in Ghana's dramatic shift from exporting no cocoa beans in 1892 to overtaking Brazil as the world's biggest cocoa exporter less than twenty years later (Hopkins 1978; Hill 1997). The combination of continued labour scarcity, the (gradual) abolition of slavery, and the greatly increased exchange value of agricultural output, resulted in relatively high real wages for unskilled labourers in the capitals of Ghana and Nigeria (and, as these were nationally and regionally integrated labour markets, not only in the cities). They were not only well above global pre-industrial norms, but were also above those of, for example, the major textile-producing centres of British India, especially before 1940 (Frankema and van Waijenburg 2012).

The land-extensive character of West African agricultural export production was epitomized by the fact that in the nineteenth century, in parts of the palm oil exporting belt, palm trees were not deliberately planted. Again, when cocoa growing was adopted (in the limited areas where rain and soil conditions suited it), while the planting of the trees necessarily constituted an intensification (more labour per hectare, creating a fixed capital stock), African farmers' approach continued to be land-extensive rather than labour and/or capital-intensive: seeking to maximize returns to labour by bringing more land under cultivation, rather than concentrating on raising returns per unit area. This was clear not only in their planting strategy but also in their method for dealing with capsid infestation: they found that temporary abandonment worked better than pesticides. In Ghana, these methods enabled them to defeat the more capital and labour-intensive approach of European planters (Austin 1996b, 2005).

Meanwhile, in a number of colonies across the continent colonial regimes tried various forms of coercion in the course of their attempts to induce savannah farmers to expand their existing output of raw cotton, but coercion usually produced very limited results—and in Mali, as late as 1948–9, French merchants were outbid for almost the whole of the cotton crop by African brokers supplying the local handloom industry (Roberts 1996 especially p. 283). In contrast, the most successful agricultural export industries of the period developed without any direct taxation, let alone explicit coercion: cocoa cultivation in Ghana and southwest Nigeria. In short, the colonial governments' promotion of primary export production was often misdirected and frequently (though far from always) coercive. But Africans had already begun to develop a comparative advantage in agricultural exports before the colonial occupation, and where that comparative advantage was deepened, it was often by African rather than European initiative. What is often called the 'colonial division of labour', whereby Africans specialized in primary exports, is to that extent a misnomer. Though promoted and reinforced by European rulers, it also reflected the factor endowment, and was rationally recognized and originated as such by Africans.

9.5.2 Settler States and Import-substitution Industrialization

The second complication to the observation that colonial regimes promoted primary exports not manufacturing is the adoption of policies of import-substitution industrialization by the two self-governing settler regimes, South Africa and Southern Rhodesia. The former became independent, as a 'dominion' within the British empire, in 1910; the latter moved from chartered-company rule to autonomy under a parliament elected by settlers, in 1923. What made it possible for them to adopt ISI was precisely that in these cases the governments were controlled by local interests, albeit white minority ones, which differed from those of the imperial government in London.

In both cases the coercive power of the state had been deployed already to drive down the reservation wages of black labour. Specifically, both states tried to drive Africans out of the produce market and into the labour market, by large-scale appropriations of land for the use of Europeans, coupled with bans on Africans working on European farms as tenants rather than labourers. Though African production for the market proved remarkably resilient in Southern Rhodesia, in both cases the policy was successful in driving down the real wages of African employees.[6] Without it, the South African gold mining industry could have been grown to only a small fraction of the size it reached by the early 1930s, when the gold price shot up following the British and United States abandonment of the gold standard (Feinstein 2005: 109–12). With mining royalties boosted by cheap labour, both governments embarked on import-substitution industrialization, South Africa in 1924 and—partly in response—Southern Rhodesia in 1933 (Phimister 2000), based on electrification and including iron and steel.

The settler regimes were inferior to at least the more prosperous of the 'peasant' colonies when it came to the welfare of the black majorities (measured by both real wages and infant mortality (Bowden, Chiripanhura and Mosley 2008). But when it came to structural transformation of the economy, because they had domestic electorates to answer to—small in number and privileged in wealth and status though they were—the 'settler' governments were more 'developmental' than the administrators of 'peasant' and 'concession' colonies. The South African move responded to the demands of white workers for jobs, and of Afrikaner nationalists for economic independence from Britain; the Rhodesian response asserted the desire for economic independence from South Africa as well as a longer-term interest in developing the economy. In 1960, when most of French Africa and the largest Belgian and British colonies all became independent, manufacturing as a share of GDP was estimated at just over twenty per cent in South Africa (Lipton 1986: 402) and sixteen per cent in Southern Rhodesia, whereas the 'peasant' (or, in part, indigenous rural capitalist) colony with the largest economy, Nigeria, and the one with the highest income per head, Ghana (independent in 1957), had manufacturing shares of only 4.5 and 6.3 per cent respectively (Kilby 1975: 472).

9.5.3 'Late Colonialism': Imperial Governments and 'Development'

Twentieth-century colonial regimes were not always indifferent, let alone hostile, to manufacturing. Even while Britain was still committed to laissez-faire, pressure from nationalists led to the beginning of infant industry protection in India, in 1924 (Dewey 1978). In Southeast and East Asia, European

---

[6] For a different perspective on the case of Nyasaland (Malawi), which was a peasant-cum-European-planter rather than a self-governing settler regime, see Bolt and Green 2015.

as well as Japanese and American colonial administrations promoted manufacturing in the 1930s as a counter to the Great Depression (Brown 1997: 203–15; Booth 2007). The story was different in Africa. In the 1940s, the British Colonial Office wanted to promote manufacturing in African colonies to counter the instability of primary product markets, but was largely thwarted by a more powerful ministry, the Treasury, which worried about loss of British export markets and the cost of subsidising probably unprofitable industries (Butler 1997). Meanwhile, the French government's promotion of imperial autarky had facilitated the relocation of part of the French textile industry to Hanoi, but Paris intervened to limit the equivalent growth of peanut oil processing in Senegal (Boone 1992: 47–9). In the last decade before the independence of Senegal and Nigeria (1960), there was a rush of European investment in manufacturing in tropical Africa. This was largely driven, not by the state, but by European trading companies anxious to retain after Independence their shares of markets for manufactured consumer goods, which were being expanded at the time by population growth and higher incomes from agricultural exports (Kilby 1975).

Even so, the combination of 'developmental' rhetoric from the postwar colonial governments with the success of nationalist parties, bequeathed to the governments of newly-independent Africa a mandate, and an expectation, that they would vigorously promote development. The outgoing colonial regimes also passed on the most effective mechanism yet devised for the taxation of agriculture, and thus for the 'socialisation of savings', in tropical Africa. This was the statutory export marketing board, which enjoyed a legal monopoly of exporting crops, and—though created in the 1930s to support rather than reduce producer prices—was able to fix the producer prices well below world market prices. Thus the marketing boards could deliver big surpluses to the state. For politicians such as Kwame Nkrumah in Ghana, this seemed to be the instrument which could make possible serious industrial investment.

9.6 The 'Developmental State' and Shifting Resource Ratios, since 1960

Most of Africa recovered independence, packaged in new 'nation-states', in or about 1960 (the Portuguese colonies followed in 1975). Besides the domestic imperative to pursue development, this was the period of maximum policy influence for the advocates of active state intervention in, and even substitution for, the market, in the cause of industrialization: from Raúl Prebisch, Albert Hirschman and, indeed, Gerschenkron. One way of looking at state-led 'late industrialization' is as an attempt to shift the country's comparative advantage higher up the value scale. The question was and is whether the distance to be travelled was and is simply too great in economic terms, and whether the political commitment was sufficiently strong, in will and capacity.

Virtually all African states proclaimed some form of state-led development policy, including the promotion of manufacturing. The results were largely discredited by the 1980s, with the developmental state being reinterpreted as a rentier state. A damning assessment was given in what became the World Bank's manifesto for Structural Adjustment in Africa, the Berg Report (World Bank 1981): a verdict which has largely stuck ever since.[7] In retrospect, rather than in the context of the high expectations of the decolonization era, this pessimism is somewhat exaggerated, especially considering that the countries' populations were growing at two to four per cent a year, making any per capita growth at least moderately impressive. From 1960 until the 1973 OPEC oil shock (and even for a couple of years afterwards) the average growth per capita of sub-Saharan Africa as a whole approached one per cent per annum. Moreover, a number of countries achieved a significant expansion of manufacturing, albeit from a very low base (Sender and Smith 1986: 94–9). As of 1982, those whose manufacturing sectors accounted for at least a tenth of GDP included (in percentage terms) Kenya (13), Côte d'Ivoire (12) and Ethiopia (11); though not Tanzania (9), Nigeria (6) and Ghana (5) (Sender and Smith 1986: 96, citing World Bank data). It should also be noted that the long-term development policies of these new, under-resourced states were (and are) particularly vulnerable to disruption from the kind of short-term fluctuations, frequently of external origin, that often preoccupy the finance ministers of richer countries (Fahnbulleh 2005). As Thandika Mkandawire commented:

> If a developmental state is not [to] be deified into some kind of omnipotent and omniscient leviathan that always gets what it wants, then the definition must include situations in which exogenous structural dynamic and unforeseen factors can torpedo genuine developmental commitments and efforts by the state, as happened recently [1997] in some of the most successful Asian developmental states. (Mkandawire 2001: 291)

Meanwhile, the fiscally and administratively strongest state south of the Sahara, South Africa, continued to preside over fairly rapid expansion of manufacturing, with tariff protection, in the 1950s–70s.

It is crucial to note that there was a wide range of variation in the performance of different countries. In several of the larger ones, the effect of economic policies was obscured by civil wars or independence wars during parts of the period (including Sudan, Ethiopia, the former Belgian Congo, Nigeria,

---

[7] A useful, nuanced, analysis is Mytelka 1989.

Mozambique, and Angola). A pattern that emerges from the other cases is that the states which made relatively modest economic interventions presided over more growth of both output and manufacturing than their neighbours who intervened more heavily (Côte d'Ivoire and Kenya compared to Ghana and Tanzania, for example) (Austin, Frankema and Jerven 2015). In other words, those which sought to diversify around export agriculture, sustaining the latter by keeping the rate of taxation of export growers low enough to give them an incentive to reinvest, did better than those who taxed export agriculture at penal rates, thereby undermining the sector whose surpluses had made (limited) state developmentalism possible (Austin 1996a). To ignore one's existing comparative advantage completely was perilous.

The 1980s saw almost all African states adopt World Bank and IMF-sponsored 'Structural Adjustment' programmes: in most cases not so much because of external debt (very few had been considered credit-worthy enough to qualify for loans from commercial banks) as because of internal fiscal crises, especially where (as in Ghana, Tanzania, and other tropical African countries outside the franc zone) state intervention had included price controls which, by the late 1970s/early 1980s, were so severe as to lead to widespread bypassing of official markets. Structural Adjustment consisted essentially in the replacement of administrative mechanisms of resource allocation by markets. Adopting such a programme therefore entailed renouncing the developmental state as understood by Gerschenkron, Hirschman, and Amsden, in favour of the Douglass North version: a state strong enough to enforce private property rights and other rules of the market, and limiting itself to that. Industrialization as a target in itself was off the agenda; the international financial institutions prodded African countries to focus on their existing areas of comparative advantage, in extraction and agriculture.

With dramatic exceptions, the initial results of Structural Adjustment were poor: coinciding with a decline in world commodity prices, the first ten to fifteen years of economic liberalization saw stagnation or actual decline in most African economies. In aggregate, according to World Bank data, the decline in GDP per capita in sub-Saharan Africa began in 1977, several years before the introduction of Structural Adjustment, and continued until 1994 (Stiglitz, Lin, Monga, and Patel 2013: 12). Again, however, initial economic performance during 'adjustment' varied: amidst the cases of decline or stagnation, Ghana and Uganda recovered rapidly from preceding periods of economic shrinkage (associated in Uganda with prolonged internal violence). The liberal economic regimes introduced by Structural Adjustment have remained very largely in place to the time of writing. Since c.1995, during a period of mostly rising or buoyant world commodity prices, sub-Saharan Africa has experienced probably its most widespread economic boom ever. If economic liberalization is blamed (credibly, only in part) for the widespread debacle of its first decade, by the same token it must be given part of the credit for the economic expansion during the following twenty years. But, as noted in the introduction, while manufacturing output has risen in absolute terms, as a share of output it is lower today than in 1990. This is hardly a secure route to joining the club of rich nations.

So, the case for states to intervene to promote manufacturing in Africa, reversing and going way beyond its recent relative decline, is urgent. Yet external and internal, political and economic doubts about the chances of success abound. These include the strength of competition from the current 'workshop of the world', China; the restrictions on opportunities for infant-industry protection imposed by the rules of the World Trade Organization (United Nations 2011: 86–91); corrupt and weak governments at home; and an underlying lack of infrastructure that compounds the present comparative disadvantage in manufacturing that arises from the present resource ratios.

To start with the most fundamental issue: the last century has seen a transformation, albeit still continuing, in Africa's factor endowment, with increasing availability of unskilled labour, and major growth in human capital formation. The aggregate population apparently started growing within a few years after the 1918 world influenza pandemic, and did so about six-fold by the end of the twentieth century. Though population density does not simply convert into labour abundance, in the long run the population explosion exerted downward pressure on African wages relative to wages outside Africa. At the time of the post-independence experiments in import-substitution industrialization, most of Africa was still labour-scarce and labour costs remained high compared to Asia. The most likely exception would have been the southern African settler states, South Africa and Rhodesia, where much of the rural male population had long been pressured into migrant labour. Even there, though manufacturing continued to expand in the 1950s and 1960s, it was behind protectionist tariffs. By the end of the twentieth century, however, the shift in factor ratios had reached the point where it was beginning to be surprising that, for instance, Ghana's labour costs in textiles were still too high to permit exports (Teal 1999). By the time of writing, wages in China have begun to overtake those in Africa and the Ethiopian government, by setting a legal minimum wage well below those of China, Indonesia and India, as well as African competitors, seems to be signalling a determination to make that cost advantage count. It is probably no coincidence that Ethiopia has begun to attract Chinese and Indian investment in manufacturing (Austin, Frankema and Jerven 2015: 26).[8] By the same token, one can hope (regarding Onoge's point above) that labour repression

---

[8] I owe this point to Ewout Frankema.

is no longer necessary for industrialization, when real wages are already relatively low, and contracts all too precarious. Again, African workforces are much more widely and deeply educated than 50–60 years ago. Arguably the biggest achievement of the era of state-led development policy was the expansion of formal education at all levels (Sender 1999). Adult literacy had reached 56.1 per cent for women and 74.5 per cent for men in 2009 (World Bank 2013: Table 1): low compared to contemporary Asia, but well above the threshold for countries successfully industrializing in the past. In the context of cheaper and better educated labour, the prospect of the 'flying geese' of investment in labour-intensive manufacturing reaching Africa becomes much more realistic.

It should be noted that both the demographic and educational expansions were in part endogenous to the 'land extensive' path of development. Labour being scarce, high fertility was socially prized: enabling the (in these terms) exogenous decline in the mortality rate from the middle colonial period onwards to be quickly converted into rapid population growth (Iliffe 1989). Again, cash-cropping farmers invested their savings, above all, in school fees, whether to attend mission schools during the colonial period or the expanded state school system afterwards.

The immediate international threat to this prospect is less the WTO rules, which allow some leeway for newcomers, than a continuation of the current Chinese slow-down, which would limit potential export markets and perhaps also further inward investment. Moreover, since the Great Recession of 2008 the IMF and World Bank have become markedly more concerned with market failures and more sympathetic to state intervention to counteract them. Two recent holders of the position of chief economist at the World Bank are among a group of former or current Bank economists arguing very forcefully for state promotion of industrialization in Africa (Stiglitz, Lin, Monga, and Patel 2013).

Again, while states in Africa remain relatively short of fiscal and administrative capacity, they have been potentially strengthened by the combination of economic growth and a larger supply of well-educated personnel. Central government expenditure in sub-Saharan Africa has remained very consistent, at about twenty-two per cent, since the decade in which Structural Adjustment was introduced, despite the rather fast growth of GDP since 1995 (Table 9.1). This suggests that, should larger budgets be needed, there is some room for expansion from internal revenue rather than necessarily from external loans or grant aid.

Government spending on what? Joseph Stiglitz, Justin Lin, and their colleagues envisage two priorities for industrial policy in contemporary Africa: encouraging the transfer of labour and other resources from low to high productivity sectors, 'including the migration of Africa's abundant unskilled rural labor to unskilled labor-intensive industries'; and further investment in education and learning, to improve the skills and adaptability of the

Table 9.1 Central Government Expenditure in sub-Saharan Africa, 1980–2010.

Years	Gross gov't fixed capital formation	Central government final consumption	Total
1980–89	6.1	16.5	22.6
1990–99	4.7	16.7	21.4
2000–10	5.9	16.4	22.3

Source: World Bank (2013): tables 2.15, 2.20.

workforce (Stiglitz, Lin, Monga, and Patel 2013: 12). The movement out of agriculture is already large-scale in most of Africa, as is visible in the accelerated urbanization of the last twenty years. The problem is insufficient employment. While labour-intensive industries can help, the comparative history of labour-intensive industrialization underlines the importance of enhancing skills if the process is to continue, and thereby contribute to rising output per capita rather than simply absorb the unemployed (Austin and Sugihara 2013). This perspective reinforces the case for further investment in education.

So does the ultimate fate of the *apartheid* economy. The last fifteen years before the regime handed over power in 1994 was a period of economic stagnation. While the slump was reinforced by the township revolt and the resultant loss of investor confidence, and eventually also by sanctions, arguably the initial and underlying cause was built into the institutions and practice of *apartheid* itself. The same system that generated cheap unskilled labour made skilled labour artificially expensive: which imposed rising costs as the economy reached the limits of extensive growth, thereby increasingly needing TFP growth to maintain overall expansion. Already from 1967, well before the international oil price shock of 1973, the marginal efficiency of investment was in decline, gradually, then rapidly (Lewis 1990: 132–3).

Along with education, investment in physical infrastructure, especially transport and electricity supply, is fundamental to the prospects of industrialization in Africa. Entrepreneurs in much of Africa (in Nigeria, notoriously) need their own generators, reflecting a gross lack of supply of an elementary public good. In addition, there will remain cases where governments can find useful ways to support specific industries: though each case has its own technical, economic and political complexities (Cramer 1999).

Relatedly, though not necessarily very expensively, African states may need to do more to help private firms develop the skills necessary to grow. So far, in most African countries, indigenous enterprises have rarely grown big—though there are notable exceptions, such as the conglomerate created by the Nigerian entrepreneur M. K. Abiola (1937–98). Mostly, where firms did not originate as a foreign or public enterprise sold to private African interests via the mediation of the state, they have been born small and remained fairly small, partly because few survive the death of their founder (Iliffe 1983: 74–5). This is especially important because there is evidence that the larger firms are the most likely to export (Rankin, Söderbom, and Teal 2006).

Much of the literature is deeply sceptical about the developmental commitment of African ruling elites, given the primacy of patrimonial politics, and the frequent allegations of corruption over the years in many African states. In this context it has been argued that, far from Structural Adjustment solving the problem by cutting the state to a minimum and allowing the market to rule, 'adjustment' was captured by the elites, who used the aid to re-fuel their patronage networks, while avoiding serious implementation of the reforms (Chabal and Daloz 1999: 119–23). But it is a mistake to dismiss the seriousness with which some of the independence leaders—backed by mass demands for higher living standards, schools and better public health—approached development: missing the targets does not mean that the targets were not real. In the early 1980s, the dominant argument in rational-choice political science was that in Africa the incentives to leaders were radically un-aligned with the interests of the population as a whole, such that economic stagnation or even absolute decline was a price that a leader would rationally accept in order to reward his followers (Bates 1981). But, while this might apply to slow or even no growth, only if time-horizons were reduced to months would it make sense for a patron to worry only about sharing the cake, and not at all about enlarging it. The left-populist 'revolutionary' government of J. J. Rawlings in Ghana in 1983, actually reversed its economic strategy—by adopting Structural Adjustment—when the initial policy led only to further shrinkage in output, and government revenue (Austin 1996a). Again, while economic liberalization certainly did not end patrimonialism and rent-seeking (and, as elsewhere in the world, privatizations provided a feast for rent-seekers), the economic reforms were implemented to a great extent: as the floating currencies and massive inflows of remittances illustrate.

What is clear is that analysts need to take the nuances and details of politics seriously. In this vein, from a study of a number of recent country cases, Tim Kelsall (2011) has argued persuasively that where 'rent management can be centralised and oriented to the long term, neo-patrimonialism . . . can be harnessed for developmental ends'. As he notes, genuine electoral competition may divert politicians' priorities from the long-term (Kelsall 2011: 84), leaving greater scope for optimism about the economic future in de facto single-party systems such as Rwanda and Ethiopia. On the other hand, states in which power seems now more or less to alternate through the ballot box, such as Ghana, may eventually be the most effective in deterring corruption: if incumbents will not allow each other to be brought before a court (Ofori-Mensah 2009), the next ruling party will be ready to see their predecessors exposed. It could be suggested that, in the East Asian industrializations of the Cold War era, the tendencies towards corruption and rent-seeking (which were real) were kept in check by the existential threat from Communist neighbours. There was no very close analogy to this in Africa. Even so, while the pessimistic views are not without foundation, to see the 'African developmental state' as a contradiction in terms would be to go far beyond reason and evidence (Mkandawire 2001).

9.7 Conclusions

This chapter has briefly reviewed Africa's developmental history in relation to the question of its chances of achieving a twenty-first century 'late industrialization'. This issue, and the insights of the Gerschenkron-Amsden tradition, need to be seen in a broader framework than that of deviations from the original, unplanned industrialization. Sugihara's notion of long-term 'paths' of economic development, responding to an original factor endowment with sequences of choices of technique and institution, provides a non-Eurocentric and less teleological approach. I have emphasised that the human responses themselves gradually or eventually change the so-called 'endowment'.

Until (often far into) the twentieth century (at least), sub-Saharan Africa was characterized by a relative abundance of land and a relative scarcity of labour as well as capital. But obstacles to the intensive use of land—partly diminished over time by innovations including the selective adoption of exotic crops— meant that the region was mostly not 'resource rich', at least not before industrialization elsewhere created or expanded export markets for various deposits that lay beneath Africa's soils and seas. These circumstances hindered, without preventing, state building before and, indeed, during and since colonial rule. They also favoured a 'land-extensive' path of development, especially in relation to cultivation and pastoralism, with a preference for maximizing returns to labour (without the environmental constraints) rather than to the abundant factor of land. As a result, though food security and probably real incomes gradually (if unevenly) improved over the centuries, African states were not in a position, economically or politically, to respond to the challenge of Western industrialization by launching, Meiji-style, a 'late industrialization'.

Factor endowments and African responses to them also help explain why Africa, especially West Africa, moved during the nineteenth and early twentieth centuries from handicraft manufacturing to primary-product exporting rather than directly to modern manufacturing. Colonial regimes reinforced rather than originated this, and the success of agricultural exporting, by land-extensive methods in what was still a labour-scarce economy, raised labour productivity and real wages in West Africa. Ironically, this—specifically, the relatively high wages—did not help industrial competitiveness when modern manufacturing finally expanded across the continent, as Independence approached, and especially during the following phase of import-substitution industrialization policies, in the 1960s and 1970s.

Whereas 'regular' colonial administrations showed either no, or little and late, interest in promoting manufacturing, the self-governing settler regimes of South Africa and Southern Rhodesia embarked on import-substitution industrialization as early as the 1920s and 1930s, respectively, using the revenues and import-purchasing power derived from their mineral wealth. The growth of their mining, and then also the manufacturing sectors, was crucially facilitated by the success of the state in driving down the real wages of unskilled labourers, through drastically reducing Africans' access to land in order to oblige them to sell their labour. These were 'developmental states', albeit only in the narrowest sense: unrelated (or inversely related) to the welfare of the vast majority of the populations. The ultra-discriminatory labour policy on which the growth of the *apartheid* economy initially relied, however, proved self-limiting: in the 1980s and early 1990s the South African economy was becalmed, primarily because the cheapness of unskilled labour went along with a scarcity premium for skilled workers. The latter cost greatly inhibited South African manufacturing when it needed to move on from essentially extensive growth to partly intensive, TFP-based expansion.

Further north, the 1960s–70s experiments of most newly-independent tropical African states with import-substitution industrialization mostly delivered only modest economic growth, the states which did best being those which sought to diversify around primary exports, rather than over-taxing the latter in the hope of making infant industries thrive. The liberal economic regimes that were inaugurated in the 1980s are still in place. With a few exceptions, they saw little or negative economic growth until 1995, since when the GDP of sub-Saharan Africa has been outpacing population growth by about two per cent a year. But, with industrialization off the agenda, manufacturing has actually receded as a share of total output since 1990.

There is currently renewed enthusiasm for state promotion of manufacturing in policy circles, including at the World Bank. What makes this more realistic than the ambitions of the import-substitution era is that resource ratios have become much more favourable. The non-settler states of late twentieth-century Africa invested heavily in spreading education, helped by the willingness of cash-crop farmers and labourers to pay school fees. Meanwhile, much of Africa is well advanced in a transition to labour-abundance, thanks to a twentieth-century population explosion that was facilitated by the high social approval of high fertility, which was an institutional component of the land-extensive path of development.

Reflecting on this story so far, the eventual demise of the *apartheid* route to industrialization is consistent with the emphasis on the importance of human capital formation in the 'broad capital' strand of endogenous growth theory. The other strand of the theory, focussed on the sources of TFP growth, is much less relevant to the growth of modern manufacturing in Africa, to date and in the likely near future, because the case fits Amsden's definition of 'late industrialization' as using borrowed technology. Amsden's dismissal of the competitive importance of cheap unskilled labour, on the other hand, does not fit the growth of South African output, including manufacturing, as late as the 1970s. It also seems to understate the value of cheap labour in contemporary international rivalry in textiles and other relatively labour-intensive industries.

Gerschenkron and Amsden's identification of the state as the organizing 'substitute' for the market in the most 'backward' economies was shared by the settler states of twentieth-century Africa, and by the governments of the newly-independent governments in the 1960s. Though the results of state-led development strategies in the 1960s and 1970s were pretty limited, it is inescapable that the state is the key agent for orchestrating any renewed manufacturing drive in the foreseeable future. Not least, this is because of the comparative paucity of large private African companies, South Africa excepted.

Perhaps the biggest difference between the trajectory of 'late development' in Africa so far and Gerschenkron's account of 'substitutions' in the context of 'relative backwardness' is the role of primary commodity exports. Gerschenkron emphasized the need for a market for industrial goods, which he considered to have been provided in Britain by rising labour productivity in agriculture. In the case of late nineteenth-century Russia, he believed that the state extracted sufficient surplus from a relatively low-productivity agricultural sector to enable it to provide both capital and demand for manufactures. By contrast, in Africa it was income from export agriculture and mining that created 'expanded' markets for industrial goods, and enabled first the settler regimes, and later the governments of the newly-independent rest of Africa, to subsidize import-substitution industrialization. Despite outbreaks of Dutch disease, notably in Nigeria after the 1973 OPEC oil price rise, any state push for industrialization in the near future is likely again to have to rely on revenue and import-purchasing power generated from primary exports.

Having seen India move from the so-called 'Hindu growth rate' to rapid 'late development' within recent decades, in principle it seems realistic to hope that Africa is not 'too late' for 'late industrialization'. Gerschenkron was right that the industrialization of even one country altered the conditions for future industrializations. The earlier industrializations provided technologies which—despite the restrictions of patent laws and WTO regulations—African countries can hope to adopt, as they already have to some extent. They also enlarged or created the export markets for the primary commodities highlighted above. However, there is a formidable disadvantage of lateness, which Gerschenkron did not predict. If African countries are eventually unable to reach the average living standards of the currently industrialized countries, it is likely to be because of the combination of the environmental impact of global industrialization to date, with the measures needed to mitigate its longer-term effects (Austin, 2016b).

Acknowledgements

In this chapter, 'Africa' means 'sub-Saharan Africa' unless otherwise stated. The essay is a 'think-piece' which should be read in conjunction with the more empirically detailed Austin 2013a and Austin, Frankema and Jerven 2015. I reviewed the 'late industrialization' literature in general comparative terms in Austin 2010. I presented a draft at session 20041 of the World Economic History Congress in Kyoto, and am grateful to the organizers and participants for their comments. I am especially grateful to Anne Booth, for extended feedback. Any mistakes are mine.

References

Abramovitz, M. and P.A. David, 1996. 'Convergence and deferred catch-up: productivity leadership and the waning of American exceptionalism'. In, *The Mosaic of Economic Growth*, edited by R. Landau, T. Taylor, and G.Wright, [21–62], Stanford: Stanford University Press.

Accominotti, O., M. Flandreau, R. Rezzik, and F. Zumer, 2010. 'Black man's burden, white man's welfare: control, devolution and development in the British empire, 1880–1914', *European Review of Economic History* vol. 14 number 1:47–70.

Acemoglu, D., S. Johnson, and J.A. Robinson, 2001. 'The colonial origins of comparative development: an empirical investigation', *American Economic Review* vol. 91 number 5:1369–401.

Acemoglu, D., S. Johnson, and J.A. Robinson, 2002. 'Reversal of fortune: geography and institutions in the making of the modern world income distribution', *Quarterly Journal of Economics* vol. 117 number 4:1231–79.

Acemoglu, D., and J.A. Robinson, 2012. *Why Nations Fail: The Origins of Power, Prosperity, and Poverty* New York: Crown.

Amsden, A.H., 1989. *Asia's Next Giant: South Korea and Late Industrialization* Oxford: Oxford University Press.

Amsden, A.H., 1992. 'A theory of government intervention in late industrialization'. In *State and Market in Development: Synergy or Rivalry?* edited by L. Putterman and D. Rueschemeyer [53–84]. Boulder: Lynne Reiner.

Amsden, A.H., 2001. *The Rise of 'The Rest': Challenges to the West from Late-Industrializing Economies,* New York: Oxford University Press.

Austin, G., 1996a. 'National poverty and the "vampire state" in Ghana: a review article'. *Journal of International Development* vol. 8 1996, 553–73.

Austin, G., 1996b. 'Mode of production or mode of cultivation: explaining the failure of European cocoa planters in competition with African farmers in colonial Ghana'. In *Cocoa Pioneer Fronts Since 1800: the Role of Smallholders, Planters and Merchants,* edited by W.G. Clarence-Smith, [154–75] Basingstoke, UK: Macmillan.

Austin, G., 2005. *Labour, Land and Capital in Ghana: From Slavery to Free Labour in Asante, 1807–1956,* Rochester NY: University of Rochester Press.

Austin, G., 2006. 'The political economy of the natural environment in West African history: Asante and its savanna neighbors in the nineteenth and twentieth centuries'. In *Land and the Politics of Belonging in West Africa,* edited by R. Kuba and C. Lentz [187–212], Leiden: Brill Academic Publishers.

Austin, G., 2008a. 'Resources, techniques and strategies south of the Sahara: revising the factor endowments perspective on African economic development, 1500–2000'. *Economic History Review,* volume 61 number 3:587–624.

Austin, G., 2008b. 'The "reversal of fortune" thesis and the compression of history: perspectives from African and comparative economic history'. *Journal of International Development* vol. 20 number 8:996–1027.

Austin, G., 2010. 'The developmental state and labour-intensive industrialization: "late development" reconsidered', *Economic History of Developing Regions* vol. 25 number 1:51–74.

Austin, G., 2012. 'Developmental "paths" and "civilizations" in Africa and Asia: reflections on strategies for integrating cultural and material explanations of differential long-term economic performance'. In *Institutions and Comparative Economic Development,* edited by M. Aoki, T. Kuran. and G. Roland, [237–53], Palgrave Macmillan; International Economics Association.

Austin, G., 2013a. 'Labour-intensity and manufacturing in West Africa, *c.*1450–*c.*2000'. In *Labour-Intensive Industrialization in Global History,* edited by G. Austin and K. Sugihara, [201–30], London: Routledge.

Austin, G., 2013b. 'Labour-intensive industrialization and global economic development: reflections'. In *Labour-Intensive Industrialization in Global History,* edited by G. Austin and K. Sugihara, [280–302], London: Routledge.

Austin, G., forthcoming, 2016a. 'Slavery in Africa'. In *The Cambridge World History of Slavery,* volume 4, *Slavery Since 1804,* edited by D. Eltis, S. Engerman, and D. Richardson, Cambridge: Cambridge University Press.

Austin, G., forthcoming, 2016b.'Africa and the Anthropocene'. In *Economic Development and Environmental History in the Anthropocene: Perspectives on Asia and Africa,* edited by Austin, London: Bloomsbury Academic.

Austin, G., forthcoming, 2016c. *Markets, Slaves and States in West African History,* Cambridge: Cambridge University Press.

Austin, G., E. Frankema, and M. Jerven, 2015. *Patterns of manufacturing growth in Sub-Saharan Africa: from colonization to the present',* Utrecht: Working Paper 17, Centre for Global Economic History.

Austin, G., and K. Sugihara (eds.), 2013. *Labour-Intensive Industrialization in Global History,* London: Routledge.

Bates, R. H., 1981. *Markets and States in Tropical Africa,* Berkeley: University of California Press.

Bates, R.H., 1990. 'Capital, kinship, and conflict: the structuring influence of capital in kinship societies', *Canadian Journal of African Studies* vol. 24 number 1:145–264.

Bénétrix, A.S., K.H. O'Rourke, and J.G. Williamson, 2012, *The Spread of Manufacturing to the Periphery 1870–2007: Eight Stylized Facts*, National Bureau of Economic Research Working Paper 18221, July 2012 (<http://www.nber.org/papers/w18221>).

Bolt, J. and E. Green 2015. 'Was the wage burden too heavy? Settler farming, profitability, and wage shares of settler agriculture in Nyasaland, c.1900–60'. *Journal of African History* vol. 56 number 2:217–38.

Boone, C., 1992. *Merchant Capital and the Roots of State Power in Senegal, 1930–1985,* Cambridge: Cambridge University Press.

Booth, A., 2007. 'Night watchman, extractive, or developmental states? Some evidence from late colonial South-East Asia', *Economic History Review* vol. 60 number 2: 241–66.

Bowden, S., B. Chiripanhura, and P. Mosley, 2008. 'Measuring and explaining poverty in six African countries: a long-period approach', *Journal of International Development* vol. 20 number 8:1049–79.

Breman, H., 2012. ' "African soils are sooo . . . fertile" '. In *What is the Matter with African Agriculture? Veterans' Visions Between Past and Future*, edited by H. J. W. Mutsaers and P.W.M.Kleene, [180–5], Amsterdam: KIT.

Brett, E.A., 1973. *Colonialism and Underdevelopment in East Africa: The Politics of Economic Change 1919–1939,* London: Heinemann.

Brown, I., 1997. *Economic Change in South-East Asia, c.1830–1980,* Oxford University Press.

Butler, L.J., 1997. *Industrialisation and the British Colonial State: West Africa, 1939–1951,* London: Frank Cass.

Chabal, P. and J.P. Daloz, 1999, *Africa Works: Disorder as Political Instrument,* Oxford: James Currey.

Chang, H., 2002. *Kicking Away the Ladder: Development Strategy in Historical Perspective,* London: Anthem Press.

Clarke, D., P. Murrell, and S. Whiting, 2008. 'The role of law', in *China's Great Economic Transformation*, edited by L. Brandt and T.G. Rawski, [337–74], New York: Cambridge University Press.

Crafts, N.F.R., 1997. 'Endogenous growth: lessons for and from economic history'. In *Advances in Economics and Econometrics: Theory and Applications—Seventh World Congress, vol. II*, edited by D.M. Kreps and K.F. Wallis, [38–78], Cambridge: Cambridge University Press.

Cramer, C., 1999. 'Can Africa industrialize by processing primary commodities? The case of Mozambican cashew nuts'. *World Development* vol. 27 number 7:1247–66.

Crummey, D., 1980. 'Abyssinian feudalism'. *Past and Present* vol. 89: 115–38.

Dewey, C., 1978, 'The end of the Imperialism of Free Trade: the eclipse of the Lancashire lobby and the concession of free trade to India'. In *The Imperial Impact: Studies in the Economic History of Africa and India*, edited by C. Dewey and A.G. Hopkins, [35–67, 331–8], London: Athlone Press for University of London.

Fahnbulleh, M., 2005. *The Elusive Quest for Industrialisation in Africa: A Comparative Study of Ghana and Kenya, c.1950–2000*, London School of Economics: PhD dissertation.

Feinstein, C.H., 2005. *Conquest, Discrimination and Development: an Economic History of South Africa*, Cambridge: Cambridge University Press.

Frankema, E., 2010. 'Raising revenue in the British empire, 1870–1940: how "extractive" were colonial taxes?' *Journal of Global History* vol. 5 number 3:447–77.

Frankema, E. and M. Jerven, 2014. 'Writing history backwards or sideways: towards a consensus on African population, 1850–2010'. *Economic History Review*, vol. 67 number 4:907–31.

Frankema, E. and M. van Waijenburg, 2012. 'Structural impediments to African growth? New evidence from real wages in British Africa, 1880–1965'. *Journal of Economic History* vol. 72 number 4:895–926.

Frankema, E. and M. van Waijenburg, 2014. 'Metropolitan blueprints of colonial taxation? Lessons from fiscal capacity building in British and French Africa, c.1880–c.1940'. *Journal of African History* vol. 55 number 3:371–400.

Gardner, L.A., 2012. *Taxing Colonial Africa: The Political Economy of British Imperialism*, Oxford: Oxford University Press.

Gerschenkron, A., 1962. *Economic Backwardness in Historical Perspective*, Cambridge MA: Harvard University Press.

Goody, J., 1971. *Tradition, Technology and the State in Africa*, London: Oxford University Press for the International African Institute.

Goody, J., 1976. *Production and Reproduction: A Comparative Study of the Domestic Domain*, Cambridge: Cambridge University Press.

Herbst, J., 2000. *States and Power in Africa: Comparative Lessons in Authority and Control*, Princeton: Princeton University Press, 2000.

Hill, P., 1997. *The Migrant Cocoa-Farmers of Southern Ghana*, 2nd edition with preface by G. Austin, Hamburg: LIT (1st edition Cambridge University Press, 1963).

Hopkins A.G., 1973. *An Economic History of West Africa*, London: Longman.

Hopkins, A.G., 1978. 'Innovation in a colonial context: African origins of the Nigerian cocoa-farming industry, 1880–1920'. In *The Imperial Impact*, edited by C. Dewey and A.G. Hopkins, [83–96, 341–2], London: Athlone Press for University of London.

Iliffe, J., 1983. *The Emergence of African Capitalism*, London: Macmillan.

Iliffe, J., 1989. 'The origins of African population growth', *Journal of African History* vol. 30 number: 165–9.

Inikori, J.E., 2003. 'The struggle against the transatlantic slave trade: the role of the state'. In *Fighting the Slave Trade: West African Strategies*, edited by S.A. Diouf, [170–98], Athens Ohio: OH.

Inikori, J.E., 2007. 'Africa and the globalization process: western Africa, 1450–1850', *Journal of Global History* vol. 2 number1:63–86.

Intergovernmental Panel on Climate Change (IPCC), 2014. 'Summary for policymakers'. In *Climate Change 2014: Impacts, Adaptation, and Vulnerability*, [1–32], Cambridge: Cambridge University Press.

Kelsall, T., 2011. 'Rethinking the relationship between neo-patrimonialism and economic development in Africa'. *IDS Bulletin* vol. 42 number 2:76–86.

Kilby, P, 1975, 'Manufacturing in colonial Africa'. In *Colonialism in Africa, 1870–1960*, vol. IV, *The Economics of Colonialism* edited by P. Duignan and L.H. Gann, [475–520], Cambridge: Cambridge University Press).

Kirk-Greene, A.H.M, 1980. 'The Thin White Line: the Size of the British Colonial Service in Africa'. *African Affairs* vol. 79 number 314: 25–44.

Law, R, 1978. 'Slaves, trade, and taxes: the material basis of political power in nineteenth-century West Africa'. *Research in Economic Anthropology* 1:37–52.

Law, R. (ed.), 1995. *From Slave Trade to 'Legitimate' Commerce: the Commercial Transition in Nineteenth-century West Africa*, Cambridge: Cambridge University Press.

Lewis, S.R., jr, 1990. *The Economics of Apartheid*, New York: Council on Foreign Relations.

Lipton, M, 1986. *Capitalism and Apartheid: South Africa, 1910–84*, Aldershot: Gower.

Lovejoy, P.E, 2012. *Transformations in Slavery: A History of Slavery in Africa*, 3rd edition, New York: Cambridge University Press.

Manning, P, 1990. *Slavery and African Life: Occidental, Oriental, and African Slave Trades*, Cambridge: Cambridge University Press.

Manning, P, 2010. 'African population projections, 1850-1960'. In *The Demographics of Empire: the Colonial Order and the Creation of Knowledge*, edited by K. Ittmann, D.D. Cordell, and G.H. Maddox, [245–75], Athens, Ohio: Ohio University Press.

Mkandawire, T, 2001. 'Thinking about developmental states in Africa', *Cambridge Journal of Economics* vol. 25 number 3:289–313.

Mokwunye, U., and A. Bationo, 2002. 'Meeting the phosphorus needs of the soils and crops of West Africa: the role of indigenous phosphate rocks'. In *Integrated Plant Nutrient Management in Sub-Saharan Africa: From Concept to Practice*, edited by B. Vanlauwe, J. Djiels, N. Sanginga and R. Merckx, [209–24], Wallingford, Oxfordshire, UK: CABI Publishing and the International Institute of Tropical Agriculture.

Mytelka, L.K, 1989. 'The unfulfilled promise of African industrialization', *African Studies Review* vol. 32 number 3:77–137.

North, D.C, 1990, *Institutions, Institutional Change and Economic Performance*, New York: Cambridge University Press.

Ofori-Mensah, M, 2009. '*The Politics of Anticorruption in Ghana, 1993–2006: Action, Inaction and Accountability*'. University of Edinburgh: PhD dissertation.

Phimister, I, 2000. 'The origins and development of manufacturing in Southern Rhodesia, 1880-1939' and 'From preference towards protection: manufacturing in Southern Rhodesia, 1940-1965'.In *Zimbabwe: A History of Manufacturing, 1890–1995*, edited by A.S. Mlambo, E.S. Pangeti, and I. Phimister, [9–50], Harare: University of Zimbabwe Publications.

Rankin, N., M. Söderbom and F. Teal, 2006, 'Exporting from manufacturing firms in Sub-Saharan Africa'. *Journal of African Economies* vol. 15 number 4:671–87.

Roberts, R.L, 1996, *Two Worlds of Cotton: Colonialism and the Regional Economy in the French Soudan, 1800–1946*, Stanford: Stanford University Press.

Schrank, A, 2015. 'Toward a new economic sociology of development'. *Sociology of Development*, vol. 1 number 2:233–58.

Sender, J, 1999. 'Africa's economic performance: limitations of the current consensus'. *Journal of Economic Perspectives* vol. 13 number 3: 89–114.

Sender, J. and S. Smith, 1986. *The Development of Capitalism in Africa*, London.

Stiglitz, J., J. Lin, C. Monga. and E. Patel, 2013. *Industrial Policy in the African Context* Washington DC: World Bank Policy Research Working Paper 6633.

Sugihara, K, 2003, 'The East Asian path of development: a long-term perspective'. In *The Resurgence of East Asia: 500, 150 and 50 Year Perspectives*, edited by G. Arrighi, T. Hamashita and M. Seldon, [78–123], London: Routledge.

Sugihara, K, 2007. 'The second Noel Butlin lecture: labour-intensive industrialisation in global history'. *Australian Economic History Review* vol. 47 number 2:121–54.

Sugihara, K, 2013, 'Labour-intensive industrialization in global history: an interpretation of East Asian experiences'. In *Labour-Intensive Industrialization in Global History*, edited by G. Austin and K. Sugihara, [20–64], London: Routledge.

Teal, F, 1999. 'Why can Mauritius export manufactures and Ghana not?' *The World Economy* vol. 22 number 7:981–93.

Trapido, S, 1971. 'South Africa in a comparative study of industrialisation'. *Journal of Development* Studies vol. 7 number 3:309–20.

United Nations, 2011, *Fostering Industrial Development in Africa in the New Global Environment*, special issue of UNECA and UNIDO, *Economic Development in Africa Report* (New York).

United Nations Economic Commission for Africa (UNECA), 2013, *Making the Most of Africa's Commodities: Industrializing for Growth, Jobs and Economic Transformation: Economic Report on Africa 2013* (Addis Ababa).

Van der Linden, M, 2012, 'Gerschenkron's secret: a research note'. *Critique: Journal of Socialist Theory* vol. 40 number 4: 553–62.

Vanlauwe, B., J. Djiels, N. Sanginga and R. Merckx (eds.), 2002. *Integrated Plant Nutrient Management in Sub-Saharan Africa: From Concept to Practice*, Wallingford, Oxfordshire, UK: CABI Publishing and the International Institute of Tropical Agriculture.

Wade, R, 1990. *Governing the Market: Economic Theory and the Role of Government in Industrialization*, Princeton: Princeton University Press.

World Bank, 1981. *Accelerated Development in Sub-Saharan Africa: An Agenda for Action* Washington DC: World Bank.

World Bank, 2013. *African Development Indicators*, Washington DC: World Bank.

10

Is Sub-Saharan Africa Finally Catching up?

Erik Thorbecke and Yusi Ouyang

10.1 Introduction

In the four decades before the new millennium sub-Saharan Africa (SSA) stagnated. Real per capita GDP for the region as a whole was only about twelve per cent higher in 2000 than it had been in 1960. Except for some outliers such as Botswana which enjoyed high and steady growth throughout much of the pre-2000 period and a few other countries that went through some temporary and relatively short growth spells, most of the region was mired in a maze of macro and micro poverty traps. The lack of economic growth combined with high population growth resulted in a situation of deep deprivation for the mass of mainly rural African households. The gap in the level of wellbeing in the developing regions of Asia and even Latin America compared to that of the African subcontinent kept on increasing in the pre-2000 period to the despair of the development community.

However, since about 2000, the SSA region has enjoyed a quantum leap in the pace of growth, a significant reduction in poverty, substantial improvements in human development indicators, and a more inclusive pattern of growth. Our tentative and optimistic message is that a combination of internal and external factors have started to free SSA from the various poverty traps and shackles that prevented a take-off into a sustainable growth path. Among the most influential internal factors are the improvement in the quality of governance and the appearance of a rising middle class. Among the external factors, one should note the improvements in the terms of trade (following climbing commodity prices for African exports) and a dramatic jump in foreign direct investment. Both of these developments are manifestations of the greater integration of the African sub-continent in the world economy under the forces of, and opportunities offered by globalization.

As a consequence, SSA is starting to catch up with the rest of the world. In some respects, the fact that SSA is a 'late comer' among developing regions, can work to its advantage in being able to import and implement more advanced technologies and finding its appropriate niche within the globalized world economy. This scenario would be consistent with Abramovitz's 'Catch up Growth Hypothesis' (Abramovitz 1986).

Even though it appears that SSA is finally beginning to catch up with the rest of the world, the question now is whether the current growth spell is sustainable. To answer this question, we must try to identify and analyze the factors that contributed to, and were associated with the dismal performance before the new millennium and the factors influencing, in turn, the new growth spell after 2000. A key issue is why the so-called *convergence* did not occur sooner. The Neo-classical economic theory suggests that the per capita output gap between poor and rich economies will only be transitory. Countries and regions endowed with little capital stock would enjoy higher returns and therefore attract investment that would allow them to grow faster than the richer countries and ultimately catch up with them. SSA, as a very underdeveloped and backward region (using Gerschenkron's terminology), would have seemed to be a prime candidate for convergence.

Given the fundamental importance of the concept of convergence, we start in Section 10.2 with a discussion of the meaning of convergence and whether and why one should expect convergence or non-convergence to occur; and the theoretical and conceptual cases in favour of convergence and against it. An important distinction is between unconditional and conditional convergence. The latter typically asserts that appropriate policies and institutions are necessary conditions for convergence to ensue.

Next, in Section 10.3, we assess the growth and poverty performance in SSA over an extended historical period from 1960 to around 2010. The contrast between the dismal performance prior to 2000, and the more successful current performance is highlighted. The assessment also includes a pre-2000 growth performance comparison between SSA and the rest of the developing world to shed light on the extent of divergence between the growth of SSA economies and that of other developing regions.

In Section 10.4, we explore how the structure and anatomy of growth in SSA appears to have become more inclusive in the current period—evolving from a narrow base often characterized by an enclave type of growth that prevailed previously centred on oil, mining, and mineral products benefitting only a few. We argue that the ongoing structural changes, and more particularly, a more successful structural transformation, have raised labour productivity and contributed to the acceleration in the pace of growth and a more inclusive pattern. Workers moving away from agriculture are starting to find more productive jobs in other sectors.

Section 10.5, in turn, attempts to identify the major anti-growth factors (correlates of stagnation) that led to stagnation in the pre-2000 period and the major factors that appear to be associated with, and have influenced the current growth spell (correlates of growth). Researchers in trying to explain the lack of socio-economic progress in the past focused on structural impediments such as ethno-linguistic heterogeneity, the peculiar historical origins of African (artificial) states, and endowment constraints such as being land-locked and a tropical climate. Yet, even after controlling for those structural obstacles, researchers relying on international growth regressions could not get rid of the so-called 'African dummy' and the belief that there was something fundamentally different in the growth pattern of the SSA region. In retrospect, it can be argued that it is the poor quality of governance that was mainly responsible for the dismal performance of SSA economies before 2000. In contrast, the main correlates of growth in the last fifteen years which we identified and discussed are (i) improved treatment of, and more pro-growth policies in agriculture; (ii) overall improved governance and appearance of a middle class; (iii) favourable global commodity prices; and (iv) a large flow of foreign investment.

Finally, Section 10.6 concludes tentatively that the current growth spell appears to be more inclusive than in the past and that there is evidence that Africa is starting to catch up. However, we warn against painting too optimistic a picture. The growth model that SSA is currently following is different from that used by earlier developers that relied heavily on industrialization. At this stage one does not yet see clearly the tracks that Africa needs to follow for the present growth spell to be firmly sustainable. Can agriculture and the service sector continue to be engines of growth or is more needed? Where are the stable (largely formal) jobs needed to provide employment to what will relatively soon become the largest labour force of any country in the world (including China and India)?

10.2 The Economics of Convergence

In this Section we address very briefly two interrelated questions: (i) what is the meaning of convergence? and (ii) what are the theoretical and conceptual cases in favour of, and alternatively against, convergence?

The study of growth has been of long-standing interest to economists since the age of Adam Smith, who titled his magnum opus with the question that still lingers in the minds of many economists today: what are the nature and causes of growth? In the recent Brisbane G-20 leaders' summit, economists added new dimensions in the ongoing debate on growth. A particularly relevant dimension, as far as our current discussion is concerned, is the debate on convergence.

The neoclassical growth model originating with Solow (1956) attributes economic growth to the joint impact of exogenous technical change and capital deepening on an economy with concave production opportunities; that is, declining marginal productivity of the capital stock beyond a certain level. An important implication of the neoclassical growth theory, therefore, is that the per capita output gap between poor and rich economies with identical technologies and preferences will only be transitory. Developing regions endowed with lower capital stocks would enjoy higher marginal returns than the more developed regions endowed with a larger capital stock. The equalization of per capita output across first and third world economies is called convergence.

Intuitively, convergence should happen as capital-poor economies enjoy greater returns to investment in human and physical capital than capital-rich ones to offset differences in initial conditions (Bernard and Durlauf 1996).[1] Further, poor economies could take advantage of globalization: they need not develop better technologies and management skills from scratch, as these can be adapted and adopted from their developed neighbours; they also need not be constrained by their limited domestic saving, as they could rely on the global capital market to finance their capital investment; openness would also allow poor economies to expand faster their output in those tradable goods in which they have a comparative advantage (Rodrik 2014: 2; Rodrik 2011: 10).

Yet convergence as predicted by the Solow model (1956) has historically been the exception rather than the norm. The Industrial Revolution and the Colonization period led to a wide divergence between the world's rich and poor economies during an extended century and a half long period between the late eighteenth and the mid-twentieth century (Pritchett 1997; Hausmann 2014). And in spite of the faster growth developing Asian economies enjoyed since the late 1970s and the economic take-off in Africa and Latin America since the early 1990s,[2] the average productivity gap between advanced and developing economies—which Rodrik refers to as 'the convergence gap'—remained as wide in 2008 as it was in 1950 (Rodrik 2011: Figure 4). Non-convergence was also the reality over the longer time span of 1870–2008 (Rodrik 2014: Figure 4).

Growth theorists responded to the empirical reality of non-convergence by distinguishing between unconditional and conditional convergence. They

---

[1] For a more technical definition of convergence and frameworks for testing convergence, see Bernard and Durlauf (1996).
[2] See Rodrik (2011) Figures 2 and 3.

argue that whether convergence should happen depends on a number of country-specific conditions including, among others, endowment, institutions, policies and human capital.[3] Two economies with similar technologies and preferences need not converge if they face very different country-specific conditions.

As will be discussed extensively in Section 10.5, in the pre-2000 period, in addition to structural constraints to growth of an ethno-linguistic, geographical and historical nature, most SSA countries engaged in rent-seeking policies that led to a variety of anti-growth syndromes and even many instances of failed states. In contrast, in the more recent growth spell, there is evidence of significant improvements in the quality of governance. Hence, if the realization of convergence is conditional on states adopting and following the 'right' set of policies and institutions, then appropriate governance becomes a *sine qua non*. In summary, bad public policies explained much of the pre-2000 growth differential between countries in SSA and those in the rest of the developing world (Easterly and Levine, 1997; Ndulu et al., 2008; Englebert, 2000); and improvement in the quality of governance has greatly contributed to the ongoing *African growth miracle* during 2000–2012.

10.3 Growth and Poverty Performance in SSA between 1960 and 2010

10.3.1 *Stagnation in SSA Before 2000*

An essential qualification that needs to be made at the outset of any quantitative analysis of growth, poverty, and inequality in SSA is the dubious quality of the statistical information available.[4]

---

[3] Note these conditions may interact. Institutions, for example, may be endogenous to initial levels of human capital. In turn, institutions may affect the pace and pattern of human capital accumulation.

[4] In the process of scrutinizing and analyzing growth, poverty and inequality trends, it is essential to confront the data problem. The World Bank's 'PovCalNet' data set is the main source used here. It is based on official statistics provided by the Statistical Offices of the member countries. Even though it is the most comprehensive and internally consistent data set available on growth, poverty and inequality, at the country level, it is particularly incomplete in its coverage of SSA and the World Bank apparently undertakes only a minimum of quality control. It could be argued even more strongly that, given the state of national income accounts in most SSA countries, GDP statistics are subject to high measurement errors. Furthermore, changing the methodologies for accounts of national income and surveys (which occurs relatively often in SSA) affects the accuracy of comparisons over time. Shanta Devarajan, who for a long time was the chief economist for the African region at the World Bank, referred to the poor quality of African statistics as 'Africa's Statistical Tragedy'. The tragedy is that while there is a strong presumption that the trends that we report are real, we cannot be sure that they are accurate.

Given the rather dismal development performance of most of sub-Saharan Africa (SSA) until the turn of the century, it is easy to overlook the fact that in the late 1950s, newly independent sub-Saharan Africa (SSA) had enjoyed a higher level of development than the rest of the developing world. According to McKay (2014), the average per capita Gross Domestic Product, across countries, estimated in constant US dollars for SSA economies in 1960 was, respectively, 2.9 and 3.8 times higher than that for South Asia and for the developing countries in East Asia the Pacific region.

Despite some growth in the early post-independence period, however, SSA economies started diverging from the rest of the developing world in the following decades. The SSA region, as a whole, suffered a steady and significant decline in per capita GDP from the early 1980s to the new millennium (see Table 10.1).

Table 10.1 gives the GDP per capita for the whole SSA region annually from 1960 to 2010. It reveals clearly the evolution from relative stagnation to growth over an extended period. More specifically, it shows that per capita GDP in constant 2005 U.S. dollars moved from 675 in 1960 to 944 in 1974 before it declined continuously all the way down to 732 in 1994 and remained below 800 dollars until 2003.

Table 10.1 Per capita GDP (constant 2005 US$) for developing sub-Saharan Africa 1960–2013.

Year	GDP per capita (constant 2005 US$)	Year	GDP per capita (constant 2005 US$)	Year	GDP per capita (constant 2005 US$)
1960	675	1980	934	2000	759
1961	677	1981	922	2001	765
1962	701	1982	900	2002	773
1963	727	1983	865	2003	785
1964	750	1984	863	2004	836
1965	777	1985	851	2005	859
1966	778	1986	830	2006	894
1967	769	1987	814	2007	931
1968	777	1988	824	2008	951
1969	814	1989	826	2009	946
1970	858	1990	815	2010	970
1971	891	1991	793	2011	985
1972	890	1992	758	2012	995
1973	904	1993	738	2013	1008
1974	944	1994	732		
1975	926	1995	737		
1976	943	1996	754		
1977	934	1997	760		
1978	915	1998	757		
1979	924	1999	754		

Source: Data is downloaded from the 2014 issue of the World Development Indicators (accessed on 18 March 2015) and rearranged by the authors for clearer presentation. The average per capita GDP above is obtained through population-weighting.

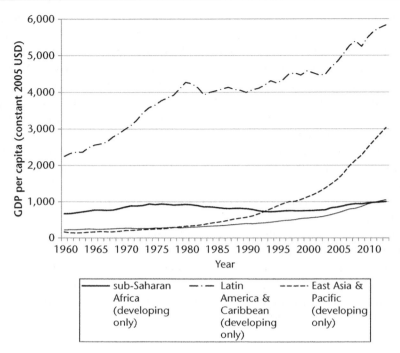

Figure 10.1 GDP per capita (constant 2005 US$) by Region during 1960–2013.

Source: Authors plotted using data from World Development Indicators (last accessed 22 March 2015).

The contrast with the other developing regions is remarkable. Figure 10.1 indicates that during the same period of 1960–2000, per capita GDP doubled in Latin America from 2,255 to 4,582 US dollars, increased almost seven times in East Asia and the Pacific region from 171 to 1,134 dollars, and rose more modestly from 229 to 555 in South Asia, where growth came significantly later and more slowly.[5]

A similar story of divergence is revealed by the studies of Ndulu et al. (2008) and McKay (2014). Ndulu et al. (2008) grouped SSA economies into three types based on their geographical location and natural resource endowment (landlocked and resource scarce, coastal and resource scarce, and resource rich) and compared each type with its counterparts in other developing regions. They found a striking growth gap between Africa and the non-African developing world during the period 1960–2000: when per capita GDP (population weighted) grew, on average, at a miniscule 0.13 per cent per year in Africa, the rest of the developing world grew 28 times faster at an average rate of 3.63 per cent per year. McKay (2014), likewise, compared the growth of SSA to that of other developing

---

[5] The 2014 Issue of the World Development Indicators database also provides per capita GDP (PPP, constant 2011 international dollars) data for these regions from 1990 on.

regions based on a sample of the 24 largest SSA countries (in terms of population) covering about 90 per cent of the total SSA population using World Bank data. His results confirm those of Ndulu et al. (2008): SSA economies stagnated in the four decades before the new millennium with an average annual growth rate of per capita GDP as low as 0.8 percentage points; while South Asia and developing East Asia and the Pacific enjoyed growth rates of 2.9 and 5.5 percentage points, respectively.

While SSA *taken as a whole* obviously exhibited a lack of growth before the new millennium, significant variations can be observed among countries and specific time-spans. Botswana was the main exception in that it performed extremely well from at least 1980 on and was consistently among the top growth performers in the developing world. Table 10.2 shows the annual growth rates for a sample of 37 SSA countries for which comparable data were available from 1980 to 2012, decade by decade.

What is noteworthy, in addition to the superlative performance of Botswana, is the generally poor performance of most countries in the 1980s and 1990s. The Democratic Republic of Congo stands out as a prime example of an economy plagued by political and social instability. In contrast, a few nations such as Burkina Faso, Lesotho, Mozambique, Sudan, and Uganda enjoyed some significant growth before 2000.

As one would have expected, the snail's pace of growth before 2000 translated into a worsening poverty incidence. The headcount ratio, for the whole of SSA, rose from 53 per cent in 1981 to 59 per cent in 1999 and the absolute number of poor increased from 210 million to 416 million over the same period (Povcalnet). However here again much heterogeneity prevailed across countries. Out of the 37 countries for which comparable poverty data were available between 1990 and 1999 the headcount ratio went up in 14 countries, fell in 15 and remained essentially unchanged in 8 countries (Thorbecke, 2013). In addition to a worsening monetary poverty picture, the general trend of human development indicators was unfavourable as well.

As will be discussed in the next sub-section, next to Latin America, the African sub-continent has the highest income inequality in the world. Given the scarcity of information before 2000, perhaps the most that can be said is that inequality did not fall and probably rose during the pre-millennium period.

10.3.2 *Post-2000 Trends in Growth, Poverty, and Inequality in SSA*

Table 10.1 confirms that economic growth started recovering in SSA around the mid-1990s, but the upward trend and magnitude only became significant after 2000. Since the beginning of the millennium, economic growth in SSA has been steady, continuous, and nothing short of spectacular. A computation

Table 10.2 Annual Growth Rate of Per Capita GDP for Selected sub-Saharan African Countries.

Country Name	1980–1990	1990–2000	2000–2010	2010–2012
Angola (earliest data: 1985)	0.6%	−2.0%	10.4%	2.1%
Benin	0.2%	1.2%	0.7%	1.6%
Botswana	10.3%	3.8%	3.6%	4.1%
Burkina Faso	0.9%	2.7%	3.3%	4.1%
Burundi	1.4%	−3.1%	0.0%	0.8%
Cameroon	0.3%	−1.3%	0.7%	1.8%
Central African Republic	−1.4%	−1.0%	−0.7%	1.6%
Chad	2.6%	−1.0%	7.2%	0.2%
Congo, Dem. Rep.	−1.8%	−5.8%	2.2%	4.2%
Congo, Rep.	2.1%	−1.2%	2.0%	0.9%
Côte d'Ivoire	−2.7%	−0.6%	−0.5%	−0.1%
Ethiopia (earliest data: 1981)	−0.9%	−0.5%	7.0%	5.3%
Gabon	−0.8%	−0.9%	−0.4%	4.1%
Ghana	−0.9%	1.8%	3.7%	9.4%
Guinea-Bissau	3.1%	−1.6%	0.3%	−0.4%
Guinea (earliest data: 1986)	0.8%	0.1%	0.4%	1.3%
Kenya	0.3%	−1.0%	1.5%	1.7%
Lesotho	1.9%	2.5%	3.8%	2.8%
Liberia	−7.2%	−0.6%	4.6%	7.3%
Madagascar	−2.0%	−1.3%	−0.4%	−0.4%
Malawi	−1.8%	1.7%	1.7%	0.2%
Mali	−1.0%	1.5%	3.1%	−2.2%
Mauritania	−1.1%	−0.1%	2.2%	3.2%
Mozambique	−0.9%	2.6%	6.2%	4.8%
Namibia	−1.9%	1.3%	3.6%	3.5%
Niger	−2.6%	−1.6%	−0.8%	2.7%
Nigeria	−1.4%	0.2%	4.3%	4.1%
Rwanda	−1.3%	−1.1%	6.7%	5.3%
Senegal	−0.4%	0.3%	1.3%	0.2%
Sierra Leone	−1.4%	−2.5%	3.4%	8.8%
South Africa	−0.9%	−0.4%	2.5%	1.8%
Sudan	−0.5%	3.1%	3.6%	3.3%
Swaziland	7.0%	0.9%	1.2%	−2.1%
Tanzania (earliest data: 1988)	2.2%	0.1%	4.8%	3.5%
Togo	−2.0%	−0.3%	−0.5%	2.5%
Uganda (earliest data: 1982)	−0.1%	3.6%	4.6%	1.6%
Zambia	−1.7%	−1.7%	3.2%	3.8%

This table reports average annual growth rate of per capita GDP (constant 2005 international dollars) during four periods: 1980–1990, 1990–2000, 2000–2010, and 2010–2012. GDP data is from the World Bank Indicators (last accessed in November, 2013).

using per capita GDP (constant 2005 US dollars) data obtained from the 2014 issue of the World Development Indicators database suggests that the average annual growth rate of per capita GDP for SSA *as a whole* has jumped from 0.3 per cent during 1960–1999 to 2.6 per cent during 2000–2013.[6]

---

[6] An alternative computation using annual percentage growth rate of GDP per capita (based on constant local currency) data, which is directly available from the 2014 issue of the World Development Indicators database, suggests that the average annual growth rate in SSA has jumped from 0.3% during 1960–1999 to 2.1% during 2000–2013.

Out of the sample of 37 countries appearing in Table 10.2, 32 countries reported higher growth rates (or lower negative growth rates) in the most recent period (2000–12) than in the preceding decade (1990–2000); three countries (Botswana, Côte d'Ivoire, and Malawi) showed essentially no change[7] and only two countries showed a worsening growth performance (Benin and Togo). The acceleration in growth, in many instances from negative growth or stagnation in the 1990s to high positive growth since 2000, is no less than a dramatic phenomenon. For example, between the 1990s and the present (2000–10) period, Angola went from a −2 per cent annual growth rate to 10.4 per cent; Chad went from −1 per cent to 7.2 per cent; Ethiopia from −0.5 per cent to 7 per cent; Liberia from −0.6 per cent to almost 7 per cent; Mozambique from 2.6 per cent to 6.2 per cent, and even Nigeria (the largest African country) enjoyed a jump from 0.2 per cent to 4.3 per cent.

The spell of rapid growth described above fueled a significant reduction in the incidence of poverty. For the whole SSA region, the poverty headcount ratio at the $1.25/day poverty line (the proportion of the population below that poverty line) fell from 59 per cent in 1999 to 49 per cent in 2010. Yet, on the downside, and pushed by still strong demographic trends, the estimated absolute number of poor continued to rise from 377 million to 414 million over the same period.

In addition to improvement in welfare in monetary terms, many SSA economies demonstrated improvement in non-monetary aspects of well-being. There are many dimensions of non-monetary poverty. The simplest and most popular indicator of progress in human development is the UNDP's Human Development Index (HDI). It is a composite index measuring average achievement in three basic dimensions of human development—a long and healthy life, knowledge and a decent standard of living.

The recent Human Development Report (UNDP, 2014) indicates that out of the twenty best performers, world-wide (including developed and developing countries) as measured by the annual growth rate of HDI between 2000 and 2013, fifteen were from SSA. Rwanda, Ethiopia, Angola and Mozambique ranked first to fourth, respectively, out of 187 countries.[8] Starting from a very low baseline, many African countries have also enjoyed significant improvements in infant mortality and school enrollment (McKay, 2014, Tables 3 and 4). McKay (2014), in his sample of 18 largest countries in SSA, used a large variety of non-monetary well-being indicators, including Demographic and Health Surveys. He concluded that (i) significant improvement

---

[7] *Changes* in growth rates of 5% above or below the prevailing level in the first period were considered as no change.

[8] Of course starting from a very low base makes it is easier to achieve high growth rates.

had occurred across most countries and most indicators between 1990 and 2011; and (ii) although the progress in those human development indicators is associated with growth, many other factors including quality of governance and effectiveness of aid played an important role.

High income inequality remains a major concern. The African Development Bank (2012) reported that the Gini coefficient in SSA rose from 43 during 2000–04 to 46 during 2006–09. A similar trend is revealed by the 2014 issue of the World Development Indicators, which suggests that the average Gini (computed across countries) for the SSA region rose from 42 in 2005 to 45 in 2013. There is little evidence to suggest that inequality is falling. Out of the 26 countries for which the World Bank's Povcalnet database reported at least two observations between the early 2000s and around 2010, there were approximately as many countries recording rising as falling Gini coefficients (Thorbecke, 2013).

Yet these composite figures hide the large heterogeneity that can be observed across countries and over time. The 2014 issue of the World Development Indicators reports, for example, that the Democratic Republic of Congo, Guinea, Mali, and Niger have managed to significantly reduce their levels of inequality between 2005 and 2013. Ethiopia and Mauritius experienced mild increases in inequality, but their Gini estimates remained relatively low i.e. below 35. Senegal and Tanzania also experienced a mild rise in inequality levels, bringing their Gini estimates up to around 40 in the late 2000s. Inequality remains stubbornly high in Botswana, Namibia, Seychelles, Rwanda and South Africa, though some improvement is seen in the latter two economies. The latter country has the dubious distinction of registering the highest Gini coefficient in the world (around 60).

10.4 Anatomy of Growth in SSA: From Non-Inclusive to More Inclusive

10.4.1 *What is Inclusive Growth?*

Inclusive growth is the new paradigm and strategic recipe in the development community. Over the last sixty years the definition of development and strategies to achieve it, progressed from the maximization of GDP in the 1950s, to employment creation and the satisfaction of basic needs in the 1970s, to structural adjustment and stabilization in the 1980s and early 1990s, to poverty reduction, followed by sustainable and shared growth that dominated the scene until recently. The evolution in the conception of development climaxed with the present broad-based concept of inclusive growth. An important contribution of inclusive growth is that it recognizes that human development is a highly multi-dimensional concept. Progress in improving human development implies, of course, poverty reduction. In that sense it builds on and expands on the Basic Needs doctrine (Thorbecke, 2014a).

There are many definitions of inclusive growth. Despite the nuanced differences among them, all definitions of inclusive growth recognize the multidimensional nature of well-being and call for a more equal distribution of the fruits of economic growth among different segments of the population.

Focusing on the specific context of SSA, the African Development Bank (2012) emphasizes three major features of inclusive growth: (i) rapid and sustained poverty reduction allowing all segments of society to contribute to and benefit from growth; (ii) both the pace and pattern of growth are important as they affect and are affected by the level and growth rate of inequality, while growth and inequality fully determine poverty levels (see Section 5); (iii) productive employment, rather than redistribution, should serve as the main and sustainable instrument of growth. It is worth noting that the African Development Bank emphasizes the need to reduce inequality to achieve inclusive growth, which is different from the World Bank's view that there is no need to advocate the reduction of inequality as long as the poor receive some benefits from the ongoing growth process.

Reducing inequality seems to be particularly relevant within the context of SSA for at least two reasons: (i) SSA countries, with few exceptions (Ethiopia is one), exhibit very high levels of inequality that have persisted for decades: (ii) despite the rapid income growth in SSA since 2000, the very low growth elasticity of poverty reduction remains a major feature of the African growth pattern (Christiaensen et al. 2013).[9] Progress in reducing inequality would, in turn, serve two functions: (i) boost economic growth as a high inequality level may dampen growth through multiple channels, such as the diffusion of political and social instability,[10] unproductive rent-seeking activities, and increased insecurity of property rights (Perotti 1993; Thorbecke and Charumilind 2002; Devereux and Sabates-Wheeler 2007); and (ii) enhance the effectiveness of growth in lowering poverty, as theory and evidence show that the impact of income growth on poverty reduction is a decreasing function of initial inequality (Bourguignon 2003; Fosu 2009).

---

[9] According to Chistiaensen et al. (2013), the growth elasticity of poverty in the developing world excluding China is estimated to be almost three times the growth elasticity of poverty in sub-Saharan Africa (−2 compared to −0.7).

[10] For example, high inequality in access to and exploitation of oil, mining, and other resources can exacerbate regional, ethnic, and tribal conflicts.

10.4.2 *Enclave-type, Extractive and Exclusive Structure of Growth in SSA before 2000*

Based on detailed studies of more than twenty-five African country case studies spanning the extended period of 1960–2000, Ndulu et al. (2008) found that two thirds of the growth gap between Africa and the non-African developing world, over this period, could be accounted for by anti-growth government behaviour; while the remaining one third of the growth gap could be accounted for by endowment constraints. The latter, within the context of most African countries, refer to both being landlocked (causing high transaction costs) and rich endowment of natural resources making African economies with weak economic and political institutions prone to the natural resource curse.

Ndulu et al. (2008) classified the anti-growth government behaviour into four groups of syndromes: (i) excessive regulation meaning heavy reliance on controls and nationalization; (ii) redistribution between ethno-regional groups to bolster domestic support; (iii) inter-temporal redistribution (including looting) and unsustainable spending by a power group expecting to lose power; and (iv) in the worse cases, systematic use of state resources to finance political allegiance which eventually brings about state collapse.

For most SSA countries during the post independent—pre-millennium years, these distortionary government policies substituted for the normal patron-client link between a state and its citizenry. Thorbecke (2014b) offered a detailed account of how anti-growth government behaviour retarded and limited growth in six groups of SSA economies with different endowments. Coastal nations in Africa performed relatively less badly than other categories of African countries during 1960–2000. But by relying on high trade barriers to seek short-term rents, they largely failed to take advantage of the global growth in trade that much of the developing Asia, including China and India, embraced and benefitted from starting in the 1980s.

In summary, most SSA countries in the pre-2000 period suffered from stagnation (or a very low pace) of growth and a narrowly-based structure of growth which can be characterized as more exclusive than inclusive. The spasmodic spells of growth that occurred tended to be generated by exports of natural resources that benefitted few, and did not trickle down. This typical growth pattern could be described as enclave-type growth.

10.4.3 *Has Growth Become more Inclusive in SSA since 2000?*

Next, we attempt to assess whether the structure of growth in SSA has become more inclusive, since 2000, through two lenses. First, the *macro lens* focusses on the overall macro-economic performance (pace of growth, poverty. and inequality impact), and a number of non-monetary welfare indicators as inclusive growth emphasizes human development, improved well-being and a wider spread of the fruits of growth. Secondly, the *intersectoral lens* centres on the ongoing structural transformation in SSA and how the latter is affecting the pattern of growth.

As discussed in Section 10.3.2, the macro-economic performance in SSA since 2000 has been remarkable. Per capita GDP growth has accelerated to the extent that one can characterize it as a quantum jump compared to the dismal pre-2000 performance. Extreme poverty remains high but has declined significantly. Despite the stubbornly high income inequality, there is strong evidence that human development in terms of access to education, health care, and other basic infrastructure such as electricity and road network has improved in many SSA countries. The tentative inference that can be drawn from the above trends is a presumption that the ongoing growth spell is contributing to a more inclusive growth pattern.

An examination through the *intersectoral lens* reinforces this presumption. Structural transformation is one of the best known dynamic regularities in economic development affecting the composition of output and employment over time.[11] In a normal (and successful) structural transformation, both the shares of agriculture in employment and in GDP decline (with the latter declining faster due to lower labour productivity in agriculture).[12] As workers move from the less productive agricultural sector into the more productive non-agricultural sectors—particularly the manufacturing sector 'where little more than manual dexterity is required to turn a farmer into a production worker in garments or shoes, raising his or her productivity by a factor or two or three' (Rodrik 2014: 13)—chronic poverty is effectively reduced. The shift of labour clearly also increases the average labour productivity of the whole society, and hence contributes to economic growth which in turn, provides more employment opportunities and further poverty reduction. A successful structural transformation therefore is a necessary condition for economic growth and poverty reduction to occur and be sustained. It contributes to economic growth in the same way as capital investment and technology advancement do, in the sense that they all boost labour productivity, which is critical to any improvement in well-being.

Based on an analysis of data from a large sample of countries, world-wide, de Janvry and Sadoulet (2010) made a convincing case that the deviation from a 'normal' (successful) structural transformation pattern explains the economic

---

[11] In the words of Herrendorf et al. (2013) and Duarte and Restuccia (2010), structural transformation is a fundamental feature of economic growth.

[12] Note that as the share of agriculture in GDP declines, total output of the agricultural sector should not so long as GDP grows faster.

stagnation in SSA in the four decades before 2000. A normal structural transformation entails that average per capita GDP increases as the agricultural share of the labour force falls. This is the type of structural transformation enjoyed by most Asian countries throughout their early development history and was a major contributor to the Asian growth miracle. In Asia, workers moving out of agriculture were *pulled* into more productive jobs in other sectors. In SSA, in contrast, the *typical* structural transformation took the form of agricultural workers being *pushed* out of the sector, and almost by default, ending up in equally or even less productive jobs largely in the informal sector. As a consequence, workers released from agriculture would perversely further depress average per capita GDP.

Such flawed migration can only be driven by lack of employment opportunities in the agricultural sector rather than any broadening of employment opportunities in the non-agricultural sectors. Lipton (2004) characterized this phenomenon as the 'migration of despair'. Though it may provide short-term relief, as poverty in urban slums displaces poverty in rural villages, this migration of despair, also 'depresses wage rates and denudes rural areas of innovators' (Diao et al. 2008).

There is some evidence that, in the recent post-2000 period, a more successful structural transformation has occurred in many SSA countries and has contributed to the acceleration in the pace and structure of growth. Thorbecke (2014a) analyzed the structural transformation pattern in fourteen SSA countries for which at least two annual observations were available between 2000 and around 2010. His tentative conclusion is that the post-2000 structural transformation appears to be closer to 'normal' for at least ten out of the fourteen SSA economies studied.[13]

The findings of McMillan and Harttgen's (2014) more comprehensive study of structural change in Africa, based on two extensive data sets including Demographic and Health Surveys[14] for nineteen African countries between 2000 and 2010, confirm that a more successful structural transformation appears to be ongoing. They showed that the share of the labour force employed in agriculture declined by roughly ten percentage points in SSA

---

[13] These ten countries are Burkina Faso, Cameroon, Ethiopia, Madagascar, Mauritius, Namibia, Senegal, South Africa, Tanzania, and Uganda. In contrast, Botswana, Ghana, and Liberia and Mali report rising shares of agricultural employment along with significant growth in per capita GDP, which could reflect increasing productivity in agriculture attracting workers back from other occupations. Such transformation, clearly, is also inclusive in the sense that workers were hired into more productive jobs.

[14] McMillan and Harttgen (2014) performed their initial analysis using a sample compiled from multiple sources and updated by several groups of scholars. They then used Demographic and Health Survey (DHS) data for robustness check. Currently 90 DHS data sets covering 31 African countries (some covered in multiple years) are available.

which was matched by, respectively, a two and eight percentage point increase in the labour shares of manufacturing and services, respectively.[15]

This structural change is associated with an impressive increase in overall labour productivity: annual growth in overall labour productivity (unweighted average) during 2000–2010 was 2.2 per cent with structural growth contributing to close to half of it (0.9 per cent of it (McMillan and Harttgen 2014: Table 5). The latter, therefore, argue that 'structural change contributed positively to growth in seventeen out of the nineteen African countries' (p. 19) and 'accounted for roughly half of Africa's growth in output per worker when data on employment shares are combined with data on value-added' (p. 5). The other half of the annual growth in labour productivity came from the increase in productivity within sectors.

Hence, while the flawed structural transformation before the turn of the century acted as a drag on the economy-wide productivity in much of the African sub-continent, the more successful transformation since 2000 appears to have contributed significantly to the improvement in the economy-wide labour productivity.

Since SSA's recent structural transformation successfully moved roughly ten per cent of the labour in agriculture into more productive jobs in services and manufacturing,[16] we can at least argue that it is broadening the employment pattern while contributing to growth. McMillan and Harttgen (2014) also find that: i) countries with initially higher shares of employment in agriculture experienced more rapid declines in those shares and more rapid increases in the shares of employment in manufacturing (requiring typically unskilled labour) and services (p.31); and (ii) an increase in rural schooling was associated with a small decline in the share of rural labour engaged in agriculture—especially for rural women whose schooling rate increased by one percentage point when their labour share in agriculture declined by 0.8 percentage point (pp. 31–32). These observations suggest that the poor and rural women benefited more than in the past from the structural transformation in SSA during 2000–2010, allowing us to conclude that the latter since the turn of the century has been more normal and inclusive than in the preceding period.

---

[15] The small growth of manufacturing employment is clearly a concern, and we return to discuss this issue and some other concerns in Section 10.6.

[16] As noted by Rodrik (2014), much of this ten percent of rural-to-urban migrants moved into 'services where productivity is apparently not much higher than in traditional agriculture' (p.9) as 'those services that have the capacity to act as productivity escalators tend to require relatively high skills' that 'required long years of education and institution building' (p. 13). In addition, the small percentage of rural labour successfully moving into manufacturing found the sector 'dominated by small, informal firms that are not particularly productive' (p.9). This is clearly a concern and we discuss it in section 10.6.

Finally, it is worth noting that the appearance of a middle class in Africa following a more normal structural transformation may also suggest that the SSA growth in the past decade has been more inclusive. A more important implication of the emergence of an African middle class, however, lies in their great potential to contribute to further economic growth in Africa, both directly through their capacity to increase domestic consumption and contribute to private sector growth, and indirectly through their pushing the African society towards more democratic (inclusive) political and economic institutions and greater improvements in human wellbeing for the poorer segments of society. We will turn to this point later in section 10.5.2.2.

Summarizing the above discussion, we conclude that growth in SSA since 2000 has been more inclusive from both a macro and an intersectoral lens analysis.

10.5 Major Factors Impeding Growth before 2000 and Contributing to Growth since 2000

10.5.1 *Correlates of Stagnation before 2000*

Given the difficulty—if not impossibility—of establishing robust causal inferences linking specific factors to growth outcomes, it is preferable to refer to correlates of growth. These correlates are factors that were associated with and influenced growth either positively or negatively. We start with some of the major factors that impeded growth in SSA before 2000.

Since probably Barro (1991), most empirical studies before the late 1990s were based on cross-country data collected between the 1960s and the early 1990s supporting the notion of a so-called African dummy, which implied that being an African country means poor growth performance. Barro (1991), for example, found that even after controlling for initial income, the level of investment in physical and human capital, school enrollment, and government consumption, the SSA African dummy in his growth regressions has a significant and negative coefficient of 1.14, suggesting that being a SSA economy contributes to an annual *decline* in per capita GDP of as much as 1.14 per cent during 1960–1985. The negative Africa dummy effect on growth remains sizable and significant when researchers further added to their regression equations other variables such as 'bureaucratic efficiency index' (Mauro 1995),[17] ethno-linguistic

---

[17] Mauro (1995) found that the negative impact of the Africa dummy on average annual growth rate of per capita GDP over 1960–1985 only decreased from 2.1 percentage points to 1.7 when he controlled for a 'bureaucratic efficiency index' including measures of corruption, excessive bureaucracy, and quality of the judiciary.

heterogeneity index (Easterly and Levine 1997)[18] or some basic indices of social capability (Temple and Johnson 1998).[19]

As Englebert (2000) pointed out, however, studies that failed to remove the significance of the African dummy must have missed some important correlates of the African growth tragedy before the new millennium. Indeed, some later studies managed to suppress the Africa dummy effect by controlling for factors such as the ratio of government consumption to GDP (Barro 1997) and unfavourable natural endowment such as landlocked position and tropical climate (Sachs and Warner 1997).[20]

In essence, scholars agree that the growth stagnation many SSA economies suffered from between 1960–2000 is not because they happen to be an African country, but mainly because they made poor public policies (Englebert 2000: 1822; Easterly and Levine 1997[21]). Easterly and Levine (1997: 1, 9, and Table 2), for example, found that about 44 per cent of the growth gap between countries in SSA and those in East Asia during 1960–1989 can be accounted for by poor public policies as manifested by low school attainment, poorly developed financial systems, large black market exchange rate premia, large government deficits, inadequate infrastructure, and political instability.[22]

Likewise, Englebert (2000: 1826 and Figure 1) using cross-sectional data collected between the year of independence (1960 for most SSA countries) and 1992 for up to 133 countries, found a significant and positive correlation between overall growth and good policy combinations, which are measured by a policy index constructed using the principal component technique to capture the compound effect of six policy variables measuring, respectively, government investment in human capital, public investments in infrastructure, the ratio of current government consumption over GDP, the degree of

[18] Easterly and Levine (1997) found that the negative growth impact of the Africa dummy during 1960–1989 only fell from 1.8% when ethnic diversity is not controlled to 1.3% when it is controlled. In all situations, the coefficient of the Africa dummy remained significant at 5% level.

[19] Temple and Johnson (1998)'s cross-sectional analysis based on 1960–1985 data shows that the Africa dummy remains significantly and negatively associated with growth after the inclusion of a social development index in the growth regression, while the effect of other regional dummies became insignificant. The social capability index is constructed using the factor analysis technique eliciting information from up to 24 social and economic indicators including, among others, the degree of cultural and ethnic heterogeneity and the extent of national integration. The main message of the study of Temple and Johnson (1998), however, is to show that some basic indexes of social development developed in the early 1960s are very useful in *predicting subsequent growth*.

[20] Sachs and Warner (1997) showed that landlocked countries enjoyed less benefits of international trade as they suffer from higher transportation and insurance cost. Tropical countries are also prone to suffer from lower agricultural productivity, greater morbidity, and shorter life expectancy (see also Bloom and Sachs 1998).

[21] 'Although an enormous literature points to a diverse set of potential causes of SSA's ills, existing work does not explain ... why so many public policies went so badly wrong in Africa' (Easterly and Levine 1997: 1).

[22] Note that Easterly and Levine (1997) did not find strong evidence for a direct link between ethno-linguistic heterogeneity and growth.

253

openness of the economy, the extent of black market exchange rate pre-miums, and the distortions in the financial market.

A later study by Ndulu et al. (2008) further confirmed the strong link between public policy and economic growth. Based on detailed studies of more than twenty-five African countries between 1960–2000, they found that out of the 3.5 per cent gap in annual per capita GDP growth between African and non-African developing countries, 2 per cent was explained by the previously mentioned four types of anti-growth government behaviour: excessive regulation, redistribution between ethno-regional groups, redistri-bution by a power group expecting to lose power (including looting), and state breakdown. It is also worth mentioning that Ndulu et al. (2008) found that the remaining one third of the growth gap could be accounted for by geographical constraints (landlocked and rich natural resource endowment leading to the natural resource curse), which is consistent with the conclusions of Sachs and Warner (1997).

The establishment and diagnosis of poor quality of governance as the main culprit in SSA's growth tragedy before the new millennium, of course, begs an answer to the further question of why African countries selected and followed poor public policies that hindered economic growth. Scholars proposed at least three explanations. The 'stupidity hypothesis' (as named by Robinson, 1996) argues that African elites chose bad policies because they did not know better. The 'ethnic heterogeneity hypothesis' (Easterly and Levine, 1997) argued that much of the bad policies African leaders chose can be accounted for by ethno-linguistic divisions leading to increasing polarization and thereby making it more difficult to reach agreement on the provision of public goods. It was therefore more appealing for the group in power to seek rents that benefited themselves than to adopt developmental policies.[23] In many instances in Africa, loyalty is to the clan or tribe rather than to the state.

The third hypothesis, namely the 'lack of state legitimacy hypothesis' (Englebert, 2000), argued that much of the policy choices African states made before the early 1990s is explained by the lack of legitimacy of the post-independent African rulers, in the sense that when they inherited the states from the colonizers in around 1960, they did not inherit the colonial power that forced the generation of modern African states and kept them together; nor had they managed to recover the pre-colonial institutional form of sovereignty. Consequently, post-independent African rulers were con-stantly challenged over even apparently benign matters of domestic politics,

---

[23] Citing from Easterly and Levine (1997:1), there exists a large body of literature linking polarization to prevalence of rent-seeking and difficulty in reaching agreement on public goods. See Alesina and Tabellini (1989), Alesina and Drazen (1991), Shleifer and Vishny (1993), Alesina and Rodrik (1994), Alesina and Spoloaare (1995).

and many issues that are not viewed as severe in other countries—such as budgetary or personnel crisis—could easily trigger constitutional deadlocks, military coups, secession attempts, and civil wars. As a result, ruling elites in African states find that it is more convenient to consolidate their power by resorting to authoritarianism and distortionary policies, which also yield the greatest relative short-term payoffs to elites. More specifically, they direct public resources to private actors through unofficial channels and networks (Englebert 2000), and even use state resources to systematically finance political allegiance which can eventually bring about state collapse (Zartman 1995).

While it is conceivable that ethno-linguistic heterogeneity, the peculiar historical origins of African (artificial) states, and endowment constraints such as being landlocked and a tropical climate could all contribute to an environment making the growth pattern in SSA different from that of the other developing regions, it can be argued that it is the poor quality of governance that was mainly responsible for the dismal performance of SSA economies before 2000. And, as we will show in the following sub-section, improvement in the quality of governance has much to do with the African growth miracle during the past decade.

10.5.2 Correlates of Post-2000 Growth in SSA

As discussed in section 10.4.3, a more normal structural transformation appears to be the main driving force behind the current growth spell in SSA. We thus start our exploration of the major correlates of the recent growth in the region by considering what could explain the region's structural transformation since 2000 based on, among others, the excellent study of McMillan and Harttgen (2014).[24]

As it turned out, two sets of factors appear to have been critical for the current acceleration of the pace of growth and the transfer from an extractive to a more inclusive pattern of growth in SSA since around 2000. The endogenous factors—in the sense that they are at least partially influenced by the development strategies adopted by SSA governments—include (i) a more friendly policy environment for agriculture that triggered a healthy structural transformation and (ii) other more inclusive (democratic) economic and political institutions that improved the quality of governance. The exogenous factors—in the sense that they are largely beyond the control of individual

---

[24] This source contains an excellent empirical analysis—using both national accounts data and Demographic Health Survey data for 19 African countries—of many growth correlates summarized here. The term 'correlate' connotes association rather than causality per se, which is difficult to establish.

African states—include (i) rising global commodity prices, and (ii) a rapid increase in Foreign Direct Investment (FDI) inflows from both the developed economies and the emerging markets.

10.5.2.1 IMPROVED GOVERNANCE AS MANIFESTED BY MORE FAVOURABLE AGRICULTURAL POLICIES

As the influential World Development Report on 'Agriculture for Development' (World Bank Report, 2008) suggested, the structural transformation represents the outcome of an underlying growth process which is not specified. The great majority of the African countries are still at an early stage of development characterized by a relatively very high share of the total labour force employed in agriculture and the bulk of total output originating in agriculture. For those countries, agriculture (and more typically the smallholder sector) is the only possible engine of growth (World Bank, 2008).[25] Only when there is an improvement in the labour and land productivity in agriculture, can an agricultural surplus (including both natural resources and unskilled labour) be released to help jump start and finance manufacturing and service activities and to engender the structural transformation. A more productive agricultural sector also contributes to economic growth by providing food at reasonable prices, which allows the non-agricultural sectors to sustain lower labour costs. Reasonable food prices also help combat poverty, narrow income disparities, and provide food security for the economy as a whole (Thorbecke, 2014b; WDR, 2008).

A lesson learned from the countries that were most successful in achieving both growth and equity throughout their development history (e.g. Taiwan and South Korea) is that a continuing gross flow of resources should be provided to agriculture—irrigation, inputs, research and credit—combined with appropriate institutions and price policies to increase this sector's productivity and potential capacity to contribute to an even larger flow to the rest of the economy and hence a net surplus (Morrisson and Thorbecke, 1990). Another lesson that can be learned from Africa's stagnation during 1960–2000, and the earlier economic disaster in China between 1950–1978,[26]

---

[25] At a recent Senior African Policy Makers seminar held in Mozambique in March, 2015 on 'Agriculture in Africa's Transformation: The Role of Smallholder Farmers,' senior policy makers from around the continent adopted a declaration as an affirmation of their strong commitment to supporting smallholder agriculture as an engine for growth and transformation on the continent.

[26] China started its economic reform in 1979 with literally 18 farming households contracting land from the collective and taking responsibility for their own production and output upon submitting a quota to the collective. This new production scheme—soon adopted by villages throughout the country—greatly increased farmers' productivity and successfully engendered structural transformation, as numerous village and township enterprises engaging in non-agricultural businesses mushroomed and many young farmers moved to urban areas and provided China's then infant export-oriented manufacturing industry with cheap labour it much needed.

is that exploiting the agriculture sector too early in the development process only short-circuits the structural transformation. The development community has therefore widely agreed that 'reaching the takeoff point (where agriculture is productive enough to provide surplus labour and natural resources) is a precondition to embarking on the next phase of development (industrialization)' (Thorbecke, 2014b).

Yet as convincingly documented by an extensive literature, agriculture was the Achilles' heel of African development (Mwabu and Thorbecke 2004). Plagued by poor agronomic and geographic conditions, exploitation by extractive leaders, and a large proportion of small subsistence farms with very low productivity, much of agriculture stagnated before the mid 1980s. Yields remained stubbornly low and there was little evidence of any significant growth in agricultural land or labour productivity.

Fortunately, most SSA countries have provided a more friendly policy environment for, and increased attention to, agriculture since the 1990s. Net taxation on agriculture in the last twenty years has been significantly reduced in SSA. A number of SSA countries are starting to diversify their agricultural exports towards higher value-added products. Ghana, for example, pushed its cocoa sector—the production of which almost doubled between 2001 and 2006. The government has taken measures to ensure a consistently high-quality cocoa bean output. Senegal, Kenya, and Ethiopia have been successful in penetrating the market for horticultural products and flowers. Significant improvements have been recorded in non-traditional agricultural exports (e.g. *Blue Skies* products such as fruit juices in Ghana and South Africa, cut flowers in Ethiopia, and fresh vegetables in Madagascar). As a result, from the mid-1980s onwards, agricultural productivity has shown gradual improvements.

Furthermore, many SSA countries also committed themselves to the Comprehensive African Agricultural Development Program (CAADP) since its implementation in 2003. CAADP's primary goals are to reduce poverty and hunger on the African continent through agriculture-led development. Participating countries are expected to achieve an annual growth rate of six per cent in the agricultural sector and to allocate at least ten per cent of the national budget to agriculture.[27]

---

[27] These appear to be overly ambitious targets—particularly the six per cent annual growth in agricultural production. According to the IFPRI's official CAADP Monitoring and Evaluation Report (known as the 2012 ReSAKSS Annual Trends and Outlook Report by Benin and Yu 2013), a total of 13 countries—Burundi, Burkina Faso, the Democratic Republic of Congo, Ethiopia, Ghana, Guinea, Madagascar, Malawi, Mali, Niger, Senegal, Zambia, and Zimbabwe—have met or surpassed the 10 per cent target in one or more years since 2003. Yet some researchers argue that the productivity growth required to achieve the targets might require expenditures even higher than 10 per cent as overall government spending rose even faster, reaching double digit rates of annual growth (Kolavalli et al 2012).

According to the International Food and Policy Research Institute (IFPRI 2013[28]), CAADP is a major source of the impressive three per cent per year growth that the African agricultural sector experienced between 2000–2013. Using a computable general equilibrium (CGE) model and historical data from Mozambique, Pauw et al. (2012) predicted that CAADP would raise the country's national GDP growth during 2009–2019 from 6.9 per cent per annum from the baseline growth rate of 5.7 per cent per annum.

In spite of recent progress, however, agricultural productivity in SSA still lags far behind other regions of the world (Fuglie and Rada, 2013).

10.5.2.2 OVERALL IMPROVED GOVERNANCE AND APPEARANCE OF A MIDDLE CLASS

A more friendly policy environment for agriculture is not the only improvement SSA countries made in the quality of governance. According to the World Bank Country Policy and Institutional Assessment (CPIA) assessing Africa's policies and institutions, twenty-one out of thirty-nine SSA economies have improved their overall CPIA score in the period 2005—2013; and countries with better policies tend to enjoy higher GDP per capita growth (CPIA Africa 2013). Further, the average overall CPIA score in Africa's non-fragile countries is now similar to that of non-fragile countries elsewhere; though the gap between Africa's fragile countries and fragile countries in other regions persists (CPIA Africa 2014).

As noted in section 10.4.3, a general improvement in the quality of governance in SSA is related to the emergence of an African middle class in the recent decade. According to Ncube and Lufumpa (2015), the size of the middle class has grown from around 66 million in 1980 to 137 million in 2010.[29] As noted in Ncube and Lufumpa (2015), the importance of this demographic transition lies in the great potential for the middle class to contribute to *further* economic growth in Africa. Indeed, the emergence of an African middle class is not only endogenous to the initial growth and improvement of governance in the region, but it would in turn make fundamental contributions to Africa's *future* growth through directly contributing to consumption and investment, and indirectly strengthening the African society's move towards more democratic (inclusive) political and economic institutions and greater improvements in human wellbeing for the poorer segments of society. Historically, there has been a close relationship between the rise of a middle class and improved governance and the appearance of democratic institutions. That said, 'many

---

[28] 'CAADP's 10-Year Report Card: An evaluation of a premier program for investment in agriculture' by Rebecca Sullivan on 7 May, 2013. Retrieved on 24-11-2015 from <http://www.ifpri.org/blog/caadp-s-10-year-report-card-evaluation-premier-program-investment-agriculture>.

[29] The middle class in SSA is defined as including individuals whose income per day ranged from $4 to $20.

obstacles still need to be overcome before a strong and sustainable middle class dominates the social fabric in Africa, a continuation of this trend is essential to the building of inclusive institutions' (Thorbecke 2014c).

10.5.2.3 GLOBAL COMMODITY PRICES

Next we turn to some of the relatively exogenous correlates of the current African growth spell. Many empirical studies—examples are Deaton and Miller (1995) and Raddatz (2007)—found a positive relationship between commodity booms and output in at least the short run, though Collier and Goderis (2008)[30] argue that there is strong evidence for the natural curse hypothesis in the long run, suggesting that those non-agricultural commodity exporters with weak institutions—many of which are located in sub-Saharan Africa—would experience slower output growth in the long run in response to spikes in global commodity prices.

Commodity price indices faced by many SSA countries doubled or even tripled between 2000 and 2010. As a result, many resource-rich economies in the sub-continent enjoyed favourable terms of trade which clearly helped fuel economic growth. McMillan and Harttgen (2014) suggest that there is a significant and positive relationship between commodity prices and the acceleration of the pace of growth in SSA from 2000 to 2010, though the significance of this relationship is weaker when the quality of governance is poorer.

The index of primary commodity prices has been falling recently, though it still remains at its 2000 level. Falling prices of oil, metal, and agricultural commodities suppressed the region's exports, which remained dominated by primary commodities. Angola, for example, was set back by a decline in oil production and oil prices.

That said, some SSA economies have shown some resilience to fluctuation of global commodity prices thanks to good governance and expansion of the nonagricultural sector. As noted in the Global Economic Prospects (GEP) recently released by the World Bank, a record maize harvest in Zambia helped offset the decline in copper production; and a strong increase in cocoa production allowed Côte d'Ivoire to enjoy higher output despite the Ebola outbreak. Nigeria, Tanzania, and Uganda managed to expand activity at a robust pace due to service sector expansion led by transport, telecommunication, and financial services (GEP 2015: 101).

It therefore seems promising that resource-rich SSA economies may continue to benefit from high commodity prices so long as they continue to improve their quality of governance. More specifically, a part of the revenues

---

[30] The study of Collier and Goderis (2008) differs from previous studies in that they used the panel cointegration approach rather than the vector autoregression (VAR) approach pioneered by Deaton and Miller (1995).

and royalties generated by commodity booms needs to be captured by the State and ploughed back internally to promote a more inclusive growth.

10.5.2.4 FOREIGN DIRECT INVESTMENT

SSA in the past decade has witnessed a dramatic increase in FDI inflows, which comes not only from the OECD economies who have long been the major contributors of FDI inflows in SSA, but increasingly from the emerging markets including particularly the BRIC countries. Since 2000, the global FDI stock in SSA has increased from about 34 billion to 246 billion US dollars in 2012. Much of this increase in foreign investment, according to the Brookings Institution (Copley et al. 2014), was directed to Southern African countries with rich precious metals and minerals reserves and Nigeria with its oil wealth.

As Adams (2009a) suggested, FDI flows had greatly contributed to economic growth in SSA through augmenting domestic private investment and thereby creating new jobs and enhancing technical and business efficiency. Weisbrod and Whalley (2011), for example, documented that Chinese FDI contributed at least an additional half a per cent to the average GDP growth of two per cent per year in thirteen SSA countries during different periods between 2003 and 2009. FDI would also, as Thorbecke (2014c) noted, promote human development in SSA countries if part of the investment returns accruing to governments can be used to provide productive social protections benefiting the poor and unskilled. As is the case with high commodity prices, the growth impact of high FDI inflows in SSA countries also depends on the quality of governance. Adams (2009b), for example, shows that the FDI inflows had a net crowding-out effect in SSA between 1990–2003, suggesting that the subcontinent needs better cooperation between government and multi-national corporations to promote the mutual benefits of both parties.

10.6 Conclusions

A historical analysis of the pace and pattern of growth in the African subcontinent spanning the period from 1960 to the present reveals that the SSA region evolved from overall stagnation in the pre-2000 period to a high pace of growth and a more inclusive pattern in the last fifteen years.

The present growth spell is still too short to draw any strong and authoritative conclusions that Africa is finally catching up with the rest of the world. What can be concluded is that the process of convergence appears to have started and that ongoing structural changes are raising labour productivity and moving the pattern of growth in a more inclusive direction.

Whereas the main culprit for overall dismal performance before the present millennium appears to have been extractive policies and institutions, significant improvements in the quality of governance in the post-2000 period clearly played a role in the acceleration and changing structure of growth. In particular, the more favourable treatment of agriculture encouraged a more successful structural transformation. Other interrelated factors associated with the new growth regime include the appearance of a middle class, high global commodity prices, and a large flow of foreign direct investment.

In addressing the key question as to whether the present spell is sustainable, a number of potential obstacles (clouds over the horizon) need to be mentioned. First, the ongoing growth model in SSA is very different than that followed by earlier developers-particularly in Asia. The typical model followed by developing countries in Asia and Latin America, when they were at about the same stage of development as most SSA economies today, relied on labour intensive manufacturing. This is not presently the case in Africa. Only a small proportion of the workers moving out of agriculture find employment in the manufacturing sector. Most of those workers end up in the service sector and often in informal rather than formal activities. Clearly, labour-intensive industrialization in SSA is not a meaningful engine of growth at this time. While, agriculture is functioning as a (puttering) engine, as the agricultural labour force continues to fall, other sectors have to be ready to absorb productively not only the labour released from agriculture but also the new entrants from what will soon become the largest labour force in the world. Traditional services do not provide the productive outlets necessary to employ this enormous labour force. Conceivably, some hi-tech services that cannot be foreseen at this time might develop in SSA.

Yet it is difficult to imagine that without an upsurge of investment in manufacturing, the increasing labour force could find the stable and formal jobs needed for the growth spell to be truly sustainable. A further handicap is that Africa is a latecomer in the production and export of labour-intensive manufactures. Already, the global market appears to be saturated in many product lines. The best hope is that, in this era of intense globalization, many nodes will be found for Africa on the many present and future value (supply) chains. In addition, the rising African middle class provides a potentially large source of internal (domestic) demand for consumer and capital goods. In order to satisfy this demand, African producers would be greatly helped by a process of regional integration particularly through investment in transport infrastructure linking neighbouring countries. A road network, joining landlocked and coastal economies, could, by reducing transport costs, provide the necessary incentives to embark on an industrialization path responding to the domestic demand within SSA. The disadvantage of being a latecomer could turn out to be an advantage if African producers imported and adopted technologies closely adapted to the underlying conditions prevailing in Africa. A recurrent complaint in the region is the low quality of many Chinese imports. Clearly, there is scope for replacing these Chinese goods with locally produced goods.

So our cautious final message is that while Africa is starting to catch up, this process will only be sustainable with the continuation of appropriate policies and institutions and a greater integration within Africa and the global economy.

Reference

Abramovitz, M., 1986. 'Catching up, forging ahead and falling behind'. *Journal of Economic History* vol. 46 number 2:385–406.

Adams, S., 2009a. 'Can foreign direct investment (FDI) help to promote growth in Africa'. *African Journal of Business Management* vol. 3 number 5:178–83.

Adams, S., 2009b. 'Foreign Direct investment, domestic investment, and economic growth in Sub-Saharan Africa'. *Journal of Policy Modeling*, vol. 31 number 6:939–49.

African Development Bank, 2012. *African Economic Outlook 2012*. Tunis, Tunisia.

Alesina, A. and A. Drazen, 1991. 'Why Are Stabilizations Delayed?' *American Economic Review* vol. 81 number 5:1170–88.

Alesina, A. and D. Rodrik, 1994. 'Distributive Politics and Economic Growth'. *Quarterly Journal of Economics* vol. 109 number 2:465–90.

Alesina, A. and E. Spolaore, 1995. 'On the Number and Size of Nations'. *Quarterly Journal of Economics* vol. 112 number 4:1027–56.

Alesina, A. and G. Tabellini, 1989. 'External Debt, Capital Flight and Political Risk' *Journal of International Economics* vol. 27 number 3:199–220.

Barro, R., 1991. 'Economic growth in a cross-section of countries'. *Quarterly Journal of Economics* vol. 106 number 2:407–44.

Barro, R., 1997. *Determinants of economic growth: a cross-country empirical study*. Cambridge, MA: MIT Press.

Benin, S. and B. Yu, 2013. *ReSAKSS Annual Trends and Outlook Report 2012*. Washington, DC: International Food Policy Research Institute.

Bernard, A.B. and S.N. Durlauf, 1996. 'Interpreting tests of the convergence hypothesis'. *Journal of econometrics* vol. 71 number 1:161–73.

Bloom, D. and J. Sachs, 1998. *Geography, demography, and economic growth in Africa*. Harvard Institute for International Development, October, Mimeo.

Bourguignon, F., 2003.'The growth elasticity of poverty reduction: explaining heterogeneity across countries and time periods'. In *Inequality and growth: Theory and policy implications*, [3–26]. Washington, DC: World Bank.

Byerlee, D., A. de Janvry, E. Sadoulet, R. Townsend, and I. Klytchnikova, 2008. *World Development Report 2008: Agriculture for Development*. Washington DC: World Bank.

Collier, P., and Goderis, B. 2008. Commodity prices, growth, and the natural resource curse: reconciling a conundrum. *Growth, and the Natural Resource Curse: Reconciling a Conundrum* (June 5, 2008).

Copley, A., F. Maret-Rakotondrazaka, and A. Sy, 2014. *The U.S.-Africa Leaders Summit: A Focus on Foreign Direct Investment*. Washington, DC: The Brookings Institution. Retrieved on 4/20/2015 from <http://www.brookings.edu/blogs/africa-in-focus/posts/2014/07/11-foreign-direct-investment-us-africa-leaders-summit#ftnte2>.

Christiaensen, L., P. Chuhan-Pole, and A. Sanoh, 2013. 'Africa's Growth, Poverty and Inequality Nexus – Fostering Shared Prosperity'. World Bank, mimeographed.

Chuhan-Pole, P., 2013. *Country Policy and Institutional Assessment (CPIA) Report 2013: Assessing Africa's Policies and Institutions*. Washington DC: World Bank.

Chuhan-Pole, P., 2014. *Country Policy and Institutional Assessment (CPIA) Report 2014: Assessing Africa's Policies and Institutions (includes Djibouti and Yemen)*. Washington DC: World Bank.

Deaton, A., and Miller, R.I. 1995. *International commodity prices, macroeconomic performance, and politics in Sub-Saharan Africa*. International Finance Section, Department of Economics, Princeton University.

de Janvry, A., and E. Sadoulet, 2010. 'Agriculture for Development in Africa: Business-as-Usual or New Departures?' *Journal of African Economies* vol. 19 suppl 2: ii7–ii39.

Devereux, S., and R. Sabates-Wheeler, 2007. 'Editorial introduction: Debating social protection'. *IDS Bulletin*, Vol. *38 number:* 3: 1–7. Brighton, UK: Institute of Development Studies.

Diao, X., P. Hazell, P.D. Resnick, and J. Thurlow, 2008. *The Role of Agriculture in Development, Implications for Sub-Saharan Africa*, International Food Policy Research Institute Research Report 153.

Duarte, M., and Restuccia, D. 2010. 'The role of the structural transformation in aggregate productivity'. *The Quarterly Journal of Economics*, *125*(1), 129–173.

Easterly, W., and R. Levine, 1997. 'Africa's growth tragedy: policies and ethnic divisions'. *The Quarterly Journal of Economics* vol. 112 number 4:1203–50.

Englebert, P., 2000. 'Solving the Mystery of the AFRICA Dummy'. *World development*, vol. *28* number 10:1821–35.

Fosu, A.K., 2009. 'Inequality and the impact of growth on poverty: comparative evidence for sub-Saharan Africa'. *Journal of Development Studies* vol. 45 number: 726–45.

Fuglie, K., and N. Rada, 2013. 'Resources, Policies, and Agricultural Productivity in Sub-Saharan Africa'. *USDA-ERS Economic Research Report*, (145).

Hausmann, R., 2014. 'In Search of Convergence'. *Project Syndicate, 20*. Retrieved on 4-2-2015 from <http://www.project-syndicate.org/commentary/ricardo-hausmann-asks-why-growth-rates-are-converging-among-some-countries-and-diverging-among-others>

Herrendorf, B., Rogerson, R., and Valentinyi, A. 2013. 'Two Perspectives on Preferences and Structural Transformation'. *American Economic Review*.

IFPRI 2013. "CAADP's 10-Year Report Card: An evaluation of a premier program for investment in agriculture" by Rebecca Sullivan on May 7, 2013. Retrieved on 24-11-2015 from <http://www.ifpri.org/blog/caadp%E2%80%99s-10-year-report-card-evaluation-premier-program-investment-agriculture>.

Kolavalli, S., R. Birner, and K. Flaherty, 2012. 'The comprehensive Africa agriculture program as a collective institution'. *Available at SSRN 2197400*.

Lipton, M., 2004. 'Crop science, poverty and the family farm in a globalising world'. Plenary Paper. 4th International Crop Science Congress, Brisbane, Australia. Retrieved on 4-2-2015 from <http://www.cropscience.org.au/icsc2004/plenary/0/1673_lipton.htm>.

Mauro, P., 1995. 'Corruption and growth'. *Quarterly Journal of Economics* vol. 110 number 3:681–712.

McMillan, M. S. and K. Harttgen, 2014. 'What is driving the "African Growth Miracle"?' NBER Working Papers 20077, National Bureau of Economic Research, Inc.

McKay, A., 2014. 'Recent Evidence on Progress on Poverty Reduction in Sub-Saharan Africa since 1990' To appear in McKay, A. & Thorbecke, E. (Eds.). *Economic Growth and Poverty Reduction in Sub-Saharan Africa: Current and Emerging* Issues. Oxford University Press (forthcoming).

Morrisson, C., and E. Thorbecke, 1990. 'The concept of the agricultural surplus'. *World Development* vol. 18 number 8:1081–95.

Mwabu, G., & E. Thorbecke, 2004. 'Rural development, growth and poverty in Africa'. *Journal of African Economies*, vol. 13 suppl 1: i16–i65.

Ncube, M., and C.L. Lufumpa, (Eds.), 2015. *The Emerging Middle Class in Africa*. London: Routledge.

Ndulu, B.J., O'Connell, S., Collier, P., Fosu, A.K., Bates, R.H., Gunning, J.W., Azam J., and Hoeffler, A. 2008. *The political economy of economic growth in Africa, 1960–2000* (Vol. 1). Cambridge University Press.

Pauw, K., J. Thurlow, R. Uaiene, and J. Mazunda, 2012. *Agricultural growth and poverty in Mozambique: Technical analysis in support of the Comprehensive Africa Agriculture Development Program (CAADP)* (No. 2). International Food Policy Research Institute (IFPRI).

Perotti, R., 1993. 'Political equilibrium, income distribution, and growth'. *The Review of Economic Studies* vol. 60 number 4:755–776.

Pritchett, L., 1997. 'Divergence, big time'. *The Journal of Economic Perspectives* vol. 11 number 3:3–17.

Raddatz, C., 2007. 'Are external shocks responsible for the instability of output in low-income countries?' *Journal of Development Economics* vol. 84 number 1: 155–87.

Robinson, J., 1996. *Theories of 'bad policy'*. Working Paper, Department of Economics, University of Southern California, Mimeo.

Rodrik, D., 2011. *The Future of Convergence*. HKS Faculty Research Working Paper Series RWP11-033, John F. Kennedy School of Government, Harvard University.

Rodrik, D., 2014. *An African Growth Miracle?* (No. w20188). National Bureau of Economic Research.

Sachs, J. and A. Warner, 1997. 'Sources of slow growth in African economies'. *Journal of African Economies* vol. 6 number 3:335–76.

Shleifer, A. and R. Vishny, 1993. 'Corruption'. *Quarterly Journal of Economics* vol. 108 number 3:599–617.

Solow, R.M., 1956. 'A contribution to the theory of economic growth'. *Quarterly Journal of Economics* vol. 70 number 1:65–94.

Sullivan, R., 2013. *CAADP's 10-Year Report Card: An evaluation of a premier program for investment in agriculture*. Retrieved on 4-2-2015 from <http://www.ifpri.org/blog/caadps-10-year-report-card-evaluation-premier-program-investment-agriculture>.

Temple, J. and P.A. Johnson, 1998. 'Social capability and economic growth'. *Quarterly Journal of Economics* vol. 113 number 3:965–90.

Thorbecke, E. and C. Charumilind, 2002. 'Economic inequality and its socioeconomic impact'. *World Development*, vol. 30 number 9:1477–95.

Thorbecke, E., 2013. *The Present Pattern of Growth, Inequality and Poverty in Sub-Saharan Africa*. Paper Prepared for the Conference in Honor of Per Pinstrup-Andersen, Cornell University.

Thorbecke, E., 2014a. *The Structural Anatomy and Institutional Architecture of Inclusive Growth in Sub-Saharan Africa*. UNU/WIDER Working Paper 2014/041.

Thorbecke, E., 2014b. 'The Anatomy of Growth and Development in Sub-Saharan Africa'. To appear in McKay, A. and Thorbecke, E. (Eds.), *Economic Growth and Poverty Reduction in Sub-Saharan Africa; Current and Emerging Issues*. Oxford University Press (forthcoming).

Thorbecke, E., 2014c. Thorbecke, E. 2014c. "How Inclusive is the Present Pattern of Growth in Sub-Saharan Africa?" in Ernesto Zedillo, O. Cattaneo and H. Wheeler (editors), *Africa at a Fork on the Road*, Yale Center for the Study of Globalization (2015)

UNDP, 2014. *Human Development Report 2014*. Washington, DC: United Nations Development Program.

Weisbrod, A. and J. Whalley, 2011. *The contribution of Chinese FDI to Africa's pre crisis growth surge* (No. w17544). National Bureau of Economic Research.

World Bank. 2007. World Development Report 2008: Agriculture for Development. Washington, DC. © World Bank. <https://openknowledge.worldbank.org/handle/10986/5990%20License:%20CC%20BY%203.0%20IGO>.

World Bank. 2013. CPIA Africa, June 2013: Assessing Africa's Policies and Institutions. Washington, DC. © World Bank. <https://openknowledge.worldbank.org/handle/10986/16504%20License:%20CC BY%203.0%20IGO>.

World Bank Group. 2014. CPIA Africa, June 2014: Assessing Africa's Policies and Institutions. Washington, DC. © World Bank. <https://openknowledge.worldbank.org/handle/10986/18939%20License:%20CC%20BY%203.0%20IGO>.

World Bank Group, 2015. *Global Economic Prospects, January 2015: Having Fiscal Space and Using It*. Washington, DC: World Bank. Doi: 10.1596/978-1-4648-0441-1. License: Creative Commons Attribution CC BY 3.0 IGO.

Zartman, I.W., 1995. *Collapsed states: the disintegration and restoration of legitimate authority*, Boulder, CO: Lynne Rienner.

11

Relative Economic Backwardness and Catching up

Lessons from History, Implications for Development Thinking

Martin Andersson and Tobias Axelsson

11.1 Introduction

The aim of the book has been to discuss the historical and current develop-ment processes across the world by addressing the question of whether poor countries can catch up. In doing that, the chapters have elaborated on the diverse nature of relative backwardness, and the possible escapes from it, in a broader geographical scope. Consequent to this, a number of issues are explored further.

A main objective has been to sketch a research agenda where Economic History and Development Economics share common ground in their pursuit of understanding the diversity in the mechanisms of development. Given that the theoretical and analytical tools employed in economic history originate in European experiences, are these also useful when studying development pro-cesses outside Europe? In this context, the role of agriculture is often ignored, yet it is evident both from historical cases and the contemporary developing world that agriculture has an important role to play. Any understanding of the transformation process must thus also clarify the role of agriculture.

Another aspect that warrants further discussion is the relative optimism in the notion of catching-up. This was arguably due to the post-war *zeitgeist* but more importantly, with this positive outlook on development, the focus was on providing strategies for success. Countries were seen as just at varying degrees of backwardness and the notion that it was merely a case of kick-starting the development process needs further qualification, especially given today's much more globalized world. We must ask ourselves if there is a limit to how backward an economy is before a potential advantage of being late is turned into a trap virtually impossible to escape.

Grounded in the chapters in the book, let us now turn to the issues above in more detail.

11.2 Development as a Historical Process

The most pertinent question addressed in this book is how useful a historical approach may be in understanding current development issues. Grounded in standard economic theory, economically backward countries may seize the late-comer advantages by emulating well- tried technologies and know-how coupled with comparative advantages. Yet, as noted by Thorbecke and Ouyang in chapter 10, the historical records show that where the universal economic growth models would predict convergence between the developed and the developing world (i.e. catching up) there has instead been divergence. If the standard economic growth theory offers scant explanation for the failure of catching up, then it is equally poorly equipped to help in the understanding of the growth surge in Africa, and in Latin America for that matter, in recent years. Consequently, standard development economics fall short of plausibly explaining different growth trajectories. One solution may be to turn to a more 'evidence based' Randomized Control Trials (RCT) which rejects theoretically derived development policy. The RCT tradition also argues that turning to history leads to a too deterministic understanding of development processes. Regarding the works of economic historians following in the tradition of David Landes's (1999) cultural determinism, and economists writing truncated history like Acemoglu, Johnson, and Robinson (2001), this concern is of course real. Instead, in this book it is argued that a historical perspective based on empirical evidence of the actual catching up process which highlights the diversity in development may help in understanding not just different growth trajectories of the past but also offer some insight into current day development issues. This standpoint is clearly reflected throughout the chapters. All authors focus on the dynamics of growth and approach it from different angles, yet they are doing so by analysing the dynamics of structural change in a historical perspective. Perhaps most clearly, Austin argues the historical perspective as a means to inform the ongoing discussions on present day late developers. In much of the current discussion, the role of good institutions, usually secure property rights, is seen as a golden key to success. Likewise, bad institutions, weak or excluding property rights, is a principal explanation to why some countries stagnate or fail. Austin argues that institutions may very well have an important role to play but in the current debate they are little more than empty words that need further qualification if they are to help us in our understanding of the development process itself. In chapter 5, Gunnarsson pushes this point even further. In his analysis of the East Asian experience he strongly argues that in the debate on the success of these countries focus is largely on the role of governance. One side argues that it is the liberal open markets with 'getting prices right' that is the main explanation, while the other side argues it is the role of the state with more regulated markets. Without a historical foundation, the base of the discussion becomes ideological, and even superficial. He continues to argue, however, that also historical accounts, such as the one suggesting that the rise of East Asia is explained by an Asia-specific story of a continuously evolving labour-intensive pathway of industrialization, fall short of providing a satisfactory explanation. None of these perspectives gives sufficient credit to actual differences and strong discontinuities in the transformation of East Asia.

Gunnarsson's standpoint highlights that we run the risk of jumping wrongly to the conclusion that a particular set of institutions, often those associated with property rights and political power found in the successfully industrialized West, need to be in place from the beginning rather than evolve, or being forced, in the process. Gunnarsson's point of view finds further support from other authors in this volume. In the Asian context, Lin, working with recent decades of Chinese resurgence as an inspiration, calls for a re-interpretation of what kind of institutional framework may be conducive to growth. Also Alston and Mueller go beyond a simplistic view of institutions by looking to history when explaining the Brazilian case. Instead of flatly arguing that institutions matter in making modern Brazil an agricultural success story, they carefully map institutional changes over time. By doing this they not only show which are the institutions that matter but also show the underlying drivers for change.

A more historical approach may increase our understanding, but is not limited the role of institutions and institutional change in the development process. Another example where the historical perspective may be useful is found in the debates on factor endowment and economic change. The importance given to factor endowments has a long tradition in economic history, and more recently spearheaded by Engerman and Sokoloff in explaining the divergence between North and South America (2002; see also López-Jerez in a study on Vietnam 2014). As is highlighted by Gunnarsson, Lin, and Austin for Asia and Africa respectively, and by Bértola in the Latin American case, differences amongst regions and countries may be traced back to population size and the sheer size of the countries. With smaller domestic markets and more limited possibilities for within country diversification, the capability to cope with international markets becomes increasingly important. It is in this context Schön argues that as the world economy has become much more integrated small open economies have largely been at the peril of trends in the world market, but have at the same time, through strong institutions guarding the welfare of its people and high levels of human capital managed to carry through structural reforms and benefit from the global pressure.

11.2.1 *Diversity in Development—the Gerschenkronian Approach*

Above we argue that to study the development process, both past and present through the lens of history is potentially a rewarding venture. The step, however, from asserting that history matters to making analytical use of it is far from self-evident. With the help of economic history, we recognize the danger of falling into the trap of creating a one-size-fits-all template for development. In this sense, we see economic history as a discipline where the discussion on the nature of the catching up processes depends on contextual conditions and endowments. If the emphasis lies on understanding the general mechanisms and processes of change, special attention must be given to these specific conditions. At the same time, one must not fall in the trap at the other end of the spectrum where each case under study becomes unique. Therefore we move away from both the deterministic and generalizing schools in the Marxist or neoclassical traditions and those exploring one country's development trajectory as an isolated story with no lessons for others to learn from.

It is in this context that the Gerschenkronian approach has its place, where general implications may be drawn from diverse development trajectories. This is a central argument in the chapter by Gunnarsson. Taking this a step further, Lin argues in chapter 3 for a new development strategy. Built on the premise that the preconditions for development differ from country to country, the need for a country to increase the overall productivity in the economy and utilize its comparative advantages in order to catch up with the richer countries is still the same.

A case in point for the merits of the Gerschenkronian approach is the contributions in the two chapters on African development, both past and present. It is clear that by analyzing the catching up process and the future prospects for development, these chapters both stress the need to step away from a universalistic approach. In both chapters industrialization is called for, but in order to understand the African context they stress the need for a more careful examination based on institutional conditions and the factor endowments as to what development trajectory may be suitable.

269

11.3 Agriculture as a Driver of Catching up

As highlighted by Timmer in chapter 4, agriculture is largely ignored in the writings of Gerschenkron. After his initial writings on the *junkers* and German agriculture, the role of the agricultural sector is rarely mentioned and it does not feature explicitly in his typology. Yet, this does not imply that he would not have considered agriculture as an important element in the development process. Nor does it mean that we cannot and should not, include an agricultural dimension more clearly in the discussion on catching up. Admittedly, changes in agricultural productivity will have effects on other parts of the economy and thereby influence the possibilities of catching up. Timmer argues further that it is not just a case of the agricultural sector indirectly contributing to the development process, but also a case of the sector itself being a driving force. The question remains open but, at the very least, an economy with a relatively backward agricultural sector will face difficulty in catching up with more advanced countries, a notion that was argued already by Ranis and Fei (1961). In the Asian context, it has been argued by, for instance Adelman (1984), that a core element in the success of the first tier Asian miracles (for instance Japan, Taiwan and South Korea) was that the productivity improvements in the agricultural sector increased income and demand from a broad base in society. By extension it also drove the catching up process. This argument finds support not just in Timmer but also in Gunnarsson, who by comparing the growth process of Japan before the World War II with that of the post-war era, show that it was not until after the war, with accelerated productivity improvements in agriculture that the transformation process could begin in earnest. Similarly, the experience from South Korea and, even more so, the Taiwanese cases, show the importance of agricultural transformation for the whole economy to forge ahead. According to Gunnarsson, the Taiwanese development path was the least substitutive among the East Asian success cases. Conversely, when explaining the lower growth rates, and slower catching up in India compared to China, Schön highlights the role of slow agricultural change. An observation also made by Datt and Ravallion (2002). This seems to hold for the Southeast Asian countries too, where the nature of the agricultural transformation process goes hand in hand with the possibilities for sustained growth (see for example Axelsson 2013).

The Latin-American experience also points up the significance of structural and agricultural transformation. In the chapter by Bértola, when looking at the continent as a whole, it is evident that although there have been periods of strong growth and catching up these have soon been replaced by dramatic periods of falling behind. This Bértola attributes to a failure in the structural transformation and poor productivity development in general. Bértola and

Ocampo elaborate on this and argue that this is very much a result of weak support for technological change (Bértola and Ocampo 2012). In the recent decade, Latin America has once again seen a growth spurt. Bértola warns that this may just be another commodity price driven process lacking any structural transformation. While this is a valid point, there are signs, in this volume presented by Alston and Mueller, but also put forward elsewhere (see for example, for Chile, Anríquez and López 2007 and Andersson 2009) indicating that where there has been a shift in Latin-American agriculture, catching up processes are likely to be more sustained.

To further assert the role of agriculture as an instrumental part of the development process, it is enough to turn to sub-Saharan Africa (SSA). Except for a few years after independence, most countries in the region have shown an increasing divergence not just in relation to the major world economies, but also to that of other developing countries. Yet in the recent decade, much like Latin America, previous growth tragedies have been partially reversed. In the chapter by Thorbecke and Ouyang they convincingly argue that the main reason for Africa falling behind, and recently also commencing modest catching up, may be found in the level of inclusiveness. To put it simply, the investments in African economies have traditionally not focussed on the sectors where they would have had the greatest impact on productivity, and in the long run on economic growth and poverty reduction. Africa, having a sizable agricultural sector, would in the second half of the twentieth century have benefited as a whole from a structural transformation process. As has been shown elsewhere, the Asian miracle in its initial phase was very much a result of productivity increases in agriculture which allowed labour and capital to be transferred to other sectors of the economy. Productivity of the economy, as a whole, increased and fed the catching up process. In Africa we saw no such thing. Since the beginning of the twenty-first century, however, African growth seems driven not just by higher commodity prices but also by more inclusive development strategies that are both an effect and cause of agricultural growth.

To conclude, the notion that agricultural transformation is at the core of the catching up process is well founded. Worth keeping in mind is that it is not enough and that structural changes unravel in different ways. The Asian accomplishments, and this seems to hold also for the more successful Latin-American cases, are dependent on the development of other high-productivity sectors which can absorb the redundant rural labour force. The structural transformation is thus as dependent on linkages between the rural and urban economies as it is on changes within the sectors. The challenge for Africa is consequently to transform agriculture and, at the same time, industrialize in an increasingly globalized market with fierce competition from manufacturing powerhouses like China.

11.4 Prospects for Development in the Twenty-first Century

The argument in this book has not been to establish the Gerschenkronian approach as a development policy or strategy. The approach does not easily translate into practical policy advice and it is quite clear that the framework is an analytical tool, created to understand the differences in the development processes rather than a manual for how to increase growth and by extension development. Nonetheless, with approximately one billion people living in absolute poverty the question why so many countries in relative backwardness have failed to live up to expectations and make the transformation to modern economic growth is highly relevant. One could rightly argue that the advantage of backwardness is nothing more than wishful thinking. On the other hand in recent decades, poverty has been reduced dramatically, there is a growing middle class in the developing world and we have seen countries shift from low to middle income status. In fact in some countries, predominantly in Latin America and Africa, which we previously thought of as growth tragedies, the ship has perhaps been turned around. While heeding the warnings of exaggerated optimism raised in many of the chapters in this book, it could also be a sign of a sustained catching up. The research challenge ahead is to more fully understand these processes.

Gerschenkron never really touched upon examples of stalled catching up, except only briefly (Abramovitz 1986). In order to understand this issue better we may instead turn to Abramovitz's argument that catching up is dependent on the social capabilities and institutional context in a country. He also argued that what holds a country back could also be what causes it to be slow in catching up (Abramovitz 1995). Booth argues along these lines when explaining the relative success of the ASEAN countries but also why they have failed, with the exception of Singapore, to catch up with the leading economies. Booth shows that the countries which have been leading the catching up among the ASEAN countries were also the richest countries at the time of independence. The institutions not conducive to growth in the past are also to blame for holding countries back in poverty causing a relatively slow catching up process with some even falling further behind. When qualifying the context she argues that it at least partially boils down to the social capabilities in the economy that determines the development trajectories in ASEAN. The countries that in a global context are often put forward as success cases are only half-way miracles because they lack the social capabilities to deliver sustained economic growth. Singapore, like Japan and the other first-tier developers in Asia, had invested heavily in human and social capital. Yet, she argues there is more to it than that and puts forward state capacity as a likely decisive factor. Many Southeast Asian countries have seen rapid economic growth, which has then slowed down due to political instability and a lack of distribution of the spoils of growth. This might suggest that the ones relatively well-endowed with social capability (such as Malaysia and Singapore) have continued to outperform the ones with initially weak capabilities. But the Philippines, initially thought of as a case with favourable capabilities, continuously fell behind the other economies of the region. And Indonesia, for example, saw a more unequal growth pattern with greater inequality and also less investment in social, human, and physical infrastructure in comparison with Japan or Singapore. Consequently Singapore forged ahead while Indonesia's catching up process has been much more punctuated with progress quickly reversed. In the case of the two giants, China and India, it is evident that the better part of the twentieth century was marred by stagnation and falling behind the leading economies. Yet as is widely recognized, in recent decades we have seen a growth surge in both cases. Schön estimates, however, that the catching up of China and India to the developed world may not be as fast as sometimes projected. In both countries the process is well underway, particularly in China, but a broad-based growth model remains to be created.

Turning to the Latin American experience, the causes behind the failure to sustain long-term convergence may also be contributed to the lack of social capabilities and institutional weaknesses. As Bértola notes, the twentieth century in Latin America has been characterized by an almost roller-coaster like development path which has been greatly influenced by international commodity prices. The prospects of catching up, Bértola argues, has, time and again, been shot down because the state has not been capable of transforming the export and commodity based growth into long term sustained convergence. In fact, this causes him to question whether the current boom is price, rather than productivity driven. It remains to be seen whether the economies showed the capabilities to sustainably capitalize on the price boom. As is recognized, in Bértola's as well as in Alston and Mueller's chapters, there seem to be signs of a structural shift which is more favourable to inclusive growth. This is the argument put forward by others who show that that the last decade or so has displayed an inter-linkage between agricultural growth and decreasing inequalities (see for instance Andersson and Palacio forthcoming). The question remains, however, if this is enough to catch up with the world leaders. Bértola argues that it is not likely, since a more thorough restructuring of the economies in Latin America also would result in slower growth. This may be true for the continent in general, but possibly less so in the case of Brazil, where Alston and Mueller argue that we have seen this institutional change already. The Brazilian success is consequently not just a result of the commodity price hike, but also increased productivity in the economy itself.

Perhaps an even clearer example is the African continent. Thorbecke and Ouyang argue that a main cause of the African growth tragedy can be explained by institutional weakness. Particularly in terms of the lack of a functioning state which has implications also for the regulatory framework and the distribution of income (for a more detailed discussion on this see for example Ndulu et al. 2008). Like Latin America, in the past decade or so, Africa has seen an economic upsurge. Many observers argue that this is the China effect, with the increased demand for natural resources to feed the growing giant. While this may be part of the explanation, the African continent has seen what Thorbecke and Ouyang call improvements in the institutional quality, much in line with Abramovitz's original idea. The most recent African growth surge is thus a result of a more normal structural transformation with improvements in the overall productivity levels in all sectors of the economy.

To conclude, it might not be too late for the latecomers. Asia is most certainly the greatest example of this. Poverty and near famine was replaced by a productivity surge in both agriculture and industry. It may be argued that the Asian experience, as was the case also in Western Europe and its offshoots, occurred before the forces of globalization were as strong as they are today. This does not, as shown by Schön, render the idea of catching up void. Globalization should of course not be ignored in the discussion, but is rather an instrumental part of the catching up processes of today. The ASEAN countries are only half way there, the process of change is still moving ahead with countries like Indonesia maturing both economically and politically. In both the Latin American and African cases, it is of course still too early to pass judgement on whether this is a catching-up process that is being observed or if it merely a repeat of previous cycles. What we have seen in the recent decade is how the increased globalization has been beneficial to the emerging economies that have been able to reap the benefits of increased commodity prices. Evidence indicates that along with the recent economic boom there have also occurred institutional changes which may carry this recent decade's growth surge to a more sustained development process. As argued by all the contributors to this volume, but perhaps most clearly by Schön, increased globalization in the past twenty-odd years has highlighted the structural transformation as the big decision maker as to whether a country will be able to catch up of simply fall behind. For many developing countries the agricultural transformation is still unfinished business and one of the prime reasons why occasional economic growth is neither inclusive nor sustained. The variety of ways in which the development process unfolds makes it reasonable to suggest that current development paths, if analyzed in historical perspective, allow for comparisons of conditions, patterns, possibilities and obstacles to draw lessons from.

References

Abramovitz, M., 1986. 'Catching up, forging ahead, and falling behind'. *The Journal of Economic History* vol. 46 number 02:385–406.

Abramovitz, M., 1995. 'The Elements of Social Capability'. In *Social Capability and Long-Term Economic Growth,* edited by B. H. Koo and D. H. Perkins, [19–47] Basingstoke: Macmillan Press.

Acemoglu, D., S. Johnson, and J.A. Robinson, 2001. 'The colonial origins of comparative development: an empirical investigation', *American Economic Review* vol. 91 number 5:1369–401.

Adelman, I., 1984. 'Beyond export-led growth'. *World Development,* vol. 12 number 9:937–949.

Andersson, M., 2009. 'More to the picture than meets the eye—Towards an institutional interpretation of the ultimate causes behind the Chilean economic transformation' *European Review of Latin American and Caribbean Studies* Number 86.

Andersson, M. and A. Palacio. (forthcoming). 'Structural change and the fall of income inequality in Latin America—Agricultural development, inter-sectoral duality, and the Kuznets curve'. In XX Edited by L. Bértola and J.G. Williamson.

Anríquez, G. and R. López, 2007. 'Agricultural growth and poverty in an archetypical middle income country: Chile 1987–2003'. *Agricultural Economics,* 36, 191–202.

Axelsson, T., 2013. 'State led agricultural development and change in Yogyakarta 1973–1996'. In *Agricultural Transformation in a Global History Perspective* edited by E. Hillbom and P. Svensson [86–107], London: Routledge.

Bértola, L. and J.A. Ocampo, 2012. *The Economic Development of Latin America since Independence.* Oxford: Oxford University Press.

Datt, G. and M. Ravallion, 2002.'Is India's economic growth leaving the poor behind?' Policy Research Working Paper Series 2846, The World Bank.

Engerman, S. and K.L. Sokoloff, 2002. 'Factor Endowments, Inequality, and Paths of Development Among New World Economics' NBER Working Papers 9259, National Bureau of Economic Research.

Landes, D., 1999. *The Wealth and Poverty of Nations.* London: Abacus.

López Jerez, M., 2014. *Deltas Apart. Factor Endowments, Colonial Extraction and Pathways of Agricultural Development in Vietnam.* Lund studies in economic history (69).

Ndulu, B.J., S.A. O'Connell, J-P. Azam, R.H. Bates, A.K. Fosu, J.W. Gunning and D. Njinkeu (Eds), 2008. *The political economy of economic growth in Africa, 1960–2000* (Vol. 2). Cambridge: Cambridge University Press.

Ranis, G. and J.C.H. Fei, 1961. 'A Theory of Economic Development'. *The American Economic Review* vol. 51 number:533–65.

Index

Printed and bound by CPI Group (UK) Ltd, Croydon, CR0 4YY